BEYOND THE BEACH

TITLES IN THE SERIES

Airpower Reborn: The Strategic Concepts of John Warden and John Boyd

The Bridge to Airpower: Logistics Support for Royal Flying Corps Operations on the Western Front, 1914–18

Airpower Applied: U.S., NATO, and Israeli Combat Experience

The Origins of American Strategic Bombing Theory

THE HISTORY OF MILITARY AVIATION

Paul J. Springer, *editor*

This series is designed to explore previously ignored facets of the history of airpower. It includes a wide variety of disciplinary approaches, scholarly perspectives, and argumentative styles. Its fundamental goal is to analyze the past, present, and potential future utility of airpower and to enhance our understanding of the changing roles played by aerial assets in the formulation and execution of national military strategies. It encompasses the incredibly diverse roles played by airpower, which include but are not limited to efforts to achieve air superiority; strategic attack; intelligence, surveillance, and reconnaissance missions; airlift operations; close-air support; and more. Of course, airpower does not exist in a vacuum. There are myriad terrestrial support operations required to make airpower functional, and examinations of these missions is also a goal of this series.

In less than a century, airpower developed from flights measured in minutes to the ability to circumnavigate the globe without landing. Airpower has become the military tool of choice for rapid responses to enemy activity, the primary deterrent to aggression by peer competitors, and a key enabler to military missions on the land and sea. This series provides an opportunity to examine many of the key issues associated with its usage in the past and present, and to influence its development for the future.

BEYOND THE BEACH

THE ALLIED WAR AGAINST FRANCE

STEPHEN ALAN BOURQUE

NAVAL INSTITUTE PRESS
ANNAPOLIS, MARYLAND

Naval Institute Press
291 Wood Road
Annapolis, MD 21402

Library of Congress cataloging-in-publication data is available.
978-1-61251-873-2 (hardcover)
978-1-61251-874-9 (eBook)

Maps created by Bobby Wright.

♾ Print editions meet the requirements of ANSI/NISO z39.48-1992 (Permanence of Paper).
Printed in the United States of America.

26 25 24 23 22 21 20 19 18 9 8 7 6 5 4 3 2 1
First printing

CONTENTS

ILLUSTRATIONS

Figure

Photos

Maps

PREFACE

While having breakfast in the Metz train station in the summer of 2007, I noticed a large marble plaque on the wall. On it, the city had inscribed the names of several hundred rail workers killed by air bombardment during the Second World War. It was apparent that the dispensers of those munitions were the air forces of the United States, Great Britain, and Canada. It simply had never occurred to me that the good guys, trying to rid Europe of the Nazi menace, could be responsible for such civilian losses against a friendly, occupied state. I considered myself reasonably knowledgeable about this conflict, having just conducted a staff ride on the Normandy beaches and driven along the route taken by American forces during Operation Cobra. It was evident that I had missed some of the details. Intrigued, I walked to the local bookstore and found a copy of French journalist Eddy Florentin's 1997 book *Quand les Alliés bombardaient la France.*[1] This sensationalist account of the air war mostly listed some of the largest aerial assaults on French towns and villages, with little analysis of why or how it happened. Back in the United States, I reviewed the books in my library and discovered little discussion on the air war in France other than the inaccurate bombing during the landings and the use of bombers during the Transportation Plan against rail centers. Nothing approached the comprehensiveness of Florentin's disjointed book. Except for the summary of the debates over the bombing of the railroad marshaling yards, none mentioned the problem of French civilian casualties. Thus began my extensive search as to the causes, conduct, and effect of the Allied air operation in France. My intent was to answer two relatively straightforward questions: What happened and why?

What I discovered is that more than seventy years ago, as part of the Northwest European Campaign against Nazi Germany, the armed forces of the United States and the British Commonwealth unintentionally waged an air war against France. Depending on where you lived, especially near airfields or ports, the bombing lasted five long years. After January 1944 the Allies targeted most of France's population centers, small towns, and even isolated villages. By the time the Allied ground forces had driven the German defenders from the country, aircraft from the US Army Air Force and British Royal Air Force had killed more civilians by high-altitude bombing, dive bombing, rocket attacks, and simple machine-gun strafing—approximately 60,000—than the Germans had killed British civilians during the same period. Unfortunately for the French, the American and Commonwealth air attack programs were far larger, more methodical, and more efficient than the German and caused greater physical damage to France's cities, harbors, and rail lines.[2] Monuments across France attest to the effects of these attacks, often naming the individual victims in the same way a war memorial commemorates the conflict's military veterans. Newspapers and civic groups alert the rebuilt communities as the anniversary of a particularly important raid approaches. Finally, cemetery plots, often entombing entire families, provide tangible evidence of the grief suffered by individuals and communities.

While the effect of these air operations is far less than the destruction inflicted on Germany and Japan, it is important to remember that the Allies considered France an allied, occupied state awaiting liberation. What makes this aerial onslaught interesting is that its scale, nature, and effects are almost unknown in the English-speaking world. Not only was it extensive, but it was all part of a comprehensive Allied plan, directed by the supreme allied commander, Gen. Dwight D. Eisenhower, with the specific purpose of ensuring that Operation Neptune, the establishment of a lodgment of Allied forces in the French departments of Calvados and La Manche, succeeded.

This book seeks to place the bombing war against France within the perspective of Operation Overlord. How did the Allied bombing operations fit into the plans for invading Europe in 1944? What did they attack? What was it like for those that lived under the bombs? Moreover, most important and most difficult, what does it all mean to the modern world? Of course, tens of thousands of words have found their way into the digital hold bucket. I have no space to spend twenty pages on French history or another dozen describing the rise of air power and the key participants. My apologies to those that know the details of these events, and I hope that those who do not will use the notes and bibliography to explore the rich history of the period. It is an uneven situation for the French who experienced the bombing. In some cases, such as in Lower Normandy, the archive in Caen has an impressive collection of personal testimony that is available to any researcher. In other localities, these stories are in the hands of local historians, if they exist at all. This can create an uneven portrayal of the scope and effects of the bombing. Unfortunately, this is a survey, and it is impossible to evaluate the story of every target and every mission. I hope it will provide others a place to begin their studies of this complex series of events.

Logistically, this has been a difficult book for an American to write. While the planning documents are available at the American and British national archives, researchers find the real details of the bombings at the local level. There, in one of France's ninety-five departmental libraries (each department comparable to an American county), or the many municipal archives and libraries located in almost every midsized city, are the official and unofficial reports of the damage done to France's communities. Because I have been able to visit only a handful of these excellent facilities, much of my material is the result of local historians' scholarship. This book reflects their passion for uncovering the details of their parents' and grandparents' lives during this difficult period.

Readers should note that all numbers, from bomb tonnage to the number of aircraft to the casualty counts, are based on the best evidence available. Particularly in regards to casualty figures, estimates vary widely. Also, specific targets are sometimes in question, as official reports might show an attack in one town while local officials note that it took place nearby. Bombing objectives may appear on a list of rail centers but might note that aircraft attacked it because of the local bridge. Hopefully, scholars will continue to investigate and refine what is found within.

One of the pleasures of writing and research is to interact with a plethora of people interested in your topic. Many of the librarians and archivists who helped me have long forgotten our discussions, but they all contributed to my understanding of the issue. To all of you, thank you for your support, advice, and inspiration. In the United Kingdom, these include Sebastian

Cox, Bob Evans, Richard Overy, Lindsay Dodd, Ross Mahoney, Sam Cates, Claudia Baldoli, and Jim Aulich. I should also thank the great archivists at the National Archives at Kew, and the Imperial War Museum in London, who made research in the United Kingdom such an enjoyable experience. In Canada, Michael Bechthold, Terry Copp, Craig Aitchison, Marc Milner, Yan Poirier, and Michelle Fowler deserve my thanks for their advice and support.

Thank you to my French colleagues, archivists, and friends, including André Rakoto, Marie-Claude Bertholet, Paul Le Trevier, Sébastien Studier, David Baillet, Alain Talon, Véronique Delpierre, Marie-Christine Hubert, Corinne Bouillot, Hervé Passot, Val Schneider, Antonine Hardy, Sébastien Haule, Arnaud Planiol, Lucien Dyan, John Barzman, Antoine Capet, Jean Canoit, Isabelle Caniot, Anne and Didier Mellini, Raphaëlle Fages, Arnaud Fages, and Julie Six.

In the United States, students, friends and colleagues who supported my work include Scott Gorman, Rich Dixon, Candi Hamm, Anna White, Kathy Barbier, Brian North, Rick Herrera, Robert Davis, Pete Schifferle, Bobby Wright, Katie Gaetke, Maranda Gilmore, Dan Mortenson, Jenns Robertson, Kenny Johnson, Tim Nenninger, Joseph Fitzharris, Robert Shafer, Kate LeMay, George Eaton, Chelsea Milner, Kevin Baily, Michael Creswell, Carol Leadenham, Herb Pankritz, Frank Shirer, Tom Hughes, Robert O. Paxton, and Dave Livingstone. International officers Giovanni Corrado and Alessandro Vivarelli helped me put these operations in a European context. At the Naval Institute Press, Paul Springer, Gary Thompson, and Paul Merzlak were a constant source of encouragement and support. Drew Bryan did a superb job of editing the manuscript.

Andrew Knapp from the University of Redding deserves my special thanks. The expert in this field, he was a constant source of advice, encouragement, and friendship. The result of his edits, challenges, and criticisms are found throughout this book. Similarly, I need to thank my wife, Debra, my best friend for more than thirty years, who has been a major part of this project from the beginning. In addition to traveling with me to many of these locations, she has read every word of this manuscript several times and has provided me the criticism and advice I needed to make it better. Of course, in spite of their best efforts, readers will discover some errors of fact and interpretation; these, of course, are my responsibility.

Finally, I want to dedicate this work to my loving aunt Patricia Currier Walsh, who has been my biggest supporter and cheerleader all my life. Thanks for all you have done to make me a better person.

ACRONYMS

AFHRC	Air Force Historical Research Center (Maxwell Air Force Base, AL)
AHB	Royal Air Force Air Historical Branch (Northolt, UK)
AHEC	Army History Education Center (Carlisle, PA)
AN	Archives Nationales (Paris)
Arch35	Archives Départmentals et du Patrimoine (Rennes)
Arch62	Archives Départementales du Pas-de-Calais (Arras)
Arch50	Archives Départementales de la Manche (Saint-Lô)
Arch59	Archives Départmentals du Nord (Lille)
Arch76	Archives Départementales de la Seine-Maritime (Rouen)
CARL	Ike Skelton Combined Arms Research Library (Fort Leavenworth, KS)
CMH	US Army Center of Military History (Fort McNair, DC)
COSSAC	Chief of Staff to the Supreme Allied Commander
DDEPL	Dwight David Eisenhower Presidential Library (Abilene, KS)
FO	Field Order
HIAL	Hoover Institute Archives and Library (Stanford, CA)
IWM	Imperial War Museum (London, UK)
KC	Kings College (London, UK)
MC	Mémorial de Caen
NARA	National Archives and Records Administration (US) (College Park, MD)

SHAEF	Supreme Headquarters, Allied Expeditionary Force
SHD	Service Historique de la Défense (Vincennes, France)
UKNA	National Archives (UK) (Kew Gardens, UK)
USAWWII	United States Army in World War II (Green Book Series)
USSBS	United States Strategic Bombing Survey

BEYOND THE BEACH

CHAPTER ONE

A MISSING NARRATIVE

In the spring of 1944, thirteen-year-old Michelle Chapron lived in a boardinghouse on the Rue Verrier, just east of the center of Saint-Lô. As the administrative center of the department of the Manche, the city had the secondary schools smaller towns did not. Michelle was from one of these, Carentan, thirty-five kilometers closer to the coast. Her landlady, thirty-four-year-old Simone Gravey, was struggling to get by under the German occupation by renting out the extra rooms in her home to transient students and teachers. Like millions of other women in France, Simone's life was difficult. She and her four young children, Jean (eight), Georgette (six), Yves (three), and Geneviève (two), had to go on with their daily lives while her husband was away. In his case, the Germans had incarcerated the monsieur in the local prison for trying to evade working for the occupation regime. Other tenants in this small home that spring included sixty-year-old Augustine Barbier, a professor at the local school, and her thirty-year-old daughter, Yvonne. Also new to the boardinghouse was a recently hired instructor who had just taken a room. Michelle had yet to have a chance to introduce herself and find out anything about him. After a weekend visit home, she returned to her room on June 5 in preparation for classes the next day. Awakened that night by the sounds of the invasion coming from the coast, she was, like everyone else, excited and unable to get back to sleep. When she ran to school the next morning, the headmaster told her, "The school is closed; it is the landing!" Her grandmother lived in another part of the city, so after returning to the boardinghouse to gather some belongings, she raced down the Rue Falourdel across town to join her. It took her some time to cover the eight kilometers and climb the hill to her grandmother's house, and she arrived around noon. Her aunt Helen was also visiting, and so three generations of French women spent the day attempting to understand what was going on around them and what was happening along the coast. Then, a little before eight o'clock in the evening, many bombers arrived over Saint-Lô, and the women watched with horror as the ancient city burst into flames. Michelle later found out that the bombing had killed her fellow borders, the Gravey family, and 350 other civilian citizens of her town. She never forgot that terrible night.[1]

In the market town of Lisieux, 135 kilometers east, six-year-old J. P. Cordier had put on his pajamas and was getting into bed. Writing forty years after the event, he still remembered his parents discussing the question of leaving their house and escaping the city to avoid the possible Allied bombs. Everyone knew the invasion was under way, and airplanes had dropped leaflets telling the residents to get away from the city. But his mother was pregnant, and his father decided it was better for them to stay put in the safest part of the house. When they heard the bombers approaching their city, the parents, according to their rehearsed routine, moved the family into its makeshift shelter. It was on the ground floor, under the staircase, in the center of the house, and seemed to offer the best protection. Suddenly the bombs began exploding outside. One destroyed the house's back wall, knocking young J. P. unconscious. He recalled briefly waking up and calling out for water. He remembered his mother answering him. Then he again passed out and apparently remained unconscious for several hours. His neighbor, he found out later, had pulled him from the debris and brought him across the street to an undamaged house. Seminary students, who were searching for survivors, carried him to the local hospital. He remembered deliriously arguing with the nurses who were cutting his new socks off his bloody feet. When he finally awoke, he was in the hospital along with his injured sister. Both of his parents were dead, the doctors had amputated his leg, and fire had burned his house to the ground. Other than his sister, he was alone in the world with nothing left. Along with his parents, at least forty Lexoviens, as they called themselves, were dead, with many more wounded.[2]

One hundred kilometers farther east, journalist Gontran Pailhès surveyed the remains of his beloved Rouen. For more than a week, Red Week as the citizens would later call it, the United States Army's Ninth Air Force had attacked the three bridges that connected the two sides of this ancient city on the River Seine. The medium bombers and fighter-bombers had not been very accurate, and little remained to show that anyone had lived and worked along the riverbank. Of course, the incredible destruction was not only limited to the American bombers. In mid-April, Royal Air Force Bomber Command spent almost an hour destroying much of the city center and killing more than nine hundred civilians in Rouen and the suburbs, adding to the damage done in 1940, when another part of the old town had gone up in flames during the German advance. Almost three hundred Rouennais had died in the preceding week, and the only respite came as the American aircraft shifted from bombing the city to supporting the invasion landings. The air attacks continued until the Canadian army arrived to drive the Germans out at the end of August. In the minds of those who lived through it, there was a strong sense of barbaric treatment in the way the American and British Commonwealth forces abused their beloved city.[3]

This book focuses on the air war over France in relation to Operation Neptune, the landing component of Operation Overlord. Because of the offensive's nature, however, it has often been necessary to visit events earlier and later in the war. The story looks at these events from three different perspectives. Each is a different narrative, a different vision, a different mythology, of a shared central story. The most prominent view is that of the Anglo-American leaders who directed the landings that spring. Working from large command posts in London and its suburbs, these army and air officers focused on the task and purpose of bombing operations. They talked about military conditions they wanted to create and what was the best way to achieve them. They based their views on historical perspective and military doctrine. But they also wrestled with new concepts and often became embroiled in personal battles based on their experience, service, and attitude. Accurate from the command perspective, and well known to those who have studied the conflict, this narrative concentrates on the senior personalities who planned and led the invasion.

A second narrative concerns the air forces that supported the invasion with their bombs. Bombing raids over Schweinfurt, Regensburg, Ploiesti, Dresden, Hamburg, Köln, and Berlin form the heart of British, American, and Canadian narratives. Descriptions of the trauma and excessive losses to

Eighth Air Force and Bomber Command crews over these cities are familiar to even casual students of this war. It may come as a surprise, however, that from January until August 1944, the Allied heavy bombers dropped 1,000,482 tons of bombs, with only 26 percent falling on targets in Germany and another 15 percent on targets in Central Europe. France absorbed more than 45 percent of the tonnage (452,919), and Italy, since its surrender in 1943 also an Allied state, another 144,521 tons (14.4 percent).[4] In addition, American medium and light bombers, from the Ninth and Fifteenth Air Forces, dropped an additional 148,032 tons of bombs on French territory during the year, primarily in May and July. By the end of the war, France had absorbed 21 percent of all American bombs of all types compared to 41 percent dropped on German soil.[5]

These attacks generally took place over lightly defended occupied Europe rather than against Germany itself. Attacks against Boulogne-Sur-Mer, Lille, Rouen, Amiens, and Paris itself are at the heart of this story. Descriptions of targets and mission reports form the basis of this narrative. The scale and scope of this perspective provide the reader with an understanding of the massive nature of industrial warfare in the middle of the twentieth century. Machines and tonnage figures dominate this view.

The final narrative belongs to the average French man or woman who lived near the bombing targets selected in London and flown by crews in the world's most powerful air forces. While those who experienced these attacks remembered them for the rest of their lives, postwar French society, on a national level, generally ignored these events in the first decades after 1945. The effects of Allied bombing competed with problems of collaboration, the role of the Resistance, the Holocaust, communist displeasure with postwar governance, problems in Algeria, returning prisoners of war, and simply rebuilding and restoring the nation. France had just emerged from what was essentially a civil war, and no one wanted to scratch the many national scabs that had just stopped bleeding. In the past twenty years, however, French historians and the descendants of this generation have begun re-evaluating that conflict in general and the bombardment in particular. French national interest in this narrative continues to grow, while the English-speaking world remains unaware of the scope and scale of the Allied air war against France.

These stories are mostly unknown to Americans, who are more familiar with movies such as *The Longest Day*, *The Big Red One*, *Patton*, and *Saving*

Private Ryan, as well as the HBO series *Band of Brothers*. French civilians that appear in these works, if they do at all, are helpful and appreciative of the Allied invasion. Some are in the Resistance, fighting alongside their Anglo-American liberators. Others are living in villages and farmhouses, trying to survive. Seldom do movies or books portray French firefighters and first responders pulling survivors and cadavers out from under destroyed buildings, or cathedrals still smoldering from a recent air attack, or children wandering the streets looking for their parents. Rarely do these accounts discuss the civilian casualties in towns, near the beach, and across the French countryside caused by these operations. For hundreds of thousands of average civilians, that was their reality. The result is that we have strikingly different interpretations of these events, which has affected how the invaders and the invaded societies relate to one another.

Most national narratives stem from actual important events, which scholars call *fundamental stories*. These form the foundation upon which political, religious, and cultural elites can help mold their arguments and affect how a population views itself and the world. Events such as the founding of the English colonies, the creation of the Constitution, the US Civil War, expansion, and Manifest Destiny are early examples. The events become more complicated as these fundamental accounts must explain the Philippine Insurrection, the First World War, the Japanese attack on Pearl Harbor, and the nation's entry into the Second World War. For the Germans, the greatness of the Bismarckian Empire, the unanticipated defeat in the Great War, and the rise of National Socialism are all part of these primary accounts. For the British, the treasured stories include their nation's victory over the Spanish Armada, the Duke of Wellington's decisive victory at Waterloo, the sacrifice of the Great War, and the Battle of Britain. Politicians help in shaping the *war narrative* that explains for the people the purpose of the conflict, identifies its context and origins, and identifies why the state is at war.[6]

A narrative is a powerful tool that helps to unify a nation by providing a common understanding of an event. It simplifies complex occurrences and actions into stories average citizens can understand. It provides a general representation as to what happened and has enough veracity to be credible. This narrative forms the foundation for a constructed reality, the accepted, and often sacred, truth that helps unify members of the national group. In many ways, it contributes to creating a social community. For military events, this condensed story contributes to explaining the role of the nation and its people in the larger story. The "Japs" attacked the peaceful United States, so the standard narrative goes, and America responded as the arsenal of democracy and liberated the occupied countries. The British escaped from Dunkerque[7] to stand alone during the Battle of Britain and then withstood the Blitz against all the odds. Joined by their American cousins, they landed in Europe to liberate the oppressed French and Belgian people. The German people have a much different narrative that includes the Treaty of Versailles, Jews, Bolsheviks, and the Great Depression. These stories are not universal, and people from one region will have different experiences than those in other parts of the country or will be caught up in a different set of circumstances. For example, many German soldiers who fought only on the Russian front have fundamentally different perspectives from those who spent most of the war in western Europe. Bomber pilots stationed in the United Kingdom but conducting several missions a week over occupied Europe have a different perspective of the war than the French and German civilians forced to live under their bombs.

As time goes by, these narratives may transform into stories embellished for personal or political reasons and may therefore become national myths. These myths help to bind different societies and contribute to issues of nationalism and community.[8] Museums, public libraries, monuments, and the public school system reinforce these interpretations. Indeed, the American and Commonwealth narrative of D-Day has provided a story of the "greatest generation" that helped make sense of the Second World War in Europe for those who lived in the United States, the United Kingdom, and Canada.[9] President Ronald Reagan captured the essence of the Anglo-American viewpoint in his historic presentations in Normandy on June 6, 1984. That morning at Pointe de Hoc, the scene of a determined struggle in 1944, Reagan described the dramatic actions of American Rangers on the cliffs overlooking the landing beaches. In front of the world's television cameras, he addressed the old men, the survivors, sitting in front of him:

> Behind me is a memorial that symbolizes the Ranger daggers that were thrust into the top of these cliffs. And before me are the men who put them there.
>
> These are the boys of Pointe du Hoc. These are the men who took the cliffs. These are the champions who helped free a continent. These are the heroes who helped end a war.[10]

The president then headed to Omaha Beach, with the white crosses of the military cemetery as a backdrop. As in the case of the previous speech, Reagan had everyone in the audience in tears. To those in attendance and watching on televisions in the United States, he described a letter he had received from the adult daughter of Pfc. Robert Zanatta, who always wanted to return to the scene of the battle. Building on the previous speech, he summarized the American view of the war:

> When men like Private Zanatta and all our Allied forces stormed the beaches of Normandy forty years ago they came not as conquerors, but as liberators. When these troops swept across the French countryside and into the forests of Belgium and Luxembourg they came not to take, but to return what had been wrongly seized. When our forces marched into Germany they came not to prey on a hated and defeated people, but to nurture the seeds of democracy among those who yearned to be free again.[11]

To Reagan and most Americans, it was a pure, noble cause. As convincing as the president was that day, however, this interpretation distorts reality, and not everyone who participated in the struggle accepted it. As Paul Fussell points out in his classic *Wartime*, "For the past fifty years the Allied war has been sanitized and romanticized almost beyond recognition by the sentimental, loony patriotic, the ignorant, and the bloodthirsty."[12] The missing civilian experience is part of that modern sanitization, as is the myth that the American and British air fleets were attacking only German targets. In their attempt to liberate the European continent from Axis control, Allied aircraft damaged or destroyed cities across the occupied states of France, Italy, Belgium, and the Netherlands, killing, wounding, and displacing tens of thousands of civilians.[13] Historian Norman Davies notes that "it is not difficult to see that powerful myths have arisen that override all accurate records or recollections of what actually happened in 1939–45. The victorious countries hang on to these myths, endlessly repeating the simplified storylines that serve both as parables of Right and Wrong and as guides to political action."[14] These nations hold on to these different perspectives since they reflect long-held beliefs based on truth and modified to reflect the changing society, not the event.

Other than the clash of Union and Confederate armies at Gettysburg in 1863, no military event has received more attention from American authors than the Anglo-Canadian-British landing on the Normandy beaches in June 1944. In this narrative, America's greatest generation came to rescue the old world from the grip of the Nazi ogre.[15] As noted by Reagan, this noble cause to liberate a people reflected the United States at its best and heralded the beginning of America's reign as a superpower. British and Canadian perspectives are similar to the American but are more somber, reflecting the significant price the Commonwealth had paid in blood and treasure by 1944 and the reality that Washington was supplanting London as the center of the English-speaking world. This is also a story of personalities. Gen. Dwight David Eisenhower, the supreme commander of all Allied forces, was an American Moses who returned democracy to Europe. Fueled by postwar memoirs and politics, it is also a story of arguments between the principals over issues of policy and strategy, operating methods, and even tactics. Authors have expended much ink arguing for or against the importance of Gens. Omar Bradley, George S. Patton, and Bernard L. Montgomery. All of this is interesting and familiar to students of the conflict.

The US Army took the lead in creating this narrative with the famous "Green Book" series of official histories. Formally called the *United States Army in World War II*, it got its nickname from the color of its primary volumes. With seventy-five different titles, the Army's history branch published it over a space of forty-five years, and the series became the standard for all subsequent ground interpretations of the operation. Missing in all these is a discussion of the effects of Ultra, the radio eavesdropping program, and bombing in the Pas-de-Calais as part of Operation Fortitude. While they discuss the importance of targeting French railways to delay the arrival of German reserve forces, they say little about the scale of the bombing or its effect on French society. These books rarely discuss unpleasant aspects of the conflict such as prisoner mistreatment, soldier misconduct, or the killing of civilians and the destruction of their homes.[16] British and Canadian official army narratives focus on their respective forces but are in the same vein as their American equivalents, although nowhere near as voluminous.[17]

Bookshelves groan under the weight of histories that tell this story from the Anglo-American point of view, with some attempt to include the Germans in the account. Most of these studies glorify the performance of this or that unit, or the decisions of a particular general, showing why this was the key to the Allied success. They are all triumphant marches that focus on the personalities of the opposing forces, with little attention paid to those caught in the middle of the conflict.[18] Most Anglo-American journalists and historians have followed the narrative path blazed by Cornelius Ryan in the late 1950s.[19] From the earliest days, therefore, the narrative for most Americans' understanding of the invasion and its aftermath was the heroic liberation of France from the oppressive Nazis.[20] This story focuses on the tactical actions to prepare and execute the landings and parachute drops. Comments concerning bombing and air support during the invasion note its ineffectiveness and inaccuracy and omit the larger perspective.[21]

In all these stories and the movies they inspired or generated, Frenchmen are usually bystanders, members of the Resistance, or ignored. For example, in *The Longest Day*, Ryan sets the tone for subsequent books by describing some of the French families who live along the beach, such as those watching Germans and celebrating first communions at the local church. Other civilians receive the message from London warning of the invasion and begin moving to sabotage sites. Others, such as Amélie Lechevalier, sat in a prison in Caen, a few miles from the beach, awaiting execution for a variety of "forbidden" activities. With the invasion in progress, German firing squads began killing the ninety-two Frenchmen behind bars. Ryan discusses these atrocities but says nothing of the Allied bombing of the same city that afternoon. When he summarizes casualties resulting from the invasion, he describes American, British, Canadian, and even German losses. In contrast, he says nothing about the thousands of French civilian lives destroyed.[22] This pattern remains consistent in the subsequent decades. In one of the best narratives of the ground invasion, *Decision in Normandy*, Carlo D'Este mostly ignores the bombing operations both on and beyond the beach as well as the existence of French civilians anywhere.[23] British author Max Hastings' comprehensive *Overlord* describes in some detail Eisenhower's air struggles but says nothing about the massive bombardment of French cities. He treats the French as interested bystanders, but takes time to discuss "overworked Norman prostitutes."[24] Stephen Ambrose's *D-Day* devotes almost two full chapters to the issue of air support, including the bombing of rail yards and Operation Fortitude. The specifics of the missions, however, are nonexistent, and according to Ambrose, the results, especially along the beach, "turned out to be a bust."[25] Ambrose says even less about the French who lived in Normandy. While adhering to the general narrative, recent authors have begun including discussions of bombing activities and French civilians. Anthony Beevor and Rick Atkinson, for example, have done a much better job of integrating the civilian and aviation component into their manuscripts. Nevertheless, in the grand narrative of events, the authors have difficulty conveying the reality of the damage to French society or the scale of the air actions across France. They seldom describe the story of incidents beyond the beach in these books.[26]

The second narrative is the perspective of the American, British, and Canadian air force units that bombed the targets in France. In contrast to the armies of all invaders, the aviation branches, especially the bomber forces, have sought to downplay their participation in Operation Neptune, the code name for the landing phase of Operation Overlord, the overall invasion. While infantry, armor, and artillery officers could describe hotly contested battles at the beach and into the bocage, the air perspective usually consisted of keeping the few German fighters away from the landing force and dropping bombs on lightly defended French targets. What the principal air commanders—Air Chief Marshal Arthur T. Harris, commander of Bomber Command, and Lt. Gen. Carl Spaatz, commander of United States Army Strategic Air Forces—emphasized was the importance of their heavy bombers against targets in Germany. For many reasons, attacking anything in France was a sideshow and not something they wished to emphasize.

Like the American, British, and Canadian armies, the air forces began work on their histories soon after the conflict's end. Historians Wesley F. Craven and James L. Cate authored a six-volume history of the conflict, with three of these volumes focused on the European theater. More than in the case of the Army, these books reflect the doctrinal perspective of the US Army Air Force's leadership, emphasizing in particular the role of strategic bombing.[27] The first volume ends with a chapter devoted entirely to the Eighth Air Force's first mission, against the rail yard at Rouen-Sotteville, in August 1942. It ends with the general theme that held through in all the official histories: "When the small force . . . took to the air on 17 August 1942 they carried with them much more than a bomb load of trouble for the enemy. They carried with them a long heritage of debate and controversy."[28] Unpleasant facts could not be allowed to distract the reader from the purpose of the history, which was to emphasize the need for a modern, independent, US Air Force and its war-winning capability of strategic bombing and delivering the war to the enemy heartland. While the second volume describes operations in North Africa and Italy, its most important chapters concern the Combined Bomber Offensive during the second half of 1943. The authors want the reader to assume that the Eighth Air Force attacked only targets inside German territory, such as Hülls, Schweinfurt, and Regensburg, and was capable of penetrating deeper into Nazi Germany and striking targets like Merseburg and Berlin. Only a few paragraphs allude to the bombing of French targets such as the aircraft factory at Nantes and submarine pens at St. Nazaire, and the "simpler tasks" of bombing airdromes and airplane factories in France.[29] But the accompanying map of targets from June through December 1943 and the appendix of targets bombed during this volume's period clearly indicate that many of the Eighth's targets were over occupied Europe rather than Germany. In fact, 138 out of 171 missions, a whopping 81 percent, were against cities in France, Belgium, and the Netherlands alone.[30] In terms of tonnage, the US Army Air Force dropped only five thousand more tons on Germany than it did on France in 1943.[31] In the third volume, the authors clearly identify the scale of the attacks and the massive bomb loads they dropped on French cities as well as against the V-1 and V-2 rocket sites (Operation Crossbow). They make no mention, however, of the cost of those missions for those living under the bombs.[32] The same applies to the extremely brief discussion of the destruction of Norman towns such as Thury-Harcourt, Lisieux, and Saint-Lô, where thousands of French civilians perished in the flames.[33] In contrast to the brief discussion of operations by the strategic Eighth Air Force in France, the tactical Ninth Air Force has an entire chapter chronologically identifying almost every target hit by its medium bombers and fighter-bombers. In general, the section describes all the missions as well executed and efficient. The authors make no mention of any civilian casualties or physical destruction to French towns or cities.[34] The official intent is clear: While medium bombers and lighter aircraft may support troops on the ground, the heavy bombers had only the mission of the strategic strike. As Conrad Crane points out, the purpose of the official history was not to tell an accurate story, but "more designed to assist the AAF (Army Air Force) in justifying independence."[35]

The Royal Air Force's Air Historical Branch produced a series of superb operational narratives during the war, which formed the basis of all subsequent official accounts. Now available through the UK National Archives and secondary publishers, they provide well-documented and detailed descriptions of almost every operation involving the RAF. Operation Neptune is the subject of three separate volumes, discussing the planning and preparation, administration, and the actual landings. Each volume provides notes and identifies the documents used in their preparation. While these authors write with incredible detail, in most regards they include almost no discussion of the effects of the bombings on French civilians.[36] Basing their work on these comprehensive reports, historians Denis Richards and Hilary St. George Saunders wrote the three-volume *Royal Air Force, 1939–1945.* The third volume covers Pointblank and Neptune, as well as attacks on the U-boat bases and Crossbow sites. While this account, sanctioned by the British government, comprehensively describes the bombing operations in France and includes several striking photographs of destroyed rail yards, it says nothing about the fate of those near the attack locations.[37] Fifteen years later, the British issued their official history, written by Charles Webster and Noble Frankland, titled the *Strategic Air Offensive against Germany.* Volume 3 examines the activities surrounding the preparation and execution of the invasion. As in all the official reports, this volume describes the intense discussions among the Anglo-Allied leadership about the problem of killing French civilians, especially when attacking the rail centers. As the title suggests, however, the emphasis is on bombing the Germans. This account ignores details about the effect these missions had on French society.[38] Published only in 1994, the Canadian official history, written by a four-person team and published by the University of Toronto, is the most scholarly of this genre. Unfortunately, it continues the tradition of erasing the civilian element from its detailed discussion of raids, statistics, and heroics.[39]

Until recently, most aviation histories have followed the lead of the official accounts. In general, they focus on describing aircraft, tons of bombs dropped, and the high loss of aircrews, especially over Germany. For these authors, the air story is taking the fight to the Germans and destroying their targets and installations. For example, Donald L. Miller's well-researched and written *Masters of the Air* ignores French sources almost entirely and bases his discussion on standard English-language books and records, in the process saying little about effects of bombing on the population.[40] Max Hastings, in his *Bomber Command* (1979), lists the German cities attacked and describes the cumulative effects of these bombardments. Unfortunately, he omits any such description of targets in Italy, France, and Belgium, reinforcing the official narrative of taking the war to the enemy.[41]

Since the turn of the century, though, new generations of historians have begun to address the issue of civilian casualties. Stephen Darlow, for example, poignantly describes the return to the rail yard at Juvisy of one of the American bomber crew members forty years after the mission that killed hundreds of civilians.[42] Claudia Baldoli and Andrew Knapp have provided the fundamental analysis of the air war over occupied countries in their work *Forgotten Blitzes*, and the bombing of occupied states is an important topic in Richard Overy's *The Bombing War*.[43] Authors are now beginning to modify the traditional heroic narrative and include the story of those affected by the use of air power to support the Allied invasion.

The French experienced the invasion period differently both from those who fought on the ground and those who dropped bombs from the air. Special memorials and plaques occupy prominent locations in train stations across France. These impressive markers, such as those in Metz and Rouen, commemorate railroad workers killed by friendly bombers trying to destroy France's rail infrastructure from April through June 1944. Others demand a traveler's attention, such as a large plaque on the side of the promontory, called the Enclos, in Saint-Lô that proclaims (in French): "To the memory of the victims of the bombardment that destroyed the city of Saint-Lô. Six June Nineteen forty-four." Others are not so grand but are still powerful, such as the tombs in the Saint-Désir cemetery outside of Lisieux, which are the final resting place for whole families killed by American and British attempts to block the flow of German reinforcements to the invasion beaches. On one of them, the community had placed a small black marble marker with letters indicating the addition of a later arrival. "J-P Cordier, 1938–1992," whom we discussed earlier in this introduction, had rejoined his family forty-eight years after his parents' demise. The burial markers have been in place for almost seventy years, but many of the monuments are of much more recent construction and represent the survivors' need to pass on to subsequent generations an understanding of the trauma of the time. Each testifies to local memory, and this represents something fundamentally unique to each locale. On a broader scale, however, these monuments and family memorials combine to form a growing element of France's collective memory of the Second World War. The resulting national narrative is essentially missing from the Anglo-Saxon understanding of the conflict.[44]

So what is this revised narrative? If you lived near a French rail yard or factory, near a harbor or along the coast in the Pas-de-Calais, you lived under the constant threat of Allied bombardment. This threat existed from the beginning of the war, but from January through July 1944, the RAF Bomber Command and the US Army Strategic Air Forces dropped more bombs on occupied Europe than on Germany. It was only after the ground forces approached the German border in August that these attacks against French and Belgian targets decreased and more bombs began to fall on the Nazi homeland. The Royal Air Force statistics are similar; from April through August 1944, more than three-fourths of all bombs dropped were against targets in France and other occupied territories.[45] In Normandy south of the Seine River, casualties were high during the invasion itself. By the end of June 8, 1944, almost four thousand French civilians lay dead, thousands more were wounded, and ancient towns and dozens of old churches were reduced to rubble. All this carnage, on the ground and from the air, was a result of Operation Overlord.[46] By the time the war was over, the liberating air forces had killed as many French civilians as the Germans had killed British civilians during the "blitz" and vengeance weapon assaults. The total French toll caused by Allied bombs was between 60,000 and 70,000 out of 150,000 French civilian deaths during the war.[47] Unfortunately for the French, the American and Commonwealth bombers were far more methodical and efficient, causing more physical damage to their cities, harbors, and rail lines than the Germans had to London.[48] Not all Frenchmen desired this kind of liberation, and it is not a narrative that comforts former allies. It certainly detracts from the wholesome image of American, British, and Canadian soldiers battling Nazis to liberate an eagerly awaiting French population.[49] The reader should also keep in mind the particular story is different depending on where one lived. For example, if you lived in the departments of the Indre, Dordogne, or along the Rhone, your memories might be based on the violent civil war fought between the Maquis and the Vichy Milice. The damage done to much of France by Allied bombardment, nevertheless, is significant and forms an important part of that generation's memory.

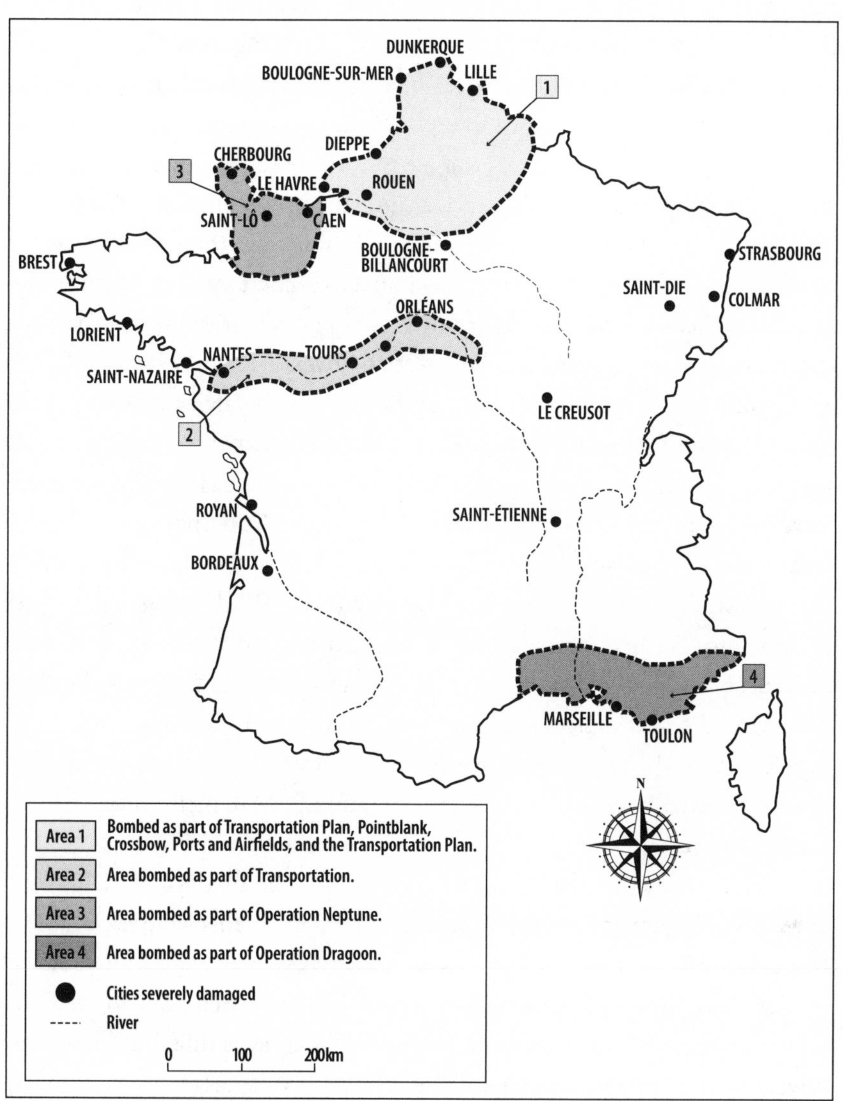

Map 1. French areas heavily bombed by Allies, 1943–44

France's tumultuous postwar history kept this part of its war experience in the background. Many issues deflected attention from a public understanding of this bombing campaign. These include the resolution of participants' roles in the occupation governments and their degrees of collaboration. Into the 1970s, tension remained between communist and Gaullist resistance movements. Participation as victims or perpetrators of the Shoah was also a primary source of the public's interest. Memories of service in forced labor organizations or as prisoners of war all contributed to a desire to forget this part of the past.[50] There is still no governmental discussion that provides citizens a common memory of these events.[51] More pressing issues, such as the wars in Indo-China and Algeria and France's place in the new Europe, also acted to deflect interest in this controversial period. With the approaching demise of the war's generation, however, their relatives and extended family are beginning to explore the history of the period. This interest began locally in Normandy after the fortieth anniversary of the invasion. In 1997, a French journalist and former member of the Resistance, Eddy Florentin, compiled local stories and archives into a national exposé on the bombing campaign.[52] Since then, French scholarly and popular interest in this story has continued to develop, with cities, such as Le Havre in 2014, hosting conferences to look into its cause, conduct, and consequences.[53] When confronted with these accounts, English-speaking audiences often defend these bombings as necessary to defeat Hitler's forces or note that many French were supporting the German war effort. Usually one hears the retort that these attacks and any resulting casualties were the "price of liberation."[54] Making such a statement is easy when one's family members are not the victims.

Two themes, therefore, permeate this book. The first is the relationship of the bombing operations to the physical invasion. The Allied Expeditionary Force's bombing of France was not an isolated air problem, but an integral part of Eisenhower's overall design. As historian Richard Overy has pointed out, "(Bombing) has all too often been treated as if it could be abstracted in some way from what else was going on." "Bombing," Overy observes, "was always only one part of a broad strategic picture, and a much smaller part than air force leaders liked to think. . . . The operational history is all too often seen as distinct from the political, social and cultural consequences for the victim communities: a battle history rather than a history of societies at war."[55] The purpose for bombing France was not an air problem, as was the case with

Operation Pointblank and the air campaign against Germany. It was the overall commander, Dwight David Eisenhower, who directed these air attacks. One should not expect to find the reason for these air operations in France in the minds of the air commanders; they did not want to do it. It was Eisenhower and Montgomery who demanded that the respective air forces provide the support they needed to prepare for the assault, securing the beachheads, and the subsequent breakout. The multiple air operations against France were all part of Eisenhower's operational concept. Everything the air forces, as well as the navies, merchant marines, and armies, did directly or indirectly supported these landings. Popular and professional studies have only tacitly acknowledged this relationship. The aviation community has ignored it because it highlighted collateral damage among a friendly population. The traditional narrative ignored it because Anglo-American writers could not see the bombing from the ground force perspective. For the liberated population, however, these attacks, *beyond the beach*, created a different narrative.

The second theme is that French casualties during the June 1944 invasion were not confined to the villages in Normandy, but occurred across France. This French-centered perspective is different from the land-based narrative so familiar to most citizens of the United States and the Commonwealth. Little they have read or seen has provided them any indication that there is another perspective. They believe the air forces focused on the war against Germany, flying missions against Schweinfurt, Berlin, and Dresden, rather than dropping bombs on friendly cities. But American, British, and Canadian bombers visited cities across France, from Boulogne in the north to Marseille in the south. From April until the end of June, from Brest in the west to Metz in the east, most bombing missions had the intent of facilitating the infantry landing on the Norman coast. The French and German casualties on Berck Beach, south of Boulogne, were part of the drama taking place on Omaha Beach. How did these distant bombing operations relate to one another?

This book explores the relationship between ground and air operations and its effects on the French population. It begins by considering the three broad groups the air operations involved: the occupied French, the occupying Germans, and Eisenhower's headquarters. It then examines the doctrine and equipment used by Allied air force leaders to implement the supreme commander's plans. Next, it examines each of the eight major operations, called lines of effort, that coordinated the thousands of fighters, medium bombers, and heavy bombers that prowled the French skies that spring and summer of 1944. Each of these sections discusses the operation's purpose, conduct, and effects upon both the military and the civilian targets. Finally, the book explores short- and long-term effects of these activities. To begin, therefore, we need to start by understanding the perspectives of those who inhabited the environment, the French civilians of 1944.

CHAPTER TWO

THE OPERATIONAL ENVIRONMENT

The first American bombing mission of the war, against the Sotteville rail center adjacent to Rouen, is one example of competing narratives. Although British Bomber Command attacked these rail yards on numerous occasions, its commander, Air Marshal Arthur Harris, was not enthusiastic about sending his admittedly inaccurate Halifax and Lancaster bombers against the occupied territory. Therefore, other than a few attacks by Blenheims and other smaller aircraft, the rail yard was untouched and full of railcars. It was an enticing first target and close enough to the United Kingdom to ensure proper air cover. Shortly after 1530 hours on August 17, 1942, twelve US Army Air Force Boeing B-17E Flying Fortresses departed Grafton Underwood Airfield in England. Watching on the runway was the American air commander Gen. Carl "Tooey" Spaatz, accompanied by a host of journalists and politicians. In one aircraft was Maj. Gen. Ira C. Eaker, VIII Bomber Command's commander. The British were determined not to let the Americans fail and provided four squadrons of Spitfires to intercept German fighters.[1] The aircraft crossed the English Channel and arrived over Rouen without being intercepted by German fighters. At 1839 hours, they dropped their bombs and headed back to England. On the way back, they took fire from an anti-aircraft battery and were the object of Luftwaffe attempts at interception. A series of intense dogfights took place, and the British lost four Spitfires and the Germans an FW 190.

When the bomb crews returned to Grafton Underwood, without casualties, there was much backslapping and cheering. As the official history notes, "Pilots and mechanics swarmed out to meet the incoming crews like, as one observer put it, the crowds at a football rally." The history's report of the bombing is typical of airmen reports throughout the war over France. Of the 36,900 pounds of bombs dropped that day, it noted that "approximately half fell in the general target area." The results were good enough for Spaatz to cable Gen. Henry H. Arnold, chief of the Army Air Force in Washington the next day: "The attack on Rouen had, he wired on 18 August, far exceeded in accuracy any previous high-altitude bombing in the European theater by German or Allied aircraft. Moreover, it was his understanding that the results justified 'our belief' in the feasibility of daylight bombing."[2] Thus, with considerable fanfare, did the new weapon of American daylight bombing enter the Allied arsenal against the Nazis. There is no comment in the Air Force's official history as to what happened to the rest of the bombs, nor did the official crew reports at the time provide any comment on possible civilian casualties. French sources, however, note that the attack killed 52 civilians and injured another 120.[3] Each affected family has a personal, gripping story. For example, in one instance a father, named Armand, rushed home to look for his family after the bombing began. He could find no one in the ruins of his demolished home. Civilian authorities surveying the damage directed him to a nearby morgue. In one room, he found bodies stored awaiting identification. He moved into another one where, on a large table, about twenty cadavers lay side by side. Up front were the bodies of his two parents and his young son. They were naked, still bleeding, and wearing only socks. There was no trace of his daughter.[4] This story is just one of many public experiences that help explain why the French narrative of the event was different from the American.

As mentioned earlier, historians seldom consider the French story, and indeed the entire French war experience, in evaluating the air war in Europe, even though France and Belgium absorbed 21 percent of all American bombs delivered by heavy, medium, and light bombers throughout the war. Dodd and Knapp argue that the RAF Bomber Command's statistics are similar, with about 30 percent of total bombs dropped on the occupied territories.[5] Standard historical accounts ignore these events and focus on the prowess of specific commanders, the motivation and skill of their soldiers, and the quality of their equipment and organization. Or, as in the case with heroic stories, the book's focus is on the bravery of the soldier in combat. That is acceptable if the intended reader understands the bigger picture and can place the book's events in the context of the larger narrative. Unfortunately, that is not the case, and readers, who are anticipating only a good story, might come away with the impression that America, General Patton, and the Band of Brothers are all they need to know about the Second World War. While these accounts are interesting and compelling, a conflict's outcome depends on a host of complex factors, all interacting with the military forces to produce unique and unanticipated results.

This chapter examines the operational environment that the Allied air forces expended so much energy attacking. To set the stage for later chapters, this one describes the traditional factors of geography, infrastructure, and history. It includes a brief description of the 1940 campaign and the outlines of the subsequent Nazi occupation and adds context to explain why certain facilities became targets for the air forces. Finally, describing the interaction of the French and German civilians, who engaged in an ideological, social, economic, and political dance throughout the occupation, it provides a human dimension to this story. In general, Neptune's planners had a relatively sophisticated understanding of their operational environment, especially regarding the region's history, geography, and culture. They had a reasonable understanding of what had happened during the campaign, how the German military had translated operational success into a military occupation, and the economic role France played in its war effort. In many ways, however, they did not appreciate the relationship of French society to the occupation. Of course, this is a limited analysis to remind readers of the European war and to show how the bombing fit into the most destructive event of the twentieth century. Hopefully, it will spark some interest in readers to consider the conflict from different perspectives.

Traditional Factors

France is an ancient country that has been a work in progress at least since Julius Caesar and the Gauls clashed in the middle of the first century BCE. While the subsequent two thousand years of history is fascinating, the environment of the first few decades of the twentieth century is most relevant for understanding the context of the bombing operations. These include the geographical environment, the nation's physical infrastructure, economic status, and the perception the population had of war at the end of the 1940 campaign. With a population in 1936 of less than forty million people, slightly more than half of Germany's, France occupied the most important terrain in western Europe, at the intersection of the critical ocean and land trade routes. While it honored its historical regions, such as Picardie, Bretagne, or Auvergne, the government, based in Paris, administered the nation through ninety *départements* (roughly the size of counties). It had an extensive land border totaling 1,709 miles (2,751 kilometers), bordering Belgium, Luxembourg, Germany, Switzerland, Italy, and Spain. Its maritime boundary was even greater, with 2,129 miles (3,427 kilometers) of coastlines opening onto the Mediterranean Sea, Atlantic Ocean, and the narrow English Channel, which the French called La Manche. At its most restricted point, the Pas-de-Calais is only 20.6 miles (33.1 kilometers) from southern England, which can easily be seen on a bright day. Its largest city was Paris, with 2.8 million inhabitants. Other large cities included Marseille (914,232), Lyon (570,622), Toulouse (213,220), Lille (200,575), and Bordeaux (258,348).[6]

Although several mountain ranges, especially the Alps, the Vosges, and the Pyrenees, border the nation on the east and south, much of the country consists of gently rolling hills, the exception being the rugged terrain of the Massif Central in the south-central portion of the state. France had an extensive road network, with some roads dating back to the Roman era, and a well-developed rail system. Rivers have always been an important aspect of French geography, with the Seine, which flows through Paris, and its tributaries the Oise, Aisne, and Marne, the most prominent. Other important rivers include the Somme and the Meuse in the north and the Loire, which passes through Nantes, and the Garonne, which flows into the Bay of Biscay through Bordeaux, farther south. Flowing north to south is the Rhone, which flows through Lyon and empties into the Mediterranean near Marseille. Part of the Rhine near Strasbourg, which flows from south to north, forms the natural border with Germany. Man-made canals connected or improved many of these rivers. The harbors at the ends of these waterways contributed to France's early engagement with the world and its development of a large colonial empire. This strategic location between the sea, where England was the principal power, and land, where Germany was the dominant power, ensured it would continue in almost perpetual conflict with one or the other. Bordering both Germany and England guaranteed the French a significant role in Adolf Hitler's attempt to redress the wrongs of the First World War.

Government-directed construction, especially roads, harbors, rail lines, and airfields, enhanced France's geographical location and river network. The country's sophisticated highway system was developed during three centuries of Roman occupation as Rome's legions designed and built thousands of miles of roads to move troops and supplies across its empire. Beginning with Louis XIV's reign, modern French governments continued to invest considerable sums in improving and extending this network. Given historical and geographical forces, almost all French roads converged on Paris. Napoleon Bonaparte introduced order into the system by designating some of these roads as imperial highways. The July Monarchy (1830–48) renamed them *routes nationales*, or national highways, in 1830 and gave them numbers beginning with the letter "N." Departments could designate smaller roads as departmental roads, which on French maps start with the letter "D." Many of these routes connect to some of the finest harbors in the world with a rich tradition of seafaring.

The old ports of Narbonne and Marseille were centers of trade in the Roman world. In 55 BCE, Roman general Julius Caesar launched his raids into Britain from harbors around modern Boulogne.[7] A thousand years later, William of Normandy departed the natural harbor of Saint-Valery-sur-Somme in 1066 for the last successful invasion of the island. Sailors from Saint-Malo, Honfleur, Dunkerque, Calais, Dieppe, and La Rochelle competed with English, Spanish, and Portuguese fishermen for the cod and other sea dwellers of the Grand Banks during the first decades of American colonization and exploration. These ports also served as bases for both explorers of the New World and the buccaneers who preyed on the Spanish treasure fleets of the sixteenth century.[8] By 1940, hundreds of harbors and anchorages dotted the two thousand miles of French coastline.[9]

As in the rest of western Europe, extensive rail facilities modified the nation's landscape during the railway revolution of the nineteenth century. By the 1930s, the French system was as developed and as dense as any in the world, with almost 30,000 miles of track. This dense rail network is mainly present in the north, where the government had expanded the system during the previous conflict. Nearly half of all rail lines had a double track (compared to less than 15 percent in the United States), and most shared the same gauge as the remainder of western Europe.[10] Even before the Great War, moreover, France was a leader in aviation. The massive conflict against the Germans required the creation of hundreds of airfields to house more than 530 squadrons of French, Commonwealth, and American aircraft. Some of these facilities remained operational after the war, and Paris-Le Bourget became one of the first commercial airports in the world, beginning service in 1919. The other main airports included those near Calais, Dieppe, Abbeville, Arras, Lille, and Valenciennes.[11]

This geography and infrastructure, along with an educated and industrious workforce, contributed to a sophisticated economic system. By the end of the Great War, France was an industrial powerhouse, producing an amazing array of tanks, trucks, aircraft, and artillery tubes. Its disciplined factory workers supplied not only its own army's needs but supported the requirements of several other allied armies. French companies produced almost all the trucks, tanks, machine guns, and artillery tubes used by the American Expeditionary Force that arrived in Europe without heavy weapons of any kind.[12] What makes this even more interesting is that the most important French mining and manufacturing infrastructure lay in the north and northeast, near the Belgian and German borders. About 75 percent of the nation's coal mines and 95 percent of iron-ore production facilities had been under German control and had been destroyed in the course of the conflict. Almost all of France's textile production was in the same region and had also suffered tremendously. After the war, French workers flocked back to the industrial cities and restored their damaged facilities. In the years following the conflict, the manufacturing sector had recovered and developed into a sophisticated consumer and civilian industrial economy. Citroën and Renault for automobiles, Michelin for tires, and Ateliers de construction du Nord for rail locomotives are just some of the major industrial firms that competed in the international marketplace. Of course, the lingering effects of the war, social turmoil, economic conservatism, and the Great Depression of 1929 all limited economic growth in the 1930s. On the eve of the German invasion, however, French industry and the French economy were reviving to levels not seen since before 1914, and the country was a leader in textiles and general manufacturing. Nevertheless, south of the Seine, except regions around Marseille and Lyon, the nation devoted most of its land and energy to agriculture, with a third of the active population working on the land as late as 1939. In many ways, France remained a conservative, rural society.

Few nations have as extensive a military history as France, with the Crusades, the Hundred Years' War, the Seven Years' War, the French Revolution and Napoleonic Era, and the Franco-Prussian War being some of the most significant conflicts. Most relevant for this discussion are its experience in the war that ended in 1918 and the 1940 campaign. Both of these had a profound effect on French society during the German occupation. As Gordon Wright commented in 1995, "No historian has yet managed to measure the consequences of the First World War,—'the Great War,' as Frenchmen still call it—on the French nation."[13] From August 1914 through the summer of 1918 the French army, and its Belgian and British allies, fought an incredibly bloody conflict with its German neighbor. Following the final enemy offensive in 1918, the Anglo-French forces, now bolstered by a seemingly unending stream of American troops, drove the Germans out of the country, causing the collapse of the Hohenzollern Dynasty.[14]

Other than Serbia, no other state suffered such a high percentage of manpower losses during the Great War; out of eight million mobilized, more than five million became casualties, approximately 10 percent of the male population. Thirty percent of all infantrymen perished in battle, an astounding statistic by any measure. In perspective, the continued loss of life was the equivalent of nine September 11 attacks each month for fifty-one months. The prolonged struggle also resulted in the spoilage of some of the nation's most productive agricultural and mining resources. French industrial production immediately after the conflict was only 60 percent of prewar levels. The fighting destroyed almost 1,700 towns and villages and more than 20,000 factories, large and small. Economists have argued that the war set industrial growth back by nearly a decade.[15] As much as the physical losses, the war aggravated the centuries-old social cleavages in French society. The war also encouraged the demise of French traditional craft production and the conversion to a machine-based industrial economy. Leaving the villages for factories in the city, the new urban workers were even more radical than their revolutionary predecessors and were open to communist and labor union proselytizers. Most of these industrial laborers escaped duty in the trenches, as the government increasingly demanded the production of war material to feed the armies in combat. It was the French farmer who found himself on the front lines, bearing the national burden of fighting and suffering as much as 50 percent of the total casualties. Wives and young children struggled to keep family farms and small shops operating while the men were away. When the fifty-one months of the war were over, many farmers no longer trusted their government and resented those who had not shared the cost of the victory.[16] The psychological effect of this human tragedy on the thirty-eight million surviving Frenchmen created a scarred narrative that made many determined never to experience such an ordeal again; the price of evicting the invader had simply been too high. The debate over this experience continued among the population throughout the interwar period. Monuments scattered across France to the dead. The *monuments aux morts*, the war memorials erected in every single French city, town, and village, as well as family struggles to find loved ones, reminded Frenchmen almost daily of the price a generation had paid. Was it worth it? Should we do it again?[17]

The Defeat

The 1940 campaign is one of the most discussed, analyzed, and misunderstood events in military history. Contrary to the Cold War perspective that the French defeat was the result of German brilliance and French cowardice, a more balanced consideration arrives at a narrative of the French military, government, and society contributing to the Wehrmacht success.[18] Anyone with an interest in the Second World War knows the campaign's general outline. When the German army Group B invaded the Netherlands and seized the Belgian fortress at Eben-Emael on May 10, 1940, the French army commander, General Maurice Gamelin, ordered his forces into Belgium. Rather than prudently occupying the best fighting positions north of the French border, however, he ordered his troops to move northeast of Brussels along the Dyle River and then continue into the Netherlands near Breda. His deputy, General Alphonse Georges, vigorously protested this movement so far from the base, remarking that with this extended distance "we could be deprived of the necessary means for a counter-attack."[19] As the Allied forces moved into Belgium, German army Group A wormed its way through the Ardennes Forest. By the morning of May 14, German tanks, generally inferior to French models but massed at the decisive point on the battlefield, crossed the Meuse River near Sedan. The French infantry conducted a determined defense along the Meuse, but it was to no avail as no help was arriving. As the German historian Karl-Heinz Frieser notes, "One could already tell on May 14 that the Allied troops had been outmaneuvered because of their false deployment and had thus lost the campaign."[20] Once the Germans were beyond the thin defenses along the Meuse, their leadership and experience took over. Commanders made decisions from the front and demonstrated the finest in tactical and operational leadership. Using the classic principles of war of mass, maneuver, and economy of force, which the French and British generals ignored, nine panzer divisions converged on a line between Cambrai and St. Quentin, only sixty kilometers wide.[21] Behind them marched the infantry and artillery, keeping the pressure on the retreating forces and establishing a line of contact along the Somme River. In the air, the Luftwaffe dominated the sky, attacking moving units and keeping Allied aircraft away from the ground troops. Allied attempts to bomb the bridges over the Meuse on May 13 and 14 resulted in little more than the loss of fifty British and French aircraft.[22]

By May 20, German general Heinz Guderian's 16th Panzer Corps had arrived in Abbeville and began moving north along the coast. By then the French army in Belgium was having serious logistical and communication problems, and the arrival of the enemy in its rear only made it worse.[23] As on the Meuse, without direction from senior headquarters, isolated French infantry units fought back against the enemy onslaught. Fighting was intense, especially at Valenciennes, Lille, and outside the Dunkerque pocket. French forces did not just surrender the ports of Boulogne-sur-Mer and Calais but defended them fiercely.[24] German frustration with the French defenders of these and other cities resulted in retaliation, including the execution of more than six hundred French civilians and Anglo-French prisoners of war.[25] With British forces on the verge of annihilation, Churchill ordered the Royal Navy to begin evacuating British troops from the port city on May 26 under the code name Dynamo. On May 30, Churchill ordered the Royal Navy to start moving French forces as well. By the time the Germans moved into Dunkerque on June 5, the mixed fleet of naval and civilian vessels had pulled 198,000 British, 140,000 French, and, several thousand Belgian, Dutch, and Polish troops across the channel. The last 40,000 French defenders surrendered and began their march to the German prisoner-of-war compounds. Most of the evacuated French forces would return to France, without equipment, to rejoin the fight. They had little chance of success, and most would join their comrades in captivity. While poorly commanded, they had fought well, as attested by the over 49,000 German soldiers who perished during the campaign.[26]

While the British public celebrated the evacuation, the French felt betrayed. William Shirer, the American journalist who followed the German army across France and had the opportunity to interview many of the participants, realized almost immediately the animosity that Dynamo caused between the former allies. Shirer learned that eighty-four-year-old Philippe Pétain, marshal of France and one of the most respected personalities to emerge from the previous war, was not happy with the British. According to Shirer, Pétain told William Bullitt, the American ambassador to France, during the evacuation that he believed the British wanted the French to "fight without help until the last available drop of French blood" and then they would make peace with Hitler.[27] According to Shirer, on June 4 General Maxime Weygand, who had replaced Gamelin as commander on May 19, had an outburst at a conference with prime minister Paul Reynaud and Pétain, who had joined the government as vice premier on May 18. Weygand exclaimed that the effort to close the gap between the northern forces and those south of the Somme would have succeeded if "the British had not continually looked back toward the sea," as they had in the first war.[28] For many, there was no love for the British allies.

One of the most important features of French society during this period, one that would later influence civilian responsiveness to evacuation warnings, was the Exode, the flight of French and Belgian civilians away from the advancing German troops. There were reasons for citizens fleeing their homes and trying to get away since it had only been twenty-two years since the Germans had last occupied Belgium and northern France. For more than four years following the invasion of August 1914, the departments of the north, with 12 percent of the French population, were under military occupation, and the purpose of the occupation was to support the enemy's war effort. They conscripted civilians for forced labor, confiscated buildings and equipment for their use, and so disrupted the economic balance that they reduced most French civilians to some level of starvation. Stories of atrocities, real and imagined, committed by Germans upon the civil population became part of the national narrative. From the French perspective, this occupation was a disaster and its memory remained embedded in the psychological makeup of anyone over the age of thirty. It was the memory of this period that sparked the stampede to get away. Many refugees remained scattered across the country, and even the world, for the duration of the war. This dispersion, some of it permanent, makes any accurate accounting of civilian casualties almost impossible.[29]

The Belgians, who had spent most of the Great War under occupation, were the first to leave, and they began flowing into French cities a few days after the invasion.[30] This civilian movement was an unplanned evacuation, and it complicated the lives of French generals and administrators alike. They moved on the same roads as military units and contested the same rest areas and water, and German aircraft routinely attacked them in an attempt to increase confusion behind the lines. There was no system in place for feeding or housing the refugees. Whole cities emptied out. For example, Lille went from 200,000 to 20,000 inhabitants and Chartres from 23,000 to only 800. Meanwhile, other cities exploded with the influx of migrants from Belgium and northern France. Bordeaux doubled in size to over 600,000, and Pau north of the Pyrenees grew from 30,000 to over 150,000. While we will never know the exact number, between six and eight million Frenchmen left their homes and tried to get away. They carried what they could by any means available, often bicycles and carts. Those who used automobiles soon had them confiscated by soldiers or left them broken or out of fuel. In some places, the roads appeared as extended trash dumps, with abandoned treasures mingling with dead horses and discarded military equipment. With most of the young men at the front, women and grandparents led the evacuation. Many never made it to a final destination and died on the way. Some, and we will never know how many, committed suicide when facing the prospect of losing it all. On the way, families separated and lost track of one another.[31] For some, this displacement would continue until the end of the war as the Germans would not allow them to return to areas they believed to be important, such as the forbidden zone in the Pas-de-Calais. Others would be thankful to come back to their homes alive. Later, when Allied aircraft dropped leaflets on French towns telling the citizens to evacuate, they were not quick to respond. They had done that already.

As the civilians attempted to keep moving ahead of the conflict, the Germans began to realize the scale of their success, and they prepared to exploit it. By the afternoon of June 5, the German units had regrouped along the Somme and were ready to complete the destruction of the French state. With the bulk of their mobile forces destroyed, their best troops reorganizing and without their heavy weapons, sixty understrength and poorly trained and poorly equipped French divisions struggled to establish a defensive line. They faced more than 120 veteran German units flushed with the recent string of victories and moving under the protection of a Luftwaffe that had almost total air superiority. By June 8, the invaders had broken through the Somme defensive line and began approaching the capital. Two days later, the French government left Paris to set up a new capital in Bordeaux. Prime Minister Paul Reynaud, in a fateful decision, decided not to defend Paris and declared it an open city, and German troops entered it on June 14.[32]

The French decision to quit the war and request peace is one of the great debates of the twentieth century. Was it the result of lingering effects of the Great War, the subsequent rise of pacifism, the political context of the Depression years, a breakdown in civil-military relations, or simple military incompetence? Perhaps all these factors contributed to the decision and public acceptance of the defeat. For certain, under intense pressure from those in his government who believed the fight was not worth continuing, Reynaud resigned on June 16. President Albert Lebrun immediately asked Pétain to form a government. The next day, as the last prime minister of the Third Republic, the old marshal asked the Germans for an armistice. He also addressed the nation around noon indicating that his government had decided "to stop the fighting." As Robert O. Paxton wrote in his seminal and provocative work *Vichy France*, "there is simply no mistaking the wave of relief which came flooding and the anguish" of Pétain's announcement.[33] No one wanted to continue the war. Only a relatively few politicians and military officers, ultimately led by the unknown brigadier general Charles de Gaulle, determined not to accept the surrender and left the country. On June 22, in the same railcar at Rethondes where the Germans had signed the armistice that ended the Great War, the French government signed the German surrender terms.[34] De Gaulle was already in London and began the long process of organizing a national resistance. He was an outlaw to the legitimate French government that had come to terms with Hitler. In July, Pétain's government, denied by the Germans permission to either stay in Bordeaux or move back to Paris, found what it hoped would be temporary quarters at the old spa town of Vichy, near Clermont-Ferrand. On July 10, the reassembled French

Parliament gave all governing powers to the marshal and named him head of the French state. It directed him to prepare a new constitution for the nation, a task the new regime would not accomplish.

While the Vichy government had administrative responsibilities across France, the physical boundary line between the occupied and unoccupied portions of the country limited its authority. While Pétain remained as its head, Pierre Laval served as his principal minister from July through December and again from April 1942 until the war's end. A politician from the Auvergne near Clermont-Ferrand, he had served as a socialist politician during the Great War and remained as one of the Third Republic's prominent politicians throughout the interwar period. After the German victory, he became an active proponent of fascist ideology and collaboration with the German authorities. It was Laval who facilitated German administration and policies across France and supervised the maintenance of security, including overseeing a 100,000-man "Armistice Army" stationed in the unoccupied zone as well as in North Africa and across the empire. The United States retained an embassy in Vichy and continued diplomatic relations until November 1942. During this period the Vichy-controlled zone was off-limits for air attack, mostly being treated by Britain as neutral territory.[35] This situation changed in early November when the British and Americans landed in North Africa as part of Operation Torch. After some fighting and political maneuvering, Vichy forces in Algeria and Morocco switched to the Allied side. As a consequence, German and Italian forces occupied the remainder of France and disbanded the Armistice Army in the occupied zone. On November 27, Nazis failed to capture the French Mediterranean Fleet at Toulon. Admiral Jean de Laborde ordered his crews to scuttle the fleet, sending sixty-one ships to the bottom of the harbor, depriving the Germans, and the Allies, the use of this still powerful fleet.[36]

The German Military in France

In 1940, much to Hitler's surprise, his Wehrmacht had conquered France. For the next four years, he would administer it as occupied territory, fortify it, and prepare to defeat the inevitable Anglo-American invasion. In the first two years of the war, he believed he had little to fear from along the coast other than raids and harassment. By the beginning of 1943, however, following setbacks in Russia and Allied successes in the Mediterranean, he realized the war's strategic situation had changed and he could no longer ignore the situation on the Atlantic coast. In March he appointed sixty-nine-year-old Generalfeldmarschall Gerd von Rundstedt as Oberbefehlshaber West (western front commander), responsible for all military operations in France, Belgium, and the Netherlands. His fifty-two years of service focused on infantry operations, and the Allies expected him to bring this experience to the impending battle.[37] By March 1943, Allied intelligence analysts believed Oberkommando der Wehrmacht, the German High Command, to have allocated fifty-five divisions, approximately 850,000 soldiers, to the western front. By the eve of the actual invasion, the Allies would raise this number to sixty divisions.

The command structure the old general supervised was, by any military standard, confusing. Rundstedt directed two army groups: Group G under Generaloberst Johannas Blaskowitz and Group B under Generalfeldmarschall Erwin Rommel. Rommel, who had a reputation for hard fighting and aggressive armored operations, was one of Hitler's favorites and could mostly ignore Rundstedt's directives. Potentially, this could be a disaster since the two field marshals disagreed on how to defeat an invasion, on the beach or in a battle of depth.[38] The Luftwaffe and Kriegsmarine (German navy), not under his command, had another 650,000 sailors and airmen in the theater. Luftwaffe ground divisions could also take their orders from Herman Goering, while the Schutzstaffel, or SS units, could also respond to Heinrich Himmler's commands. Most of the heavy guns along the coast were under the navy's control; it had not yet completed many of its fortifications and emplacements. By any measure, it was an organizational nightmare, and it is a wonder that it functioned at all.[39] The fundamental confusion continued down to the divisional level as it became almost impossible to describe with any precision the Wehrmacht's actual order of battle. In April 1944, to make some sense of what they observed, the Allied intelligence staffs began to classify units into two general categories: infantry and panzer. Mainly, they counted divisions with tank or assault gun battalions in the panzer class. Planners considered these units capable of counterattacking the invasion force. Most of the rest they classified as infantry; these were either field divisions, those capable of movement, or "LE" or limited employment units, those that occupied the coastal fortifications. These limited employment units often had nonstandard organizations, used captured French or Soviet equipment, and often contained companies of captured or conscripted Polish or Soviet soldiers from the east forced into German uniforms.[40]

By 1944, no military force in the world had more experience with the conduct of defensive operations then the German army. Any invading force would face both an impressive initial defense and violent counterattack. Wherever the Allies chose to land, they would encounter the Atlantic Wall, a fortification system designed to make an invasion difficult. Stretching from the Netherlands to the Spanish border, 2,685 miles, it was an uneven collection of artillery emplacements, infantry fighting positions, machine-gun bunkers, and other fortifications often supported by mines, barbed wire, and other obstacles. Its purpose, as spelled out in an initial High Command order of December 1941, was to allow the smallest number of troops to repel a massive invasion force. Hitler's Directive Number 40, issued on March 23 the following year, amplified its purpose: set the conditions for throwing the invaders back into the sea.[41] On November 3, 1943, his War Directive 51 made the defense of western Europe an equal priority with stopping the Red Army in the east.[42] By early May 1944, Allied intelligence identified thirty-four limited employment divisions along the coast. They had confirmed the organization and location of nine infantry field divisions and identified six more that the German commander could move to threatened zones. These fifteen units would serve as the tactical reserve force, to conduct local counterattacks and restore the front line.[43]

From a simple analysis of geography, the Wehrmacht's leaders believed the most dangerous potential landing area was the region closest to England, the Pas-de-Calais. At the narrowest point in the English Channel, between Dover and Calais, observers could see the other side. The expansive French beaches were within range of the fighter aircraft, ensuring Anglo-American dominance in the air. The region's several great ports could serve as logistics bases for the drive inland. Moreover, it was the shortest route from the coast into Belgium and then into the heart of the German industrial region along the Ruhr. It is not surprising, therefore, that this was the best-defended region on the coast. General Hans von Salmuth's Fifteenth Army controlled this sector, which extended from Antwerp in the north to Caen in Normandy. In the Netherlands and Belgium, he arrayed six divisions, one a field infantry unit, to defeat any landing in the Low Countries. On the French portion of his defense area, with little ability to move, he placed nine limited employment infantry divisions. In the Calais sector, he thickened the defenses by adding four field divisions and setting only one in the area near Rouen, and only one limited employment infantry unit, the 711th, south of the Seine near Caen.[44]

General Friedrich Dollmann's Seventh Army defended the coastline from Caen to Nantes along the Loire River south of Brittany. This sector was hard to protect because it contained two different and dispersed landing areas. In the north, the Cotentin Peninsula offered many landing areas and the large port of Cherbourg. The southern rim of the Brittany Peninsula also provided some good landing sites and ports at Lorient and Nantes. But these landing locations would stretch the capability of Allied air cover, so the Germans did not believe this sector would host the main event. Dollman had to defend nine hundred miles of coastline and had to protect it with the forces available. He had nine limited employment divisions, and he placed one of them along the Norman coast and two others near Cherbourg. The general deployed one of his seven field divisions to the Saint-Lô area and another farther north, in the center of the Cotentin Peninsula. The remainder of his infantry divisions he scattered from Brittany to the Spanish border. Depending on the landing area, he would march these units to the invasion sector.[45]

What bothered Allied commanders and planners the most were those units in the panzer category. These included panzer, panzer grenadier, and panzer training units. To further complicate the issue, as mentioned earlier, some organizations belonged to the Luftwaffe or SS. These latter groups were often larger than their Heer, the German army, equivalents and had more modern and better equipment, such as Panther and Tiger tanks, the most dangerous weapons on the battlefield. Rundstedt arrayed these forces, his operational reserve, thirty to fifty miles behind the threatened beaches. Their mobility and armored component made them exceedingly dangerous to recently landed infantry. While many of these divisions had relatively few tanks, often between fifty and a hundred, their fighting capabilities remained impressive. As would be demonstrated during the ground campaign, a few well-led panzer companies could wreak havoc with American and Commonwealth tank battalions. The theater commander had nine of these units available, with five of them concentrated in the area just west of Paris.[46] The original Allied planning staff document from March 1943 estimated that the Germans could mass at least thirteen divisions in the first week of the landing, against the handful of disorganized Allied units on the beach. By the week before the invasion, the intelligence analysts at SHAEF (Supreme Headquarters Allied Expeditionary Force) believed they had to worry about ten of these units during the first week of the landing. Four could arrive within twenty-four hours if not interdicted and the remainder within seven to ten days.[47]

To add weight to the fears of Gen. Dwight D. Eisenhower, the overall commander, and Field Marshal Bernard Montgomery, the ground force commander, Hitler's most aggressive and dangerous tank commander, Rommel, Montgomery's old North African opponent, was now in France. By early April, Allied analysts began to notice the improvement the feared German leader had brought to the Atlantic Wall.[48] The G2's Weekly Intelligence Summary in late April emphasized the problem. In the first of a series of profiles on enemy commanders, the initial presentation was, not surprisingly, of Rommel. His arrival, according to the report, resulted in "increased vigor of German defensive preparations." It noted the "dispositions of mobile reserves had assumed a more businesslike pattern." The report reminded Allied ground commanders they could expect Rommel to act offensively, concentrate his mobile forces, and strike at the enemy's flank. Like a "caged tiger," he "may be expected to employ them with vigor and decision."[49]

The Occupation

While this book considers France in the context of its traditional borders, the Germans had already begun to make long-term administrative and territorial reorganizations. As Frenchmen started recovering from the shock of the defeat, they understood that these boundary modifications anticipated changes that would permanently break up France and undermine its social cohesion. A sophisticated German bureaucratic structure intersected with France's civilian administration and organized, controlled, and redirected the nation's population and resources to support the German war effort. While this was not as onerous as Nazi rule in the east, there was no doubt the French were a conquered people. Military commandants (Militärbefehlshaber) in Brussels and Paris mostly governed France. Department capitals and major towns housed subdistrict or field commanders. Under the commandant's general direction was a confusing array of security and police units that, especially after November 1942, operated in every major town and city in

France. The French gendarmerie, who remained in place during the occupation, acted in support of the local German commander. Most feared, and generally beyond the authority of local leaders, were the various state police organizations, most notoriously the Gestapo (Geheime Staatspolizei) and associated groups.[50] Also, Organisation Todt, the massive government civil and military engineering organization, had a significant presence in much of France. As will be discussed later in this book, this bureaucracy, directed by Albert Speer, was responsible for designing and building the Atlantic Wall on the coast, the submarine pens in Brittany, and the vengeance weapon installations primarily in the Pas-de-Calais and Cotentin Peninsula. Often working through French subcontractors, it directed the effort of more than a quarter of a million laborers in 1942. The status of these workers ranged from reasonably well-paid French and Belgians to those paid less by the *service du travail obligatoire*, or French conscripted labor, to slave laborers on loan from concentration camps in the east. Most of the workers lived in camps that had their own infrastructure and security units.[51] The German presence in France was not solely military but had economic and security aspects as well. German directors assumed control of most factories, and they focused on the short-term output with little concern for maintenance and reinvestment. More than 40 percent of all industrial production went to support the Nazi war effort, a figure greater than in any other occupied country.[52]

In fact, it becomes difficult to refer to France as an organized entity during the years of occupation, as the occupiers modified both the external and internal borders. The Nazi state also began annexing parts of France. As most observers expected, Alsace and the Moselle areas of Lorraine came back under German control, as they had been from 1871 until 1918. The cities of Metz, Sarrebourg, Strasbourg, and Colmar became major administrative headquarters under the umbrella of Nazi government. Along with the standard security and government agencies, the National Socialist Party also introduced its hierarchy. The new administration forced those French people who would not accept the return of German authority to leave and, as a result, another 115,000 Frenchmen headed south looking for a place to live. Most in France and Germany expected these territorial changes to be permanent.[53] More alarming to French citizens were changes taking place in the departments of du Nord and Pas-de-Calais, where their conquerors were beginning to separate them from the remainder of France. Rather than receiving administrative direction from Paris, the Militärbefehlshaber in Belgian und Nordfrankreich (Military commander in Belgium and northern France) supervised this region from Brussels. Often referred to as the "Zone Rattaché," or rejoined zone, many feared it would ultimately become part of a different administrative district, separate from Paris, at the end of the war. This union with Belgium was not, as many Frenchmen believed at the time, part of a master plan of conquest, but simply the military response to the situation on the ground. From the Wehrmacht's perspective, it made sense to combine the region north of the Somme River with Belgian Flanders. The Germans established the regional headquarters, combining both French departments, in Lille. This local government mostly ignored the laws and directives emanating from the distant leaders at Vichy, which still believed it had authority over all of France.[54]

The Germans also modified traditional boundaries and began by prescribing two forbidden zones (Zones Interdites) to restrict the return of French civilians back to their original homes. One area was in the Pas-de-Calais and Nord region and corresponded to the territory most damaged during the 1940 Campaign and the likely landing area for an Allied invasion of Europe. This area, about twenty kilometers wide and extending along the coast, was called Zone Rouge (Red Zone) and initially had a military purpose. It was logical to keep French citizens away from fortifications, airfields, and other military facilities in the region the Germans expected to use in their invasion of England. Only people with special permission and those who were registered as living there were allowed to enter this area. Soon it also took on an economic aspect as the occupying authorities began to confiscate facilities and lands not reclaimed by their missing owners. Of course, those civilians that desired to remain or return faced a daunting existence, especially after the increase in American and Commonwealth bombing in 1944. The second restricted area comprised the departments bordering Belgium and Germany. The Nazi leaders saw these lands as regions for settlement of German civilians and the expansion of the Reich. By the time of the Russian invasion, the logic of these areas had broken down. French peasants were simply too persistent in returning to their homes and farms. The occupying administration simply did not have the security assets to prevent their movement across the boundaries.[55]

In November 1942, as the Axis occupied the rest of the country, the Italians enlarged their small occupation sector in southeast France. Now separated from central control were the Alpine areas east of Lyon and Marseille. As in the case of much of northern France, this area faced the prospect of permanent annexation to Italy if the Axis prevailed in its war against the Soviet Union. During this early period, the Italians acted as protectors of Jews fleeing persecution in the Vichy-controlled departments. This illusion of safety ended in September 1943 when the Germans occupied the Italian sector after the overthrow of Italian dictator Benito Mussolini and the subsequent capitulation of General Pietro Badoglio's government to the invading Allied forces.[56]

Finally, there was the remainder of France under Pétain's personal control, governed from the resort town of Vichy, one of the most improbable locations for a capital. Over thirty miles from the nearest large city, Clermont-Ferrand, the new government selected it as a temporary haven because of the reasonable number of hotels servicing the resort centered on its mineral baths. The government never intended to stay there, but a variety of circumstances never let it leave.[57] Although remote, the Vichy government had significant reach across the old state. It had influence with the *préfets*, or administrators, across France and still directed the Gendarmerie. After 1942, these French national police supervised the assembly and transportation of Jews and other undesirables to national internment camps, such as Drancy, north of Paris. From there, they traveled in sealed trains to the Reich's concentration camps. At least in the early years of the occupation, the Germans were more than happy to allow the administrative organizations of the Third Republic to continue operating on their behalf. The final organizational changes would happen at the end of the war.[58]

Although the occupation affected daily life, local French institutions continued and helped to prepare the nation for its months of bombardments. Communities continued with traditional city governments with mayors and municipal councils, providing a robust administrative system. French schools continued operating, although the curriculum changed to support the authoritarian government. For this study, two organizations were particularly important, civil defense (*défense passive*) and fire and rescue departments (*sapeurs-pompiers*). The communities had standing fire departments, often augmented by volunteers, of various sizes. Rouen, a city of approximately 122,000 inhabitants, had a department with an authorized strength of 150. In addition to extinguishing fires, it also was responsible for removing debris from damaged structures and rescuing survivors. In reality, these fire departments were always short-handed, so often they supervised rescue and fire-fighting efforts. In 1935 the French government required each community to establish a civil defense organization. Like the fire departments, they connected laterally to nearby communities and vertically to the departments. The government authorized the Rouen unit to have 3,500 members, mostly trained volunteers, but on a regular basis, it fielded less than one-third that number. Untrained citizens joined the ranks in time of need, and local hospitals, sometimes operated by religious orders, supported firefighters and civil defense actions in time of emergency. While neither perfect nor sufficient, France had a structure in place to help combat the effects of city bombardment.[59]

In addition to bureaucratic and administrative changes, the occupation created or exacerbated national social divisions. Few Frenchmen challenged Pétain in the early years after the defeat, and most considered de Gaulle a renegade and a traitor. Many perceived British behavior, especially at Dunkerque, as unacceptable, and they only increased their support for the social changes taking place in France. German behavior during this period was correct, and its soldiers would face court-martial if they misbehaved.[60] Men not in prisoner-of-war camps went back to work, many of them producing material for the German war effort. Others helped to remove the debris of war, especially in harbors and airfields. Later, others would take contracts from Organisation Todt to build the Atlantic Wall and vengeance weapon facilities. With the absence of so many men, young French women made their peace with the young soldiers from across the Rhine. To most observers in the spring of 1941, the National Socialist domination of France was going to be a long one, and it made sense to cooperate.[61] The defeat and experience of occupation helped make French society a whirlwind of change, especially regarding those who left the country, those who supported the Vichy regime, and those who changed their attitudes as the war progressed.

The German victory and subsequent occupation distorted French society by removing a significant portion of the population from the nation. Those who remained, primarily women, the elderly, and children, adjusted to the world without their principal source of emotional and economic stability.

The Battle of France that lasted from May 10 until June 22, 1940, removed almost two million young men from French society. Never to return were the 55,500 soldiers the government confirmed as killed during the fighting. The 123,000 wounded may or may not have returned to the workforce, depending on the severity of their injuries.[62] Still alive, but mostly not coming home, were approximately 1.85 million young men who marched off to prisoner-of-war camps in Germany, a greater loss than the total killed in the previous war and representing a significant portion, approximately 30 percent, of the country's male population. Since there was no actual peace treaty between the French and German governments, the captives were essentially hostages who ensured good French behavior and collaboration. For the families, however, it was a painful period of physical and mental separation. In our modern age of instant communications, it is worth remembering how difficult it was for prisoners and their families to communicate with each other. In fortunate cases, there was some notification that the soldier was healthy and safe, and there was occasional mail. In others, the wife could go the whole time without knowing if her husband would ever return. There was no plan to end the captivity other than at the promised end of the Anglo-German war. While the Vichy government was successful in getting some of the hostages released, others died in captivity. At the end of the war in 1945, 1.5 million Frenchmen, now five years older, began the journey home to a very uncertain reception.[63]

Beginning in 1942, several hundred thousand Frenchmen volunteered to work in Germany. Generous contracts and good working conditions were an enticement to those now looking for ways to support their families. By the middle of 1943, work in Nazi factories no longer had the same appeal, as the changing fortunes of war caused a deterioration in working conditions. Therefore, in 1943, under pressure from the Germans, who were struggling to simultaneously operate their factories and man their combat units in Russia and the Mediterranean, the Vichy government passed a law requiring labor service in Germany. The Service du Travail Obligatoire was unpopular from the beginning. Those workers sent to factories or to work in cities became targets of the increasingly effective Allied air bombardment. Many sought to evade the forced labor, and some joined the growing Resistance movement. Most others, however, only hid out and attempted to stay ahead of the authorities. More than any other program, it was the deportation of French labor that destroyed any possible positive relationship with the German occupiers, as well as long-term French support for Vichy, however much Pétain might remain an object of respect. Ultimately, 650,000 men and some women found themselves working and living under generally abysmal conditions in Germany.[64]

As in other Nazi-occupied states, France contributed to Hitler's intended Final Solution of killing Europe's Jews, initiated in 1942. As in the case of forced workers, French governmental officials and police were an integral part of the persecution process. Gendarmes rounded up Jews as individuals or by families, depending on the requirements given them by the French officials, to meet German quotas. For example, on July 16 and 17, 1942, nine thousand gendarmes rounded up 12,884 Jews and packed 7,000 of them into the Vélodrome d'hiver indoor sports stadium near the Eiffel Tower, with the rest housed at other camps, such as Drancy, outside of Paris. Four thousand of these unfortunates were children, and they suffered in horrible conditions for several days, under French guards. Finally, after days of horror, the guards put their catch on trains and escorted them to Germany and extermination at Auschwitz. Although knowing the exact numbers continues to be a problem, French and German governmental officials sent approximately 75,000 Jews to Germany for extermination, with only 2,500 returning alive. The horrible conditions at internment camps and on crowded trains killed another 4,000. In the end, one-quarter of all Jews who lived in France at the beginning of the conflict perished as a result of persecution. The complacency of French officials, police officers, and even everyday citizens would haunt postwar society into the twenty-first century.[65]

No issue in postwar France was more contentious than that of collaboration. While it is hard for Americans to understand, Frenchmen greeted Pétain's announcement that the war was over with almost universal relief. No one wanted a repeat of the previous conflict, with its great casualties and destruction. With memories of the 1871 Commune and the interwar crisis still fresh, only the old field marshal was seen as possessing the gravitas to restore some sense of stability and prevent a civil war. As Jean Berthelot, who would become Vichy minister of transportation, noted, Pétain deserved the gratitude of all Frenchmen "as the leader who saved us from the abyss."[66] There would be no civil war, and if the new leadership in Vichy had its way, they would become part of the new Europe Adolf Hitler was constructing.

As Robert Paxton clearly pointed out in his 1972 landmark *Vichy France: Old Guard and New Order, 1940–1944*, the new French government desired collaboration with the German occupiers. French civilians had little love for their former British allies, especially following the retreat at Dunkerque and the Royal Navy's assault on the French fleet at Mers-el Kébir (July 3, 1940). By October, even the Germans realized that the French government was extremely hostile to both the British government and to the small group of Frenchmen assembling around Charles de Gaulle in London.[67] Paxton's arguments sent shock waves through Cold War French society, which had tried to forget the confusion of those early days. Less than twenty-seven years after the war, Paxton destroyed the myth that only a few French supported Vichy and the Germans. There were few in the first six months of the war that actively challenged the new regime or the occupation forces, and most embraced the policy of collaboration.[68]

Underlying and informing this entire book is the idea of the French Resistance. One of the foremost French historians of the period, Olivier Wieviorka, admits it is not easy to define. Referring to the different groups, organizations, and individuals, he notes, "Their variety hinders us from proposing a comprehensive definition of a phenomenon that is surely marked by diversity and pluralism."[69] Defining its composition and relevance has been at the core of one of France's most intense and divergent debates since the end of the war. The scope of activity of the Resistance ranged from individual noncompliance with German or Vichy directives, to providing information to Allied agents, to rescuing downed pilots, to sabotage of major factories or rail tracks, and finally to armed combat against German regular forces. From the beginning of the occupation, various groups, such as Jews and soldiers not wishing to surrender, went into hiding. Their armed efforts against the German occupiers were ineffective, as was the British Special Operations Executive, or SOE as most refer to it, which tried to provide logistical support. The German invasion of the Soviet Union on June 22, 1941, began to change the nature of the internal opposition, as the French Communist Party began to confront the German occupiers actively. Since Germany and France had never signed a peace treaty, prisoners of war remained in captivity, which continued to anger the population. Since Germany needed workers and began conscripting young men to labor in its factories, young people began to go into hiding and join the armed groups forming up throughout the country. Wehrmacht forces rotating back from the Russian front were not as respectful of French civilians as the original occupiers had been, which created more animosity. As Jewish deportations increased, more people took to the countryside. And as armed opposition to the Germans continued to grow, the occupation authorities reacted harshly against the local population, increasing discontent.[70]

Allied success in North Africa and Italy, and an apparent stalemate in the east, gave indications that the Nazis were not going to be successful. By 1944, the Resistance, now generally referred to as the French Forces of the Interior under the vague direction of General Marie-Pierre Koenig, was a potentially viable force. Although many in the SHAEF high command sought to harness the growing eagerness by the French to assist in the final liberation, disagreements in political and military circles over the value and need to involve the Resistance limited its participation. General de Gaulle, determined to impose his mark on postwar France, also limited both its employment after he secured Paris and its ultimate inclusion in the restored French military. It was never unified and never had enough equipment. Yet no matter what the Allies or de Gaulle wanted, civilians of all creeds, political views, and nationalities contributed to the removal of German forces from France, and this became an increasing source of pride in the postwar years.[71] But the buildup of this force depended on the course of the war and took a great deal of time. As German fortunes waned, recruits joined the Army of the Shadows. As Robert Gildea pointed out in his study of the Loire Valley during the occupation, "The moral universe of occupied France was notoriously murky. What was right and what was wrong, what patriotic and what unpatriotic, may have been clear in the summer of 1944, but not before."[72]

The German occupation is thus a complex event that France still, more than seventy years later, is struggling to resolve. The attitude Frenchmen had at the beginning of the Vichy era was not the same after three years of occupation and the impending invasion of Allied forces. At the beginning of 1944, France was an elaborate system of citizens, geography, industry, infrastructure, and occupiers. Personal narratives depended on where one lived, the nature of the prewar experience, their experience in May and June 1940, the state of their family and the absence of a loved one, and the evolving relationship with the German soldiers and police who controlled varying aspects of their lives. The French narrative of the war years is different, and the survivors of these tumultuous years would struggle for the rest of their lives to reconcile events such as the defeat, occupation, deportations, and their personal behavior. It is a social complexity that most contemporary American, Canadian, and British citizens can scarcely comprehend. It is against this operational environment that the Allies turned their attention in the spring of 1944 in preparation for their landings later that summer. Building on operations conducted in the preceding four years, this string of connected air bombardments signify one of the largest offensives ever conducted against a friendly state in the twentieth century.

CHAPTER THREE

EISENHOWER'S COMMAND

Jean Larue was only eighteen in 1944 and lived in Condé-sur-Noireau, forty-five miles from the coast and between the larger cities of Vire and Falaise. The farmers in this regional market town of about 4,800 produced the standard Norman products of pork, cheese, wine, and, of course, calvados. Americans, still recovering from prohibition, would soon discover the potency of this addictive apple brandy. Larue worked at a local printer, and all day on June 6 he and his boss tried to find out what was happening with the invasion. The town was filling up with refugees from the coast, trying to escape the fighting. Back home on a beautiful evening, he was outside around 2000 hours. While his sister played with their two cousins in the street, he noticed white streaks in the sky off to the east and "suddenly very low flying planes arrive with a deafening noise. I see bombs dropped by aircraft. We enter the house running, and we put ourselves under the table. My father closes the door. The explosions continued for several minutes." When it was over thirty minutes later, they went outside. It looked like the house had moved from its foundation, and the streets were a mass of burning, falling buildings, but they were alive. The carnage, however, was everywhere. "But alas, there are victims. Madame Brion, the wife of a laborer, was crushed by a beam, her face is purple. Her daughter Adrienne, 21, recently married to Henri Jeanne, died on the sidewalk."[1] And he had much more to say about the destruction of his small town by 45 American B-17 Flying Fortresses, which killed a hundred villagers in less than thirty minutes. But there would be more destruction. The next morning, 112 Avro Lancaster heavy bombers from RAF Bomber Command appeared over the center of the town and destroyed the rest of the community. When the bombing stopped, Allied heavy bombers had killed 246 of Condé's citizens. They wounded many more and left almost everyone who survived without homes.[2]

Both the US Army Air Force and Royal Air Force liked to call Flying Fortresses and Lancaster aircraft "strategic bombers." Their purpose, according to bombing theory and doctrine, was to attack deep into the heart of Germany to decisively destroy its industrial centers. Operation Pointblank, conducted against factories and oil targets in Germany, and the employment of the atomic bomb against Japan are examples of strategic bombing roles. In these kinds of examples, politicians may enter into the targeting process and often approve or deny the specific targets.[3] With Eisenhower's assumption of command in January 1944, however, most bombing missions in France took on *operational* characteristics, the military aspect of a conflict that lies between strategy and tactics. For these missions, bombers responded to the needs of the campaign's commander and attacked beyond the area occupied by ground forces. SHAEF (Supreme Headquarters Allied Expeditionary Force) planners sought to create conditions for a successful ground invasion by destroying, degrading, and deceiving enemy forces months in advance of the actual landings. In other words, these operational strikes, the dropping of bombs, helped set the physical conditions for later tactical success. In some instances, Eisenhower assigned these potent weapons to his ground generals so they could use them in direct support of infantry and armored troops; this is tactical employment. It was an operational task that explains why heavy bomber units were flying missions against French towns only 150 miles from London rather than against the Ruhr that June. This employment was the aviation commander's worst nightmare, as Eisenhower used these powerful weapons not for a strategic, independent purpose but to support his ground forces, just like long-range artillery.

This chapter examines the policy and strategy, operations, and tactics that framed the Allied air war against French cities and countryside. The strategy resulted in a massive series of bombing operations beginning months or even years before the soldiers landed on the Norman beaches. All these seemingly unconnected, especially to the French, attacks focused on Eisenhower's operational objective: landing ground forces on the French coast and preventing the German armor from forcing his troops back into the sea. More than just a name, Operation Neptune was a complex series of written plans that spelled out what every element of the command was supposed to accomplish. For the air forces, detailed guidance came from two parts: The Overall Air Plan and the Joint Fire Plan. The creation of these documents is a story in itself.

Policy and Strategy

The British and Americans fought the campaign in the European theater as a coalition, a temporary military alliance to accomplish a common objective. Neither state could successfully invade Europe and drive the Germans out of its occupied territories alone. Necessity forced the political leaders to cooperate. The necessity, the political requirement, was the elimination of the Nazi state. Carl von Clausewitz, the often quoted but least understood Prussian theorist, noted that the political purpose (*Der politische Zweck*)—"the original motive for the war—will thus determine both military objective to be reached and the amount of effort it requires."[4] In a coalition, the political purpose affects every aspect of the war's conduct. In the case of the Allied powers, it was British prime minister Winston Spencer Churchill and US president Franklin Delano Roosevelt who provided the political direction.

From the British perspective, the original purposes of the war were survival and restoring the Empire. Churchill personified these goals and made it clear that it was his war. Born into a prestigious and aristocratic family that included the Duke of Marlborough, no wartime leader could match his political-military experience. His colorful career as a soldier, journalist, member of Parliament, and minister gave him a unique perspective on military affairs. Of particular note was his role as first lord of the admiralty in planning the disastrous operation in the Dardanelles Straits. While strategically and operationally sound, the landing at Gallipoli ranks as one of the worst tactical disasters of the twentieth century. The inability of military officers to plan and direct this operation had a profound effect on Churchill's later conduct. He genuinely admired France's First World War prime minister Georges Clemenceau, and Churchill's actions reflected his agreement with the often-quoted line, "War is too important to leave to the generals."[5] From the beginning, he warned of the danger Adolf Hitler posed to European peace and was one of Prime Minister Neville Chamberlain's most vocal critics after the Munich Agreement. At the outbreak of the war in September 1939, he returned to his former post at the Admiralty. On

Chamberlain's resignation in May 1940, King George VI asked him to form the new government. He did so, and he also assumed the role of minister of defense, thus assuring there would no confusion as to the source of the war's political direction. He was deeply involved in the final moments of the German invasion of 1940 when France lost its opening campaign against the Wehrmacht and all political will to continue evaporated. Under his watch, the Commonwealth endured an unending series of military disasters: the evacuation at Dunkerque, setbacks in Greece and Egypt, near-fatal losses in the Battle of the Atlantic, and the humiliation of the Japanese offensives against the Pacific enclaves of Hong Kong and Singapore. He had supervised a host of operations from the Battle of Britain through the replacement of various commanders in North Africa. Although America was now in the war, he did not intend to change how he operated. Three significant concerns affected his actions as the Allies prepared to return to the continent: his political fear of another defeat, his practical need to limit the drain on Commonwealth manpower, and his refusal to allow his generals and admirals to conduct war without political supervision. By January 1944, he was sixty-nine years old, had been in office for forty-three months, and was personally involved in every military operation.[6]

Although lacking his peer's military experience, Roosevelt could match Churchill's political and social background. His family's roots went as far back as any in the United States. His fifth cousin, Theodore Roosevelt, had a military-political career that paralleled Churchill's in many regards, serving with the Navy Department, fighting in the war with Spain, and serving as president of the United States. Franklin also served as assistant secretary of the Navy during the Great War and was a constant presence in state and national politics in the 1920s. Disabled by polio in 1921, he spent the remainder of his life fighting its effects. His performance as governor of New York as the Great Depression struck thrust him into the middle of the presidential race. By 1944, he had been president years longer than any previous officeholder. Like Churchill, he never forgot that policy was the driving force of military action, although he gave his military subordinates more flexibility in the conduct of the war. He had watched President Woodrow Wilson pay the political price for ignoring domestic politics at the end of the previous conflict, and he never lost sight of his domestic priorities. Also, the scope of his federal responsibilities, including industrial mobilization, two different theaters of war, recovering from the Depression, and local progressive politics, prevented him from interfering in routine military operations. He avoided involvement in the minutiae of strategy and military actions. When it was required, however, he was most decisive. For example, overriding military advice, he forced the invasion of North Africa (Operation Torch) in November 1942 because of the domestic requirement to get American soldiers into the ground war. Unlike British desires to restore the status quo ante, Roosevelt envisioned a postwar world in which empires gave way to national sovereignty and a United Nations, backed by American economic and military power, maintained international stability.[7] While Churchill and Roosevelt agreed on the first task of destroying the German and Japanese empires, their political goals were fundamentally different. The similarity in their short-term objectives and differences in long-term goals affected the conduct of coalition military operations.

It is the process of developing a strategy that links political purpose with military force.[8] Alternatively, in Clausewitz's words, "Strategy is the use of the engagement for the purpose of the war."[9] In simpler times, the state's leader might be able to direct both policy and the formulation of strategic plans. By the twentieth century, the complexity of political-military operations conducted over vast distances made this an increasingly difficult undertaking. It was not a task that could be directly handed over to those in uniform since, as the great historian Gordon Craig reminds us, "All operations have political consequences."[10] Both leaders formed and directed strategy through the senior officers of each military service. These two groups, the chiefs of staff, became the link between the political leaders and the commanders in the field.

The Chiefs of Staff Committee coordinated British military actions. In his role as minister of defense, Churchill often participated in this body's discussions. Its chairman from 1941, Field Marshal Alan Brooke, had commanded artillery units during the First World War and the British II Corps during the 1940 Campaign in France. After the evacuation from the continent, he supervised the reorganization of the army's survivors as commander of the Home Forces.[11] In this role, he worked closely with the prime minister as they prepared to repulse the anticipated Nazi invasion. When his predecessor, Field Marshal John Dill, moved to Washington to coordinate with the Americans in November 1941, Brooke was the obvious choice to become chief of the Imperial General Staff. Admiral Dudley Pound supervised naval operations until just before his death in October 1943. Admiral Andrew Cunningham, Britain's most successful naval commander thus far in the war, moved to the Admiralty to fill Pound's vacant post. The youngest Allied chief, only fifty years old in 1944, Air Chief Marshal Charles Portal, led the Air Staff. A protégé of British bombing advocate Hugh Trenchard, he commanded Bomber Command in the early months of the war. Considered by many to be the service's most promising airman, he assumed the role of chief of Air Staff in October 1940. Until the arrival of the Americans almost two years later, he was the primary architect of British air policy, and he continued to coordinate the Combined Bomber Offensive after the Americans' arrival. General Hastings Ismay served as Churchill's personal military assistant and often represented him in the Chiefs of Staff Committee.[12]

The American Joint Chiefs of Staff was a new organization. The traditional War and Navy Departments had been sufficient for planning operations in the early stages of the conflict. Although the Joint Army-Navy Board had operated since the Spanish-American War, it had little actual effect on policy since the respective secretaries and senior officers effectively ran their services independently. This ad hoc operation was not sufficient in the age of global, multidimensional war. When the Army and Navy chiefs began coordinating military policy and plans with the British in 1941, they discovered they were at a serious bureaucratic disadvantage. The primitive American planning staffs could not match their ally's in the scale and comprehensiveness of planning efforts and the quality of advice given to the political leaders. Therefore, in February the senior leaders reorganized themselves as the Joint Chiefs of Staff and added a robust joint plans committee to mirror the British organizational structure. In addition to Gen. George C. Marshall, Army chief of staff, and Adm. Ernest J. King, chief of naval operations, the group included Lt. Gen. Henry H. Arnold, the commanding general of the Army Air Forces. Marshall knew the old land-sea paradigm had shifted with the advent of aviation and realized he needed this veteran aviator on the staff to coordinate air operations and match the quality of advice Portal was giving to the British leadership. Arnold was one of the pioneers of aviation and a disciple of William Mitchell, the most influential American flight officer of the interwar period. Adm. William D. Leahy, a former chief of naval operations and, until America's entry into the war, the ambassador to Vichy France, also joined the new organization as the president's personal liaison to the service chiefs.[13]

For a wartime coalition to be successful, political and military leaders from both states need to meet often and work together in good faith. Personal, cultural, national, and organizational differences ensure that friction will always be present at all organizational levels. Soon after the Japanese attack on Hawaii, Churchill, Roosevelt, and their respective military advisors met in Washington at the end of December 1941. Code-named Arcadia, this three-week meeting formed the basis for Anglo-American cooperation for the remainder of the war. Among other issues, the national leaders decided to combine national resources and organize a unified command, the European Theater of Operations, with its headquarters in London. They agreed to form a Combined Chiefs of Staff with its headquarters in Washington, and they decided to begin deploying US Army combat divisions and heavy bombers to the United Kingdom.[14] To facilitate coordination between the two national military establishments, the prime minister directed his chief of the Imperial General Staff, Field Marshal John Dill, to remain as chief of the British Joint Staff Mission. Dill became close friends with both Marshall and Arnold and had no problem representing the American perspective to his British masters. Leaders on both sides credit him with smoothing over the bureaucratic and national differences that were bound to appear in such an undertaking.[15] Before the campaign on the European continent could begin, however, they had to select a commander.

Operational Organization

The American and British chiefs of staff bickered continuously over the European war's strategic direction. For many reasons, the British preferred to concentrate their operations in the Mediterranean and postpone the final meeting with the Wehrmacht on the continent as long as possible. The Americans, led by General Marshall, wanted to land as early as possible in France and begin the liberation of the occupied states and destroy the German army. Soviet premier Josef Stalin, whose forces had been fighting Hitler's legions for two and half years almost alone, supported the American position. As Stalin knew, until the Western political leaders identified an invasion date and selected a commander, there would be no plan of operations. By January 1944, a commander was in place, his command was organized to execute the campaign, and the principal subordinate commanders were beginning to organize for the invasion.

Stalin forced the Western leaders to make the critical decisions following the Tehran Conference that ended on December 1, 1943. Compelled to act before they departed the conference, Churchill and Roosevelt agreed to launch Operation Overlord in May 1944 as the primarily Allied effort for that year, promised to name a commander soon, and to start a second invasion of southern France (Anvil) to open the Mediterranean ports later that summer. The political leaders and the combined chiefs then organized the European theater into two theaters of operations, with northwest Europe as the primary theater and the Mediterranean as the secondary effort.[16] A few days after the Tehran meetings, Roosevelt and Churchill renewed their discussions in Cairo. Several candidates were in the running for the role of European campaign commander, including British generals Montgomery and Alan Brooke. Most in the Roosevelt administration assumed that Marshall would get the nod. In one of his most important decisions, Roosevelt decided to retain Marshall and recommend Gen. Dwight David Eisenhower, who had been leading the Allied effort in the Mediterranean, to be the supreme commander of the Allied Expeditionary Force for Operation Overlord. British general Sir Henry Maitland Wilson took command of the Mediterranean theater of operations, with responsibility for all actions in Italy, North Africa, and the Middle East. From then on, this was a supporting effort, and Eisenhower could call on Wilson for additional resources. Also, Wilson would supervise the planning for Operation Anvil later that summer. The political leaders also agreed to reorganize the Eighth Air Force in the United Kingdom and the Fifteenth Air Force in the Mediterranean under a new headquarters, the United States Strategic Air Forces in Europe under the command of Maj. Gen. Carl A. Spaatz, one of the pioneers of army aviation. Spaatz intended to provide more operational direction for the heavy bombers in their conduct of Operation Pointblank and support of Overlord, although he agreed with Harris that strategic bombing could probably end the war without landing troops in France.[17]

Fifty-three-year-old Dwight David Eisenhower was easily the right choice to assume direction of the Allied invasion of northwest Europe. It was not an accident that he was in command, as he had been preparing for this role since the end of the First World War. While not serving in France during the conflict, Eisenhower had supervised the training of America's infant armored force and had spent time there after the peace studying the American operations of 1918 with Gen. John J. Pershing and walking across all of America's battlefields. He produced the most comprehensive evaluation of the American portion of the war, *American Armies and Battlefields in Europe*, which remains in 2017 the starting point for any discussion of operations by the US Army in this conflict. A graduate of West Point, he was also the top graduate of both the US Army Command and General Staff School and the Army War College. His personal mentors included Pershing, Douglas MacArthur, Fox Conner, and Marshall. In almost every case, he was usually the general's most important assistant.[18] In June 1941, he demonstrated his expertise as chief of staff of the Third Army during the Louisiana Maneuvers, a testing ground that trimmed inept officers and organizations from the peacetime force.[19]

After the attack on Pearl Harbor, Marshall brought Eisenhower to the War Department to prepare the initial strategy for conducting operations in the Pacific. Few officers could equal his experience in the Philippines and his detailed knowledge of the field commander, MacArthur, during the early days of the conflict. Eisenhower helped Marshall construct the 1941 memorandum that provided the overarching vision of Army deployment until the Casablanca Conference of 1943.[20] After months as the Army's principal planner, Eisenhower, who was a lieutenant colonel in March 1941, received several rapid promotions and had advanced to lieutenant general by July 1942. By the end of that month, Marshall directed him to plan and command Operation Torch, scheduled for November. During 1943, he was the principal Allied commander in the Mediterranean, supervising ground, air, and naval operations in Tunisia, Sicily, and the initial landings in Italy. Appearing to be mild-mannered to the American public, he was a masterful manager who knew how to make a coalition function.

In February 1944, American and British planners needed a code name to identify the revised landing plan on the Norman coast. The campaign's original name, Overlord, was too broad and encompassing. Given England's relationship to the sea and its traditional affection for Athens, it should not be a surprise that they chose a maritime god's name to identify this amphibious operation. But Britain no longer dominated the oceans and, like the ancient Greeks, had surrendered control of their marine world to a rising power from the west. With an American commander directing the assault, it is not surprising the invasion took the name of the sea god's Roman transformation: Neptune. It was under this operational umbrella that the Allied air forces conducted most of their missions against targets in France.[21]

Eisenhower began to show his bureaucratic infighting skills as soon as he took command. As he was leaving his Mediterranean assignment in December, he discovered that the British chiefs of staff had forwarded a recommendation to their American counterparts, including Marshall, proposing detailed guidance on how they wanted to organize the tactical air forces for the invasion. Simultaneously, he discovered that the British had appointed Air Marshal Trafford Leigh-Mallory as air commander, over his choice of Air Marshal Arthur Tedder. Eisenhower was furious and fired off a telegram to Marshall asking for support in keeping his British colleagues out of his business.[22] As soon as he arrived in London on January 16, he began organizing his staff and arguing for a clear directive that specified his scope of command. The combined chiefs had started developing such a document as early as the previous October, with little to show because of disagreements between the two military organizations. Eisenhower would not operate without one, and on February 12, after many heated negotiating sessions, the Combined Chiefs of Staff signed the directive making him the supreme Allied commander.

The chiefs designated his command the Supreme Headquarters Allied Expeditionary Force, generally referred to as SHAEF. His task was to "enter the continent of Europe, and, in conjunction with the other United Nations, undertake operations aimed at the heart of Germany and the destruction of her armed forces." He was responsible to the Combined Chiefs of Staff and had authority to consult with each organization separately. With Marshall as his primary supporter, he was always able to negotiate with specific military and political leaders from a position of strength.[23] This directive changed the character of the war in Europe. In modern parlance, he was the operational artist, the commander who used the tactical forces at his disposal to accomplish the coalition's strategic purpose. His experience in the Mediterranean had convinced him that he needed unity of command and authority, without interference. Now he was responsible for the conduct of the campaign. Although he had much help from a host of dedicated and motivated subordinates, the campaign was his, and he could organize his forces and his means of war to accomplish the strategic objective. From then on, there was little doubt as to who was in command of Overlord, although he would often have to remind others, both seniors and subordinates, of that fact from time to time.[24]

Eisenhower's primary task as operational commander was to develop a coherent campaign to achieve the combined chiefs' strategic objective, the liberation of occupied Europe and Germany's military defeat. Building on the previous work done by planners in 1943, the new commander identified hundreds of tactical tasks needed to build up forces, secure the sea lanes, deceive the enemy, land on the far coast, secure a lodgment, and then prepare to move forward into France. He and his superiors appointed subordinate commanders to develop *lines of action* to accomplish these objectives.[25] Often ignored by historians are the many critical lines of action his headquarters had to supervise. Lt. Gen. John C. H. Lee directed the massive logistics operation in the United Kingdom. The SHAEF staff had to plan for civil governments in the territories they liberated, an operation ultimately coordinated by Lieutenant-General A. E. Grassett. It was the age of radio and mass-produced newspapers and newsreels, and in the Mediterranean Eisenhower had learned that the public message had to be controlled both for domestic and hostile audiences. Gen. Robert McClure supervised these tasks for the forthcoming invasion. SHAEF, along with French general Koenig, attempted to coordinate resistance and commando operations in France. Eisenhower required that a reorganized French army be re-equipped and sent back into the field. In addition, his staff was planning a subsequent invasion that would eventually result in Gen. Jacob L. Devers' Sixth Army Group landing in southern France and joining with the original Overlord armies.[26] The most prominent lines of action took place on land, on the sea, and in the air. From one perspective, crossing the English Channel and building up forces on the European coast was a complicated but rather straightforward problem. Organize the troops in England, ferry them across, deposit them on the far side, and then continue to move inland. What made it extremely complicated, and the focus for most air activity against France in the spring and summer of 1944, was the dynamic and adaptive German defensive environment as personified by Field Marshal Erwin Rommel.

The two most distinct lines of action took place on land and sea. Historically, they were also the most developed in regards to military theory and doctrine. The Twenty-First Army Group was the ground force senior headquarters during the assault. For political reasons, the combined chiefs planned to assign an experienced British general to command. After some discussion of various candidates, Churchill decided in mid-December to pull General Bernard Montgomery out of Italy and send him back to England to assume command.[27] Fifty-seven years old in 1944, Montgomery is, as far as Americans are concerned, one of the most controversial generals of the Second World War. Almost every historical account of the northwest Europe campaign contains some reference to Montgomery's clashes with Eisenhower, Bedell Smith, Omar Bradley, or George S. Patton.[28] The fact is that he was exactly the kind of general Churchill and Eisenhower required in the opening phase of the operation. He was a conservative commander who liked to have his operations synchronized and designed to maintain the morale of his troops and to limit the number of soldiers lost in combat.[29] For almost a year and a half, he had been fighting against some of the best forces in the Wehrmacht, including Rommel in North Africa and Albert Kesselring in Italy. Once Montgomery received his notice of command, he began considering and improving on the draft plans that had been at work for a year. As he continued to think about the landing, one of his chief concerns was building up enough forces to withstand the inevitable German counterattack. He concluded that while the Allies were moving enough troops into position, "the air would have to hold the ring, and hinder and make difficult the movement of enemy reserves by train or road towards the lodgment area."[30] From his perspective, air operations in France must support the needs of the amphibious invasion. It was this kind of firsthand experience that Churchill and Eisenhower required in the landing zone.

From the beginning, the combined chiefs planned to appoint a British admiral to command the naval portion of the invasion. The Royal Navy would provide the bulk of the seagoing support to Neptune, and they knew the channel environment in detail. Prime Minister Churchill, in one of his symbolic gestures, appointed sixty-one-year-old Admiral Bertram H. Ramsay as the Allied naval commander, Expeditionary Force, often referred to as the ANCXF. It was under his command that the fleet and private supporting vessels had executed Operation Dynamo in May and June 1940. Although he does not indicate it in his memoirs, Churchill must have relished the opportunity to assign the same commander who removed British troops from French soil the task of returning them.[31] The Royal Navy had been fighting in the English Channel since the beginning, so many of its invasion tasks were simply to continue what they had been doing. These included destroying German *Unterseeboot* or submarines (U-boats) and torpedo boats, called *Schnellboote* or S-boats. Ramsay organized his force into two groups, one to support the American landing sectors and the other for the British. Each force had approximately 64 vessels ranging in size from battleships down to destroyers and minesweepers. These combat ships were in addition to more than 3,500 landing craft of all sizes that would continue to ferry troops across the channel and deposit them on the hostile shore. In addition to protecting the troop carriers from S-boat and U-boat assault, the Navy had to remove mines and obstacles along the landing beaches and drop mines in French harbors and approaches beyond the invasion area. Thirty minutes before the assault landing, the battleships and cruisers would bombard twenty targets along the French coast. During the landing, naval vessels would remain on station to provide direct support to the troops on the beach.[32] Since this book discusses bombing operations, it is appropriate to delve a little more deeply into the third line of action, the air domain.

Allied Air Forces

The third aspect of Neptune's lines of effort was the air component and the heart of this book. Unlike the land and sea domains, the use of airplanes in a war was still a relatively new phenomenon. The theory of air warfare could look back only as far as the First World War for historical examples on how to use military aircraft. As a result, military leaders had a wide range of opinions on how they should use this rapidly developing technology.[33]

An early theorist of strategic bombing was the Italian airman Giulio Douhet. Based on his observations of the Great War, he believed the way to prevent another exhausting ground war was for a state to create an independent air force, use its aircraft to dominate the air, and take the offensive to the enemy's heartland. The targets were the hostile cities the bombardment of which would compel citizens to evacuate and sap the will and ability of the enemy to continue the war.[34] Written in the years following the Great War's horrific casualties, Douhet's words have a hard tone to the modern reader. "The purpose of aerial warfare" is to gain command of the air and then attack "surface objectives with the intention of crushing the material and moral resistance of the enemy." Dismissing ideas of supporting ground troops, he argued there was no other role for aerial forces "if we want to avoid

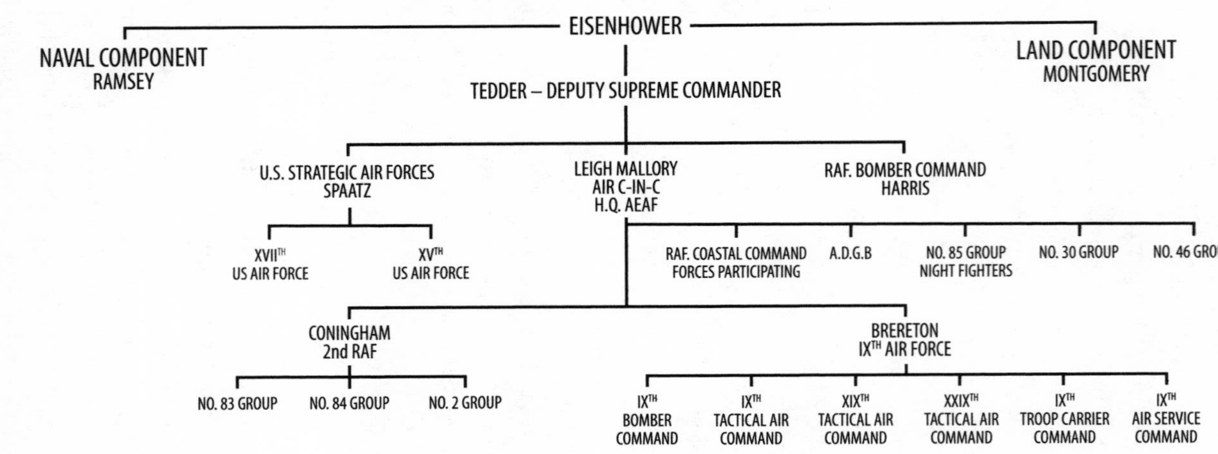

SOURCE: *Air Ministry, Air Historical Branch, "RAF Narrative (First Draft): The Liberation of North West Europe; Volume I: The Planning and Preparation of the Allied Expeditionary Air Force for the Landings in Normandy," Air 41/66 (Kew, UK: National Archives, 1946), 35.*

playing the enemy's game." The way to fight this kind of conflict was with an independent air force, with its only purpose of bringing the war to the enemy's homeland. It should not be diverted to "secondary purposes, such as auxiliary aviation, local air defense, and antiaircraft defenses." He dismissed the idea of air defense, declaring that the independent air force "admits of no defensive attitude, only the offensive."[35] Douhet saw no distinction between combatants and noncombatants; it was the entire society that was now at war. At the beginning of war, the state's independent air force must be prepared to conduct massive bombing attacks against enemy centers of population, government, and industry. The intent was to shatter civilian morale and force the enemy to ask for peace. There was no need to develop defensive options since the speed and altitude of the bombing force made it impossible to stop.[36] These ideas in the postwar environment were provocative and influential and contributed to the development of strategic bombing doctrine and, ultimately, the development of heavy bombers. Douhet's vision of an all-out war between states, however, excludes consideration of alternative situations, especially the possibility that the enemy's land forces might be successful and result in their occupation of friendly territory. What is the role of the bomber in this case? One suspects the Italian theorist would have repeated his second principle: not being diverted from the aim of getting command of the air and taking the fight to the enemy.

Based on limited experience in the First World War, and informed by Douhet's writings, American and British airmen struggled with developing doctrines of strategic bombing. The most passionate of these thinkers believed *the* best way to win a future war was by a bomber attack on the industrial heart of the enemy. Factories, utilities, oil refineries were all valid targets. A successful bombing campaign, added to the physical effects on targeted population centers, would bring an enemy belligerent to his knees. William Mitchell in the United States and Hugh Trenchard in the United Kingdom were the intellectual predecessors of the bomber barons of the Second World War. Trenchard, the father of Britain's independent air force, developed his ideas independently of Douhet, but he agreed on the importance of bombing civilians and targeting the enemy's morale.[37] By the beginning of the war, centralized control and targeting of the enemy's national infrastructure were at the core of the Royal Air Force bombing doctrine, even if it could not deliver on the promise of taking the war to the enemy.[38]

Mitchell's main contribution to aviation doctrine was his demand for centralized control and an independent air force. Although Douhet contributed to his ideas, the concept of deliberately targeting civilians was politically unacceptable to the American government and people. Once out of the US Army following his court-martial in 1926, Mitchell continued to develop his theories of paralyzing the enemy's industrial centers, food supplies, and transportation network.[39] The vision that emerged from the Air Corps Tactical School at Maxwell Field near Montgomery, Alabama, focused on an independent air force conducting precision bombing against "carefully selected elements of the (enemy's) industrial system."[40] Former Maxwell faculty members occupied most important positions in the Army Air Force's War Plans Division in 1941. Responding to an inquiry from President Roosevelt, they produced Air War Plans Division-1 (AWPD-1), "Munitions Requirements of the Army Air Force," that August. This document, which formed the basis for air development, equipment procurement, and doctrine for the remainder of the war, identified three missions:

1. To wage a sustained air offensive against German military power, supplemented by air offensives against other regions under enemy control that contribute toward that power.
2. To support a final offensive if it becomes necessary to invade the continent.
3. In addition, to conduct effective air operations in connection with Hemisphere Defense and a strategic defensive in the Far East.[41]

While its authors recognized the possible need to employ bombers against other targets, such as submarine pens and ports, they saw this as a "diversion from the true objective."[42] Written before the Japanese attack on Pearl Harbor, it acknowledges the decisions made by the American and British staffs on how to prosecute the war after the United States joined the conflict. During the American-British conversations (ABC-1), held in Washington from January through March 1941, the senior military leaders agreed that one of their important tasks would be to build up forces and launch an offensive against Germany. It goes into detail concerning the number of airplanes and types of munitions the Army Air Force would need to destroy German targets. Although the Nazis had occupied France more than a year earlier, it says nothing about the problem of attacking targets in friendly, occupied nations. It assumes that the bombing of ports and other diversionary objectives would take place in a sterile environment, devoid of civilian inhabitants. That perspective is ironic since a large portion of the bombs dropped by the Allies in Europe were against targets in occupied France, Belgium, the Netherlands, and postsurrender Italy.[43] Therefore, neither the British nor American air force leaders had developed a vision of how to address methods of using their heavy bombers against targets with friendly populations. Isolated in solving their technical problems, the doctrinal writers ignored the existing political realities.

Of course, Eisenhower and Montgomery, backed by decades of military experience, thought that aviation was just another weapon and that its primary purpose was to facilitate the land campaign. Knowing what soldiers would face in battle, and backed by current military doctrine, they had no doubt that aviation's primary requirement was to support the invasion.[44] From the beginning, Montgomery was a believer in the use of air power, as he used his Desert Air Force "as the long range hitting weapon" at Alamein.[45] As he refined the plans for the ground invasion in January after his arrival in London, he realized that air was a critical component to the operation's success and that "air would have to hold the ring and make difficult the movement of enemy reserves by train or road networks towards the lodgment area."[46]

Eisenhower was even more determined to use the heavy bombers as one of his tools for war. As early as August 1943, before the landings in Italy the following month, he was demanding more heavy bomber support for the landings at Salerno.[47] He received three additional groups of B-24 Liberators just in time to defeat the German assault on the beachhead. In his mind, air power had prevented the Nazis from throwing the invasion force into the sea.[48] Air Marshal Trafford Leigh-Mallory, the person the British chiefs of staff intended to command the tactical air arm for the invasion, visited Washington at the beginning of November 1943. Most observers then believed that the US Army chief of staff, Gen. George C. Marshall, would be the invasion's supreme commander. After a meeting with Marshall, Leigh-Mallory wrote a letter to Charles Portal informing him that the American general, if placed in command, would never accept any arrangement other than control of all air assets. He "would insist on deciding when the time had come to switch from Pointblank to operations in direct support of Overlord, and, thereafter, against what targets the strategical effort should be directed."[49] Eisenhower, Marshall's protégé, was in complete agreement and would not compromise on the principle of unity of command. Like the sea and ground components, the organizational theory was that one commander would coordinate all air activities in support of Neptune and report directly to the supreme commander. Even before he arrived in London, though, General Eisenhower had to begin resolving the bureaucratic divide between land and air organizations to gain full use of the heavy bombers for the invasion. Disputes among the air commanders, each a strong-willed individual determined to defend his position, made the problem even more complicated.

Fifty-two-year-old Leigh-Mallory, who took command of the Allied Expeditionary Air Force (AEAF), was a fighter pilot by training and experience. He had commanded the 12th Fighter Group during the Battle of Britain and was, by 1942, leading Fighter Command, which was responsible for defending the island's air space. An energetic leader, he seemed to be the right person to coordinate the air support needed by the landing forces. Portal recommended him for the AEAF assignment, and the combined chiefs approved it in November 1943.[50] His contemporaries and most historians of the air war, however, have not treated Leigh-Mallory kindly. His "Big Wing" ideas during the Battle of Britain undermined the authority of the then head of Fighter Command, Hugh Dowding, creating bad feelings among all involved. Historians and biographers have implied that he was less capable than his peers. His early death in November 1944, in a plane crash while on the way to take command in Southeast Asia, ensured that he would not be able to participate in the postwar glut of personal memoirs and fawning biographies. More than seventy years after the invasion, there is still no full-length account that does justice to the scale and complexity of his tasks as air commander in chief. The documentary record of conferences, orders, and reports make it quite clear that he effectively supported Eisenhower and Neptune.[51] As his chief planner, Air Vice Marshal E. J. Kingston-McCloughry, noted, Leigh-Mallory's task was almost impossible. His subordinate tactical air commanders, Air Marshal Arthur Coningham and Maj. Gen. Lewis Brereton, each wanted to be an air commander in chief of their respective national armies and gave their boss unenthusiastic support. The two strategic leaders, Lt. Gen. Carl Spaatz, commander of the United States Strategic Air Forces, and Air Marshal Arthur Harris, commander of Bomber Command, were utterly hostile, as Leigh-Mallory believed he needed the growing fleet of American and British heavy bombers to support the invasion.[52] Although technically responsible for the operation's air support, he became more of a coordinator and planner than an actual commander. Tasks he gave to his assigned organizations were always subject to debate and referral to a more senior leader. The official draft Royal Air Force narrative frankly admits that Leigh-Mallory "had in fact no control of the air forces nominally under his command."[53]

Like most British bomber commanders, British aviation pioneer Hugh Trenchard greatly influenced Arthur Harris, who wanted nothing to do with Leigh-Mallory or with providing support to the land battle. A ruthless advocate of total war, he argued that destroying the enemy's cities and its civilization was the best way to end the conflict. He hated Germans and was more than happy to lead England's heavy bombers against their cities.[54] He was also opposed to any subordination of his bombers to an American ground commander or, even worse, a British fighter pilot. Using heavy bombers in support of Neptune would, according to Harris, be "committing the irremediable error of diverting our best weapon from the military function for which it had been equipped and trained to tasks which it cannot effectively carry out."[55] In January 1944, Harris sent both Montgomery and Leigh-Mallory a paper that argued that "the best and only efficient support which Bomber Command can give to OVERLORD is the intensification of attacks on suitable industrial centers in Germany." He went on to argue that while bombing gun emplacements, communications, or military dumps in occupied territories may look like the bombers are supporting the troops, the fact was "in reality, it would be the gravest disservice we could do them. It would lead directly to disaster."[56]

Lt. Gen. Carl Spaatz, commander of the United States Strategic Air Forces, agreed with Harris that any diverting of his bombers to Normandy was incredibly wasteful.[57] On April 10, he told Maj. Gen. Hoyt Vandenberg, Leigh-Mallory's American deputy, that Overlord was not necessary and quite dangerous.[58] Harris and Spaatz were adamant that their bombers would never operate under Leigh-Mallory's direction. In fact, the bomber commanders believed that if they could continue the air campaign unhindered by other requirements, ground forces might not even be required and Hitler's dictatorship would collapse under its ruins. They did not intend to give command of their strategic assets to Eisenhower.[59] Nevertheless, there was a way to resolve the impasse among this group of strong, experienced, and stubborn leaders. One of Winston Churchill's wisest appointments was fifty-four-year-old Air

Marshal Arthur W. Tedder as the SHAEF deputy commander.[60] Eisenhower and Tedder had worked well during the Sicily and Italy operations, and upon his appointment to supreme command, Eisenhower was perturbed to "hear that Tedder, who I have assumed to be my chief air man is really intended to be an officer without portfolio, and that a man named Mallory is to be my chief air man."[61]

But Tedder was in the right position, and because of the command impasse, Churchill proposed that he should coordinate the activities of Harris and Spaatz with Leigh-Mallory and become the de facto coordinator of all air operations in the period just before and after the invasion. Portal and Tedder worked through the details and arrived at an acceptable solution on March 9. The bottom line was that the Eighth Air Force and Bomber Command would support the invasion, under Tedder's direction, and Leigh-Mallory would command the tactical air forces.[62] Harris and Spaatz remained angry that Eisenhower was diverting their large bomber force away from its primary task, and Leigh-Mallory was limited in how he could use the heavy bombers. By April, the senior commanders worked out a method of allocating targets by forming a joint Bomber Operations Planning Staff with representatives from SHAEF, Leigh-Mallory's AEAF, both strategic air forces, the Railway Research Service, and the Twenty-First Army Group. In the end, the only one satisfied with the solution was Eisenhower.[63] He got what he wanted: control of all air activities.

His struggle over this issue, however, had not yet ended. When Leigh-Mallory, on March 14, presented his plan for bombing rail centers, the British chiefs of staff challenged the wording of the project and the entire Portal-Tedder plan. The final decision on how to use the heavy bombers took place on March 25. On the eve of that conference, Eisenhower wrote out a memorandum for record on progress of his command so far. At its end, Eisenhower noted, "If a satisfactory answer is not reached I am going to take drastic action and inform the Combined Chiefs of Staff that unless the matter is settled at once I will request relief from this command."[64] Eisenhower had no need for such action, and two days after the meeting he received the formal authority he needed from the combined chiefs.[65] On April 15, Eisenhower, through Tedder, took control of Bomber Command and the US Strategic Air Forces. Without having to negotiate with other commands or senior organizations, he could use all the military assets in his theater of operations to achieve his goal of landing on the Norman coast and defeating the expected German counterattack.[66] The result of this compromise was that Tedder directed the largest air force ever to support a single campaign. Leigh-Mallory, Spaatz, and Harris collectively had 12,617 aircraft assigned to operational squadrons on June 5, 1944. This combat power's primary task was to ensure Montgomery's infantry-heavy invasion force could land on the French coast, expand the lodgment, and beat back any German counterattacks. The preparation for these landings began in earnest in April, long before the first landing craft approached the shore.[67]

Leigh-Mallory supervised a diverse collection of units and aircraft in his AEAF. From the beginning, the command's purpose was to provide direct support to ground actions, generally tactical actions. Air Marshal Arthur Coningham's (British) Second Tactical Air Force had the primary role of providing close air support for British ground units during the invasion, while Lt. Gen. Lewis H. Brereton's US Ninth Air Force had the same mission in the American sector. Coningham was an experienced commander, called "Mary" by his fellow generals for his New Zealand (Maori) roots. He had fought with Tedder against Rommel in North Africa.[68] One of the least known but most important airmen of the Second World War, Brereton was the unfortunate air commander in the Philippines when the Japanese attacked in 1941. After a series of commands in the Pacific, Brereton was ordered to Cairo by Marshall in June 1942 to help strengthen the Allied air force's defense of the Egyptian frontier. Here he organized the Ninth Air Force, commanding alongside Coningham and working for Tedder.[69] In addition to this experienced team, Leigh-Mallory could, through Tedder, request support from several independent fighter groups, including the aircraft assigned to the Air Defense of Great Britain Command, formerly Fighter Command, and a variety of aircraft allocated to Coastal Command, which had the primary role in preventing intrusion into the invasion zone.[70]

These units had an extensive array of roles to perform before, during, and after the invasion. In general, they had three different kinds of aircraft: fighters, fighter-bombers, and bombers.[71] Fighters had the primary role of engaging enemy aircraft in air-to-air combat with their machine guns, small cannon, or even rockets. They did this either above troops on the ground or while escorting bombers on raids against inland targets. They were often fitted with light bombs or rockets and could assist the ground fight by attacking unprotected ground targets. These were also the aircraft for conducting reconnaissance missions and could be fitted with sophisticated cameras for examining targets before or after a raid. The two most common aircraft in these roles were the British Supermarine Spitfire that had served as Fighter Command's backbone during the Battle of Britain, and the US Air Force's North American P-51 Mustang. Fighter-bombers could engage enemy aircraft, but their primary task was fighting troops or specific targets on the ground. In theory, they were the best planes for engaging targets when precision was needed. The British aircraft for this role was the Hawker Typhoon, which had better crew protection than the typical fighter and carried a large load of bombs, rockets, and 20-mm cannon ammunition. For the Americans, the Republic P-47 Thunderbolt performed that role. Heavily armed, it could carry a mix of rockets, machine-gun ammunition, and up to 2,500 pounds of bombs.

Light and medium bombers gave each of the tactical air forces the ability to deliver heavy munitions against targets requiring more bombs, such as bridges and concentrations of enemy troops. In theory, they could provide their ordnance with more precision than their heavier counterparts could. The Martin B-26 Marauder was the primary weapon for the Americans, while the B-25 Mitchell was used by the British. These systems could carry between three and four thousand pounds of bombs and would play a significant role during the forthcoming campaign. Two aircraft are difficult to place in a particular category because of the wide range of tasks they performed. For the British, it was the de Havilland Mosquito, one of the most unusual aircraft produced by any nation during the war. A very fast, high-flying aircraft built entirely of wood, it could be used in a wide variety of roles including night bomber, night fighter, pathfinder, and precision bomber. For the Americans, the Lockheed P-38 Lightning performed a variety of air superiority, ground attack, and reconnaissance tasks, and it could act as an air superiority fighter. A versatile aircraft, it served throughout the war. By June 6, Leigh-Mallory had over six thousand fighters, fighter-bombers, medium bombers, and other assorted aircraft under his command.[72] By itself, this was one of the largest air forces ever assembled, but the air component commander also planned for the employment of the massive bomber fleets assigned to Bomber Command and the US Strategic Air Force.

Harris, directing Bomber Command, and Spaatz, leading the US Army Strategic Air Forces (Eighth and Fifteenth), commanded more than five thousand heavy bombers, the largest force of its kind ever assembled. Bomber Command had been in the war since the beginning, carrying out its first raid against German ships at Wilhelmshaven on September 4, 1939. In the early days, it conducted ineffective pinprick raids against German targets with no apparent focus.[73] Until 1942, it was relatively ineffective and did not measure up to the promises of Trenchard and other bomber advocates. Part of the problem was technology, as the early aircraft did not have the capability to do much damage to the German war effort, but partially it reflected the mismatch between, as Tami Davis Biddle has pointed out, rhetoric and reality. The air leaders promised the politicians more than they could deliver.[74] This poor performance and lack of focus changed in February 1942 with the arrival of Arthur Harris, who never deviated from his goal of destroying Germany's morale and industrial capability. He believed it was England's decisive weapon for attacking Germany, and he fought against any diversion of his forces for missions other than killing Nazis.[75] Bomber Command also attacked targets in France, concentrating on airfields, ports, and transportation centers for the first two years of the war.[76] Harris' arrival also coincided with an improvement in the quality and quantity of the tools he had at his disposal. For the next two years, he waged an intense war, especially at night, against German cities and selected industrial targets in France, since the latter were acceptable to him when weather conditions prevented operations against the Reich.[77] By June 1944, Harris had 1,786 aircraft at his disposal, including 856 Avro Lancaster heavy bombers, arguably the best such aircraft in Europe during the war. Its average bomb load was more than 10,000 pounds, but it was capable of carrying the 12,000-pound Tallboy bomb used on reinforced concrete targets. Handley Page Halifax bombers, with an average bomb load of 7,650 pounds, made up the bulk of his remaining force. Bomber Command also employed the ubiquitous Mosquito, primarily as a pathfinder to mark the targets at night.[78]

The US Army Air Force flew its first raid, against Rouen, on August 17, 1942. For the next sixteen months, the United States continued to build its bomber strength and attack targets in Germany, France, and the Mediterranean theater of operations. From his position as Army Air Force commanding general, Lt. Gen. Henry H. Arnold wanted the heavy bombers attacking Germany under one command. In addition to issues of efficiency, such a commander would rank as Harris' peer. The American Joint Chiefs of

Staff agreed, and with Roosevelt's concurrence, Spaatz took command of the US Strategic Air Forces in Europe on January 1, 1944.[79] His main unit was the Eighth Air Force, based in England and commanded by Maj. Gen. Jimmy Doolittle, who had received the Medal of Honor for his audacious raid on Japan in April 1942. The Eighth had forty-one bomb groups, each with about 45 aircraft, split between Boeing B-17 Flying Fortresses and Consolidated B-24 Liberator bombers, organized into three bombardment divisions. While short of his authorized strength, Doolittle could still put more than 1,850 heavy bombers into the air.[80] Often ignored in calculations of forces available for employment in support of the landings is Maj. Gen. Nathan F. Twining's Fifteenth Air Force. Flying from Foggia, Italy, its primary mission was supporting operations in the Mediterranean and southern Europe. By June, Twining's twenty-one bomb groups had approximately 1,000 heavy bombers available for operations.[81]

According to their doctrine and culture, both air forces considered themselves as strategic commands, giving notice that they did not work for ground commanders but responded directly for missions specified by their national leaders. In the case of the Combined Bomber Offensive, the war against the German air force and industry, this was true. The combined chiefs, the strategic commanders, issued the final objective for Operation Pointblank in June 1943, directing the US Strategic Air Forces and Bomber Command to fight a coordinated campaign against Germany. Air Marshal Portal provided general coordination between Harris and Spaatz, who mainly fought independent operations: Americans bombing by day and the British by night.[82] On April 15, however, the situation changed, as these bomber fleets now worked for Eisenhower and Tedder. Until Eisenhower determined that the landings were secure, most of the heavy bombing missions would be either operational or tactical. In most cases, planners at Leigh-Mallory's headquarters, in coordination with those at Twenty-First Army Group, selected the targets. While the record clearly describes debates among leaders concerning target selection and suitability, in the end Eisenhower had the authority to make the final decision.[83] As we will see, challenges to Eisenhower's decisions usually involved the senior political and military authorities from both coalitions.

As Spaatz and Harris knew, and French civilians living in the target area would learn, these missions required a degree of precision that the heavy bombers simply did not have, and they told their leaders so.[84] At the beginning of 1944, heavy bombers were an incredibly inaccurate and blunt military instrument. Commanders considered missions successful if 90 percent of the bombs landed within a mile of the actual aiming point.[85] An extensive list of technical and physical reasons contributed to this inaccuracy. Navigation aids that guided aircraft to the target, while steadily improving, were still primitive in 1944. Sometimes formations bombed the wrong objectives in the wrong countries. Identifying and hitting prescribed targets, in particular through thick cloud cover, was almost impossible. The Norden bombsight, which worked reasonably well in the western United States, was ineffective in the European weather environment. For example, the United States Strategic Bombing Survey discovered that for every one hundred bombs dropped on an oil refinery, only two hit the buildings or equipment and only thirteen ever got close. The spatial array of bomber formations ensured that most bombs would fall outside the target area. Finally, because of the need to avoid anti-aircraft fire, commonly known as flak, the crews attacked from relatively high altitude, generally around 25,000 feet, ensuring the dispersion of the bomb load.[86] Since civilians worked in and lived near these target areas, they would pay the price of imprecision.

Along with the land, sea, and logistics lines of action, Leigh-Mallory, backed by Tedder, developed an *air line of action* made up of separate primary operations. These operations used the air weapon to create specific conditions that would enable Montgomery's infantry-heavy landing force to establish itself on the French beaches facing a degraded German defense and counterattack force. Lieutenant-General Frederick E. Morgan had developed the original concept for employing fighters and bombers during Overlord, while the AEAF staff and air force commanders continued to adjust these plans right up to the eve of the invasion.

Soon after the Torch landings, with North Africa reasonably secure and the British and American chiefs of staff deadlocked over the strategic direction of the Allied forces, Churchill and Roosevelt agreed to meet in the Moroccan city of Casablanca. From January 14 to 24, 1943, the political leaders and their military staffs wrangled over the larger issues of policy and strategy. The question was simple: How should the American and Commonwealth forces proceed now that American combat units were entering the war in strength? The scope of discussion was global in scale and unprecedented in the history of combat. This small group of men determined the logistical requirements for their efforts around the world in all theaters of war. In addition to the controversial political objective of unconditional surrender by the Axis powers, they made several important decisions bearing on the war in France. Most important, they agreed to begin planning the invasion and appointed Morgan as the chief of staff to the supreme Allied commander, and the headquarters became known as COSSAC. Forty-nine years old in 1943, Morgan set up his offices in Saint James' Square, London, and began selecting a staff to start planning.[87] When they began working on the invasion plans, they could hardly imagine the scale of resources that would be available a year later. Therefore, the original concept, based on the 1943 planning environment, was conservative in both the commitment of men and equipment. They anticipated an initial assault by only three divisions on a relatively narrow sector between the Orne River and Carentan, with three more units to follow immediately.[88] While these details are familiar to many, less well known are the details of the draft air plan.

COSSAC's integration of the air forces into the overall scheme of operations was the most sophisticated up to that point in history. Between June and July 1943 the air planners, led by Brig. Gen. Robert C. Candee, considered how aviation could ensure "freedom of action" between Cherbourg and Dieppe.[89] Fighter aircraft radius of action had been one of the primary considerations for selecting the landing area near Caen in Normandy. Fighter aircraft had only a limited distance to fly so could ensure constant coverage above the landing area. As envisioned by Candee, the operation would have three phases: preparatory, assault phase, and a follow-up and buildup. During the preliminary phase, in addition to destroying the German air force (an essential Pointblank aim in any case), the plan envisioned the use of air attacks "against communications more directly associated with movement of GERMAN reserves which might affect the CAEN area." A short air bombardment would precede the assault phase. The thrust of the planning documents is that the greatest threat to the landing was the Luftwaffe, the German air force.[90] But these were all planning considerations. The invasion's commander would be the one to confirm and adjust these plans to address the actual situation on the eve of the invasion.

Two documents provided the direction planners and commanders needed to prosecute air operations in support of Operation Neptune. The first was the Joint Fire Plan approved on April 8 and signed by all of the component commanders, Ramsay, Montgomery, and Leigh-Mallory. It described the general framework of the fire support for the invasion so that the three service commanders could develop their specific operational plans. It identified the ships, aircraft, and ground units each leader intended to use and how he would organize them for the assault. It identified specific responsibilities, such as how to resolve issues with underwater obstacles, civil affairs responsibilities, the use of chemical weapons, and who owned what portion of the battle space and when. Finally, appendices identified specific targets for bombardment from air and sea before, during, and after the actual invasion.[91] A week later, Leigh-Mallory published the AEAF Overall Air Plan. Like the Joint Fire Plan, this would be revised and adjusted well into the actual invasion. It specified the principal air tasks concerning the discrete phases of the assault. It also provided specific guidance for anti-aircraft defense, air and sea rescue, and the use of air transports.[92] Although attacks against rail centers had been taking place since March, these documents provided the authority for most of the bombing done in France in the spring and summer of 1944. But they were only outlines. Commanders and even political leaders would challenge the specifics of how and when the air forces could bomb targets in France.

As historian Richard Overy has pointed out, the bombing war in Europe has often appeared as if it were something separate from what was happening on the ground.[93] Eisenhower, in his role as commander of all Allied forces in northwest Europe, was determined that they would work in harmony toward the common goal of landing on the French coast and defeating the Wehrmacht, especially its counterattacking panzer forces. In spite of the bomber commanders' severe protests over the diversion of their assets, all aircraft based in England worked for Tedder and Leigh-Mallory. Eisenhower, backed by Marshall and Roosevelt in Washington, controlled Allied bombing policy in the European theater of operations. While there were many arguments over what and how to bomb, the overall issue was never in doubt. If the ground force commander believed he needed to destroy a target, then it would be destroyed. Military necessity, the need to protect the invasion force in the field, overrode any objectives from civilians or the air commanders themselves. Only the political need to respond to German vengeance weapon attacks would divert aircraft from Eisenhower's control.[94] Some of the operations, such as attacks on the military infrastructure (ports, submarine pens, airfields) and Operation Pointblank (attacks on German industry), had been going on almost since the beginning of the war and had become part of the overall line of action. The next two chapters will describe these actions in detail.

CHAPTER FOUR

AIRFIELDS AND PORTS

For English speakers who lived through the war, few events captured their imagination more than the evacuation of Dunkerque, mentioned in the previous chapter. For a week starting on May 26, 1940, a ferocious battle took place as British air and sea forces struggled to withdraw the remnants of its expeditionary force and a portion of the French army in the port area. By June 3 it was over, with the surviving British and French troops safe on the other side of the English Channel. Winston Churchill devotes an entire chapter in his memoirs to the drama of Operation Dynamo, calling it the "Deliverance of Dunkirk (English spelling)."[1] As the British fleet withdrew, German troops marched into the city, capturing the remaining French defenders and sending them off to five years in prisoner-of-war camps in Germany. The city was in flames, and the intense bombing and artillery fire that landed throughout the city killed more than three thousand civilians.[2]

Following its evacuation from Dunkerque in June 1940, Britain stood alone (with its vast empire) against the German threat, but, much to Hitler's chagrin, it remained defiant. On June 18, in one of his finest presentations, Winston Churchill addressed Parliament and the nation: "What General Weygand called the Battle of France is over. I expect the Battle of Britain is about to begin."[3] Churchill had little doubt that the first round of this contest would be in the air.[4] By June 22 France was under Nazi domination and its infrastructure was available for continuing Hitler's war against England. German air units occupied abandoned Allied airfields and began reorganizing and re-equipping for their next missions.[5] On July 16 the Nazi leader issued Directive No. 16, which spelled out the details of the landings in the British Islands.[6] Two weeks later, he issued another directive detailing how the German air force and navy would conduct operations in preparation for the landings.[7] Even before Hitler's directives, the British Air Staff issued the first of its bombing policy directives to RAF Bomber Command. They would attack all vessels in ports "from Calais to Le Havre and airfields in France" with the purpose of preventing a German invasion.[8] This first line of effort against airfields and ports, followed two years later by attacks against the submarine pens, would continue until the end of the war. The purpose of these attacks on France's airfields and ports would change from preventing invasion, to stopping air and sea attacks on shipping, to securing the invasion fleet's crossing lanes, to supporting the deception plan, to finally assisting ground troops in contact with German defenders.

Because of the French surrender, some of the world's finest ports and most sophisticated airfields were under the control of the German military. These facilities now became the primary staging areas for Operation Sea Lion, the anticipated assault on England. From the beginning, the British attacked many of these facilities with an intense desperation. In the spring of 1941, after failing to knock RAF Fighter Command out of the war, Hitler abandoned his invasion plans and turned his attention to the Balkans and the Soviet Union. Air operations, however, continued against targets in France. For the next three years, the Royal Air Force, joined by the US Army Air Force in mid-1942, continued to attack these targets with ever-increasing bomb tonnage and effectiveness. By spring of 1944, Allied bombing had rendered most French airfields capable of only marginal use, and the intensity of this operation only increased as the invasion date approached. While the air raids had damaged most port areas, the Germans converted several into impressive submarine bases, which resisted all Allied efforts to put them out of operation.

Unlike most French citizens who lived in the hinterland, those who chose to remain in their homes near ports had a unique perspective of the war. For five years, German forces of varying quality dominated their city life. They confiscated homes and public buildings. Many Frenchmen who remained worked, either voluntarily or by force, on fortifications or in the port area for Organisation Todt or one of the various French and Belgian subcontractors.

Slave laborers, primarily Russians and Poles, joined the workforce. The fishermen who remained were unable to go to sea without an escort and always remained under surveillance.[9] When they went home, Allied attacks from the air or sea often disrupted the night and, on occasion, destroyed significant portions of their towns. While we have little difficulty identifying the major attacks on each port, it is a highly time-consuming task to list each strafing, mining, nuisance bombardment, and naval raid on each of these towns and cities. They were the natural targets for land attacks. Although the Canadian Dieppe raid in August 1942 is the most famous, commandos attacked almost every port from Dunkerque to Saint-Nazaire, with the obvious exceptions of Cherbourg and Le Havre.[10] Other than Cherbourg, none of the major ports was in the invasion area and their story, therefore, is unknown to most American readers.

Airfields

The British, French, and American armies had used hundreds of landing strips across northern France during the First World War. In the interwar years, some became major civilian and military airfields, while others remained little more than grass landing strips. After they declared war on the Germans in 1939, the French and British air forces reoccupied and restored more than one hundred of these bases in preparation for the conflict.[11] The Germans attacked first and by the end of June 1940 had captured all these airfields.[12] On the heels of the ground forces, the Luftwaffe moved into the abandoned bases, occupied a host of civilian airfields across the country, and constructed many others within the range of the United Kingdom. When the German air assault against England began in August, they had more than four hundred fields of varying quality available for their offensive, with about sixty in the Pas-de-Calais alone.[13] After four years of war, and despite their overextension in all directions, the Germans still had more than one hundred airfields in use across France and dozens more in Belgium and the Netherlands. Defending the major routes into its national airspace, the Luftwaffe had more than thirty air bases, primarily for use by fighters, concentrated in the four departments of the Somme, Nord, Pas-de-Calais, and Eure.[14]

In the war's early years, Bomber Command struck back and continued counterpunching against the German air force, hitting targets across France and Belgium. The first Bomber Command missions were unproductive. For example, the airfield at Merville, southeast of Hazebrouck, was one of the first occupied by German air units and became the first one the British bombed on June 14, 1940. Damage to the airfield was very limited. The most common bomber of the time, the Bristol Blenheim, was only a two-engine aircraft with limited capabilities.[15] On a July 10 mission, in the early stages of the Battle of Britain, Bomber Command sent forty Blenheim bombers to attack the airfields at Amiens and Saint-Omer. They lost five aircraft and caused no report from those on the ground.[16] In general, these raids were small, usually thirty to forty aircraft, and relatively ineffective. Long term, this period of bombing appears to have had little effect on the French population or the German military operations. Aircrews could quickly identify airfields from the air, and most of them were a reasonably safe distance from most private homes.

By the end of September, Hitler accepted that his Luftwaffe would not be able to defeat RAF Fighter Command, and he began refurbishing his land forces and moving them east in anticipation of operations against the Soviet Union. From September until May, however, German attacks against British cities continued, probably with the hope of causing civilians to reject the war. Raids against Coventry (November 14–15, 1940) and London (December 29–30), were especially damaging, killing hundreds. In four months of bombing, the Germans had killed almost 30,000 British civilians, removing any moral hesitation Churchill's government may have had about killing German civilians.[17]

By the summer of 1942, the Royal Air Force, now joined by American airmen arriving in England, began challenging the Germans for control of the skies over France. Allied air raids continued against occupied French airfields through 1943 and into 1944 as Allied pilots sought to deprive German fighters and bombers of their bases. While these Allied attacks were productive, the primary reason Luftwaffe aircraft moved out of France was a combination of its requirements to support ground troops in Russia and the increasing pressure of the Allied Combined Bomber Offensive against targets in Germany. And once long-range fighter escorts, in the form of P-51 Mustangs equipped with extra fuel tanks, were available, American raids over Germany in February and March 1944 inflicted punishing losses on German fighter aircraft, which tried to defend vital industry and resources.[18]

All winter and into the spring of 1944, Allied aircraft continued to attack airfields across France, such as on March 27, when the Eighth Air Force sent more than seven hundred bombers to attack a host of runways including those in Pau, Mont de Marsan, Bordeaux, Cayeux, La Rochelle, Tours, Chartres, and Biarritz. The attack on this last airfield, a training base for German pilots near the Mediterranean, apparently caught everyone by surprise. In addition to killing between 40 and 100 Germans, it also severely damaged the French resort, killing between 100 and 150 civilians and wounding almost 200 more. The names of 109 citizens are displayed on the city's monument to the dead.[19] By May, with the Joint Fire Plan in place, the attacks became more focused as the AEAF's primary task during Neptune's preparation phase was the "rendering unserviceable and destruction of German airfields within 130 miles of the assault beaches."[20] From the time of the final buildup to the invasion, German fighters had pulled back into the French and German interior and were using none of the airfields in the landing area.

But Allied planners expected that the enemy could deploy 850 front-line aircraft of all types against them during the early days of the invasion. Therefore, if the airfields were still capable of use, the enemy could concentrate fighters and light bombers in the forward area at the last moment and attack the invasion fleet.[21] Planners in the British Air Ministry drew up two lists of targets. The first, about forty air bases, were within 150 miles of Caen and were the primary objectives. The second list contained fifty-nine airfields, mostly bomber-capable bases, across western Europe. Because of the reduction of air units on the western front and the sustained bombing these fields had endured during the spring, planners considered only about two dozen as still dangerous as the invasion approached. Leigh-Mallory directed an increase in the intensity of attacks against these installations at the beginning of May.[22]

Any doubts about the imminent invasion in the minds of German soldiers and French citizens should have begun to disappear in the first ten days of May. The Allies struck at seventeen different airfields across thirteen different departments, none of them in the actual invasion area. Seven of the raids were small, with 17 or fewer heavy bombers. Another seven used between 30 and 58 bombers. Juvincourt, Rennes, Montdidier, Nantes, and Laon bore the brunt of the most massive attacks. Bomber Command struck the Nantes airfield in the early morning hours of May 8 with 93 Lancaster bombers. That same night, 55 Lancasters attacked the airport at Rennes and the ammunition depot at Bruz. Apparently, the aircraft were unable to locate the ammunition depot and dropped their bombs in the center of Bruz, killing 167 civilians, including 50 children.[23] The next day the Eighth Air Force attacked Laon-Athies airfield with 113 B-17 Flying Fortresses. Altogether 811 heavy and medium bombers attacked air facilities during this period.[24] At least one raid was either a mistake or an attack on a secondary target, the German interceptor base at Vitry-en-Artois. French officials on the ground noted 30 bombers were attacking the airfield the afternoon on May 11. Some bombs fell in the village, killing one and wounding another civilian. The bombs also killed several cows, a description that one often finds in these reports, and damaged a few buildings.[25]

Air attacks continued, with more than eighteen raids over the next two weeks. The offensive's goal was to prevent the Luftwaffe from moving aircraft from the rear to more forward bases. They attacked Caen-Carpiquet, the only airfield in the planned invasion sector, twice. The Eighth Air Force conducted its biggest raid during the period against the airfield at Orleans-Bricy. This large installation, already bombed many times, had been a bomber base during the Battle of Britain. It was centrally located and served as the primary air staging area in the Loire region. On May 23, 184 heavy bombers, primarily B-24 Liberators, dropped 513 tons of bombs on the airstrip, ensuring that it and its facilities would not be useable during the invasion. The Americans also launched two raids on the Orly airfield outside of Paris. Because of its proximity to the city, it was a significant operational and training base. Eighty-eight heavy bombers attacked the field on May 20, followed by a return visit four days later by 151 B-24s. That same day 168 bombers attacked the airfield and aviation repair facilities at Melun, southeast of Paris on the Seine.[26]

The airfield destruction operation entered its final pre-invasion phase on May 29. All the targets were outside the invasion zone. In the north, the Luftwaffe had abandoned the Mardyck Air Field, outside of Dunkerque, in May 1941. German troops still occupied it, and it could serve as a staging field for fighters attacking the invasion fleet. Soon after midnight, Bomber Command sent 49 Lancasters to destroy the base. Farther inland, the Ninth Air Force dispatched more than 100 A-20 Boston bombers against the air base at Achiet in the old Somme battlefield near Bapaume. To the south of the Brittany peninsula, 80 P-47 Thunderbolts dive-bombed and strafed the Luftwaffe bases at Vannes and Kerlin-Bastard. Another 35 bombed each of the fields at Gaël and St. Brieuc, near Rennes, and 50 more went after Lanvéoc, near Brest.[27] The next day 120 aircraft attacked three airfields, including Mardyck again, in the Department du Nord. [28]

After a short two-day break, the Allies continued their assault on airfields on June 2. Fifty B-17 Flying Fortresses bombed the base at Conches, and another 50 P-38 Lightings dive-bombed the important Luftwaffe interceptor base at Saint-André, both near Évreux. These were the most dangerous airfields in regards to the invasion because of their proximity to the Normandy beaches. Also, the Eighth Air Force bombed the major German facility north of Paris, Creil, with 64 B-17 Bombers, while 12 visited Bretigny, to the south.[29] The Allied attacks on the airfields continued through the invasion on June 6. Critical postinvasion assaults included 134 Flying Fortresses attacking the large Kerlin-Bastard airfield near the harbors of Lorient and Vannes, and several B-17 and B-24 attacks on airfields at Le Mans and Rennes.[30]

Few soldiers landing on the beaches in early June appreciated the scale of the Allied effort to prevent the Luftwaffe from interfering in the landings. French airfields and their German occupiers absorbed more than 3,000 tons of bombs in April, almost 10,000 in May, and more than 16,000 in June.[31] From a military perspective, the air operation's success is essentially beyond debate. Against 5,600 Allied fighter aircraft the German defenders had only about 170 interceptors able to fly, and only a handful of these fighters were able to reach the beach and cause any damage at all.[32] Most famous was the near suicide attack by two FW-190s piloted by Joseph Priller and Heinze Wodarczyk and memorialized in Cornelius Ryan's *The Longest Day*. These planes strafed the British beaches early on June 6, causing a great deal of temporary confusion.[33] Most of the others who were able to take off never reached the beach. Reports on June 6 and 7 indicate that aircraft providing protection to the beaches intercepted about twenty aircraft before they caused damage, and they shot down eighteen.[34] With the success of Allied bombers and fighters in forcing the Luftwaffe to withdraw most fighters to defend German industry and the destruction of most airfields within fighter range of the beaches, the skies were mostly free from interference. Although Luftwaffe-occupied airfields in France were among the most bombed targets, they have produced the least comment from French historians and officials. Perhaps it is because most inhabitants of air bases were Germans or forced laborers. Another reason may be because the runways were large targets and easy to identify and hit. Finally, unlike railways and some factories, no one disagreed that bases that supported the Luftwaffe were legitimate military targets. The result appears to be, as indicated by the archives in the Pas-de-Calais, relatively few civilian casualties during this period near most airfields.[35]

Ports

In addition to its large number of airfields, France had one of the world's most developed systems of maritime ports. In most cases, these complexes had developed from natural harbors with some particular geographical characteristic, such as a strategic location or a nearby mouth of a river. Over time, the nearby community improved each site by adding jetties and breakwaters to provide ships additional protection from storms and tides. In some instances, such as the case of Cherbourg and Brest, the French government directed the harbor's construction for strategic reasons and provided land access by constructing roads and railways. By the early twentieth century, a good port included pilots and tugboats to guide large cargo vessels to their designated berth, and cranes, ramps, and other equipment to unload each ship. Small trucks or rail then moved the cargo to nearby storage and sorting buildings and delivered it to receiving company officials. Local workers then transferred the sorted cargo to trains for distribution across the country or into the heart of Europe. From north to south, Dunkerque, Calais, and Dieppe had long been the primary terminals for ferry service between the continent and England, while Boulogne-sur-Mer included larger terminals for transatlantic trade. Farther south, Le Havre, Rouen, and Cherbourg all provided access to the English Channel. Opening directly out to the Atlantic, Brest, Nantes, La Rochelle, and Bordeaux were major centers of maritime trade. The ancient port of Marseille was an important transportation center in France's south, while Toulon served as its primary naval base on the Mediterranean coast. In between these major hubs were hundreds of medium and smaller ports that served maritime trade and the fishing industry.

With France's collapse, Hitler now controlled most of these superb facilities and intended to use them in continuing his war against England. One major exception, mentioned in chapter 2, was Toulon, where, following the British-French naval battle in at Mers-el-Kébir in July 1940, the survivors joined the remainder of the Vichy French fleet. Almost eighty ships, including the powerful battleship *Strasbourg*, three heavy cruisers, two light cruisers, thirteen destroyers, and ten submarines sat in the harbor until November 1942, when the Germans occupied the remainder of France following Operation Torch. The Kriegsmarine wanted these ships, but the French had no intention of giving them up. When the Nazis attacked the base and attempted to seize this still powerful fleet, its commander, Admiral Jean Laborde, was ready. On his command, preset explosive charges went off and seventy-seven fighting ships sank to the bottom of the harbor.[36]

The first threat that caused the British to bomb French ports was the prospect of a German invasion. On July 16, 1940, Hitler issued his Directive Number 16, which spelled out for his service chiefs his vision of the assault. He wanted a surprise amphibious assault on a broad front.[37] Churchill, while respecting the Wehrmacht's combat power, was confident he could defeat the invasion before it ever reached British shores. In a speech to Parliament on June 18, he noted that the Royal Navy would detect the enemy invasion armada and intercept it "long before it reached the coast, and all the men drowned in the sea or, at worst, blown to pieces with the equipment while trying to land."[38] Later in August, as the air battles were intensifying, he noted, "Our first line of defense against invasion must be as ever the enemy's ports." The detection of a buildup of barges and landing craft "should be followed by resolute attacks with all our forces available and suitable upon any concentrations of enemy shipping."[39]

Even before Hitler's Sea Lion directive, the British Air Staff issued its first bombing policy directing Bomber Command to attack French ports, and they followed up with more details in September, with the purpose of preventing a German invasion. French civilians began experiencing indications of what they could expect, as at least 292 perished because of bombing before the end of the year. While the British took the German threat seriously that summer, neither the Heer's generals nor the Kriegsmarine's admirals were anxious to cross the channel. They knew the Royal Navy, the world's most powerful, would fight to the death to defend the crossing. Even without the enemy fleet, the weather could play havoc with the invasion force. In July the naval staff argued that given the current state of affairs, they should postpone the assault until "May 1941 or thereafter."[40] Hitler had no desire to wait. He ordered the continuation of a buildup of supplies and landing craft and ultimately set a target date for September 21. Of course, the Luftwaffe proved incapable of defeating RAF Fighter Command, and on September 17 the German leader called the whole thing off.[41] In the meantime, however, the Royal Air Force continued attacking German concentrations in ports and along the rivers feeding into the channel.

The most famous of the ports is Dunkerque, mentioned earlier, which has the infamous honor of being the longest-occupied city on the western front and one of the most bombed places on earth. The intense fighting and bombardment by both sides during Operation Dynamo virtually destroyed the city. Given the breakdown of the government, disorganization of the medical services, and the thousands who fled the fighting, it is still almost impossible to determine exactly how many civilians died during the battle, and any numbers remain a guess.[42]

For the next four years, aerial attacks on the city and the port area continued almost daily. In the beginning, the bombardments were relatively small, such as the case of the raid by six Blenheim bombers on February 10, 1941. This attack was part of a larger program called Operation Circus, which consisted of bombing raids with fighter escorts, designed to draw German aircraft into combat. The planes arrived around 1330 hours that Monday, and most of the bombs fell in a residential area on the east side of town, far from any apparent military target. This small force managed to kill twenty-one civilians and wound another eighteen. The Kfourn family lived at 6 rue d'Est, around the corner from the old college (high school) Jean Bart. After the bombers had hit their house, rescuers pulled Olga (ten), Mauriette (nine), André (four), and Alfred (three) from its wreckage. Mauriette died almost immediately, and the explosions wounded the other three.[43] Similar attacks took place almost daily, often doing little damage. In other cases, such as the vain attempt of twelve Boston bombers on June 21, 1942, to attack a cargo ship in the harbor, civilians paid the price. In this case, the raid killed twelve and wounded thirty-three. As both Bomber Command and local records point out, however, most raids were mining missions, designed to prevent the Germans from using what remained of the harbor.[44] Fighting had damaged most of the port area in the first few months of the war, so it was no longer a serious threat by the time of the Allied invasion.

In early September 1944, the Canadian 2nd Division arrived outside of Dunkerque, after breaking out from Normandy and crossing the Seine and Somme Rivers. After some sharp fighting outside the city, the Canadian commander decided to encircle it with one of his brigades and continue north toward Boulogne and Calais. There was no reason to waste time and precious manpower on a port the Allies could not repair in time to support the campaign into Germany. The 13,000–15,000 German soldiers and sailors under Vice-Admiral Fredrich Frisus, and what remained of the civilian population, were now isolated from the outside world.[45] For the next seven months, Allied brigades would rotate around the fortress' perimeter to ensure its isolation. Occasionally, they would launch limited attacks to seize important positions on the perimeter. Finally, two days after German general Alfred Jodl capitulated to Eisenhower in Reims, Frisus surrendered his command to Brigadier General Alois Liška's 1st Czechoslovak Armoured Brigade, then operating under the control of the Twenty-First Army Group. From the evacuation of the last British and French soldiers on June 5, 1940, until May 9, 1945, the city experienced one of the longest hostile occupations of the war. The city was little more than a pile of ruins, its ancient port destroyed and useless, and only 750 citizens remained of the 31,000 who called Dunkerque home before the war.[46]

Nantes was another port that took a beating. This ancient city was famous in French history for the Huguenot protective edict that Louis XIV revoked in 1685 and for the ruthless *noyades*, or drowning executions, of enemies of the French Revolution in 1793. The Allies attacked its docks with heavy bombers at least thirty-one times during the war. In one instance, on the pleasant afternoon of September 16, 1943, seventy-nine heavy bombers from the Eighth Air Force appeared without warning over the city. Its streets were full of shoppers gathering food from the country markets. The exploding bombs caused panic in the city center. Projectiles hit the hospital, killing forty of the sick almost immediately. While the raid itself lasted only seven minutes, it was, in the words of Paul Caillaud, the director for local civil defense, "a dismal surprise" ("*une funèbre surprise*"). American bombers returned on September 23, and just these two attacks killed at least 1,463 civilians, injured another 2,500, destroyed 700 houses, and made another 3,000 too dangerous to occupy.[47] It is an interesting commentary that the destruction of this historic city receives only a passing comment, with no details, in the Air Force's official history of the conflict.[48] The bombing of September 16 destroyed the Maison du Prisonnier, which coordinated support for French soldiers in German POW camps, and killed fifteen of the staff. This perceived atrocity caused those in these camps in Germany to send money and food and to offer to adopt children orphaned by the Allied attacks. As historian Robert Gildea pointed out, "The wheel had come full circle (and) . . . those in exile who should have been helped were in their turn helping those at home, who, for once, had greater need than they."[49] Nantes, of course, was just one city, but these were the deadliest attacks yet suffered by a French city.

When the threat of an invasion had passed in 1940, the British turned their attention to the ports that housed surface raiders and U-boats. After the war, Churchill remarked, "The only thing that ever really frightened me during the war was the U-boat peril."[50] Remembering the effectiveness of these vessels during the previous war, he anticipated that the Kriegsmarine would improve its performance. What made this threat even more dangerous was the German occupation of the French ports that opened up onto the Atlantic, four hundred miles farther west than their German bases. The Breton Peninsula had been particularly dangerous in this regard. The excellent harbors at Lorient, Saint-Nazaire, and Brest provided natural facilities readily convertible to accommodate the most modern vessels.

Even before the submarines could bite, the Kriegsmarine began with conventional naval operations. It started the war with four large warships, the *Bismarck*, *Scharnhorst*, *Gneisenau*, and *Tirpitz*, and about a half dozen cruisers. Individually these were powerful warships, but this small fleet could do little to affect the war's outcome. In the early stages of the conflict, though, they caused the British Admiralty lots of concern because of what they did to merchant shipping when they escaped onto the high seas.[51] Most notably were the January–March 1941 sortie by the *Scharnhorst* and the *Gneisenau*, which sank twenty-two Allied vessels. The short-term effect of the attack prompted the dispatch of almost every British warship to convoy duty. At one point, according to Churchill, the fleet had only one battleship in home waters for combat.[52] After this foray, the British took the prospects of German surface raiders on the high seas seriously. When the *Bismarck* and the *Prinz Eugen*, a cruiser, entered the North Sea in late May 1941, the Admiralty launched the largest British naval operation since the Great War. It did not start well as the *Prinz Eugen* destroyed the battle cruiser HMS *Hood*, Britain's "largest and fastest," in a few moments on May 24, killing all but three of the 1,417-man crew. Ultimately, the Royal Navy prevailed, and a task force that included the aircraft carrier *Ark Royal* sank the *Bismarck*.[53]

Brest became Germany's main Atlantic base and as a result attracted the wrath of Bomber Command and RAF Coastal Command. The city rests in an amazingly rich natural harbor that dominates the tip of the Breton Peninsula that juts out into the Atlantic Ocean at the intersection of the English Channel and the Bay of Biscay. Cardinal Richelieu, the de facto dictator during Louis XIII's reign, recognized its strategic significance and began construction of a port that became the principal base for the French navy. So it remained though monarchies, empires, and republics until the Germans arrived in the city on June 21, 1940, and occupied the harbor. The British bombed it for the first time on August 9 and continued on a small scale for the rest of the year. In January, after the threat of invasion had passed, Bomber Command began paying attention to this important port with a raid of 53 bombers on January 5, and they continued with light bomber attacks and mine laying.[54] Following their North Atlantic raids in February and March 1941, the battleships *Scharnhorst* and *Gneisenau* arrived for repairs, prompting a significant response from the RAF. In the early morning hours of March 31, 109 Wellington medium bombers attacked the ships, doing little damage. Large British attacks continued, and the bombers scored some success, in particular against the *Gneisenau*, which had moved into the harbor.[55] In June, following its action in the North Sea, the *Prinz Eugen* made good its escape and made it back to Brest.

By January 1942 the German navy had concentrated all three large ships in the harbor, which the RAF bombed almost daily in an attempt to destroy them before they could do more damage. In February, making a mockery of British attempts to destroy them, they made a mad dash up the English Channel. As the ships departed, their crews watched as Bomber Command attacked their recently evacuated locations. Fighting off RAF air strikes and encountering mines, the small fleet arrived in safer North Sea harbors.[56] With the squadron's departure, Brest's population surveyed the damage. Since January, sixteen bombing and mining missions had induced almost half the population to flee to the countryside. The raids killed 200 citizens and wounded over 300 more. Much of the city was in ruins, and the war still had three years to go.[57] Brest would find itself bombed sporadically as part of the Allied attempt to destroy the submarine bases threatening its vital sea lanes with the United States and the Commonwealth. The Americans reached the city after the breakout from the Normandy beaches in July 1944. When it was over in September, only 3,000 civilians remained from its original population of almost 60,000.[58]

The Atlantic campaign resulted in the German adaption of some ports into bases for U-boats. Failing to attack these ports when they were under construction and most vulnerable was one of Bomber Command's greatest errors. The workers were able to build these facilities without fear and with a steady supply of building materials. After Organisation Todt finished them, the Royal Air Force, joined by the United States Army Air Forces in mid-1942, began attacking these targets with ever-increasing bomb tonnage, destroying the French structures in the area but having little effect on the U-boat shelters themselves.[59]

The first submarine base, complete with tools, repair parts, and ammunition, opened on July 6, 1940, at Lorient, on the southern Brittany coast. Between February and May 1941, the Todt organization finished submarine shelters in Brest, at La Pallice near La Rochelle, and Saint-Nazaire that were almost impervious to bombing with the available technology. As U-boat attacks began having a severe effect toward the end of 1942, the Allies dropped any pretense of precision bombing and began area attacks designed to destroy the pens "even if the resultant bombing causes complete devastation of the inhabited areas of the town."[60] When the Allied leaders directed the heavy bombers to destroy these facilities, it was too late. Not until the British introduced the Tallboy bomb later in the war were they able to do any damage to these structures. By that point, the Allies had already won the Battle of the Atlantic: at sea, not in the ports.[61]

These bombing missions were truly a waste of effort. For example, the Allies bombed Saint-Nazaire, in southern Brittany at the mouth of the Loire River, almost two hundred times during the war.[62] On February 28, 1943, 413 British heavy bombers attacked these submarine pens without damaging the German installation. Allied bombers burned the city to the ground. The toll would have been much higher but, fortunately, only a few hours earlier, more than twelve thousand citizens had heeded the warnings found in leaflets dropped by Bomber Command and had left the urban area to seek shelter in adjacent towns. Hitler declared what remained of the city a fortress in January 1944, and its soldiers prepared to defend the base and the Loire River entrance in all directions. These bombings, especially mining, continued until American forces arrived outside the city in July. Rather than attack the position and waste lives, the Americans continued to surround it until its commander finally surrendered on May 8, 1945, the last day of the war. When it was over, this once great port was in ruins, and the city of Saint-Nazaire had fewer than one hundred of eight thousand buildings intact at the end.[63] The French rebuilt the port in the postwar years. Near the submarine base, a public beach, generally unremarkable-looking housing, and an unimpressive shopping center have replaced the ancient structures. Across the street from the center, the massive submarine base remains for all to see.

The ports took on a new significance as Eisenhower's planners began to consider the dynamics of crossing the channel in 1944. The Kriegsmarine had been in position for more than four years and had organized its forces in France under Naval Group Command West (Marinegruppenkommando West), commanded by Admiral Theodor Krancke. He had three subordinate commands, the Channel Coast Command that had control from Ostend in Belgium to Saint-Malo south of Normandy, the Atlantic Coast Command that controlled operations from Brittany south to the Spanish border, and South Coast Command that controlled forces along the Mediterranean Sea. He had a relatively small force with only 3 destroyers, 6 standard torpedo boats, 38 Fast Attack torpedo boats, Schnellboot, called E-boats by the Allies, and 116 various kinds of smaller patrol boats. The potential was there for U-boat flotillas from Brittany to join the fight and interfere with the Allied invasion forces. The German navy also had responsibility for all artillery batteries on the coast and air defense batteries around the ports.[64]

Krancke demonstrated his potential for doing damage in April, when nine E-boats slipped out of Cherbourg and attacked a convoy full of troops practicing landings at Slapton Sands, killing more than six hundred American soldiers and sailors.[65] Eleven of these ports also became fortresses. Dunkerque, Boulogne, and Calais in the Pas-De-Calais were obvious choices for extra defensive construction because of their proximity to England and the fear that this would be the Allied invasion site. Le Havre protected the Seine River Valley that led into the heart of France. Cherbourg and Brest were the key ports on the nation's two most significant peninsulas and apparent invasion alternatives. Lorient, Saint-Nazaire, La Rochelle, and the Gironde River Estuary dominated the coast along the Bay of Biscay. The Germans had already augmented defenses at all of these facilities because of their other roles as a submarine or naval base. With their designation as Festungen, commanders

Bombing Dieppe by the Ninth Air Force, May 1944. *NARA RG 342 US Air Force Photo Collection*

now paid attention to all-around defense. Machine-gun positions, command posts, and artillery batteries now moved into concrete-protected shelters. Workers cleared fields of fire, often by destroying buildings and homes, on the landward side of the port to prevent its capture from the rear. Around the periphery, barbed wire and land mines encircled the defenders. While much of this work had already begun at the local level, the fortress designation now indicated that soldiers would defend these positions after the Allied troops surrounded them. The implied promise was that reinforcements would come to their aid; the reality was it would not happen.[66]

Le Havre is one of the most profound examples of the fate awaiting such fortresses. It had one of the earliest state-sponsored ports, founded by King Francis I in 1517 specifically to support the long-distance trade that the smaller ports of Honfleur and Harfleur, subject to silting from the Seine, could not handle. The city and new port also occupied a strategic location on the north bank of the river.[67] It remained a vital naval and trade port into the twentieth century. By 1936 it had more than 164,000 inhabitants and was the second most productive port in the country, only slightly trailing Marseille.[68]

By May 1944 the Allies had bombed, mined, or strafed the city, its port, enemy positions, and suburbs well over one hundred times. As June approached, the missions began adding attacks on radar and German military posts. The city was close to the invasion beaches, and for almost three months its citizens had been able to hear, and occasionally see, the fighting on the Calvados beaches only twenty or so miles away along the coast. Colonel Eberhard Wildermuth's mixed force of about 11,000 soldiers defended this important fortress, and approximately 50,000 civilians remained in the city.[69] General John Crocker's British 1st Corps, part of the First Canadian Army, arrived outside of Le Havre in early September and determined to capture the city. With the apparent success of the bombings outside of Saint-Lô in July, commanders wanted to use heavy bombers when they could to avoid casualties. This attitude was particularly true for General Montgomery, who was determined to prevent friendly casualties and was eager to use massed artillery and aircraft in a direct support role to attain his objective. As should have been obvious, though, such an attack would devastate the terrain on the target the ground troops were trying to capture. They also should have known by this stage of the war that such bombardments usually did not destroy enemy forces in defensive bunkers.[70]

The assault, named Operation Astonia, began on September 10 with 65 heavy bombers attacking the main artillery battery overlooking the water approaches from the west. Then the British monitor *Erebus*, the battleship *Warspite*, and eight regiments of artillery (approximately 192 guns) fired against selected targets in the city. At 1615, more than 900 bombers returned and, in two waves, plastered the city with 4,719 tons of bombs. At 1745, the British ground attack began and continued into the late evening. Early the next morning, Bomber Command returned with 146 aircraft dropping another 742 tons of bombs. All day, rocket-firing Typhoons continued to attack strong points and provide support for the advancing ground troops. At noon on September 12, British infantry captured the wounded Wildermuth in his bunker. Soon it was over.[71] Canadian historian Terry Copp called Astonia, the capture of Le Havre, "a model of combined operations, one that involved close cooperation between army, navy, and air force."[72] The Canadian official historian had earlier referred to the city's capture as "a neat and expeditious three-day operation."[73] If the measure of success was the number of British casualties suffered in the operation, 322 soldiers killed and wounded, then it was successful. But a more detailed examination of the object of the attack, the use of air power, and the ultimate results may raise questions about the veracity of that judgment.

The first intense day of bombardment took place on June 14. That morning the Royal Navy executed a short but intense attack of the docks housing the E-boats. That evening Bomber Command joined the fight against the waterfront. Beginning around 2120 hours, 221 Lancasters and another 13 Mosquitoes attacked with a host of bombs, including the new Tallboy, 12,000-pound bombs. The attack on this military objective resulted in 76 civilians killed and another 150 wounded.[74] As the Allies began their breakout from the beaches, Bomber Command turned its attention back to the city with more raids. One 50-aircraft raid on August 2 against the port area failed as smoke covered the target. Although they could not see, they continued dropping their bombs, and the attack killed 33 civilians and wounded 50 more.[75]

After the ground troops had arrived, raids became incredibly intense. At 1900 hours on September 5, 348 bombers struck at the city's center, seeking to destroy German positions. The 1,800 tons of bombs did little damage to German targets but ravaged the heart of the town near city hall. The

Le Havre subprefect reported to Wildermuth that these attacks killed more than 2,500 civilians and that perhaps twice as many were still missing and perhaps under the wreckage. These figures would turn out to be an exaggeration.[76] The British survey team concluded that this last attack "contributed little except, possibly, by increasing the demoralization of the enemy."[77] The next evening, another 344 bombers attacked enemy fortifications. The preassault phase continued with a raid by another 333 bombers on September 8 and another on September 9. Therefore, before the actual ground attack had even begun, Bomber Command had launched more than 1,000 heavy bombers against Le Havre. Its goal was to neutralize the defenders before the infantry's attack. According to the fortress commander, though, these attacks did little damage, only destroying two gun positions that were under construction, damaging the telephone system, and turning the streets into rubble. The infantry fighting positions remained intact.[78] The sad fact is that the air bombardment had little effect on the defender's rapid collapse, and its use reflected the British and Canadian armies' penchant for using all of the firepower available against the enemy defenders to prevent friendly casualties. Bomber Command's massive attacks on September 10 and 11, discussed earlier, contributed to the city's carnage but little to the ground attack's success, other than keeping the German defenders in their bunkers. Solly Zuckerman's survey team, which visited Le Havre after the battle, determined that the bombardment put out of action only 25 to 30 percent of all artillery exposed. English artillery had destroyed many of the guns in a more precise counterbattery effort, which did not require the town's destruction.[79]

The idea that the British army would have to destroy an old French city to liberate it from demoralized German defenders reflects poorly on the Allied conduct of the campaign. The evaluation summary, written by Zuckerman's team, is a significant indictment of the army's operational approach: "(iv) The air attack on the town itself contributed little to the subsequent success of our ground forces."[80] Wildermuth, the fortress commander, concurred. His interrogation report notes that he remarked, "The air bombardments and the shelling from the sea had only a general destructive effect, but did not create much military damage. The real effective fire came from the Allied concentration of artillery."[81] Infantry and armor, attacking with good artillery support, against an enemy with low morale, captured the city. But the ground commanders would take no chances. The army group commander's entire operational approach was one of preventing friendly casualties and, at what appeared to be a turning point in the war, of taking this important port without delay and with minimal commitment of ground forces. Montgomery could count on no more young men to train as soldiers, and in the post-Normandy period he would begin breaking up divisions in search of replacements. Overwhelming firepower was the key to victory and preserving the army.[82] The First Canadian Army commander, General Henry D. G. Crerar, was a product of the artillery branch and was an enthusiastic believer in using heavy aerial bombardment to pave the way for his troops.[83] Although Crocker, an armor officer, planned an attack that would probably have succeeded without Bomber Command, he had no reason to refuse the massive firepower placed at his disposal by Montgomery and Crerar. Moreover, he believed it would help lower the enemy's morale.[84] While that may have helped the offensive to some degree, it also reflects an unwarranted lack of confidence in the fighting capability of the British commander and his soldiers. Apparently, as most of the secondary literature concerning the operation indicates, leaders displayed little concern for either civilian casualties or the impending destruction of a great city. As a result of irresponsible planning, Le Havre would end the war as France's most damaged city, with 82 percent of it destroyed and more than two thousand citizens killed and wounded and 58 percent of the remaining population homeless.[85] As Andrew Knapp, who has studied this event more than anyone else, argues, the Havrais have a different narrative. For them, "liberation was synonymous with catastrophe."[86] Today, wandering into the restored underground shelter used by doctors and nurses at L'hôpital Flaubert, in the center of Le Havre, one encounters a poster portraying sixteen young women. All of them were nurses, hospital employees, or members of the area's passive defense. The simple caption reads: "*Elles n'avient pas 20 ans.*"[87]

One more port deserves our attention before we conclude this chapter. In January 1945, while American and British armies drove the Germans back from the French border and out of the Ardennes, another drama took place along the Atlantic coast at the seaside resort of Royan. Some English-speaking readers may know of the solid performance by the reconstituted French army in Italy in 1943 or its performance later as part of Operation Dragoon in southern France. Others may know of the French 2nd Armored Division's dramatic liberation of Paris, and the French First Army's intense fighting outside of Strasbourg and the Colmar Pocket in January and February 1945. Not mentioned in most histories of the campaign, however, are the tragic events that took place at the same time 450 miles west of the fierce fighting. In late 1944 French general Edgar de Larminat, working under the direction of French chief of staff General Alphonse Juin, had organized the various French Resistance forces, which had been fighting the Germans during the occupation, into standardized infantry divisions. Larminat now commanded three of these against La Rochelle, Pointe de Grave, on the left bank of the Gironde estuary, and the seaside resort of Royan on the right. All three of these positions were fortresses and, as 1945 arrived and Allied armies headed into Germany, were still under Nazi control. Starved for manpower, it made operational sense for these reconstituted units to release the regular US Army forces for combat at the front. At Royan, Colonel Henri Adeline, a former Resistance leader, led a force of about 10,000. Its mission was to encircle the fortress, prevent the Germans from breaking out, and, if possible, capture it. Adeline's force, however, was neither equipped nor trained for urban operations, so everything was essentially at a standstill. Liaison with air and sea units, by all accounts, was tentative at best. Unlike Le Havre, there was no need to capture the city, as sufficient Allied supplies were now flowing into the continent and the end game was in sight. Initially, with a population of about 12,000, about 2,000 civilians remained inside the pocket.[88]

The complexity of modern industrial war now intervened in this stable environment. During a discussion between Larminat and the commander of the First Tactical Air Force (Provisional), Maj. Gen. Ralph Royce, the topic of air support for the siege arose. Royce pointed out that the Eighth Air Force was developing a special force for night bombing, and the targets the French commander was describing would be excellent for training the new American night bombers. The general convinced the American that the French civilians were gone and that the attack would be helpful.[89] Larminat, with his small staff, probably did not know that the civilians were still there. Royce, as a good Air Force officer who wanted to support and demonstrate the utility of air power, turned the mission over to his staff, which forwarded the request to senior headquarters. Across Europe, the same staff actions took place hundreds of times a day.[90] In this instance, no one questioned the wisdom of destroying this nonthreatening village so far behind the enemy lines. It was just another staff action, like the ones that had been going on for years. What made it different was new Air Force headquarters with a temporary staff, supporting an ad hoc division made up of citizen soldiers without an experienced team of leaders, attempting to coordinate with an efficient cell hundreds of miles away. Add the exhaustion of air planners that had just helped defeat the German assault in the Ardennes, and the potential for a mistake was high. In the early morning hours of January 5, Bomber Command deployed 347 Lancaster heavy bombers in two waves above the town, dropping 1,476 tons of high explosives. To add a sense of irony to this senseless attack, 285 of the bombs were of the 4,000-lb. "blockbuster" variety, which was certainly excessive for a nonessential target. The second wave took place an hour after the first and caught many civilians, passive defense members, firefighters, and others out in the streets trying to recover from the first raid. As a result, between five hundred and eight hundred civilians perished in two attacks that wiped the town off the map. The attacks did little to the German defenders.[91] General Juin was furious and demanded an investigation.[92] Air Marshal James Robb, the deputy chief of staff for air operations, chalked it up as a misunderstanding and recommended against any further investigations. He also directed no more heavy bomber missions in western France "unless the request for the attack is made by JUIN himself."[93] Eisenhower agreed and had his chief of staff, Bedell Smith, draft a personal letter to the French commander with apologies and assurances it would not happen again.[94] This bombardment should have been the end of this tragic event, but it was not.

For reasons that make little military sense, the French decided to renew the attack on Royan in April. The war was almost over and Allied troops, even French troops, were across the Rhine and into Germany. Nevertheless, several veteran French units arrived to reinforce General Larminat's command, including elements of the 2nd Armored Division that had led the assault into Paris the previous summer. While it might be acceptable to grant the French leaders a victory, what is certainly questionable is the need for a massive air bombardment before the attack. This time, it was the Americans, bomb groups from both the Eighth and Ninth Air Forces, that softened up the fortress. More than 1,400 B-17s, B-24s, and B-26 bombers plastered the same target attacked previously, as well as positions across the estuary at Pointe de Grave.[95] Flying that day as a bombardier in a B-17 assigned to the 490th Bombardment Group was twenty-three-year-old Howard Zinn, who helped drop the thousands of pounds of bombs, including one of the first uses of napalm on the French city below. In 1966 Zinn, now a postdoctoral student, returned to Royan to better understand the nature of his mission. His research, which included talking to survivors of the attack, had a profound influence on his later life and leadership in efforts to prevent civilian casualties in America's next wars. In the conclusion to his short article on the bombing, he writes, "More and more in our time, the mass production of massive evil requires an enormously complicated division of labor. No one is positively responsible for the horror that ensues. But everyone is negatively responsible because anyone can throw a wrench into the machinery."[96] Zinn's point is quite important. Royan was a sideshow and not essential to the conduct of the war. Larminat later commented to local leaders that the city was "destroyed by mistake."[97] Sadly, as Zinn pointed out, this destruction could have been stopped at any point, not the least by the planners back in London who approved both of these needless missions. Today, the citizens of this region continue to struggle with its cause, trauma, and consequences.

The Allied bombing of airfields and ports began long before America entered the war and before COSSAC and Eisenhower designed their various approaches to the Neptune air operation. By the spring of 1944, however, they fit well into the plan. What is important, especially in the case of the ports, is that some of these operations continued until the last day of the war. They get little attention in American and Commonwealth literature because they were so far away from the invasion zone. Later in this book, we will visit other ports, especially those in the north. In all cases, especially in those harbors designated as fortresses, the citizens that remained suffered longer than any other French group. Casualties were often severe, and the memories and trauma has lasted well into the twenty-first century. In most cases, the targets were legitimate. The problem was using imprecise weapons, heavy bombers, to go after relatively precise objectives. In some cases, the use of heavy bombers was irresponsible and poorly directed by the ground commanders. No matter what, this history is a fact of the war. In almost all these cities, citizens have restored the ancient churches. Usually, they have rebuilt the old marketplaces and homes, using the familiar, prefabricated style common in the postwar era. For those who survived, this bombardment, rather than liberation, is their central narrative of the Second World War.

CHAPTER FIVE

INDUSTRY

Taking the war to the enemy by destroying its factories, electrical power plants, and petroleum refineries, and attacking those who worked in these facilities, had always been an important aspect of British and then Allied strategic bombing doctrine. Destroying factories and demoralizing those who worked there was, from the perspective of aviation visionaries, the fastest way to end a war. For the United States Army Air Force, AWPD-1, the planning document mentioned earlier, included petroleum, power generation, and German aircraft as its principal targets. British Bomber Command, handicapped by problems in developing sound aviation doctrine, a shortage of heavy bombers, and the strain of worldwide war, was mostly ineffective against German industry until at least 1942. In that year performance began to change as Bomber Command continued to convert to a fleet of all heavy bombers (Lancasters and Halifaxes), Harris took command and provided stronger leadership, and American aircraft began arriving in force near the end of the year.[1]

The most important change was the Allied implementation of Operation Pointblank, the Combined Bomber Offensive. Although referred to as an operation, it was a campaign under the direction of the Combined Chiefs of Staff. For the bomber commanders, this around-the-clock-bombing of German industry by the British and American air forces was the centerpiece of their participation during the Second World War in Europe. Certainly, it is the aspect of the conflict that both the American and British air forces are most proud. Developed by the Combined Chiefs of Staff during the Casablanca Conference in January 1943, the plan called for each service to attack targets based on the capabilities they had planned for and developed during the early stages of the war. Harris' RAF Bomber Command would continue mass night attacks against German industrial areas. Spaatz' US Strategic Air Forces would continue to execute daylight precision bombing raids against selected elements of the enemy's military and industrial infrastructure. In priority, the heavy bombers were to destroy German submarine construction facilities, aircraft industry, transportation system, oil plants, and other facilities supporting the enemy's war effort. The campaign's overall objective was the "progressive destruction and dislocation of the German military, industrial, and economic system." As a caution, the original directive noted, "In attacking objectives in Occupied territories, you will conform to such instructions as may be issued from time to time for political reasons by His Majesty's Government through the British Chiefs of Staff."[2] As an official Army historian noted, the Casablanca directive "marked a strategic milestone in assigning airpower a definite place in Allied planning against Germany."[3] It is one of the few times in modern history that a single military capability, in this case, the heavy bomber, was given an independent task from national political leaders. Of course, the directive, ultimately formalized in June when the leadership moved German fighter factories and bases to the top of the target list, remained extremely broad and subject to interpretation as the war progressed.

The key to the directive was the codification of the two commands' particular ways of conducting the air war. For Bomber Command, it was night bombing and area attack. In spite of the prewar concerns that the bomber would always get through, enemy fighter aircraft and anti-aircraft fire demonstrated, by the middle of 1940, an ability to prevent many aircraft from hitting their targets during the day. By night, however, the bombers were often able to approach their objectives without loss. Therefore, as the year went on, the British conducted most of their bombing missions at night, which became Bomber Command's standard mode of operation for the remainder of the war.[4] Along with night missions came the realization that the bombers, if they were able to navigate to the correct area (which was by no means certain), had little probability of actually hitting what they were aiming at. A study of the command's performance between June 2 and July 25, 1941, prepared by the economist David Bensusan-Butt, indicated how bad things were early in the war. On average, only one aircraft in three got within five miles of the intended target. For the thirty-eight missions launched against the German industrial area of the Ruhr, only one aircraft in ten got anywhere close.[5] Therefore, rather than aiming at precise targets, they focused on area bombing. A city's factories became the "aiming point," but everyone knew the damage to both facilities and civilians would be great.[6]

American policy, developed in the interwar period, focused on precision bombing during daylight. American aviation enthusiasts believed that massed formations of the heavily armed B-17 Flying Fortress, unescorted by fighters, would be able to fight their way through to the designated target. Then, once overhead, the bombardier would use the sophisticated Norden bombsight to hit the target with precision.[7] In spite of high casualties on raids into Germany, Spaatz never abandoned the principle of daylight operations. Besides, for a host of reasons involving calculations of air speed, altitude, cloud cover, crew fatigue, and enemy fire, the Norden did not live up to its publicity.[8] Under the Pointblank directive, therefore, American Liberator and Flying Fortress bombers were to attack German industry during the day, while British Stirling, Halifax, and Lancaster bombers bombed at night. With few exceptions, and with some setbacks on the American side, this around-the-clock bombing effort continued until the end of the war.[9] Both commands realized they were killing German civilians. Although there were some moral issues, by 1943 most leaders accepted that civilians would die and that the lowered morale might even contribute to Germany's demise. Harris, for one, had no inhibitions in killing as many enemy civilians as possible.[10] But the inaccurate bombing of industry in occupied, friendly countries was a different matter.

The Operation

France has always been one of Europe's major commercial and industrial states. It emerged from the First World War as a more efficient industrial powerhouse, equipping not only its own forces, but also those of the US Army, which sent only soldiers and little else to Europe for the war.[11] Its postwar recovery efforts, reabsorbing the Alsace-Lorraine region and rebuilding the destroyed mines and factories in the north, was one of Europe's greatest achievements in the interwar years. Although it suffered during the Great

Depression like the rest of the Western world, by 1932 it ranked as the world's fifth industrial power, behind Germany, the Soviet Union, Britain, and the United States.[12] For example, Renault, Peugeot, and Citroën produced some of the world's best automobiles. Ford, an American multinational corporation in 1935, had just completed a state-of-the-art factory, with machinery based on Henry Ford's mass-production techniques, at Poissy, northwest of Paris.[13] The quality of French weapons, especially tanks and artillery, was superb and usually superior to those of any army, especially the Germans. But problems with the late rearmament and training the conscript army to use and maintain this equipment contributed to the Nazi victory in 1940.[14]

It is interesting that in most comparisons of weapons and material produced during the war, French statistics abruptly end with the 1940 campaign. For example, the standard Second World War desk reference entirely omits French weapons production in its tables. This omission is perplexing since France was in the process of a massive rearmament program when the Germans arrived and had already produced thousands of tanks, artillery, and weapons. Did this massive industrial system, essentially untouched during the weeks of combat, disappear?[15] The answer, of course, is no. Nazi economists and factory owners, following in the wake of their conquering armies, incorporated the French industrial system into the overall war effort. Soon, French firms began producing, or retrofitting to Wehrmacht standards, a broad range of equipment from aircraft engines to tanks, artillery, tires, and military trucks.[16] They also served as repair facilities for military equipment, which compensated for the Germany economy's inability to produce sufficient weapons and ammunition. Automotive and aircraft companies were more than willing to combine their efforts with German industrialists.[17] Companies such as Schneider, Renault, Ford, Hotchkiss, and Michelin were some of the many prominent brands that now served the Nazi war effort. Eighty-five percent of all trucks and automobiles produced in France went to Germany.[18] For example, by 1941, almost 63,000 French workers labored in factories, such as the Gnome et Rhône facilities that built aircraft engines, that supported the German aviation industry.[19] That same year the new Ford SAF plant at Poissy sent almost 4,000 trucks to German forces struggling against Soviet forces on the eastern front. This same factory also delivered another 4,109 truck engines, 4,173 rear axles, and 4,000 different automotive parts to other facilities producing vehicles in Belgium and the Netherlands.[20] The most important

English-language study of this topic notes that "French automobile companies had made a major contribution to Germany's war effort."[21] The same was true with other aspects of production. For example, French firms provided sophisticated design capabilities that were lacking in Germany. One such firm was Technique de Châtillon, which spent much of the war researching and designing long-range bombers and aircraft.[22] So important was supplying the German war effort that the number of French unemployed dropped from almost a million in September 1940 to zero in September 1942.[23]

These facilities were exactly the kind of targets planners for Pointblank wanted to destroy. As in the case of bombing airfields and ports, this campaign was already well under way when Eisenhower arrived in London in early 1944. Bombing French targets had a positive effect on crew morale since, as Arthur Harris pointed out after the war, they were relatively easy to find. They could attack them "in bright moonlight, or even by day" because air defenses were much weaker than those surrounding German factories, although, in practice, the vast majority of heavy RAF raids on French industrial targets took place at night.[24] Like those in Germany, French industrial targets were a priority for several reasons. Naturally, their destruction reduced the material flowing to the Wehrmacht, which in 1943 was fighting for its life in the Soviet Union. The destruction of factories might dissuade skilled French workers from supporting the war effort. Finally, the bombing provided French civilians, eager for an Allied victory in the conflict, with tangible evidence of the increasing power of the Anglo-American war machine. While bomber legend is all about the great raids against big factories in Germany, authors have written much less about attacks involving French facilities. Also, because these factories often had large rail yards nearby, air planners would sometimes try to destroy both in a single raid. The raids against Lille, which we will discuss later, is an excellent example. The problem, of course, was that industrialists built these facilities in French cities near the homes of potential labor. In the nineteenth and early twentieth centuries, people usually walked to work.[25]

Renault-Boulogne-Billancourt

Few Parisian tourists take the Metro 9 line to its end at the Pont de Sèvres and the commune of Boulogne-Billancourt. No renowned museums or art exhibits attract those looking for cozy cafés and monuments. It is a wealthy, densely populated part of the city and home to several major international corporations, movie studios, and a large football stadium. If you head a kilometer southwest on Avenue Leclerc, you arrive at the Seine and confront the Île Seguin in the middle of the river. In 2017 this island, and a portion of the right bank, was a major construction site, as new buildings and green space struggled to cover the earth that once housed the great Renault factory complex the company demolished in 2005. Beginning in 1890, workshops on both sides of this stretch of the river produced cars and trucks until the last rolled off the assembly line in 1992. Today, a company-constructed heritage and information pavilion are all that remains of this important factory, a reminder of the role Renault played in France's automotive industry.[26] In 1940 French automotive barons had, with some degree of enthusiasm and anticipating profits in the postwar world, embraced the new political situation and sought to integrate their industry with the German war effort. Louis Renault had already met with Hitler at his chancellery in February 1935 and argued that it was in both nations' best interests to form a unified cartel to counter competition from England and the United States.[27] By the spring of 1942, Billancourt was, according to an Office of Strategic Services report, "the largest single armament, truck and tank works in France."[28] The factory kept busy converting its military vehicles, such as the B-1 and R35 tanks captured by the Wehrmacht, for service with German units, in particular on the eastern front. By 1942 it was producing about a thousand military trucks, a hundred tanks, and three hundred airplane engines per month. This output equated to one panzer division every two months.

Parisians had begun ignoring the alert sirens they had heard since the beginning of the war, and the ones that went off on the night of March 3, 1942, probably seemed no different from any other. But there was a difference, as Arthur Harris had taken over Bomber Command a week earlier. Into February, Britain's strategic air force had not been successful. After an ineffective raid against Berlin at the beginning of November, which resulted in more than 9 percent of the aircraft not returning, Churchill told its commander, Air Marshal Sir Richard Peirse, to cease offensive operations over the winter. Poststrike investigations convinced the prime minister that he needed a new leader, and he sent Peirse off to Asia. For six weeks (January 8 to February 22, 1942), an interim commander, Air Vice-Marshal John Baldwin, managed affairs. He was no more effective; under his command the German capital ships made their dash up the channel from Brest on February 12.[29] So poor was Bomber Command's performance that some in the government were arguing that the organization should be broken up. Churchill had already decided to recall Harris from Washington, DC, where he was coordinating with the Americans, to take over the struggling command effective on February 22, 1942.[30]

Ten days later, Harris launched Bomber Command on its largest mission of the war to date, and he did it by scraping together half of all the aircraft he had available. He saw this as a relatively harmless way to experiment with different bombing techniques at a close target that would not be well defended. He also probably wanted to make a statement that there was a new commander in charge. Business would not be as it had been in the past. The assault consisted of 89 Wellington, 48 Hampden, and 23 Whitley medium bombers joining 29 Stirling, 26 Manchester, and 20 Halifax heavy bombers. Only the 20 Halifax bombers, out of the 235 dispatched, were first-rate aircraft, and the RAF had only 29 of these in its entire inventory.[31] The mixture of different aircraft, with different capabilities, indicates the degree of determination Harris displayed in showing his leaders that Bomber Command was under new management. He intended this mission to be a demonstration of the organization's power. It was impossible not to be able to locate Paris from the air, and the factory complex along the Seine on the south side of the city was easy to find in the bright moonlight. He correctly anticipated that, unlike German targets, it would have little night fighter and anti-aircraft gun protection. He planned the attack carefully, with the aircraft grouped in three waves according to the planes' capabilities. They approached at a low level, with flares illuminating the target area. Harris wanted precision and hoped to dampen the command's reputation for inaccurate bombing. They carried a larger than normal bomb load, and the aircraft went after the factory with 1,000- and 4,000-pound bombs. The raid, as planned, was a success from the British perspective, and it went as well as any up to that point in the war. Only one aircraft failed to return, and from crew observation and later poststrike photographs, the factory looked utterly destroyed.[32]

Analysts later announced, though, that the actual results were not as good as the initial reports, designed primarily for propaganda purposes, had suggested. The raid destroyed only about 40 percent of the factory, and it had to stop making trucks for only a few weeks. The workers spent several weeks repairing their facilities, and by June most of the nine thousand workers were back on the job, producing trucks and other equipment around the clock.[33] Harris' biographer, after describing the success of the raid, notes that in addition to the five French workers killed, "Several others, including their families, had unfortunately been killed in neighboring houses."[34] In reality, the bombers killed at least 367 workers and their families and severely injured another 341 while they slept in their beds or shelters in this crowded arrondissement. Only about half of the almost 100,000 citizens had access to any bomb-proof shelters. Rescuers discovered dozens of victims in demolished cellars.[35] Many of the wounded would later die of their injuries. Significantly, in this raid on a French city, Bomber Command inflicted twice as many casualties as they had on any German habitation up to that point in the war. Almost 10,000 civilians had become homeless and had lost all their possessions and food. Surprisingly, in spite of the casualties, many French citizens greeted the raid as proof of British power. These factories were legitimate military targets, and the growing French Resistance published accounts in their underground newspapers justifying the attacks and that "these French workers fallen on the field of battle are the victims of the policy of collaboration."[36] The German and Vichy governments, of course, responded to the British bombardment with outrage, with ceremonies and a day of mourning for the fallen.[37] This early attack would pave the way for much more violent Allied raids against factories over the next two and a half years.

Schneider: Le Creusot

Almost two hundred miles to the southeast of Paris is the Schneider factory at Le Creusot. The Schneider brothers, Adolphe and Eugène, purchased the region's iron mines and metal forges in the 1830s and developed them into a massive industrial empire, producing steel, railways, ships, and armaments. In 1912 the Breuil family constructed steel works nearby that grew to be quite large and supported Schneider's construction. By the eve of the First World War, they were among the greatest exporters of steel and artillery, competing with the German firm Krupp for military contracts across Europe, especially with Russia, and Asia.[38] Before the war, these firms produced a broad range of artillery and other weapons for the French army, and after the occupation, the Wehrmacht incorporated the captured weapons into its inventory. The Schneider factory was also a major producer of heavy guns, electric turbines, and railway engines. Allied intelligence analysts also believed it made tanks and armored cars.[39] Schneider was a massive complex of several facilities producing different kinds of equipment and supported by the impressive Montchanin electric transformer station. Again, just like the Renault plant, Allied planners considered it a legitimate military target, on a par with any similar facility in Germany.[40] Like Boulogne-Billancourt, the laborers lived close to their place of employment, ensuring they and their families would suffer just like anyone working in a factory.

By the fall of 1942, Harris had a much more powerful bombing force than he had had in the spring. With some exceptions, such as raids against the Gnome et Rhône aircraft plant at Gennevilliers, north of Paris, and the Ford plant at Poissy, Bomber Command had limited its attacks on France to coastal targets and concentrated its efforts against western German cities for the remainder of the spring and summer. He had been able to remove from the bomber squadrons most of the ineffective Blenheim, Hampden, Manchester, and Whitley bombers. He retained the Handley-Page Halifax and the Short Stirling, both four-engine heavies, but was not happy with their performance. Arriving in increasing numbers, however, was the Avro Lancaster, arguably the best bomber of the European war. It had all the attributes of "speed, height, and range" that Harris required.[41] It also had the largest bomb-carrying capability of any Allied bomber until the B-29 Superfortress and was one of the easiest to fly.[42] In mid-October, he had enough of these superior aircraft to test them in a concentrated strike. Again he was looking to demonstrate the power of his command against a high-profile target, and he chose Le Creusot. Because it was deeper into France, it was harder to locate than the Parisian suburbs, and it was an excellent test range for Harris' new aircraft. Also, bombing the Schneider complex would evoke a propaganda and publicity response from the French and German authorities, adding to the command's reputation.

On October 17, 1942, eighty-one Lancasters flew south into the Bay of Biscay, evading the concentration of German radar and coastal observers, and then due east, crossing the coastline between Nantes and La Rochelle. Harris determined to execute this attack with a degree of surprise and hoped for precision by attacking at dusk. By 1900 hours they arrived over the target at relatively low level, between 2,500 and 7,500 feet. As was the case with most missions over occupied France, no German fighter aircraft rose to intercept the raiding force. No one on the ground anticipated the raid, as the bombers approached out of the setting sun with an excellent view of the target area. There was no alert for either the factory workers or the civilians. German anti-aircraft crews, not anticipating a British raid so early in the evening, were unprepared to engage. In seven minutes, the bombers dropped almost 140 tons of munitions on the target. The raiders returned with the loss of only one aircraft, and the crews reported a successful attack. Photographs taken later, however, indicated that the attack did little damage to the factory. Many of the bombs had fallen short and struck the workers' housing area, with some of the first hitting the city hospital and causing widespread damage. Sixty-two civilians died in this raid and five hundred families lost their homes in the resulting fires caused by the incendiary bombs.[43]

Following the October raid, Harris had felt confident enough to begin his concentrated assault on German industrial cities. His boss, Charles Portal, who had a broader view of the global conflict from his pew as chief of the Air Staff, derailed his desire to take the war to Germany by requiring him to divert bombers to support the Battle of the Atlantic, which in 1942 was still a threat to British survival. Churchill ordered Bomber Command to repeatedly hit the submarine pens at Saint-Nazaire, Brest, and La Pallice. Harris was furious at this diversion, and Bomber Command, along with the Eighth Air Force, did little other than complete the destruction of the towns surrounding the large Nazi facilities. By March 1943 everyone realized that the Germans had won the battle between bombs and concrete, and Harris was ready to resume what he had wanted to do from the day he assumed command: destroy the German cities. His first target in what his report calls the called the Battle of the Ruhr was Essen, home of Schneider's prewar competitor Krupp. He went well beyond the German industrial region and sent his bombers, in fleets of more than one hundred at a time, against many German cities such as Munich, Berlin, Nuremberg, and Stuttgart.[44]

Several months after the October raid it became evident that the Schneider complex was continuing to produce weapons and trucks for the German war effort, and the Air Ministry wanted another attack, which Harris scheduled for June 20, 1943. For this strike, Harris gathered an array of second-class aircraft, such as the Stirling and the still inadequate Halifaxes. But this time he sent 290 aircraft, more than three times as many aircraft as he did on the first raid. This Schneider attack was a night raid, and two Lancasters, acting as pathfinders, led the way and dropped flares on the target. Although the aircraft bombed only from altitudes between 5,000 and 10,000 feet, this strike was no more effective than the first. Only one-fifth of the bombs managed to hit targets, with many falling as far as three miles from the factories into the city. This attack finished off the hospital and destroyed a church and other structures. According to Vichy's director of passive defense, it also killed 270 civilians, wounded 207 others, and destroyed 800 structures, presumably outside of the factory area.[45]

Le Mans

Located on the Sarthe River, a tributary of the great Loire, Le Mans is one of France's oldest communities, occupied by the Romans at the end of the Gallic Wars. A city of devout Catholics, with a beautiful cathedral and one of the most impressive ancient walls in France, it was sacked by the rebellious Huguenots in 1562. During the French Revolution, it again suffered as an army of the Revolutionary Republic defeated rebelling Catholic and Royalist troops during the Vendée uprising in 1793 and massacred many of the survivors and civilians living in the city. It was also the scene of one of the last battles of the Franco-Prussian War. In 1923 the Automobile Club de L'Ouest began organizing annual twenty-four-hour-long races in and around the city, making it the world's oldest active sports car race. With its central location and excellent transportation network, it was a natural center for industrial facilities, which included a Renault tractor plant, a Gnome et Rhône Aero factory, a large rail marshaling yard, and a Junkers aircraft repair plant and airfield. These were all on the south side of the city.[46] During the war, the Allies launched eleven bomber attacks and twenty-one fighter strikes against the city's various targets.

Renault built a factory there after the First World War, with the primary purpose of making tractors. Tractors may seem like harmless products, but, like everything produced in France during the war, they were part of the war effort. Renault sent more than three thousand farm tractors to German officials supervising agricultural operations in the Ukraine. The factory also produced some tanks and aircraft engines.[47] It was one of the region's largest employers, with more than 1,500 workers. The strike by fifteen RAF Mosquito bombers on March 9, 1943, severely damaged the factory, with direct hits in two of the three production buildings. The attack also killed six workers and wounded twenty more. The air planners appeared to be satisfied with the results of the mission, as they did not target it again. Of course, it was adjacent to the large Arnage rail yard, which Allied bombers visited several more times, so it received additional damage during those raids.[48]

The facility that most interested the Allied planners was the Gnome et Rhône plant. This complex was one of six company plants across France that produced engines and other material for the government. Originally developed to provide motors for final assembly in Paris, it fell under the direction of the German firm Bayerischen Motoren Werken (BMW) after June 1940. By 1943 the BMW directors were also converting part of the plant to build engines for German trucks. Little had changed with the new directorship as the Germans allowed the French managers to conduct day-to-day operations. The management took good care of its workers and managed to compensate them for their work at a competitive level. Postwar interviews with workers, conducted by a US Strategic Bombing Survey team, reflect a contented workforce. The factory employed approximately six hundred workers, primarily men. The factory itself was located on a narrow strip of land between the airfield and the rail yard, making it an easily identifiable target. The workers lived, along with their families, in a company-sponsored housing area constructed about a kilometer northeast of the factory and just north of the airfield. Given the intensity of the Allied bombing operations, it was a dangerous location.[49]

The Eighth Air Force conducted the first major bombing attack against the engine plant around 2000 hours on June 29, 1943. Eighty-four B-17 Flying Fortresses appeared 23,000 feet over the factory, dropping 726 500-pound bombs. None of them hit the target, but they did kill two and wound four civilians nearby.[50] The Eighth returned on July 4. This time, 105 B-17 Flying Fortress again tried from relatively high altitude, above 26,000 feet. Bomb crews reported that the attack seemed very concentrated and accurate, with severe damage to the factory, the rail yard, and the airfield. With so much smoke on the ground, the crews believed they were hitting the target. The actual image interpretation report shows otherwise, with bombs scattered throughout the area. While the bombers did hit the factory several times, more than 95 percent of the bombs fell outside the target area. In addition to the high altitude, German anti-aircraft fire appeared efficient, and a number of enemy fighters made the bombing run difficult. Most of the bombs fell near the town of Guécélard, sixteen kilometers south of the factory.[51]

Guécélard was a pretty little village of about four hundred inhabitants on the banks of the Sarthe River, astride the Route Nationale, called the Rue de Tours, between La Flèche and Le Mans. In 1943 the Montager and Païrel families were sharing a home near the Tours Road. Forty-six-year-old René Montager was the patriarch of this extended group. It included his wife, Jeanne (forty-eight), his mother-in-law Emilia Tillier (seventy-eight), his son René (seventeen), his daughter Jeanine (nineteen), and Jeanine's husband Henri (twenty-six). Jeanine and Henri had two children, Serge (one) and Roger (one month). July 4 was a beautiful summer day, and shortly after 1230 the whole family sat down for dinner. It was a joyous occasion as they were going to baptize the two babies. René was a mechanic who worked at the nearby rail yard that supported the massive Gnome et Rhône factory. Suddenly the alarm sounded, indicating that bombers were on the way. The Americans had bombed the factory several days earlier, so the family knew the drill, and they ran out of the house to a nearby ditch that served as their shelter. Suddenly, flares floated down over the target area, and the first formation of 105 B-17s appeared overhead. A neighbor, Aline Deroy, watched the spectacle as hundreds of 500-pound bombs exploded around her. She saw that several hit near the Montager home, creating thick clouds of smoke and flame. Nothing remained of the home. Only Emilia was alive when rescuers arrived, and the seventy-eight-year-old woman died several days later.[52] In addition to the Montager-Païrel family, Blanche Tedeschi, Alexis Robin, and Henri Besnardeau and his son Bernard also died in this senseless display of American firepower. The authorities buried the victims three days later at the cemetery at Saint-Martin de Pontlieue church, on the south side of Le Mans. Sixty-five years later, the victim's relatives were still trying to understand what had happened to this entire family.[53] What is most amazing to someone reading the official report, prepared by the US Strategic Bombing Survey analysts, is how ineffective the two missions of June 29 and July 4 were. One hundred and eighty-nine B-17 bombers, all equipped with the supposedly sophisticated Norden bombsight, dropped 1,764 500-pound bombs and only hit the target seven times! It was an abysmal performance, certainly not the kind the Air Force would want to share with the general public, and few Americans would ever learn about the reality of precision bombing in France.[54]

Raids in 1944

Bombing industrial targets in France continued as the war moved into 1944. By this time the air war had intensified and the Allies had prepared a much larger air machine to conduct operations against factories across Europe. The increasingly large England-based US Eighth Air Force and Bomber Command now included a robust Fifteenth Air Force, with ten heavy bomber groups, of about 720 B-17s and B-24s, flying from Italy. With the sky over Germany clearing in February, Spaatz' US Strategic Air Forces began Operation Argument, the focused attack on Germany's ability to produce and maintain its fighter aircraft. Primary targets were airframe assembly plants and factories that produced essential components such as engines. Harris cooperated with the Americans by coordinating Bomber Command's nightly raids with the American daily objectives. Most of these targets were deep in Germany, near cities such as Schweinfurt, Leipzig, and Regensburg, which the heavy bombers had previously attacked at a high cost to the bomber crews. No one doubted that the Luftwaffe would fight viciously to defend these critical facilities. The attacks that began on February 20, referred to in US Air Force history as "Big Week," did not destroy, but only slowed, Germany's aircraft production capability. But what the American fighters that participated in this phase of Operation Pointblank did do was destroy one-third of the Luftwaffe's fighter strength and kill approximately one-fifth of its fighter pilots. From March until the end of the war, the Allied air forces maintained almost total air superiority over occupied Europe.[55]

One of the first targets the Allies attacked in the new year was Limoges, on the banks of the Vienne River in central France. Military historians remember the city as the post to which the French high command banished its disgraced commanders during the First World War, creating the verb *limoger*, to dismiss.[56] The ubiquitous Gnome et Rhône aircraft company built one of its many factories two miles northeast of the city, on the river's banks. Nearby was a small rail yard that also served the region's needs. This plant produced engines for German ME-323 transport aircraft. The ME-323 was one of the largest aircraft of the Second World War, capable of carrying light tanks and artillery, and it gave Germany a robust airlift capability. Hitler wasted most of these precious aircraft in his futile attempt to resupply Tunisia in 1943. In one dramatic event, American and British fighters destroyed sixteen of these aircraft and another thirty transport aircraft packed with reinforcements, a massive loss of cargo aircraft needed on the eastern front. This factory produced most, if not all, of the engines for this mammoth transporter, but the Allies hesitated to attack it because of the proximity of French civilians. Although not in Germany, it was well within the parameters of Operation Argument.[57]

Bomber Command struck this target on February 9, almost two weeks before the Eighth Air Force's big raids in Germany. The 617 Squadron, best known for its dramatic attack against Ruhr River dams in May 1943, conducted the attack. Since this elite unit had not found many opportunities for subsequent precision raids, it seemed like a good chance to hone the crew's skills. Marking the target seemed, in the mind of the squadron commander, Wing Commander Leonard Cheshire, the essence of the problem. He modified the standard technique by flying over the target twice at low level before dropping his flares, giving ample warning to anyone nearby to get away. He then accurately delivered his markers on target and the following eleven Lancasters dropped 5 12,000-pound bombs, 55 1,000-pound bombs, and 340 30-pound oil ignition bombs squarely on the target. By all accounts, this was a model of precision bombing, as the raid injured only a French civilian.[58] Bomber Command returned on June 24, and this time there was no attempt at precision as the primary target was the rail yard near the factory. Ninety-six Lancasters and four Mosquitoes dropped 146 1,000-pound bombs and 1,343 500-pound bombs.[59] This last raid virtually destroyed the plant and the rail center for the remainder of the war.

Clermont-Ferrand was another French industrial target attacked as part of Operation Pointblank. One of the oldest cities in France, it was the capital of the Gallic Averni tribe. Under its chieftain Vercingetorix, who was born near the city, the Averni rebelled against the Romans in 52 BC. Defeated by Julius Caesar at the climactic Battle of Alesia, the tribe surrendered and turned its leader over to the Roman general, who marched him in a parade through Rome. Vercingetorix's murder, apparently on Caesar's orders in 46 BC, ensured his status as France's first national hero. In 1903 Frédéric Auguste Bartholdi, who sculpted the Statue of Liberty, created a giant statue to the Averni chieftain that rests in the city's center at the Place de Jade. Nearby is a statue of Pope Urban II, who in 1095 at the Council of Clermont preached a war to take back the Holy Land from the Seljuk Turks. A year later, princes from across France marched off in the First Crusade. Until the early twentieth century, Clermont-Ferrand remained a market town and center of Auvergne culture.

This quiet existence partially changed at the beginning of the twentieth century with the creation of the Michelin Tire Company and the construction of several factories around the city. The company prospered during the First World War supporting the massive increase in wheeled motorized vehicles. By 1940 it had three major plants to the north and northeast of the city, all in residential areas. Under the German occupation, Michelin management had little hesitation in adapting production to supply tires to the Wehrmacht. By the spring of 1944, these factories were sending 294 tons per month of tires and other rubber-based products to the German military, especially badly needed truck tires for the Nazi war effort on the eastern front. The Cataroux facility was the main factory, about a mile northeast of the city's center. The original French management operated the plant with little German supervision.[60]

Bomber Command's first mission against the tire factory complex took place on the night of March 11–12, 1944. Although the official report claims to have successfully bombed the target, there is no indication from ground reports that it did much damage to either the facility or the local population.[61] Twenty-one Lancaster bombers, most from 617 Squadron, reappeared a week later on March 22. As in the case of Limoges, the squadron commander tried to warn the city's inhabitants, and as the sirens blared shortly after 2200 hours, his aircraft began dropping leaflets, telling the city's residents to get away. The local passive defense adequately supervised the evacuation of the citizens. Many took shelter in the medieval cellars scattered below the modern city. Shortly after that, the bombers began their attack on Cataroux. Again, striving for precision, the squadron flew low, at 10,000 feet, and put five of the ten 12,000-pound Tallboy bombs right into the middle of the factory. The raiders also dropped 50 1,000-pound bombs and 1,100 30-pound incendiary bombs.[62] The factory would produce no more tires until the end of the war. Not everyone escaped the effects of the raid, however, as twenty-one civilians perished and another thirty were wounded. The raid also destroyed many residential homes, and hundreds of workers and their families were now homeless.[63] It is interesting that the primary guide to Bomber Command's operations makes only a small mention of this important and hugely successful raid.[64] Along with its raid at Limoges and other cities, Commander Leonard Cheshire demonstrated the standard of precision that was possible in 1944, but only from a crack unit.

That spring American and British aircraft would complete their raids against France's factories. Those in Toulouse, Arras, Metz, Lille, and Vélizy-Villacoublay, among others, would experience to a lesser extent the massive bombing beginning to take place place in Germany. As economic historian Adam Tooze has pointed out, the heavy bombers attacked Albert Speer's crumbling industrial empire with a vengeance after Eisenhower relinquished control of the heavy bombers in September 1944 and allowed Harris and Spaatz to return to their primary task. From October until December, Bomber Command and the US Strategic Air Forces dropped 333,573 tons of bombs on the Nazi heartland, and they added 504,000 more tons by the end of the war. In addition to destroying most industrial centers, bombers killed German civilians almost without hesitation. The most famous of these raids was the Allied destruction of Dresden on February 13 and 14, which left the once beautiful city destroyed and killed between 18,000 and 25,000 of its citizens.[65]

In the last few decades, critics of the total war approach to bombing have questioned the resulting civilian deaths. Ronald Schaffer examined the transition from precision attacks on German factories to a more, in his words, "Douhetian war" in his 1985 book *Wings of Judgment.* Several years later, Conrad Crane continued this analysis of the change in air force bombing practices in his *Bombs, Cities, and Civilians* (1993) and prepared a revised edition in 2016. Alexander B. Downes, John Tirman, and many other authors have produced books and articles critical of the Allied, and especially the American, bombing war against Germany, Japan, and other states in the postwar era.[66] What is common to each of these texts is not only their concern about killing German and Japanese civilians but their almost total omission of the Allied bombing of French factories and the resulting civilian casualties. None of them mention, even in passing, the bombing of Boulogne-Billancourt, Le Creusot, and Le Mans. Perhaps they are too insignificant for works that examine the destruction of Dresden, Berlin, and Hiroshima. But for those who experienced them, such as the Montager and Païrel families from Guécélard and their descendants, they were important events. And although Operation Pointblank was in place before Eisenhower's arrival in London, as was Operation Crossbow discussed in the next chapter, they are part of the narrative of Allied bombing of France in support of the war against Germany.

CHAPTER SIX

CROSSBOW

On Sunday morning, June 18, 1944, Clementine Churchill, the prime minister's wife, visited London's Hyde Park to see her daughter Mary, who was a young officer serving with the local anti-aircraft battery. It had been a busy week on the home front. Almost two weeks prior, the invasion force had departed British ports and landed on the Norman coast. Early optimism over the landing's success had receded slightly as the Germans had launched a new aerial assault, this time with unmanned, pilotless bombs. Mrs. Churchill arrived while the guns were firing at one of these strange contraptions, which sounded like a truck struggling, with its engine sputtering, to climb a steep hill. This particular aircraft passed overhead unharmed and destroyed a nearby house. As the mother and daughter were talking, another bomb appeared in the sky, and the battery again fired frantically at this machine as it flew overhead. Not hit, its engine stopped as scheduled, dove to earth, and exploded beyond the view of the women. Mrs. Churchill did not realize until later that morning that the explosion took place at the Guards Chapel at Wellington Barracks near Buckingham Palace. A service was in progress, and the bomb killed or wounded more than two hundred active and retired members of the brigade. This incident was the most destructive V-1 attack of the war.[1]

The German flying bomb and rocket offensive came as no surprise to Allied leaders. Although the first attack did not take place until the middle of June 1944, British intelligence had known about German research in this area since 1939. Throughout 1942 and 1943, evidence continued to accumulate that this research had progressed beyond the simple experimentation stage. For several years, German scientists had been laboring at several locations, especially Peenemünde on the Baltic Sea, to perfect these systems to strike at the English enemy.[2] By early 1943 it became apparent to British intelligence specialists that these programs were potentially dangerous and that the government needed to take action. It was ironic that this news arrived just as the prospects for Allied success in the war against Nazi Germany were improving. America had been in the conflict for more than a year, and its forces were now fighting the German army in North Africa. Its buildup of troops in the British Isles continued, and the US Eighth Air Force had joined RAF Bomber Command in its campaign against German industry. The Soviet Red Army had thrown back the Nazi offensive at Stalingrad and appeared to have turned the tide in the east. But it was premature to celebrate as new weapons emerged that seemed to threaten the foundation of the Anglo-American war effort.[3] From the week after D-Day in June 1944 until the end of the war, British civilians lived under the constant bombardment of Hitler's so-called vengeance weapons (*Vergeltungswaffe*). Most students of the Second World War are aware that the V-1 pilotless bomb and the V-2 rocket wreaked havoc on London, eastern England, and Antwerp until March 1945, when Allied forces overran the last launcher units. When it was over, the V-weapons had killed approximately 9,000 British and 1,400 Belgian civilians and wounded more than twice that many.

This shooting war, however, began almost a year earlier, under Operation Crossbow. From June 1943 until the end of the war, Allied heavy bombers attacked Peenemünde and other construction and testing facilities in Germany. These attacks fit into the already established parameters of the Combined Bomber Offensive, so there was no actual diversion of effort.[4] What was a controversial deviation from the strategic forces' intended role, however, was their large-scale employment to attack these systems and their facilities in France. Crossbow was a massive effort that from August 1943 until August 1944 consumed more than 15 percent of the total tonnage dropped by the RAF Bomber Command and the US Eighth Air Force. This operation also drained the resources of the two tactical air forces, the US Ninth Air Force and RAF Second Tactical Air Forces, as medium bombers and fighter-bombers attacked suspected V-weapon facilities. So important was it to the

Combined Chiefs of Staff to find these launchers that from May 1943 until April 1945 it dispatched more than four thousand reconnaissance sorties in search of these weapons, more than 40 percent of the total.[5] Across northwestern France, most of these attacks, often with more than fifty bombers at a time, took place near the small villages that dot the departments of Pas-de-Calais, Somme, and Nord. Few remember these events. Unlike the bombing of Rouen, Le Havre, Caen, and Saint-Lô, whose citizens have commemorated the Allied destruction of their cities, there are few memorials to the French citizens of this region. The number of casualties caused by this and related bombing efforts is not insignificant. Although exact losses are always difficult to estimate, Allied air attacks collectively killed approximately 8,460 civilians in the departments of the Pas-de-Calais, the Nord, and the Somme. If just 10 percent of those were as a result of the Noball offensive, which is reasonable considering the dispersion of the various launchers, then it is a figure worth noting in the historical record.[6]

The descriptions of the V-weapon war fall into several incomplete historical narratives. One group of historians focuses on the technical aspects of these advanced weapons systems and the construction of the French launching sites. These works, while essential to understanding the vengeance weapon programs, generally fail to describe the effect of the bombing of these facilities on the French.[7] British historian Norman Longmate typifies the second group of authors, who focus on the German use of these systems against targets in the United Kingdom. His books chronicle the suffering of the British living under these attacks and the determined efforts of fighter pilots to shoot down the flying bombs before they could do any damage. His is the narrative that most Englishmen who lived through that period can identify with.[8] The third group of books is the official histories, which are the traditional sources for understanding the relationship of Allied bombing operations against these weapons, their launchers, and support facilities. In general, these historians see the commitment of bombers against these rocket sites as a diversion of precious air resources from their primary tasks, and they downplay their overall importance.[9] All these traditional accounts fail to grapple with the damage bombing raids caused among the French towns and villages. Some historians have begun correcting this imbalance and are going beyond English-centric narratives and descriptions of construction and technical data. Regional historians, those who have grown up among the concrete ruins and have heard from their elders the stories of the bombing, have done the best work in this field.[10] Finally, absent from almost all discussions are the forced laborers who constructed the massive concrete facilities. The thousands of people the Germans worked to death pouring concrete and digging into hillsides have been all but lost to history and assimilated into general discussions of the Holocaust. This group probably suffered from the Allied bombing in the same manner as other French civilians.[11]

Vengeance Systems

Ultimately, three major systems emerged as Hitler's vengeance weapons, his attempt to punish the English tormentors who refused to surrender to the logic of Nazi domination and continued to bomb German cities. Collectively, they represented a significant threat to the United Kingdom, the Allied war effort in general, and the invasion of northwest Europe in particular. Building the infrastructure for these systems was a massive effort that strained the German wartime economy. Constructing the dozen or so large launcher facilities, approximately ninety smaller launching sites, and a host of supply and storage installations drained workers and resources away from other construction priorities. Organisation Todt, the Nazi building contractor, had hoped to accomplish this work with volunteer and conscripted workers. There was never enough civilian labor, and ultimately it needed to resort to slave labor to keep the work on schedule.[12] The first weapon placed into use was the Luftwaffe-designed flying bomb, the FZG-76 (Flakzielgerat 76), better known as the V-1 (Vergeltunswaffe 1) or Vengeance Weapon 1, intended to be launched from permanent sites. It was essentially a pilotless aircraft with a one-ton warhead and a unique-sounding pulse-jet engine. A magnetic-gyro compass guided it toward its destination. It flew at approximately 300 miles per hour until it ran out of fuel, a distance of 120 to 140 miles. Once it stopped, its one-ton high-explosive warhead crashed into the ground.[13]

The second system was the Aggregat 4 or A-4, better known as the V-2 (Vergeltunswaffe 2) or Vengeance Weapon 2. Werner von Braun, who would later contribute to the American space program, developed it for the German army based on ideas developed by American scientist Robert Goddard.[14] It was a long-range ballistic missile originally designed to be fired from fixed facilities in France and Belgium. In the last years of the war, this was the Nazi regime's most expensive armament project and, in Hitler's view, the best way to defeat the Anglo-American invaders. Each of these forty-five-foot systems traveled at more than three thousand miles per hour and carried a one-ton, high-explosive warhead. In open terrain, it could create a crater thirty-forty yards in diameter and ten to fifteen yards deep. Obviously, it was capable of doing widespread damage if it hit a city.[15]

Crossbow Overview

As early as 1939, the British government was aware of several military rocket programs under development in Germany, and by the end of 1942 the intelligence services were receiving regular reports of rocket tests along the Baltic coast. Between January and June 1943, long-range reconnaissance flights had confirmed the existence of a testing area at Peenemünde, ninety miles east of Rostock, and had clearly identified the presence of rockets. At the same time, reports continued to accumulate about large-scale excavations and construction in the Pas-de-Calais and Manche departments of northern France. In April 1943 Churchill received his first detailed briefing on the possibility of long-range rockets aimed at London. The British Chiefs of Staff formed a special committee to monitor the developing threat and appointed a member of Parliament and Churchill's son-in-law, Duncan Sandys, to head it. The primary task of this group was to figure out what the Germans were up to, what was the actual threat, and how the Allies could defeat it. A few members of the government doubted the existence of a rocket program, arguing it was a German hoax, but the evidence continued to accumulate as Sandys continued his investigation. Soon he had silenced their protests.[16]

By early November 1943, the nature of the threat had become relatively clear as intelligence analysts realized that Organisation Todt was constructing three different types of installations in the Pas-de-Calais and the Cotentin Peninsula. Some of these were enormous, with deep excavations surrounded or covered by large amounts of concrete. These experts were still unable to determine their precise purpose but strongly suspected some innovative weapon. As a result, the Air Ministry, which had the best means of responding to enemy actions across the channel, took control of the investigation from Sandys' committee and began to focus on the military aspects of the problem. Information continued to flow into London from a variety of sources, and by the beginning of 1944 it was evident that there were at least two different long-range weapon threats. Analysts reported that they had identified Flak Regiment 155W, with a headquarters in Amiens, which commanded 108 flying-bomb catapults designed to launch these unique aircraft. The prospect of rockets raining down on the United Kingdom could affect the nation's will to fight and the Allies' ability to invade the continent. Experts presented Churchill with estimates indicating that these rockets could inflict severe casualties upon the capital's population, upwards of 30,000 killed and wounded.[17] The British Chiefs of Staff were also concerned about the potential damage these weapons could do to the preparations for the landings in France. In the middle of December, they asked Frederick Morgan, still serving as the chief Overlord planner before Eisenhower's arrival, about the potential effects of the rockets on the staging and execution of the invasion. They also inquired if he should consider mounting Operation Overlord from bases out of range of the vengeance weapons, such as harbors in Ireland, Northern Britain, or even the United States. The staff needed to know the chief planner's thoughts and when they would have to make this decision. Morgan argued that the invasion had to be launched from the south, and he needed to know "at once" if he needed to make any significant changes in his plan. The chiefs directed no changes to the current preparations.[18]

As the plan to deal with these weapons, known as Crossbow, emerged, it contained several distinct sets of action. Most immediately, the government developed a civil defense and security plan that integrated observers, detection devices, balloons, and interceptor aircraft. These improved on the measures developed earlier during the German air force's bombing of London, but the staff was not overly optimistic about their effectiveness. The second aspect of the plan was the destruction of test sites and factories in Germany. The third and final portion of the operation was to destroy launching sites on the continent. They called this process Noball, which is the code name used for all missions and target lists against vengeance weapons in France.

The British public first became aware of this threat with the first V-1 attack, code-named Diver, a week after the Normandy invasion, during the night of June 12 and 13, when four bombs hit targets around London. A few days later, the barrage began in earnest with Flak Regiment 155W sending as many as one hundred flying bombs toward London each day.[19] The most intense phase of this bombardment took place from June through the end of August 1944. During this period, the Germans controlled the French Pas-de-Calais region and used the plethora of modified launching sites scattered across the countryside. By June 18 the political panic within the British government was such that Eisenhower felt the need to pointedly tell Tedder that destroying Noball targets "are to take first priority over everything except the urgent requirements of the battle."[20] By July the British cabinet was debating using poison gas to contaminate launchers in France and as retaliation against the German homeland.[21] Allied success on the battlefield muted such discussions, and as the Allies broke out of the Normandy bridgehead in July and began heading north, they overran these sites, sending the launch crews scurrying toward the Netherlands and Germany.[22]

The first V-2 rocket attack, code-named Big Ben, hit London on September 8. There were few defensive measures the British could implement to stop the attacks. The rockets simply traveled too fast to be stopped by any system in the Allied inventory. The only effective defense was to continue to attack supply sites and factories in Germany. Rocket attacks continued against London and other cities in Europe until March 1945, when Allied ground forces overran most of Germany's industrial area.[23]

Executing Noball

British intelligence eventually identified four kinds of Noball targets in France: heavy sites, ski sites, modified sites, and supply and support facilities. It was the discovery of the nine large construction sites in the Pas-de-Calais region and the Cotentin Peninsula near Cherbourg that first captured the attention of British intelligence analysts. Throughout 1943 Organisation Todt's building units, supported by thousands of slave workers and conscripted civilian labor, began excavating and building what British documents refer to as the "heavy" Crossbow sites. After the war, the Allies discovered that the German air force had responsibility for four of these, which were intended to store, assemble, and launch a large number of V-1 flying bombs. Code-named "Wasserwerk," or water works, by the Germans to hide their purpose, these were primarily long tunnels with gaps in the ceiling to fire rockets toward London. In the Cotentin, they built one in Tamerville, northeast of Valognes, and the other at Couville, southwest of Cherbourg. The US Army's VII Corps overran both of these installations in late June 1944. The other two were Lottinghen, east of Boulogne, and Siracourt, west of Arras in the Pas-de-Calais.[24] Siracourt was typical of these kinds of launching sites. The dozen or so houses at the beginning of the war contained fewer than 140 citizens, mostly farmers and their families. The German army evacuated the French civilians as Organisation Todt arrived in the spring of 1943. On a little hill, just west of the village, contractors began construction in September. This facility was to be the first of four to process, store, and possibly fire the V-1. The main construction was 625 feet long and 132 feet wide and oriented at a right angle to London. The 1,200 workers, primarily Russians, Poles, Yugoslavs, and French forced labor, lived in a camp at Croix-en-Ternois a little more than a mile away. Under the supervision of Organisation Todt's guard force (Schützkommando), the workers ultimately built the structure and poured more than 50,000 cubic meters of concrete to make it invulnerable to Allied bombers.[25] Because of the bombing, however, it was impossible to finish its construction. As a result, the Germans never fired a flying bomb from it, and it fell to Canadian troops in September 1944.[26]

The German army controlled the V-2 rockets, and it designed large concrete installations, capable of launching seven to ten rockets per day, with sophisticated storage and assembly capability. For example, the launchers at Wizernes, next to Saint-Omer, lay beneath a massive concrete cupola twenty feet thick and were capable of launching their rockets from two platforms. Other sites at Watten (Éperlecques), near Calais, and Sottevast, near Cherbourg, were just as massive and required millions of tons of concrete.[27] Forty-four miles north of Siracourt and eleven miles northwest of the Luftwaffe airfields at Saint-Omer is the three-square-mile complex at Watten. On its southwest corner, Organisation Todt built a massive structure that came to be called the Blockhaus. It was an incredibly large structure that absorbed thousands of tons of concrete and the forced labor of thousands of unfortunate workers. Based on experience at the submarine pens along the coast, the German engineers expected it to withstand the bombardment of whatever the enemy could drop on top. The Allies never understood its exact purpose but knew they had to destroy anything that was consuming so much German effort. It was the first site detected by British reconnaissance. Duncan Sandys never believed it had an offensive capability and, even after his visit in October, considered it to be a plant for the production of hydrogen peroxide, which the Germans were using as a fuel.[28] Postwar records and analysis indicate, though, that it may have served as a general storage, assembly, and launching facility in, according to one researcher, "a bomb-proof environment." Most experts believe it was capable of launching rockets on its own.[29]

Twelve miles south of the Blockhaus near Saint-Omer is the village of Wizernes. In an old quarry, Organisation Todt constructed one of the largest installations of the war, the V-2 launcher site known as La Coupole, or the dome, for the most impressive aspect of the facility. Todt designed it to assemble, fuel, and fire rockets from within the protected site. Upwards of 1,300 forced laborers worked on this project twenty-four hours a day. Like the Blockhaus, it had two launcher ramps that could fire rockets simultaneously and was probably the most sophisticated of the vengeance weapon launching sites. By March 1944 British intelligence was convinced that it needed to be added to the list of Noball targets. The most sinister of V-2 launcher sites was the silo complex west of Cherbourg near La Hague. These, generally overlooked by Allied intelligence, resemble the later American nuclear missile silos of the Cold War. It never became operational, and the US VII Corps occupied this region in July 1944.[30] The problem for the Germans was that the construction crews could not hide the extensive work sites from the hundreds of Allied reconnaissance aircraft searching for signs of activity. The continuous bombing of the extensive excavations in France meant the Germans could not complete the launching facilities, which ended any possibility of the German air force using them. Ultimately, the Germans would fire no V-2 rockets from fixed sites but would employ mobile launchers that were essentially impossible for the Allies to detect in advance.[31]

Eleven miles from Cap Gris-Nez, across the channel from Dover and ninety-five miles from the center of London, is a facility unique among the heavy sites. The British knew the Nazis were developing a long-range gun, but they did not know any details. The German army had done this before, and Allied commanders had visions of a weapon similar to the artillery used to bombard Paris in the previous conflict or the large guns deployed along the French coast. Therefore, most analysts believed the construction at Mimoyecques, France, was a variation on a V-2 launch site, since it bore no resemblance to anything with which they were familiar. Also, since most of the workers were German, few details emerged as to its actual intent. In reality, the site housed something revolutionary, a large battery of long-range guns, called *Hochdruckpumpe* (high-pressure pump) guns, later referred to by the Allies as Vengeance Weapon-3. Each 330-foot smooth-bore gun was to be capable of firing a six-foot-long dart about a hundred miles. Its range was the product of added velocity created by solid rocket boosters arrayed along the edge of the tube. Each projectile could carry about forty pounds of high explosives. The plan was to construct banks of five guns each with the potential of firing six hundred rounds per hour toward London. British intelligence knew little about what was going on inside the facility. After the war, Duncan Sandys' investigation of the large sites discovered the true nature of the threat they had faced. Fortunately, Allied air attacks prevented Organisation Todt from ever finishing its work and German gunners were never able to fire these weapons.[32]

The second kind of targets identified by Allied analysts were the so-called ski sites, named from the configuration of several buildings that looked like snow skis on their side. By late 1943 British intelligence officers had identified between seventy and eighty of these, hidden in the hundreds of wooden patches that dot the northwestern French countryside, with their launchers pointed directly at their intended target. If left alone, each one of these small installations could hurl fifteen FZG-76 flying bombs across the channel each day. The cumulative effect of hundreds of these striking London daily would not help civilian morale. They also posed a direct threat to the harbors from which the Allies would launch and sustain the invasion. One of the first sites identified by intelligence analysts was in the Bois Carré (Square Woods) about three-quarters of a mile east of Yvrench and ten miles northeast of Abbeville on the Somme. A French Resistance agent was able to infiltrate the construction site in October 1943 and smuggle out some of earliest detailed descriptions of a ski site layout. The long catapult, generally visible from the sky and quickly identified by reconnaissance aircraft, became the signature target indicator. As a result, even with extensive camouflage, they were identified, targeted, and destroyed by Anglo-American aircraft. As a result, none of these installations ever became operational.[33]

Soon after the first air attacks, German leaders began considering an alternative method of launching the V-1. Security and concealment now became a priority, and these modified launcher sites were better camouflaged and of simpler construction. These new launchers no longer had many of the standard buildings, especially those that resembled skis, which had contributed to their rapid discovery by intelligence specialists. With minimal permanent construction, the only identifiable features were an easily hidden concrete foundation for the launch ramp and a small building to set the bomb's compass. Other buildings were designed to blend into the environment or to look like the local farmhouses. All this took less than a week to fabricate, and forced labor no longer did the construction work, as German soldiers prepared each site in secret. Supply crews delivered the flying bombs directly to the launcher from a hidden location, assembled and ready to launch. All the teams needed to do was set the compass and mount it on the catapult. Difficult to locate from the air, these launchers would remain operational until overrun by Allied ground troops in early September 1944.[34] After that, the Germans launched their V-1 rockets from sites in the Netherlands or from German bombers specially configured to fire these weapons.

One week after the last V-1 flew from French soil, the V-2 rocket made its first appearance when it slammed into a French village southeast of Paris, killing six civilians.[35] The German army had abandoned any hope of using large fixed sites for anything other than storage, and they now organized the delivery of their rockets as mobile systems, structured around less than a dozen vehicles and trailers. While the rocket was still hidden, crews prepared it for launch, a process that took between four and six hours. Within two hours of mission time, the firing unit deployed to a previously surveyed site and erected the rocket on a mobile pad. As soon as it was on the way, the soldiers disappeared into the woods, leaving little trace of the launch. Unless an Allied fighter happened to catch the Germans during the short preparation process, there was little the air forces could do to prevent launches. The Germans fired none of the mobile V-2s from French soil, but fired them instead from Belgium, the Netherlands, and Germany.[36] While not part of the discussion of bombing France, these rockets are an important reminder that the Germans continued to use mobile sites until the end of the war.

The final kinds of Noball targets were the supply sites that provided rockets for the individual firing units and the transportation network that supported them. By February 1944 the Allies had determined that seven facilities existed, one on the Cotentin Peninsula and the remainder arrayed just east of the belt of launchers. These, however, were relatively difficult to attack and were often located within underground bunkers or railroad tunnels, under fortresses, or deep within thick woods. They also were often protected by extensive anti-aircraft artillery. More vulnerable were the various rail yards that served as offload and staging points for these systems. Rail stations in Saint-Omer, Bethune, Lille, Lens, and Arras were the crucial nodes in this network. Attacking these transportation nodes also supported the goals of the Transportation Plan, the Allied attack of bridges along the Seine and Loire, and Operation Fortitude, the effort to deceive the Germans as to the actual location of the invasion.[37]

Effect on France

The standard British narrative omits or minimizes the effect of this campaign on the environment and people who lived near the concrete launcher facilities. War is not merely a sport played on a designated field between military teams, but is a multidimensional tornado of violence that scars the land and people through which it passes. The skies of this small corner of Europe—three departments, the Nord, the Pas-de-Calais, and the Somme, together smaller in size than the state of New Jersey—were never empty of combat aircraft as the Allies searched for these vengeance weapons. As pointed out earlier, these aircraft were not extremely accurate. American and British air commanders, especially those in charge of the heavy bombers, seldom made claims about bombing precision. In almost every case, no matter how small the target, a minimum of a dozen B-17s or Lancasters, the general flight configuration of operations over Germany, executed the attack. Unlike during raids against the Ruhr or industrial complexes across the Rhine, few Luftwaffe fighters defended these sites. Flying high above the objective, in the same formations they used in the heart of Germany, crews dropped their munitions with the intent to pulverize the installation by the cumulative effect of the explosive tonnage. As the authors of WPD-1 anticipated, most bombs missed the target. Some got close and affected the facility's supply routes, while others only tore up farmers' fields and killed their livestock. Many others physically destroyed the farms and villages near the objective, killing or wounding those who lived there. Therefore, in evaluating Operation Crossbow's effect on France, we can examine it from three different aspects: the intensity of the air attacks, the inaccuracy of the attacks on these targets, and the killing and wounding of those near the bombing attacks.

The intensity of the bombing effort against Noball targets is difficult to understand in the contemporary era of precision munitions. According to the *United States Strategic Bombing Survey*, published soon after the war, this operation consumed 13.7 percent of all sorties, almost 37,000, launched by the Allied strategic air forces from August 1943 until August 1944. From December 1943 through June 11, 1944, more than 15.5 percent of all bombs dropped by heavy bombers were aimed at fixed sites in France. The tactical air forces conducted more than 4,000 reconnaissance sorties, 40 percent of the total between May 1943 to April 1945, to find the launchers and their supporting facilities. The northern French departments of Nord, Pas-de-Calais, and the Somme was one of the most heavily bombed parts of France if measured by individual missions. During the first three months of 1944, more than 50 percent of all bombs dropped in the country fell on these three small departments.[38] The bombing's scale is reflected in three ways: the number of attacks in the region, the number on a given target, and the intensity of a bombing mission. For example, in the space of just one month, February 1944, the towns of the Pas-de-Calais, an area smaller than the state of Delaware, absorbed 124 separate attacks, ranging in size from one or two aircraft to several dozen. Some areas, such as the installations at Siracourt and Éperlecques, were each hit several times. By spring, the weather had improved and the Allies had more aircraft available. On just one day, April 20, the region endured thirty-six separate attacks.[39] The following month, during the week of May 7–13, this same small area absorbed more than seventy-one separate raids. The Allies increased the pace of these attacks as the June landings approached, and, shortly after that, the German air force began to launch flying bombs from the improvised sites toward London.[40]

A second way to understand scale is to consider the number of missions flown against the individual sites. The large installations in the Pas-de-Calais absorbed an incredible number of bombs. The facility at Mimoyecques, what British investigators later discovered as the home of the *Hochdrukpumpe* (V-3), is typical of the offensive against the most prominent targets. Beginning with the first raid on November 5, 1943, the entire complex remained in a state of increasing pulverization. Determining the exact number of sorties that attacked this or any target is difficult. Records usually include reports of the intended target and what pilots thought they were attacking. Some hit the wrong objective without even knowing it. Other crews, especially those in the tactical air forces, hit targets of opportunity. Observers on the ground reported Allied air attacks on days not mentioned in the documents now stored in London or American archives. In the case of Mimoyecques, Allied bombers attacked seventeen times between November 1943 and July 6, 1944. Most missions ranged in size from 10 to 40 aircraft. Several raids were enormous in relationship to the targets, with more than 280 heavy bombers pulverizing the area on November 5, 1943, another 300 on March 19, and 350 on March 26. Two raids on July 6 essentially ended all work on the site. The morning strike of more than 85 Lancasters was with conventional munitions, mainly 500-pound bombs. An afternoon attack of the RAF's crack 617 Squadron, equipped with 17 Lancaster bombers carrying 12,000-pound Tallboy bombs, finished the destruction of the facility.[41]

In the case of the Wasserwerk at Siracourt, for example, 74 US B-24 Liberator bombers arrived overhead on January 31, 1944. Each bombardier aimed to place his payload on top of a building the size of a modern football field. As the Air Force knew, the probability of actually hitting the target was quite small.[42] The 189 tons of ordnance had little effect on the construction, as most bombs fell in fields far from the actual target. The attack destroyed one building and damaged nine in the village. Bombs also hit two buildings in the local village of Croix-en-Ternois, where the workers who built the facility lived.[43] This attack was the first of thirty-three, conducted by more than 1,200 bombers, which would take place over the next year. The Eighth Air Force struck six times in February, twice in March, four times in April, and six times in May. The Ninth Air Force attacked Siracourt on March 18 and April 22. These were, from the airmen's perspective, relatively easy missions. During a May 21 mission, for example, each aircraft carried eight 1,000-pound bombs. The 99 B-17 bombers had P-47 Thunderbolt fighters as escorts all the way and encountered no enemy fighters or anti-aircraft artillery. Dropping their bombs at 21,000 feet at ground obscured by clouds, crews had no idea of what kind of damage their explosives caused. As one crewman remarked in his journal, "This raid was short and sweet. . . . Hope I have 27 more just like this one."[44] The Allies continued to attack this target, just in case, until the end of June.[45]

Another good example is the Blockhaus at Watten in the Éperlecques forest. The Eighth Air Force sent more than 180 B-17 bombers to take out the site on August 27, 1943. The first aircraft hit as scheduled at 1845 hours. Allied planners, based on reports from the French Resistance, planned to arrive at 1830, when the work site was unoccupied because of a shift change, to avoid killing the workers. But because they were behind schedule, Todt's contractors had kept the day shift on the job to catch up. The 374 2,000-pound bombs found the slave laborers at their stations. Hundreds died as American bombers continued to drop their cargo for almost an hour. When it was over, five bombs had hit the target, with the remainder landing in the forest and nearby farmland. Contrary to initial positive reports, the raid inflicted little actual damage, and the Germans continued the construction.[46] Over the next year, British and American bombers would attack this massive structure at least twenty-four more times, and each time the workers repaired the damage and continued working.

The last attack in this series was an Operation Aphrodite mission on August 4. Aphrodite was an American attempt to use worn-out bombers, loaded with explosives and equipped with newly developed radio guidance systems, to destroy important targets. Essentially each bomber was an early version of a cruise missile. Unfortunately these bombers required live pilots to fly the aircraft from the airfield to a point over the English Channel. Then, the two-person crew was supposed to parachute out of the plane, while a crew in another flew the unmanned bomber by radio control. The goal was to crash the explosive-laden aircraft into the target. Unfortunately the technology was still in development, and these missions were almost always unsuccessful. Such was the case of these two old B-17s that never made it to the objective. The US Navy followed the Air Forces' lead in these experiments, with as little success. Joseph P. Kennedy Jr., brother of future president John F. Kennedy, died when the converted B-24 he was flying to the launch position exploded in mid-air.[47]

The massive La Coupole near Wizernes is another example of a heavily bombed target. The Allies were late as the massive dome was already in place and and mostly invulnerable to attack by March 1943. The first strike, consisting of 34 B-24 bombers, hit on March 11. The 248 1,000-pound bombs did little but damage the local countryside. Nine more raids, comprising 348 heavy bombers and more than 2,000 large bombs, did little damage, and work continued inside, although affected slightly by the damage outside. Bomber Command began attacking La Coupole in June and July with raids of between 80 and 100 aircraft and dropping hundreds of tons of bombs, including several dozen Tallboy 12,000-pounders.[48] The July 17 attack caused the dome to shift and block the entrances, but it did little to affect the site itself. Of course, the countryside was a bombed-out mess, and it was almost impossible for workers and material to get to the construction site. The Germans were long gone when Canadian and Polish troops arrived in the Saint-Omer region at the end of August.[49]

A final way to consider the scale of this operation is the intensity of the attacks on individual sites by specific missions. In addition to the intense bombing of the large sites described above, the V-1 sites absorbed an incredible amount of ordnance. Typical was the installation near Wisques, west of Saint-Omer in the Pas-de-Calais. With fewer than three hundred people, it was a typical farm community. Its most prominent feature was a beautiful nineteenth-century Benedictine abbey on the western part of town on the edge of the local forest. Hidden in that forest was a standard "ski" launch site. Thirty-six A-20 Havoc light bombers arrived overhead on the evening of March 19, 1944, and for almost three hours these aircraft took turns dropping their payloads on the small patch of woods, obscured by fire from antiaircraft guns and smoke from the burning forest. When they had departed, they were not quite sure if they had damaged the target. The Eighth Air Force sent six B-17 heavy bombers on April 20, and the Ninth Air Force returned with B-26 medium bombers two days later on April 22.[50] Twenty-one B-17 heavy bombers returned to attack the installation five days later, and thirty-three P-47 Thunderbolt fighters worked the woods over on June 2, the last recorded attack on the Wisques launcher.[51] Cumulatively, it was a massive amount of combat power directed against a relatively small and insignificant target.

The intensity of these attacks was made worse by the bombers' notorious inaccuracy. By early 1944, after years of practice, the Eighth Air Force had improved its bombing accuracy to the degree that 36 percent of its bombs fell within one thousand feet of an actual aiming point. Against targets in Germany, this was acceptable, but from the French perspective, most raids conducted by heavy bombers still resembled area attacks. Add considerations such as inclement weather, German ground and air defenses, and simple human error, it is not surprising that bomb runs were often wide of the intended target.[52] Photographs of craters in target areas testify to the broad impact spread of a typical attack. Beyond the damage done to the weapons sites, these runs often hit nearby French villages and individual structures. In some cases, such as the bombing of rail yards, the damage was apparent to all. In most cases, however, the Noball offensive was characterized by the destruction of small farms and villages far from most observers. This "collateral damage," to use a modern term, is seldom mentioned in reports or dispatches by attacking units. To those who owned these structures, their destruction was an emotional event. The fundamental community structure of the region, dating back to the premedieval era, was a small central cluster of farmhouses and barns with a forest nearby that provided a source of game and lumber. Most of the surrounding open area was devoted to growing grains and potatoes and raising cattle. The nature of these clusters was that if they were near a target, the odds were high that the carpet bombing would destroy them. Reports provided to the local prefect confirm the damage, as do photographs of the bombed areas taken by poststrike reconnaissance aircraft. Immediately after the war, French farmers and property owners filed reports with the local authorities documenting their losses and requesting assistance in rebuilding, reports that can be seen in departmental archives today.

Often the Allies attacked these small villages only once or twice. For example, the town of Blendecques, the location of a V-1 ski site, had about 3,500 inhabitants at the beginning of the war. The town was southeast of the highly militarized region of Saint-Omer, and it is hard to know how many of the original residents were still there. On April 22 the Ninth Air Force raided it for the first and apparently the only time. At around 1900 hours fifty B-26 bombers attacked the site. When the attackers were gone, at least fifty bombs had hit the town, killing five civilians and wounding another three badly. The attack destroyed eleven homes and damaged forty-three others.[53] Month after month, correspondence from the local prefectures across the region identified the damage or destruction to individual homes and structures. While not as dramatic as the bombing of Caen or Rouen, this damage had a substantial effect on the local population, which had now lost their homes and source of livelihood.

Those villages in the shadow of the large sites provide more dramatic examples of the effects of Allied bombing. One good example is the small village of Helfaut, on the south side of the woods near the La Coupole at Wizernes. At the beginning of the war, it had fewer than fifty structures of all kinds: homes, barns, and small shops. One attack on March 19 destroyed ten of those and severely damaged twenty more. By the end of the war, the bombing attacks had mostly destroyed this town and driven its inhabitants away.[54] Apparently aiming for La Coupole on June 20, an Eighth Air Force bombing mission could not find its target, and fifteen B-24 bombers dropped their bombs over the town of Guarbecque, sixteen miles to the southeast. The bombs hit the center perfectly. When the fires were out, the citizens

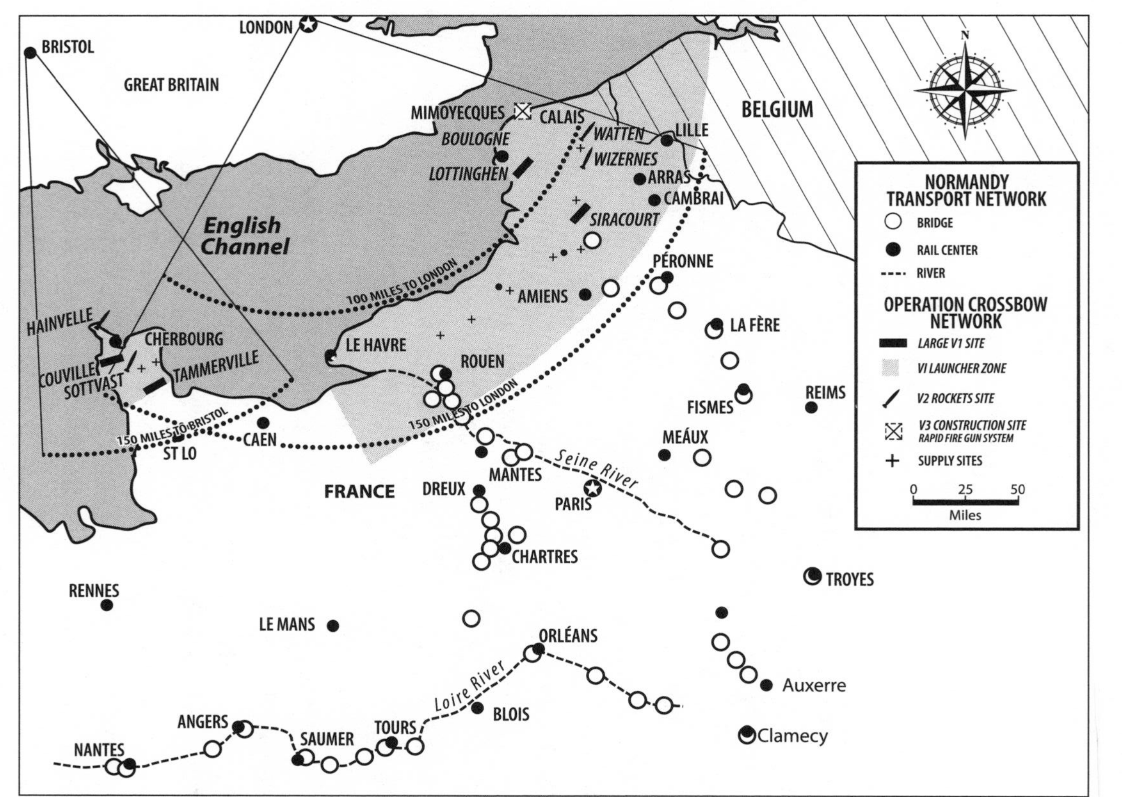

Map 2. Interdiction and Crossbow

discovered that the attack had damaged their church, destroyed the town hall, and burned more than ninety buildings to the ground. Two weeks after the Normandy landings, American aircraft had almost wiped this French village of slightly less than a thousand inhabitants off the map.

Most dramatic was the destruction that took place near the rail yards and transportation centers that supported the construction of installations and the supply of rockets for the firing batteries. These missions were not part of the Transportation Plan, discussed later, but an integral part of defeating the vengeance weapon threat. Béthune, located in the center of a triangle formed by the cities of Lille, Saint-Omer, and Arras, provides one example of the level of destruction wrought by these bombings. Located along the battle lines of the First World War, this was a rebuilt version of the ancient city. It was a relatively large town, with a densely populated city center of approximately 20,000 inhabitants. In addition to its rail yard, it was a center of regional mining, especially coal. Bombers struck the town and its suburbs on April 20, 21, 22, 23, and 27. In the wake of the bombing, hundreds of buildings were gone, including the rail yard and the housing for miners and railway workers.[55] These are just several of the examples of communities in northwestern France damaged or destroyed as part of the Allied Noball operation.

Each of the material examples described above has a human cost. Each month the department's *préfet*, the state's representative, compiled a list describing the effects of the bombing. Organized by date and community, the report identifies every town bombed or machine-gunned. Most often, the numbers are not large, especially in comparison to the carnage on the eastern front. Six wounded and seven killed at Sallaumines outside of Lens on April 20, 1944. Another five wounded and three dead on May 6, and another seventeen killed and fifteen wounded on May 12, and so on, often with other notations such as that the bombs landed in the field.[56] These casualties continued to accumulate well into July 1944, more than a month after the invasion at Normandy.[57] Sometimes the numbers in the right column attract attention, such as the attack on April 27 that left forty-eight dead and thirty-six wounded at Béthune, or on June 20 at Guarbecque that left eighteen wounded and twenty civilians dead.[58]

The more detailed reports, written by the local officials, are often quite gripping. The bombing on May 12 of the village of Saint-Venant, on the road between Hazebrouck and Béthune, is one such example. The attack killed only one victim, forty-eight-year-old André Pierru, who was working in the field. He was a veteran of the Great War and the 1940 Campaign and a knight of the Legion of Honor. He left behind a wife and a fifteen-year-old son. Reading the report it is evident that to the local police official, Monsieur Pierru was not a simple number, but a friend.[59] Another perspective is the one presented by police officials in the larger town and cities. Here we find reports that describe the nature of the attack and list the dead by name, often including the deceased's address. For example, the police commissioner of Arras reported by name those killed and wounded during the bombing of April 30. The raid wounded twenty-three citizens and six "sujets russes." Then he continues with a list of the eight dead:

- Vasseur, Yvette
- Greuin, Gaston
- Fleurquin, Oscar (48 years old)
- Seneca, Miss
- Lefebvre, Marcel (15 months old)
- Rifflart, Kléber
- Haudiquet, Lucien
- Van Rokeghem, François (61 years old)[60]

As the weeks went by, officials refined these reports and passed the new information to the national government. Often they reported the subsequent deaths of the wounded in the hospitals and more detailed information as to the scale of the damage to the community. From the countryside, these documents are brief, often only a simple letter. Reports from the larger cities, such as Lille, Calais, and Boulogne-Sur-Mer, provide a similar but longer list of casualties. In the end, it is hard to assess the actual human cost of Noball attacks in isolation from the other operations going on. A local historian, Hugues Chevalier, believes that approximately 5,000 civilians perished in just the Pas-de-Calais under Allied bombs from 1943 to 1945. Of the approximately 60,000 to 70,000 civilians killed in France by aerial bombing, perhaps 10 percent died as a result of the Allied search for German vengeance weapons. Probably two or three times that number were wounded. For many reasons, we will probably never have an accurate accounting of the human toll in this region.[61]

Absent from both the Allied and French narratives of the Noball operation is any commentary on the forced laborers who constructed these sites for Organisation Todt. As Jim Aulich, one of the few scholars to address this aspect of the war, notes, these camps are at the "margins of memory." Aulich's father was a forced laborer and helped construct the Blockhaus near Éperlecques, and he passed on some of the details from this camp, of which there were many along the French coast. Officially named Organisation Todt Watten Zwangsarbeiter 62 (Forced Labor Camp 62), it had more than 35,000 workers living there at some point in 1943 and 1944. During peak construction, between 3,000 and 4,000 slaves worked on each twelve-hour shift, seven days a week, with few breaks. The German masters, and perhaps their French contractors, worked most of these unfortunates to death.[62] At Wizernes, 1,300 workmen labored on the site day and night. Badly nourished and abused, they were forced to continue working, even under air attack, until the Germans abandoned the site in July 1944. The last 500 Soviet workers working in the Coupole were sent by train to Germany and "never seen again."[63] As the bombers approached, German guards ran for cover, often leaving the workers to their own devices. Many, such as Aulich's father, escaped.[64] The raids were costly nevertheless. As one Dutch prisoner of war, Luc Vandevelde, working at the camp near Watten, noted, after three attacks carried out by more than 320 bombers in 1943, they had more than 1,500 dead.[65] Without question, the nature of this forced labor, and the fate of those workers caught under Allied bombs, is still one of the least discussed and explained aspects of the Second World War in the west.

In the end, the Noball operation was relatively successful. Because of the bombing, neither the Heer nor the Luftwaffe was able to launch a single rocket from the large facilities or ski sites from Normandy or the Cotentin Peninsula toward the overcrowded ports of Plymouth, Bristol, Portsmouth, or Southampton. The three-month delay in V-1 flying bomb launches and as much as a six-month delay in deploying the V-2 rocket were crucial to the ultimate Allied success. But anyone interested in the Second World War in Europe, or those fascinated with the technical aspects of the conflict's weapons, knows most of this story. The British experience with these attacks, because they were so concentrated in London and southeastern England, is also amply documented and reported in histories of the conflict.

The continental perspective is less well known, even among the French who, as we shall see, are more prone to remember the effects of raids on the larger ports and rail yards. The rural population near each site was small, and the civilian casualty rates relatively insignificant. Even the French who lived near these war ruins understood these were legitimate targets and were taking a risk by remaining. Fortunately, local French historians are doing a marvelous job of researching and explaining the nature, scope, and effects of the attacks on these sites in the three northern departments.[66] Their efforts illuminate the scope and details of a portion of the air war Spaatz and Harris considered a significant diversion from their larger goal of taking the fight to the Germans. Churchill, however, after hearing the British people's complaints, had a pressing political need to defeat the V-weapon menace, and it was one of his highest priorities, as reflected by Eisenhower's memorandum to Tedder on June 18. The bombing of these installations in France was thus an important aspect of the Allied air war against France.

CHAPTER SEVEN

FORTITUDE

In April of 1944 Eisenhower wrote to Marshall "Dear General Marshall, This morning I sent you a telegram about the Patton case. Frankly, I am exceedingly weary of his habit of getting everybody into hot water through the immature character of his public actions and statements. . . . But the fact remains that he simply does not keep his mouth shut."[1]

Eisenhower was voicing his frustration over his most tactically gifted commander's recurring ability to become a public embarrassment. His seemingly harmless comments at a women's club in Knutsford near Manchester, concluding with assurances of Anglo-American friendship and an "evident destiny . . . to rule the world," set off a political firestorm back in the United States, where Congress was becoming fed up with certain generals, notably Douglas MacArthur, who seemed to be flirting with politics. Although he considered replacing Patton as the designated commander of Third Army, the supreme commander instead called him into his office and severely chastised him. Apparently, sentries down the hall heard Ike yelling. He later wrote him a letter of reprimand in case he had to take further action.[2]

Of course, besides giving speeches, Patton also had a second task, which he was accomplishing magnificently. Allied planners knew that German leaders expected them to use their most aggressive combat leader in the invasion. Patton's command of the mythical "First US Army Group" would help keep the Germans guessing about where and when the actual landing would take place. Sowing confusion and doubt were the essential objectives of Operation Fortitude South.[3] Although he had few responsibilities other than to attract attention, he became the image of the grand deception plan. Patton worshipers, and there are still plenty among military history buffs, will argue that it was a waste of a good commander. Others will make fun of the German officers, and Adolf Hitler, for not releasing German forces north of the Somme River for redeployment against the Allies landing on the Norman beaches. Few realize the scale of the deception effort that spring or that the French paid a physical and psychological price for this deception plan. Operation Fortitude was not simply a comical charade, but an extremely bloody and concentrated bombing effort against German fortifications, command posts, and other installations in the departments of the Pas-de-Calais and Du Nord. This chapter examines this intense bombardment of France on the eve of Neptune.

West of the Crossbow targets, along the coast of the Pas-de-Calais, between Dunkerque and the Baie de Somme, is an amazingly beautiful stretch of beach. At low tide, the white shore is wide, hard, and flat. At high tide, the water runs up to sand dunes that act as the first line of defense against the rough seas that can erupt when winter and spring storms stir up the water at the point where La Manche meets the North Sea. To the south of Calais are two impressive hills, Blanc-Nez (White Nose) and Gris-Nez (Grey Nose), that dominate the region on all sides. From these locations, on sunny days, the cliffs of Dover are clearly visible to all. South of Gris-Nez is the ancient port of Boulogne-sur-Mer. For an Allied invasion force seeking to breach the Atlantic Wall, the Dover-Calais avenue of approach had it all: Wide beaches, good ports, close to friendly air bases, a narrow channel, and fast shipping turnaround to staging areas in the United Kingdom. To German staff officers, aware of all these facts, this was the most dangerous approach into the heart of the Reich. Seizure of the natural ports of Calais and Boulogne would give the Allies the logistics bases they needed to sustain a drive into the Reich. As a result, German planners had no choice but to assume the primary assault would come this way, and they gave it the priority in developing defenses in depth.

As described in chapter 2, the Germans declared Zone Rouge here along the Opal Coast, and Organisation Todt constructed the primary defenses of the Atlantic Wall. Except in the cities, the Germans had removed many of the French inhabitants from this forbidden zone that stretched from the

Belgian border to the Somme. Major defensive areas, called by the Germans fortresses, or *Festungen*, dominated the approaches to the coastline at Dunkerque, Calais, Cape Gris-Nez, and Boulogne-sur-Mer. Long-range artillery positions could range English positions on the far side of the channel and cause havoc with any naval force attempting to cross it. Dominating the northern water approaches to Boulogne, Batterie Lindeman, near Sangatte, consisted of three large casements, each housing a Krupp 406-mm SKC/34 gun, designed for deployment on battleships.[4] Performing the same function farther south, near Wimille, was the Marineküstenbatterie (Naval Coastal Battery) Friedrich Augustus, also called La Trésorerie. Each of this facility's three large concrete casements housed a 305-mm SK L/50 gun, also intended for mounting on First World War–era battleships.[5] Other artillery complexes defended the coastline, with one of the most famous at Haringzelle near Cape Gris-Nez. The four large casements of Batterie Grosser Kurfürst, popularly called Batterie Todt after the German construction service, each mounted a massive 380-mm gun prominent enough to be featured in the period's Nazi propaganda. In addition to artillery, all the installations included fortified complexes with infantry trenches, machine-gun positions, mortar firing positions, and anti-aircraft guns.[6]

Between these fortifications, overlooking every possible landing site, was an array of bunkers, machine-gun positions, mortar firing points, field artillery batteries, anti-aircraft guns, and infantry fighting positions. Within the defending Fifteenth German army sector, engineers emplaced more than 1.2 million land mines and an array of other obstacles. Behind the defensive belt, the Wehrmacht deployed a broad range of radars, radio intercept stations, and electronic jammers, inaugurating an era of electronic warfare practices that would become common during the Cold War. Four infantry divisions, each with 8,000 to 12,000 soldiers, defended the coastline of this narrow sector. Entrenched ten to twenty kilometers behind the beaches, another four units of varying qualities added depth to the defensive zone. All these units were dug in and prepared to defeat the forthcoming assault. In line with German defensive doctrine, two panzer divisions, the 2nd and 116th Panzer, were within a day's march of the infantry defenders and capable of seriously interfering with the landing. Other mobile units could arrive within seventy-two hours. Finally, being close to Germany and its robust rail system, other counterattacking units could be expected to reach the battle zone on a regular basis. What Operation Fortitude intended to do was help the defenders believe what they wanted to believe and keep the defending units and their reserves focused on the Pas-de-Calais.

The Plan

Lieutenant-General Frederick E. Morgan, who prepared the preliminary Overlord plan in his role as COSSAC, originated the deception plan in late 1943. He knew it would be impossible to hide the massive buildup of ground troops in Great Britain from Axis intelligence agents and that the best course of action was to develop a cover story as to their organization and intended employment. His planners, especially Roger Hesketh, who had overall responsibility for the program, developed a cover plan, with two potential objectives: Norway (Fortitude North) and the Opal Coast (Fortitude South). Churchill was always a proponent of external operations, so it was not difficult to imagine him demanding such an invasion of Norway to start chipping away at the German empire. This scenario suggested to the Germans that the Allies would conduct landings on the Norwegian coast, with two divisions linking up with the Soviets in the north and the second landing of a reinforced division at Stavanger on the southwest coast with the intent of capturing an airfield for future operations against Oslo. While interesting, its primary limitation was that it did not directly threaten the German heartland and would have little effect on German actions.[7] The primary deception operation, and the one this chapter is concerned with, was Fortitude South, with the area across from Dover as its target. The imaginary organization, which integrated real soldiers in the United Kingdom, consisted of two assault corps and two reinforcing corps organized into two armies, under the command of Patton's First United States Army Group. Morgan had set the stage for one of the most sophisticated fabrications in western military history.[8]

The intent of the operation as published in the Plan Fortitude at the end of February was:

> 5. Induce the enemy to make faulty dispositions in North-West Europe before and after the NEPTUNE assault, thus:
>
> Reducing the rate and weight of reinforcement in the target area (Normandy).
>
> Inducing him to expend his available effort on fortifications in areas other than the target area.

> Lowering his vigilance in France during the build-up and mounting of NEPTUNE forces in the United Kingdom.
>
> Retaining forces in areas as far removed as possible from the target area before and after the NEPTUNE assault.[9]

While this is not the venue for discussing the details of Operation Fortitude, it is appropriate to remind the reader of its various elements. The plan for Fortitude South, from here on referred to simply as Fortitude, gave subordinate units the general guidelines they needed to execute the deception. The code name for the various components required for the command to implement the farce was Quicksilver, of which there were several. Quicksilver I gave commanders a detailed overview of the overall cover plan and Eisenhower's intent. Operations under code name Quicksilver II established an imaginary order of battle, described earlier, and put in motion a series of communications exercises between the appropriate headquarters. The intent was for German radio operators to intercept these communications and to focus their attention on the activities of this command post in anticipation of the invasion. Patton's role was a most important element of this operation. Quicksilver III directed the construction of dummy landing craft and other equipment that German reconnaissance elements could match to the radio traffic they were monitoring. Also, it required the marking of areas and roads in eastern and southeastern England to reflect the messages sent by the false radio traffic.

The last element of the plan was Quicksilver V, which directed the increase of activity in the Dover area, including additional communications stations, construction work, and additional night lighting to give the impression of vehicle movement and beach lighting. As summer approached, anyone passing through the region could see dummy tanks, trucks, and landing craft in selected areas of the imaginary staging area. The program also included an extensive counterspy operation with double agents, with code names such as Garbo and Brutus, feeding false information to the German intelligence service.[10] Most of this story is familiar, as most standard Overlord accounts discuss some aspect of the deception. None of them, however, discuss the details of Quicksilver IV: the air plan.[11]

In many ways, the essential element of Quicksilver IV was for the Anglo-American air forces to continue their bombing program as originally planned. They were already attacking ports and airfields across France. Heavy bombers continued to attack the French factories that supported the German war effort. The Allied air forces were already executing the Transportation Plan, which we will discuss in the next chapter, with a vengeance along the Seine and against railroad yards north of the river. Finally, Operation Crossbow continued the hunt for V-1 and V-2 launching sites in the departments of the Pas-de-Calais and the Nord, with hundreds of reconnaissance flights each month followed by concentrated bombing on construction locations.

With most of these targets in northwest France, those Germans keeping score would already notice that most reconnaissance and bombing missions were in this region. German intelligence units would have noticed a change in tone when the Allies began to attack German military targets in the landing area, as though they were softening up the enemy defenses. It was an area rich in military installations; fortifications, unit headquarters, supply dumps, assembly areas, artillery batteries, and air defense sites were exactly the kinds of facilities any invading force would need to neutralize, destroy, or at least disrupt before an invasion. The message of Quicksilver IV to the air force commanders was simple: for every pound of bombs you drop in the actual landing area, make sure you drop two in the north.[12] In practical terms, that meant that French (and Belgian) civilians would perish under American, Canadian, and British bombers for an obtuse purpose. As the Eighth Air Force after-action report admits, "The idea of deception was paramount and outweighed the recognized factor that actual damage to coastal defenses would be for the most part negligible." Everyone understood that "these targets were uneconomical from a damage standpoint." Furthermore they were difficult to find and "their size and the identification problems which they presented made the probabilities of direct hits slight and even if hit the concrete emplacements were of such thickness that little harm was likely to result."[13] What was certain was that civilians, and their homes near the targets, could expect to suffer during this onslaught. Like others in targeted areas across France, they were participants in Operation Overlord even though they were not near the landing zone.

Some Examples

A good illustration of these missions is Boulogne-sur-Mer, one of the most defended locations on the Atlantic Wall. The German High Command invested an incredible amount of men and material in retaining the city.

As one of France's key ports, it also represented the convergence of multiple lines of effort—infrastructure, Crossbow, and Fortitude—on one target. Founded by the Romans to support their invasion of England, Boulogne has always been a critical port in England's struggle with hostile powers on the continent.[14] It changed hands between the English and French several times during the Hundred Years War and was Napoleon Bonaparte's base of operations for his intended cross-channel invasion in 1805. Although the Germans temporarily captured it in 1914, the British retook it after the Battle of the Marne, and it remained one of the main British support bases during the conflict. Captured again by the Germans in 1940, its importance as a port was increased as they prepared for Operation Sea Lion. The British bombed the port for the first time on June 14, 1940, and continued doing so for the remainder of the war.[15] By the spring of 1944 the city was no longer a base for an invasion but one of the critical nodes in Hitler's Atlantic Wall. The 104th Infantry Regiment, commanded by Generalmajor Wilhelm Künz, was the fortress' primary combat force. Augmenting these defenses was a conglomeration of military units from all elements of the Wehrmacht. These defenders manned large concrete artillery positions, anti-aircraft gun positions, beach defensives, and some small naval attack ships. In addition to the manned defenses, at least thirty-six minefields of all shapes and varieties surrounded the city.[16] The fortifications and artillery installations continued both north and south of the city, along with units positioned in depth to counterattack or provide support as needed.[17] Approximately 20 percent of the original 52,000 civilians remained within the boundaries of Festung Boulogne, its official name. If the Americans and Commonwealth forces were going to land in this region, these fortifications needed to be neutralized and, ultimately, the harbor captured.

Because of its location and importance, the Allies bombed the city, its port, its airfield, or its suburbs often throughout the war. The *préfet*, the state's representative in each region, monthly summaries, and daily reports indicate the toll on the citizens who remained. Some bombardments were especially destructive. The first major one took place on August 6, 1941, when Bomber Command attacked the city with a mixed force of 38 medium bombers: Handley Page Hampdens, Vickers Wellingtons, and Armstrong Whitleys. The official war diary indicates that the crews could not identify the target and only fourteen were able to bomb. The French sources are adamant that this inaccurate attack killed 120 civilians and wounded 126.[18] Most of the air attacks against the city remained light until May 1944, when another major attack took place in the early morning hours of May 12. Bomber Command, now with a fleet of first-class heavy bombers, dispatched 143 aircraft, Lancasters, Halifaxes, and Mosquitoes, to destroy the central city's rail yard. The official report, reflected by Middlebrook and Everitt, indicates that the bombing was accurate and that they killed only 33 civilians,[19] but that is not accurate since the community of Outreau, just across the small Liane River from the rail yard, lost another 67 dead and 45 wounded. There is also no indication that the attack also wounded 63 other French citizens in Boulogne. So rather than 33 civilians as reported and now published in a variety of texts, the actual casualty count for that evening in the Fortress Boulogne was 212 French civilians killed or wounded. The report also fails to note that this one attack also destroyed 900 buildings and damaged another 800. It was good that much of the city's population had already departed the center, or the casualties would have been much higher.[20] Bomber Command returned on May 19, 20, 22, and 24, and the casualties continued.

Bombardment of Boulogne, June 1944. Notice cloud cover. No one on the aircraft could see the target. *NARA RG 342 US Air Force Photo Collection*

The bombing of May 25 was especially destructive. Around 0130 hours, 50 heavy British bombers appeared over the city. The alleged targets were coastal gun positions, and some bombs hit those targets in the Le Portel area on the coast southwest of Boulogne. There was not much left of this town of slightly more than eight thousand inhabitants. As part of an earlier deception effort, Operation Starkey on September 8, 1943, 72 US B-17 bombers attacked Germany artillery positions around 1900 hours. Bomber Command followed the initial raid with 257 aircraft, primarily Wellingtons and Stirlings, later that night. Neither of the raids were accurate and they did little damage to the German facilities, but they almost entirely destroyed the town, killing 554 civilians and wounding more than a thousand.[21]

In this case, the bombers again missed the German installations and struck the suburb of Saint-Martin to the west, the industrial city of Outreau, and the ancient château above the port. As many as 200 people, we will never know for sure, crowded into the castle's old arsenal. Converted into an air-raid shelter with a ceiling thirty-two inches thick, it seemed impenetrable. It was not. At least two bombs slashed through the weak roof and exploded. When the rescuers arrived, it was a scene of horror. Almost immediately, they pulled 39 bodies and 62 wounded from the still-burning structure. As the fires subsided, they pulled 45 whole bodies from the cellar, but they were only able to identify 37. In an era before scientific tools, the rescuers were unable to identify the many other body parts they discovered. With that raid, city life ended, and there was no water left in the city. Those who remained tried to depart.[22]

So by the time the Eighth Air Force turned its attention to Boulogne on June 2, it was already a wrecked city.[23] Thirty groups, each with eighteen B-17 Flying Fortresses, headed for artillery in reinforced bunkers and batteries in open fields on the coast and above the city. There was no possibility of being accurate since the aircraft were flying above thick clouds, at 20,000 to 25,000 feet. In fact, it did not matter if any bombs actually hit a German artillery piece.[24] Where did the 871 tons of ordnance go? Certainly it damaged or destroyed some German installations. In other cases, the local reports indicate that the bombs landed "*dans les champs*," or in the fields. The French *préfectoral* reports are accurate enough to tell us the damage done to towns and villages within five miles of the city's center. The bombs destroyed the rail center and water tower at Outreau, killing forty civilians.[25] Another 150 bombs fell on the small town of Wimille, just north of the city, killing three civilians and wounding ten more. Among the reports from the forty-nine local villages that day that experienced this attack was the notation on the report of Équihen-Plage, a small beach village a few miles from the city: Two hundred bombs killed thirty-three civilians, wounded thirty more and "*commune entièrement détruite*" (completely destroyed the town).[26]

Although the weather continued to deteriorate, the Eighth Air Force continued to pound the area around the city. It returned on June 4 with thirty-eight B-17 bombers, dropping 423 500-pound bombs on supposed German defensive positions. The cloud cover was so thick that they could not see the target. The mission's after-action report indicated that the results were "nil."[27] Twenty-four B-24 bombers from the 2nd Division attacked Boulogne's defenses the next day, but the thick clouds made it impossible to determine if the attackers hit the German installation.[28] Casualty reports for these attacks were light, with only several civilians killed or wounded by the attacks.[29] The Allied landings in Normandy the next day diverted most Allied air units away from Boulogne as every aircraft in the inventory concentrated on ensuring the first waves reached shore. For more than a week, few Allied aircraft appeared over the city, except for the periodic raids by individual fighters and aircraft on mining duties.

Nine days *after* the Allied landings in Normandy, however, Bomber Command carried out the most destructive attack on Boulogne of the war, this time against an actual threat. The target was a formation of German patrol boats in the harbor, which appeared to be threatening the invasion's sea lane. A force of 184 Lancasters, 130 Halifaxes, and 12 Mosquitoes struck the port and the surrounding city area late that evening. There were still around nine thousand civilians in the city, apparently hoping for liberation by the Allied armies still stuck in Normandy. In addition to the standard 500-, 1000-, and 2,000-pound bombs, the RAF was now dropping 12,000-pound "Tallboy" super bombs on selected targets. This attack killed another 220 French citizens and wounded at least as many. Fire, fueled by the wind, raged throughout the city, magnifying the effect of the bombardment. The physical damage caused by this raid virtually wiped out the city, with authorities reporting at least six thousand buildings and structures destroyed or seriously damaged.[30] One witness, Louis Monard, noted in his journal, "that which is not demolished by the bombing, the flames take care of. The burning oil flames in the harbor." The fire spread everywhere, and the bombardment's destruction of the waterworks "complicates the work of firefighters." The day after the bombing, Monard was dismayed to find the church of Saint-Pierre's bell had fallen from its perch and was discovered "under the heat of the fire."[31]

Unfortunately for the city's remaining civilians, Hitler had declared their city a fortress that was not to surrender, so their nightmare continued. The First Canadian Army arrived on September 5 after participating in the destruction of the German forces at Falaise and the long pursuit north. It remained under siege for seventeen days, as the Canadians moved their troops into position. Finally, after six days of determined air and ground assault, called Operation Wellhit, the 3rd Canadian Infantry Division penetrated the German positions and forced the defenders to capitulate on September 22, almost four months after the Allied landings in Normandy.[32] The city's destruction, primarily by air bombardment, was complete. Before the war, a little more than 52,000 Frenchmen called Boulogne-sur-Mer home. But because of the 1940 exodus away from the German invaders, the city's status as a fortress in the forbidden zone, and four years of constant bombardment, the war ultimately reduced the population by the end of the war to less than 10 percent of that number. More than five hundred air attacks had killed 726 civilians and wounded thousands more and had destroyed or seriously damaged most of the 10,500 buildings that existed before the war. Records indicate that only about five hundred structures were still habitable when the liberation took place. It is with good reason that its citizens today consider it "*une ville martyre*," a martyred city.[33]

Caught up in the massive assaults on the Pas-de-Calais that first week of June was the old fishing town of Berck. It was on the Opal Coast twenty-one miles southwest of Boulogne-sur-Mer, sitting just north of the small Authie River, the boundary between the departments of Pas-de-Calais and Somme. Berck-Plage (Berck Beach) has long been a summer vacation destination for Parisian city dwellers attracted by the cool, breezy summer weather and magnificent landscape. Its beautiful coastline attracted a host of painters such as Édouard Manet and Eugène Boudin. It also had a famous hospital dedicated to treating tuberculosis, a task made easier in the invigorating coastal climate. By 1936 it had almost 17,000 residents, although many of them had departed when the Germans cleared out the Forbidden Zone along the Pas-de-Calais coast.[34] From the German perspective, an Allied invasion force would have to secure this vital terrain if it hoped to capture Boulogne and move inland.

Therefore, it had some of the most formidable defenses anywhere along the Atlantic coast. To defend the beaches, the Fifteenth Army commander placed both the 344th Static Infantry Division and 49th Infantry Division in the Berck area. These troops had turned the area into a massive array of artillery positions, infantry trenches, and concrete blockhouses. While these infantry units often contained a mixture of old soldiers and foreign recruits, they had little problem turning this region into an important defensive zone. All these positions were legitimate targets for any invasion force. Of course, the Allies were not landing on this beach, but 150 miles farther south.[35]

The Eighth Air Force contributed to the German perception during two days of intensive bombing. Although the weather was terrible, the Americans began their assault when 862 heavy bombers from the Eighth Air Force headed for the Pas-de-Calais coastline late in the morning of June 2. All these bombers had one task: to deceive the Germans as to the actual location of the Allied invasion, set to take place several days later. Eleven squadrons of B-24 Liberator bombers from the 2nd Bomb Division, 132 attacking aircraft plus several to assist in navigation, headed toward the German emplacements at Berck. Overhead, more than 350 fighters, primarily Mustangs with support from several squadrons of Lightnings and Thunderbolts, dominated the sky. A little after 1340 hours the bombers attacked their designated targets of three artillery batteries, a radar installation, and a collection of machine-gun and mortar positions. In the space of only a few minutes, bombing through relatively thick clouds, the not-so-aptly-named Liberators dropped 591,500 pounds (almost 296 tons) of 500-, 1000-, and 2,000-pound bombs. Other than doing damage to one of the artillery batteries, the massive quantity of explosives appeared to have affected none of the other targets.

The crews and their senior commanders realized their slim prospects of actually hitting anything through the dense clouds. For them, the mere act of dropping the bombs near the enemy positions was what was important. Even in the bad weather, the aircraft could get close since the Eighth Air Force began using the H2X navigation radar, adapted from the British H2S system in the fall of 1943. But while it improved the ability of the bombers to fly to and identify a large town, it was of little use in hitting a specific target, especially one as small as an array of bunkers and trenches. In effect, the "overcast bombing technique," as reports routinely call this kind of attack, was an attempt in bad European weather, using H2X mapping radar, to get bombs as close to the target as possible. The radar allowed the squadrons to find Boulogne-sur-Mer, but after that almost anything could happen.[36]

Maj. Gen. James P. Hodges of the 2nd Bombardment Division returned to Berck the next day. Around noon, sixty B-24s were over the village and its defenses. Again, they used what the planners euphemistically called "through the cloud bombing techniques" to identify and drop their explosive load on the targets. Of course, it again meant that they had no idea as to whether they hit their targets. Three hours later, another bomber flight attacked the defenses along the beach. This time, the clouds were even worse, and the crews could not identify their targets. The official report for these two days of attacks and the dropping of more than 676 tons of bombs noted "no observable damage done to the assigned targets."[37]

On September 4, the Canadian Army moved into the remains of the once picturesque resort.[38] On a superficial level, the village recovered quickly. Within a few years, the French (with the forced assistance of German prisoners of war) removed most of the unexploded munitions, cleared the rubble on the beach, and rebuilt most of the hotels and cafés. Historians and citizens looking for clues and commentary on these events in early June 1944 can find little published but the single fact that the Eighth Air Force had bombed the region as part of Operation Fortitude. It was a small village, the Germans removed most of the citizens from the beach area, and the impending invasion overshadowed the tragic drama. Local governmental officials were struggling to hold together a disintegrating bureaucracy and found it difficult to investigate the massive Allied attack. Twenty years later, a young American poet living in England, Sylvia Plath, visited the beach. As she strolled among bright umbrellas and busy crushed-ice stands, placed next to the hulking ruins of German fortifications, she sensed that something "sinister" was lurking behind the cheerful façade. Her famous poem "Berck-Plage" captures that dissonance between the present joyful expression and the reality of the horror experienced on this site earlier: "Why is it so quiet, what are they hiding?"[39]

Several miles north of Boulogne are the villages of Wimille and Wimereux, which became prime targets during Operation Fortitude. A town of a little more than two thousand people located on the banks of a stream several kilometers from the coast, Wimille spent most of its existence as a mill town and site of several chateaux, which in 1944 served as headquarters for the German army and naval commands. The town is best known as the location for Napoleon's grand encampment of 1804. Although he never invaded England, a fifty-three-meter column, the Colonne Napoléon, finished in 1821, commemorates the creation of his Grande Armée and the inauguration of the Legion of Honor. Directly west, along the coast, is the beach town of Wimereux and the site of a Vauban fortress, which Napoleon converted into a staging area for part of his invasion fleet.[40] These towns bordered the major fortified installation of La Trésorerie, built around three large concrete casements, each with a 305-mm SK L/50 gun. It was a significant defensive area of machine-gun positions, anti-aircraft defenses, and all kinds of defensive works. It was a natural target that needed to be destroyed before any force could land north of Boulogne.[41]

Like that of Berck, the bombing of La Trésorerie began in the early afternoon of June 2. Three groups of fifty-eight B-17s each from Maj. Gen. Curtis Lemay's 3rd Bombardment Division arrived above the artillery zone at 1300 hours. The bombardiers could see nothing as thick clouds totally obscured the ground, but hitting the target was not a priority. The first group's aiming point was the massive battery while the other two sought field artillery units that could range the coastal area. Although one group claimed to have hit the target, the German defenses were unharmed.[42] Not so, of course, for those on the ground. The aerial attack virtually erased Wimille from the map, damaging or destroying almost all the small town's structures. Fortunately, most of the civilians had already evacuated this village and reports indicated three dead and ten wounded civilians.[43]

The next two days saw these attacks continue, but with lesser intensity. That night Bomber Command joined the fray. Soon after 0100 on June 3, 65 Lancaster bombers, part of a fleet of 271 aircraft Harris launched against the channel coast, arrived over these two villages. As was the case earlier in the day, the weather made it impossible to identify anything below other than the outline of Calais in the distance. That afternoon Lemay's bombers returned, this time with only 36 aircraft. While the raid made noise, there is little evidence it did much more than drop bombs into nearby fields. Harris sent another 36 heavies against the complex around 0100 the next morning, June 4. Lemay returned with another 36 B-17s the next day at 1345. Wimille and Wimereux each suffered several civilians killed and wounded in the raids, which reflects the small number of civilians remaining in the region.[44]

Observations

For three days, from June 3 through June 5, Allied bombers and fighter aircraft attacked targets on the coast from Dunkerque to Berck, hitting forty-one separate towns and villages. The raids varied in size but usually consisted of between twelve and thirty-six aircraft. The subprefect for the Boulogne area wrote his departmental supervisor soon after the bombing ended on June 5. "I am told now that following the recent bombing there are in Calais about 2,000 homeless persons. There is great concern; these victims are wondering what will happen to them and if their relief will be granted." He asked his boss to come in person to investigate the damage. He did not have the resources to cope with the flood of citizens seeking help. He suggested that the departmental *préfet* "consider urgently whether despite the current circumstances an evacuation outside my district can be considered, since my Desvres [a community twenty kilometers east of Boulogne] [evacuation] center is crowded and I've already sent disaster victims from Boulogne and Outreau to centers made available to me by my colleagues in the districts of Montreuil and Saint-Omer."[45] Later in the month the Préfecture of the Pas-de-Calais reported the month's casualties and described what had happened to the region. One can only imagine how difficult it was to get any accurate description of the damage done along the department's beaches. The partial reports indicate that the Allied bombing killed 253 French civilians throughout the department between June 1 and June 5. In Berck, the official reports indicate the attack killed at least 50 civilians and wounded many others. The raids either destroyed or seriously damaged every building in the city. The report suggests that these attacks also killed many North African and Belgian workers in the area.[46] On June 5 the authorities ordered all remaining civilians out of the city.

Today the Fortitude target area has recovered from the effects of German military construction and Allied bombardment. In the north, between Calais and Boulogne, the war's evidence is visible as farmers' fields still display the massive German artillery bunkers, usually showing the limited effects of the bombing missions. At Cape Gris-Nez the craters from bombs aimed at the radar stations remain, a visible reminder of the air offensive's intensity. Farmers continue to damage their plows on the scrap metal that remains in the soil. From time to time, an unexploded bomb works its way from the ground's depths and threateningly emerges to the top, requiring a visit by local ordnance disposal experts.[47] Enterprising Frenchmen have turned some of the bunkers into museums, and others are now basements for the beachfront property. Others, damaged more by erosion than by the enemy, are visible along the dunes and at low tide. In Boulogne and Calais a few remain visible, but the local governments had mostly filled them in and covered them with grass and shrubs. Between Boulogne and Berck-Plage in the south is prime beachfront property and a destination for French and British tourists in the summer. The tourist towns show little evidence of German occupation and damage. Often the Nazi bunkers are now part of the sand dunes and the local anti-erosion program. But in the hype that surrounds Patton's missteps in Knutsford and dummy tanks on the British coast, it is appropriate to realize that there was a negative side to this masquerade. As one historian of the deception plan has noted, it is hard to assess the importance of Fortitude (South) in keeping the Germans away from the Norman beaches in the early days of June.[48] But there can be no question that it was a major component of Operation Overlord and the air war against French towns and villages.

CHAPTER EIGHT

THE RAIL CENTERS

A simple monument, approximately twelve feet high, stands in the corner of the main lobby of Rouen's train station. Inscribed upon it are the names of almost two hundred rail workers from this French city killed during the Second World War. Numerous train stations throughout France display similar monuments and plaques reminding citizens of the service and sacrifice of these workers more than seventy years ago. Some modern commuters probably know that the names of their family members are engraved in stone above them, whereas tourists will simply notice and move on. Emerging from these stations, especially in larger cities like Rouen, Metz, Caen, and Nantes, an alert observer will see additional indicators of the scale of violence around these transportation hubs. Most obvious are the old town centers, now dominated by 1950s-era construction, or churches and other buildings with bombed-out portions still prominently displayed. Few visitors probably ponder the nature of this damage. Yet across France and into Belgium, heavy and medium bombers reduced once great rail centers into moonscapes of carnage that in many cases have never been rebuilt to their previous condition.

After Eisenhower's struggle with his strategic air commanders for control of the heavy bombers, Tedder and Leigh-Mallory developed three lines of action to hinder enemy movement to the invasion zone by air attack, what military professionals call "interdiction." The first of these, the Transportation Plan, focused on destroying the French rail system. Unlike almost all of

SHAEF's joint plans, this one had no code name. Its name described what it was about: stopping transportation. Specifically, the planners designed it to slow the arrival of Germany's strategic reserves to the French theater of operations. These reserves included any forces the German High Command could spare from the Russian or other fronts and was generally outside of France.[1] It was the Transportation Plan that caused Churchill the most concern regarding French civilian casualties.

The Process of Interdiction

In military parlance, stopping German reinforcements from reaching the landing beaches before his forces were in place and prepared to halt them—Eisenhower's primary goal for the Transportation Plan—is an example of interdiction. Interdiction encompasses all actions to divert, disrupt, delay, or destroy an enemy's following military force before they can employ it on the battlefield.[2] The more one side can do to interfere with an opponent's reserve forces behind the lines, the better the prospect for troops in contact. By 1940 these ground support missions were the ones bomber advocates wished to avoid, but the power of the new air weapon had impressed ground commanders, and they were intent on adding this capability to their palette of military capabilities. American operational manuals of the period clearly supported the use of air forces to interdict lines of communication and supply installations.[3] The prospect of extended operations, with aircraft attacking targets far beyond the range of any other weapon systems, was a new way for ground commanders to gain superiority on the battlefield. No matter what air force commanders wanted, bombers would be part of the main effort. Eisenhower, as supreme commander, was always clear as to the importance of this capability. "The virtual destruction of critical points on main roads and railroads leading into the battle area was a critical feature of the (Overlord) battle plan."[4]

Before the twentieth century, cavalry units or local guerrillas conducted these operations by blowing up bridges, blocking roads, or harassing enemy troops on the march or in camp. The effect of these activities was limited, and the enemy force ultimately continued on its way. The advent of combat aircraft in the twentieth century opened a broad range of possibilities for army commanders, who now had the ability to strike enemy road and rail networks far behind the lines. During the latter stages of the First World War, the Royal Air Force used the large Handley Page Type 0 and smaller Airco DH9 bombers to strike at rail yards, airfields, and supply depots far behind German lines. American aviators joined these missions, flying Liberty DH4 and Breguet 14 B2 light bombers. During the Meuse-Argonne offensive of October and November 1918, Allied pilots attacked rail yards, such as Metz, Saarbruken, and Kaiserslautern, and troop concentrations in French towns on a daily basis.[5] The bombing of logistical centers and rail lines, with the purpose of preventing or delaying the arrival of enemy reserves and supplies, had been one of the fundamental US Air Force functions since before the Second World War.[6]

For the Allies, North Africa became the testing ground for Second World War interdiction. Air leaders Tedder, Coningham, and Brereton began developing procedures for these operations, especially against roads and supply ports, in North Africa in support of Montgomery's 1942 campaign against Rommel. This western desert air force conducted most of these missions with fighters and medium bombers.[7] As the Allies moved into Sicily and Italy, now with heavy bombers, they began targeting rail traffic. But rather than attacking sparsely populated towns or isolated transportation points, the Italian targets were major rail centers near the major cities. The result was catastrophic for the civilian population and foreshadowed later operations in France. Before the Italian surrender in September, these attacks on military targets had killed almost 11,000 civilians.[8] Nevertheless, in 1943, air commanders were confident these raids were producing the desired effect. Tedder, who was the chief airman in the theater, employed an Oxford professor with good political connections, Solly Zuckerman, to inject a degree of scientific rigor into the process of evaluating bombing effectiveness. Planners at AEAF headquarters used his studies for designing the future campaign in France. By the time Tedder left Italy for his role as Eisenhower's deputy, he clearly understood that bombing accuracy was "about half of what we had estimated."[9] It was also his view, however, that these attacks were effective, and he took this perspective with him when he moved to England.

It is important to remember the purpose of the interdiction operations undertaken as the war moved to northwest Europe. From a strategic perspective, Germany was fighting from a central position and could use inner rail and road routes to move combat units from any portion of its theater of war to the Norman coast. If unhindered, the Nazis had the capability to defeat the invasion. Although most of the Wehrmacht's thirty-two panzer divisions were engaged on the Russian front, the High Command had the ability to deploy several to France, which they ultimately did by the middle of July. Two or three rested, veteran panzer divisions arriving in the invasion area within a week of the landings could have been the deciding factor in the success or failure of the assault. The Germans had performed exactly such movements in November 1942 in response to Operation Torch and again in March 1944, when Hungary attempted to back out of the coalition. As the SHAEF Intelligence Summary for April 29 noted, the German High Command was able to assemble fifteen to twenty divisions from all parts of the empire, including Poland, Denmark, Yugoslavia, Greece, Albania, Austria, and northern Italy. Were Hitler and his generals flexible enough to do it again when the Allies invaded?[10] Those officers planning the invasion could only assume that Hitler and the German High Command would not be hesitant to move reinforcements to the front immediately. Central to any troop relocation effort was the European rail system.

The primary means of moving troops and their equipment long distance was rail. Beginning as a simple device for moving coal to factories and ports in England in 1825, it soon carried passengers and had expanded to an elaborate international system by the 1860s. Especially in the western states of England, Germany, France, and Belgium, the rail system was a complex and redundant web of iron that could reroute rail traffic the same way utility companies can adjust electric power based on overloaded systems and changing requirements.[11] It was the German General Staff that pioneered the science of moving troops by rail during its wars against Denmark, Austria, and France in the middle of the nineteenth century. For these officers, the use of their national rail lines was at the core of their military strategy. They gained dominance in a theater of war by concentrating their forces faster and in greater number than their opponents. By 1914 Germany had almost 40,000 miles of rail lines supporting its military operations. In addition to moving tanks and artillery great distances quickly, the use of rail also prevented wear and tear on vehicle engines and track systems, saving them for combat operations.[12] The system functioned well throughout the conflict in spite of massive bombing. Its robust design and an almost limitless supply of prisoner-of-war and slave labor to make repairs, allowed the Nazi trains to keep moving.[13]

The French rail system was one of the most robust in the world and essential to any German reinforcement effort. Nationalized in 1938, rail systems and their workers were part of the Société Nationale des Chemins de fer Francais, generally abbreviated as SNCF. With nearly 30,000 miles of track, the French system was just as developed as the German and thoroughly integrated with it. Close to half of all rail lines had a double track (compared to fewer than 15 percent in the United States), and most shared the same gauge as the remainder of western Europe. It had about 18,000 locomotives, although about half of these were either out of service or obsolete. The SNCF designed its 31,000 passenger cars and 480,000 freight cars for international travel. By 1943 however, the rail system was no longer acting independently; it was part of a European-wide system supporting the German war effort. The Gebietsverkehrsleitung-West (Area traffic management) controlled all rail movement from Germany into the occupied nations. Within western Europe, two regional headquarters supervised track usage, administration, and rail system repair. In Belgium, Netherlands, Luxembourg, and northern France region, the Hauptverkehrsdirection-Brussels (Main traffic direction) supervised German economic and military transportation. These rail lines, which ran from Amsterdam, Köln, and Bonn through Brussels and Liege to Lille, were the most direct and important routes. Hauptverkehrsdirection-Paris administered rail traffic from Frankfurt and Mannheim, through Reims, Metz, and Chalons, to the Paris region.[14] Rail lines connected to rail centers. At the lowest level were the train stations for small towns along the tracks. In addition to a passenger and freight platform, they would have sidetracks for holding railcars and unloading cargo. At the other extreme were the large rail centers, which became the primary focus of this aspect of the Transportation Plan.

Each large center had several key components: the locomotive depot, the marshaling yard, other facilities, and housing. The locomotive depot represented a significant investment in personnel, infrastructure, and equipment. The largest contained a circular structure, often incorporating a large turntable, for major engine repair work, engine storage, and maintenance. The center usually had an additional repair shop for major repairs, and facilities for loading and storing coal and water. It had pits for storing and disposing of coal ash, oil, and sand. This facility was also a management center, with various kinds of communications capabilities (telephone, teletype, radio, for example), and dormitories for workers, food centers, and office space for crews and management. Each center also contained a marshaling yard, mainly a collection of fifteen or more tracks that small tug locomotives used to arrange the cars, depending on their destination. Once the routing manager assigned an engine, it joined the cars to become a train. The responsible engineer then moved this assembly over to a waiting, or departure, track while SNCF management communicated by telegraph with stations down the line. Once the transportation director cleared the way, the train headed to its ultimate destination. Each rail center also had other facilities for loading and unloading freight, smaller repair shops for the train cars, storage facilities, and electric power stations. Nearby there was usually a smaller railroad station designed to handle passenger traffic.[15] Usually missing in the official American and British reports is a discussion of the people who worked at the rail centers. It was an era when people took streetcars, walked, or bicycled to work, so they lived nearby. Civilian homes, churches, and schools were directly adjacent to these extensive facilities. Nearby were the stores and services supporting these vital hubs such as butcher shops, bakeries, tailors, fire stations, and hospitals. For every engineer or mechanic at work on the system, his family of two or three were living their lives less than a mile away.[16] People, however, were not the issue, the rail centers were, and the original COSSAC planners believed they needed to destroy these complexes before the actual invasion.[17]

The Transportation Plan

The planning for attacking these systems evolved from a straightforward staff analysis into as heated and angry a debate as ever took place in the Allied command.[18] From the beginning, the COSSAC staff had agreed on the threat enemy reserves posed to the invasion and that aerial bombardment was one of the several means the Allies could use to stop them.[19] Morgan's planners put more effort into evaluating the problem and concluded that the first two weeks of the invasion would be critical. "COSSAC Staff Study 6, Delay of Enemy Reserves," (December 30, 1943), argued that it was essential to delay these forces as far away from the bridgehead as possible.[20] The final edition, published several days later, identified the different French and Belgian rail yards and provided a priority for attacking them and other facilities.[21] By the time Eisenhower arrived in London, discussions on how to implement this concept were well under way. Several major concerns affected the debate. From a fundamental perspective, not everyone agreed that it was possible to affect German long-distance movement. Churchill and Portal, for example, believed that the French road and rail system was too dense for air to be efficient. As mentioned earlier, there was a grave concern over causing substantial French civilian casualties. Finally, others feared that bombing the rail and road network would give away the location of the landing area.[22]

At almost the same time as the COSSAC study was nearing completion, Professor Zuckerman arrived in England with the results of his analysis of the rail bombing in support of the Sicily operation. The science advisor's paper argued that destroying the enemy's communications was a strategic problem, not a tactical one. The best targets were the locomotive repair facilities, found at the largest yards, and the precious rolling stock. He also argued that bombing bridges, one of the other proposals under discussion, was not an economical use of air power.[23] Tedder, now deputy supreme commander to Eisenhower, was sufficiently impressed with the former biology professor to appoint him his scientific advisor for the upcoming invasion. Given the materials and information at hand, it was as reasonable a study as could have been done in the middle of the twentieth century.[24] As supreme commander of Allied forces in Europe, General Eisenhower was determined to use all the assets he had available to ensure the success of his planned invasion, and he tended to side with his trusted deputy. As mentioned earlier, he grasped better than any other leader the importance of synchronizing all elements of combat power to gain and maintain that initial beachhead.

But the Transportation Plan was anathema to the strategic "bomber barons"—Spaatz for the Americans, Harris for the British. They opposed it for cultural, practical, and personal considerations. Since the Casablanca Conference of January 1943, the strategic bombers' goal, under what became known as Operation Pointblank, had been the "destruction and dislocation of the German military, industrial, and economic system." They wished to take the war to Germany, defeat the German air force, and "destroy the enemy's means to make war."[25] Spaatz and Harris opposed any interruption to Pointblank, believing that to divert the bombers from their primary mission would prolong the war. The Americans were also dreaming of an independent air force on the RAF model, and the subordination of their bomber fleet to the Army ground forces was anathema to serious aviators. Therefore, both leaders refused to allow Leigh-Mallory, whom they disliked, to take command of their bombers.[26] At the crucial meeting on March 25, Spaatz made one last effort to retain his independence from the ground forces and continue executing Operation Pointblank. He prepared a paper arguing for attacking not French rail yards, but enemy oil supplies in Germany, a mission for an independent air force. He claimed that the enemy oil situation was precarious and that the destruction of the enemy's synthetic production could cripple the entire German war machine. The problem, of course, was that no one knew with any precision how much oil the enemy possessed and how long such a mission would take. Time was not on Eisenhower's side, as he had to execute Neptune in less than three months, and he remained determined to maintain control of all air force units.[27]

The meeting on March 25 convinced Eisenhower that the destruction of the rail centers was the best use of the heavy bombers. He noted, "The greatest contribution that he could imagine the air forces making to this aim is that they should hinder enemy movement." Furthermore, "the transportation plan was the only one which offered a reasonable chance of the air forces making an important contribution to the land battle during the first vital weeks of OVERLORD; in fact, he did not believe that there was any other real alternative."[28] He fundamentally changed Harris and Spaatz' focus from *strategic* (bombing targets in the heart of Germany, answering only to the Combined Chiefs of Staff) to *operational* (attack targets in France and Belgium at his direction). As a sop to the bomber commanders, he agreed that Tedder was his planning agent rather than Leigh-Mallory, whom they continued to despise. Two days later the combined chiefs issued their directive, and the AEAF staff began preparing the details.[29]

Prepared to resign over this issue, Eisenhower had won his battle for a unity of command. Except for the continuing struggle against Crossbow launchers, he directed the heavy bombers in a coordinated effort focused on preserving the landing force. Against stiff opposition from bureaucratic experts, politicians, and senior airmen, Eisenhower's vision on how to use air power prevailed. The Transportation Plan was an integral part of the Neptune operation from the beginning and was one the key lines of effort in his overarching operational vision.

The Transportation Plan, at its core level, focused on the "maximum destruction of motive power potential anywhere in France, Belgium or west

Germany and the maximum dislocation of all the other elements in the rail system in the areas concerned with OVERLORD."[30] Air Commodore E. J. Kingston-McCloughry, Leigh-Mallory's principal planner, prepared the original target list long before the March meeting. In February the planners submitted to the Air Staff a list of fifty-seven rail centers in France, Belgium, and the Netherlands that he needed the combined chiefs' clearance to bomb. The staff would continuously modify this list, based on better intelligence, needs of the Army planners, and estimates of potential civilian casualties. Each of the individual air forces had specific targets, and in some cases Bomber Command raids in the evening complemented American attacks during the day.[31] Appendix B contains a list of those centers identified for destruction. It also identifies those rail installations the Allies attacked but were not included in the original plan.

We should note that the issue of civilian casualties was usually in the mind of the planning staffs. Air Vice-Marshal G. A. Coryton, who submitted the target list, noted in his cover letter, "There is no doubt that heavy French casualties will ensue if all the targets referred to are to be effectively attacked."[32] Several days later the Air Staff produced a document listing the seventy-eight requested targets by risk to the French population and provided an estimate as to the number the raid would probably kill. In Sotteville, near Rouen, the staff estimated that 10,000 civilians were at risk and that 640 would probably perish. For the Juvisy rail center near Paris, the committee estimated that 24,000 were in danger and that 960 would die. The analysts pulled two targets in Paris, the rail yards at Batignolles and Le Bourget, off the list, believing the civilian losses would be unacceptable. Original estimates anticipated that the bombing could kill or wound as many as 160,000 civilians. The Air Ministry considerably reduced this estimate to suggest that while 282,100 French citizens were at risk, most likely 16,000 would perish or be seriously wounded in the bombardment.[33] Portal expressed his concern in his note attached to the final bombing directive on March 29. "There is one point which I should mention to you now. In the execution of this plan very heavy casualties among civilians living near the main railway centers in occupied territory will be unavoidable, however carefully we may be over the actual bombing. Eisenhower realizes this, and I understand that he is going to propose warnings to be issued to all civilians living near railway centers advising them to move. I hope you will agree that since the requirements of Overlord are paramount the plan must go ahead after due warning has been given."[34]

By the end of March, the British government had grown alarmed about the long-term repercussions that would result from killing many friendly civilians during the impending bombing operation. On April 3 Churchill wrote to Eisenhower, explaining the British position and reminding him "that they are all our friends, this might be held to be an act of very great severity, bringing much hatred on the Allied Air Forces."[35] On April 29 Churchill again wrote Eisenhower and pointed out the government's alarm that such a bombing campaign "is apt to poison our relations with the French people not only during the invasion but for a generation afterwards, the Government feel justified in asking to be convinced that this plan will actually bring great military advantage."[36] Eisenhower responded to Churchill on May 2 expressing his sympathy for his political concerns and ensuring him that his planners had done their best to limit the damage, but he indicated that he "had modified my plan as far as possible without vitiating its value. If it is still considered that the political considerations are such as to limit the Operations to centres where the casualties are estimate at 100/150 (a lower figure requested by the government), such a modification would emasculate the whole plan."[37]

As the bombing intensified, French officials on the continent began to bring the effect of the casualties to the attention of the Allied leadership. On May 7 the French Committee of National Liberation warned that while the French population understood that bombing was a natural precursor to an invasion, their morale would severely suffer "if it appeared that the destruction and loss of human life which the air attacks bring are not in relation to the technical results obtained." The committee continued: "in some cases the losses and damage that the aerial bombardments have brought for the population seem out of proportion to the military results obtained."[38] Churchill appealed directly to Roosevelt that same day, asking him to look at the operation from not only the military but also from the political perspective.[39] Roosevelt ended the discussion several days later. Understanding Churchill's concerns, he openly backed his commander on the scene. "However regrettable the attendant loss of civilian lives is, I am not prepared to impose from this distance any restriction on military action by the responsible Commanders that in their opinion might militate against the success of OVERLORD or cause additional loss of life to our Allied Forces of Invasion."[40]

Eisenhower was concerned enough over this issue to get support from the generally ignored Free French government's military leaders. Tedder and Eisenhower's chief of staff Bedell Smith had a meeting with General Marie-Pierre Koenig, de Gaulle's representative to SHAEF, on May 16. Koenig was one of the best French commanders. At the end of May 1942, when Rommel tried to outflank the British lines at Gazala in the Libyan Desert, they ran into Koenig at Bir Hakeim, who secured the line's exposed southern flank. For two weeks Koenig and his 1st Light Division stopped the German and Italian forces in their tracks. For ten days the major portion of Rommel's air and ground forces, led by the Desert Fox in person, tried to crack the line. Finally, after running out of ammunition and against overwhelming odds, the French fought their way out of their positions and reached the safety of the British lines. This defense, one of the first post-1940 French victories, received praise from British commanders and did much to support the Allied investment in Charles de Gaulle's resurgent military forces.[41] In March 1944, after Koenig had held a series of military and diplomatic posts, de Gaulle appointed the tough commander to be his representative in London, supporting the impending invasion. Because he had worked with the British since the beginning of the war, and the Americans since North Africa, he was probably the best choice to coordinate French interests in London's complex environment that spring.[42] By early May, French agents and officials on the continent had been complaining for some time about the effects of the Allied bombardment on civilian morale.[43] When Tedder and Smith asked for his reaction to the bombing effort, he noted in an often quoted phrase, certainly not the position of those who were affected by the bombardment, that "This is war, and it must be expected that people will be killed. We would take twice the anticipated loss to be rid of the Germans."[44] It was one of the few times at this stage of the war that SHAEF bothered to consult with the French on military operations. For certain, the comments of this veteran soldier helped provide cover for the intensive bombardment already under way.

Readers should note that twenty of the numbered targets were in Belgium and one was in Luxembourg. Almost all rail traffic from north Germany, the Ruhr, and the area near Frankfurt-am-Main passed through Belgium and Luxembourg. Although beyond the scope of this work, it is important to remember that the destruction of rail centers did not stop at the French border. For example, Courtrai (Kortrijk) suffered extensive destruction, with heavy bombings in March and July 1944. Reports indicate that between 400 and 620 civilians perished in these attacks. Overall, perhaps 10,000 Belgians perished in these transportation attacks.[45]

The Targets

The reader should probably pause and realize what had transpired since the end of March. With the aim of reducing Allied casualties amongst the invasion force, Allied commanders decided to destroy an allegedly friendly nation's rail infrastructure and, in the process, kill eight to ten thousand civilians. When the British, who lived close to the French and would have to work with them directly in the postwar era, grew alarmed, the American commander and political leader decided that the French loss was worth the price. Eisenhower rejected an alternate suggestion by Spaatz and accepted the Transportation Plan because it "was the only one (option) which offered a reasonable chance of the air forces making an important contribution to the land battle during the first vital weeks of OVERLORD; in fact he did not believe that there was any other real alternative."[46] As the supreme commander implied, however, the staff work was shoddy: "He had not realized however that the War Office Staff had not been consulted on whether if the plan were successful it would have the desired effects on the enemy's military movement."[47] No one, as expressed in the minutes of this decision briefing, could explain how much of a reduction in German rail traffic would take place. The phrase that participants used several times is "some reduction."[48] In fact, it appears that Eisenhower was as determined to get the heavy bombers into the fight as he was to interdict the Germans' transportation. Missing from this discussion are any serious alternatives to the presented Transportation Plan. Could attacks against fewer rail centers just preceding or during the invasion, thus limiting the fallout from civilian casualties, have produced the same results? Could a combination of selective bombing, supported by French Resistance operations in high-population-density areas, yielded similar effects? Apparently, if these options were discussed, Leigh-Mallory's planners never presented these options to the commander at this critical meeting.

The result would be a prolonged bombing operation against French civilian targets with the object of creating some reduction in German rail movement. Of the fifty-seven rail centers attacked in occupied northwest Europe, several provide us good examples of the nature of the rail yard missions and how they affected the French citizens. In most cases, the Allied air forces attacked these targets on more than one occasion. Most resulted in significant loss of civilian lives and left the nearby communities with profound memories of the disaster. Only one, Sotteville, a suburb of Rouen on the Seine River, was close to the Norman coast.

Rouen-Sotteville

The Allied bombing of rail centers had begun before the March meeting, but its pace increased after April 15, when Eisenhower assumed the direction of Spaatz' and Harris' bombers for use in the assault on Normandy. That same day, Air Marshal Arthur Tedder, now responsible for providing direction to the bomber commanders, issued the formal instructions for the execution of the Transportation Plan.[49] Three days later, Harris, knowing he had exhausted his arguments against bombing targets in France, complied with Eisenhower's instructions and launched more than eight hundred bombers against transportation centers at Noisy-le-Sec, Tergnier, Juvisy, and Rouen.[50] The Allies had been to all these locations previously. In fact the first American bombing mission of the war was against the Sotteville rail center in August 1942.[51] It had been a target of repetitive British attacks since the beginning, and by April more than 165 civilians from this small town had perished as a result. These assaults ranged from individual fighter-bomber strikes against road traffic to light bombing of the rail yards. In general, citizens living near the rail yard were accustomed to the attacks and learned how to take precautions. From January until the middle of April the alarm sirens had sounded more than ninety-three times.[52] They went to bed on April 18, however, with little anticipation of what was to follow.

From the beginning, Rouen was an obvious military target. It was one of France's premier shipping ports, and its extensive harbor facilities were an important military concern for both sides. In the early years of the war, it was to have been a principal point of embarkation for German troops during Operation Sea Lion. During the occupation, its many factories served as facilities for repairing German naval vessels. The rail line between Paris and Rouen was the nation's oldest, and the suburb of Sotteville developed into the center of the regional rail traffic. Sotteville had many important railroad facilities strung along the tracks, including a locomotive depot, rail yards, holding tracks, coal yards, and other establishments essential to the operation of a modern rail system. The rail yard was massive, with the triage, or sorting area, consisting of fifty-six track sidings, capable of holding and rearranging up to four thousand railcars.[53] In addition, major French and German communication trunk lines ran through the city, linking Caen and Cherbourg with the rest of the German empire. In the years before wireless and microwave networks, these wire-cable lines were the lifeblood of operational and strategic command, control, and communications.[54]

Shortly after midnight on April 19, 16 two-engine RAF DeHavilland Mosquito bombers arrived over the city and the Sotteville rail yard and began the assault. Their job was to evade detection, locate the targets, and drop small illuminating munitions that would mark the bombers' objectives. The mission planners identified two aiming points. Target A was the central tower that controlled rail traffic and its movement across different tracks. Target B was the locomotive repair depot at the northern end of the rail yard.[55] Behind the Mosquitoes, in two waves flying approximately 10,000 to 15,000 feet above the ground, came 273 Avro Lancaster bombers, each capable of carrying about eight thousand pounds of bombs. They emptied their massive loads in only fifteen minutes. The planes attacking Target A, the center of the rail yard, were relatively accurate. Approximately half of the munitions fell inside the target area and put it out of action. The Lancasters vectoring on Target B were not so precise; most of their bombs missed the rail yard. They either fell short, exploding in the center of Sotteville, or long, in the heart of Rouen. The results of the accidental bombing were disastrous. The official Bomber Command report noted that only 338 of 3,871 bombs hit the target.[56] Air reconnaissance interpreters, looking at the poststrike photographs, noted that while there was substantial destruction among the tracks and rolling stock, "considerable damage is also apparent outside the target area." The photo analysts noted damage in the residential area near the rail yard as well as damage in the "old town," meaning Rouen, several miles from the rail yard.[57]

Sleeping in their beds, tucked away in centuries-old wooden structures, many citizens of both Sotteville and ancient Rouen never had a chance. In the larger city, several high-explosive bombs hit Cathédrale Notre-Dame, demolishing part of the structure. Other bombs hit the Palais de Justice, penetrating the roof and destroying the interior.[58] As soon as the bombers left, the passive defense forces moved to their stations. The casualties quickly inundated the hospital. Firefighters moved to save the structures, especially those that were most valuable, such as Le Gros Horloge, a large clock tower from the sixteenth century, and the old market, not yet destroyed. They concentrated on fighting the fires at nine prominent locations across the burning city. The task was daunting with no telephone communications to coordinate operations and limited water to use in fighting fires. The flames digested the old wooden houses. The city requested firefighting support from as far away as Le Havre and Dieppe.[59] The French use the word *patrimoine*, or heritage, to describe their historical treasures. Much of this treasure dissolved into ash into the red sky that night. In the target area, including Rouen, Sotteville, and some smaller suburbs, authorities identified where most of the bombs had exploded, destroying almost 2,800 buildings and damaging another 1,500. Many of these were schools, hospitals, and churches. The damage was extensive, from little streets containing homes of the local citizens to ancient treasures. To those in the United States, distant from the scene of conflict, this accounting has little meaning, just an aspect of modern war. But to the people of Rouen, it was their inheritance. The local resistance leaders sent a message to the Allies warning them that the bombing was hurting the morale of the citizens and confirming the worst of the German propaganda.[60]

The British and French had different perspectives as to what had happened. The *Times* of London reported the next day that one thousand Royal Air Force bombers pounded four railway yards with four thousand tons of bombs. It informed its readers that the bombing techniques they used "were designed to keep the bombs within the comparatively small areas occupied by the yards and workshops. Every possible check was made to ensure containment of bombing well within the target."[61] The *New York Times* report from the same day paints a similar picture of successful, almost surgical, air strikes, with bombs falling within the target area. It labeled as "propaganda" reports from "the enemy" that Rouen and other cities had suffered severe damage. It noted that Vichy radio had "caustically" commented, "If German bombers had performed last night's massacre, Frenchmen would have clamored for revenge."[62] Other reports were reaching Eisenhower that let him know the bombing was eliciting a reaction. For example, a British

Rue de Republic-Sotteville. Main street of the town near the rail yard following the RAF bombardment on April 19–20.
Bibliothèque Municipales Sotteville-Les-Rouen

Sotteville refugees evacuating after April 19–20 bombardment. *Bibliothèque Municipales Sotteville-Les-Rouen*

War Cabinet note sent to him by Churchill contained an intelligence report indicating that the attacks on April 19 were "catastrophic" for French morale, and Rouen's municipal council passed a resolution of protest and adjourned. One survivor commented, "They bring us liberation with wooden crosses."[63]

The citizens of Sotteville and Rouen have not forgotten the bombing on that spring day. Today in Sotteville, a small stone monument and placard commemorates the toll suffered by this small town. The rail yard is still operating, and the authorities have rebuilt the destroyed homes. Rouen restored its Palais de Justice, and, although its interior looks untouched, the outside still displays dramatic damage from the bombing of April 19. A few hundred meters away, in a nearby square, the survivors reconstructed the buildings destroyed by the attack. Casual diners in the quaint cafés have little knowledge of the events that took place here that spring. If they look around, however, they will note that this square is the Place du 19 Avril 1944. In the middle is a statue of a mother kissing her young child as the father and older son look skyward. This poignant monument pays homage to the civilians who perished in the fires and whose lives changed forever that night. It remains difficult to assess the exact personal toll with any accuracy, but the local prefect reported to his superiors that Rouen had 341 citizens killed and missing,

Sotteville had lost 531, and other local areas had suffered about 27 killed, for a total of more than 900 that terrible night. Hundreds more lay wounded in local hospitals and facilities.[64] At Noisy-le-Sec, Tergnier, and Juvisy, Bomber Command's other targets that evening, civilian casualties also reached the hundreds.[65]

Amiens/Longueau

Located almost one hundred miles north of Paris, Amiens is the historic capital of the Picardie region and a prominent French city. Its strategic location on the Somme River ensured it would play a significant role in France's economic and military history long before the Second World War. Julius Caesar referred to it as Somme bridge (Samarobriva), and it became a Roman military base and a center of military and commercial activity. In 1220 its citizens laid the foundation for the Cathédrale of Notre-Dame, the largest Gothic building in France. In the Middle Ages, it was a center of the textile industry. Spared the destruction of Louis XIV's and Napoleon's wars, the city continued to prosper. The railroad arrived in 1848, and the city flourished as a manufacturing and commercial center. Jules Verne moved to this pleasant city in 1856 and proceeded to write his series of Extraordinary Voyages novels including *Around the World in Eighty Days* and *Twenty Thousand Leagues under the Sea*. Briefly occupied by the Prussians following the Franco-Prussian War in 1871, it was again overrun by the German army in 1914. Following the Battle of the First Marne, British and French troops recaptured it. It remained a major British supply base until the German offensives of 1918. The German drive towards Amiens created one of the turning points in the war when Marshal Ferdinand Foch took command of all Allied armies and decided to make a stand in front of the city and north of the river. While the attackers did not capture the city, their aircraft and artillery bombarded the city intensely, destroying several thousand buildings. The Allies went over to the offensive on August 8, driving the exhausted Germans back from the city in what General Erich Ludendorff called the "black day" for the German army.[66]

In 1939 Amiens was a relatively large city, with a well-developed infrastructure and almost 94,000 citizens. It was a vibrant center of trade between Paris, northern France, Normandy, and Great Britain, and it was critical to the movement of resources in the region. Traffic moved along the Somme Canal, the harnessed river that connected the city with the English Channel, and the city was connected by road, rail, and barge with the interior. A few miles to the southeast was the community of Longueau, with about 4,000 inhabitants, with its large rail yard centrally located to facilitate rail traffic in northern France. Glisy airfield lay just east of the rail yard and was an important part of the cross-channel air network. Within the city, two other rail stations served the community. Gare St. Roch handled traffic on the west side of the city and, less than a mile across town, Gare d'Amiens served the eastern side.

Amiens was a clear German objective again in 1940. This time there would be no heroic defense, as General Heinz Guderian's panzers moved too quickly for the overextended French army to recover. The Luftwaffe bombed Amiens on May 12, causing a fire that consumed part of the city. Because of its critical location, it would be attacked and repeatedly strafed over the next few days. On May 20 the 1st Panzer Division swept to its outskirts, forcing an RAF fighter unit, caught on the ground, to scramble into the air under tank fire. Moving into the city, the Germans encountered only British troops from the 12th (Territorial) Division, who had little chance against Lieutenant-Colonel Hermann Balck's veteran tank commanders. Guderian arrived shortly after that to visit the community they were unable to capture in the first war.[67] Amiens found itself a key hub in the Nazi war effort as it became an important center for the Luftwaffe in its air offensive against England, for the construction and deployment of the V-1 and V-2 systems, and for the Atlantic Wall. Almost immediately, Amiens, and especially its rail yard, became a target for Allied bombers, with the first recorded mission against the airfields coming on June 19, 1940.[68]

On August 20, 1942, soon after the first American bombing mission at Rouen, twelve B-17s from the 97th Bomb Group attacked the Longueau rail yards as one of its practice raids, dropping 64,000 pounds of bombs.[69] Image interpreters who reviewed photographs taken during the attack noted, "No bomb bursts observed in the target area, but 4 bombs can be seen bursting near the intersection of five crossroads 1 1/4 miles approx. W.S.W. of the target."[70] The Eighth Air Force returned on March 13, 1943, raiding the rail center with eighty B-17s dropping more than 447,000 pounds of bombs on the complex, killing at least thirty civilians in this attack. Of course, the official report gives no indication of damage to nearby civilian facilities.[71]

For almost a year, the Allies ignored Amiens' rail yards, until they returned on March 2, 1944; this time it was the Ninth Air Force. Three waves of bombers attacked the rail yard in sequence. First, thirty-six medium bombers from the 323rd Bomb Group appeared at 1716 hours, 11,000 feet over Longueau. A pathfinder aircraft led the group and marked the target with flares. As was standard practice, the remainder of the aircraft arrived in two "boxes" of eighteen aircraft each. Each box approached shaped like an arrow, with nine aircraft across, and four deep. Once the bombardier in the lead center aircraft identified the marked target, he began dropping his eight 500-pound bombs. All the other aircraft dropped their loads on that cue, sending 144,000 pounds of bombs hurtling toward the earth. Fifteen minutes later the 391st Bomb Group arrived with another thirty-six B-26 Marauder bombers, again in two groups of eighteen, and dropped its load. Finally, fifteen minutes later, the 387th Bomb Group tried to join the mission with its thirty-six aircraft. This strike did not go well. The group's pathfinder had trouble finding the rail yard through the smoke and cloud cover. Unable to locate the target, the first box's leader circled for a second attempt at attacking the target, but he failed to allow for the high winds and drifted too close to the rail yard to make a good bombing run. The lead bombardier released his bombs early, and the remainder of the eighteen aircraft in his flight did the same. Most of the 72,000 pounds of bombs completely missed the target area. The second box of eighteen aircraft only had time for a ten-second bomb run, but the lead bombardier for this group was right on and found the rail yard in his sights. His bombs, according to the official report, hit the aiming point.[72]

Bomber Command launched 900 aircraft into France late on the evening of May 19, 1944. Rail yards at Boulogne, Orléans, Tours, Le Mans, and Amiens were its principal targets. The attack on Longueau began according to the command's well-practiced tactics. The RAF had visited this city earlier, most recently on March 15 through 17.[73] Approaching the cloud-covered city around 0110 hours, 9 Mosquito light bombers from the 8th Group illuminated the target. Behind them came a stream of 112 Lancaster heavy bombers from the 5th Group, each dropping its 8,000 pounds of bombs on the marked target. The clouds and confusion ensured that the target was no longer visible, and the master bomber ordered the attack stopped after 37 aircraft had dropped their loads. The reconnaissance reports indicated that the attack destroyed the locomotive servicing operation and that 80 percent of the marshaling yard was unusable, but most of the through lines were still in operation, meaning that the trains were still moving through the center.[74]

The sirens began wailing at 0115, and almost immediately the pathfinders' markers illuminated the sky. While some bombs hit the rail yard, many did not and landed short of their target, exploding in the residential areas south of the city center. One of the illumination rounds fell on a house in the residential area (Rue du Bellay) three miles from the rail yard, burning alive three young children. The Vichy propagandists had little trouble exploiting such a tragedy.[75]

The attacks most remembered by the citizens of Amiens were those by the Ninth Air Force, part of Leigh-Mallory's tactical command, on May 27 and 28, 1944. The target in this case was not only the massive rail yard but also the smaller Gare d'Amiens, in the heart of the city. Shortly after lunchtime on Saturday, May 27, forty A-20 Havoc bombers from the 410th Bomb Group struck at the core of the city, aiming at the Gare d'Amiens. The A-20 was an American light bomber, referred to by the British as the "Boston," that carried two thousand pounds of bombs and four machine guns in its nose. The mission got off to an awful start. As the group approached the target, they came under heavy anti-aircraft fire, which shot down the first two aircraft. One of them made it back to the English Channel and the other crashed in the German-held territory. Five other aircraft crews became totally disoriented and headed back to England. Soon another aircraft took fire in an engine and turned back, just reaching the English coast. Of the nineteen aircraft in the first formation, only eleven continued to Amiens, and only two were not damaged. The second group of eighteen continued to the target, with German ground defenders damaging two more.[76] While most raids against facilities in France were easy, this was a notable exception. The target was difficult to hit, and the disorganized formation had little chance of a successful strike. Spooked by the earlier encounters with anti-aircraft fire, the American pilots dropped their bombs in areas not protected by German guns. The result, of course, was destruction in residential areas as bombs scattered across the city. The local paper reported 146 dead and many more civilians wounded.

The following evening, at 2030 hours, two more flights of American bombers arrived over Amiens, this time aiming for the Longueau, led by thirty-six B-26 Marauders from the Ninth Air Force's 391st Bomb Group.

Again the German air defense system was active, and the Americans encountered medium to intense fire. Attacking from 12,000 feet, the first group of six aircraft hit the rail yard, but few bombs from the later flights fell on the target. As was usual, the increased air defense fire affected the subsequent flights. The next two groups dropped their munitions way outside the target area. Fortunately the final group saw what was happening and wisely did not drop their ordnance.[77]

Ten minutes later, thirty-six more medium bombers, this time from the 344th Bomb Group, attempted to hit the rail center. According to one of the trailing crews, the lead bombardier released his bombs too soon. His aircraft was apparently trying to evade the air defense fire, one of the planes in his group had been hit and was going down, and he could not get back into position in time. Most of the trailing aircraft followed his lead. The final group of six aircraft, paying attention to the confusion in front of them, declined to attack. The damage on the ground from this confused mission was extensive as many of the projectiles landed far away from the rail yard and exploded in the nearby homes.[78] This violent attack lasted only ten minutes, but it destroyed the city center the citizens had rebuilt since the previous war.[79]

After the two days of raids, differing interpretations emerged from the Ninth Air Force and the French. Reconnaissance reports issued over the next few days indicated locomotive sheds on the south portion of the yard took some direct hits. A repair shop was out of action, and the western part of the yard was about 80 percent destroyed. The reports also noted that the mission air defense was significant and one of the most intense in France of the war to date, downing two and damaging 60 percent of the aircraft. This expenditure of air defense weapons was an indication of how essential the Longueau rail yard was to the German war effort.[80] The AEAF operations report for May 29 noted that the Amiens rail center's "goods depot was heavily damaged and at least 50 % destroyed. Some damage has been inflicted to the tracks and stock in the sidings, but the through roads have not been affected."[81]

The French, of course, had a different perspective. These attacks killed more than 200 civilians, wounded 250 more, and destroyed more than four thousand homes. The citizens gathered the dead and moved them to a mass grave in Madeleine Cemetery on the northwest portion of the city. Sixty years after the event the memories of these days remained with the survivors. One, Youlande Malgras, remembers her mother crying, "My God! Look at those

Americans! What do they have left to do? They will kill us in our homes!" Her father replied, "It is well they bomb us to deliver us." Shortly after that, he perished in the attack.[82]

The air attacks against Amiens did not, of course, end with the raids on May 27 and 28. Fighter-bombers were in the sky constantly looking for moving German forces. The city and its rail stations suffered more than eighteen identifiable rail attacks in June, July, and August. For example, a week after the Normandy landings, Bomber Command returned on June 12 with more than two hundred heavy bombers, pulverizing the three rail yards and much of the city, one more time. When it was over, more Amiénois were dead and wounded, and thousands of homes and shops were destroyed.[83] Finally, on August 31, tanks from the 29th Armoured (UK) Brigade, 11th Armoured Division, crossed into the city and captured surprised German troops, who were unaware of the pace of the Allied advance following the battle of the Falaise Pocket.[84] As the British secured the city, Amiens' agony began coming to an end, and its rebuilding and recovering was about to begin.

Lille

Lille certainly qualifies as one of the most bombed cities in Europe. Located on the Franco-Belgian border, it was a gateway to France and at the center of historic trade routes. Its location as a business center, especially for textile production dating from the early medieval era, contributed to its becoming a major transportation center. Its significance was not lost on the great nation builder, Louis XIV, who invested lots of energy and treasure for its capture from the Spanish in 1667. His famous engineer, Sébastien de Vauban, spent the next three years constructing one of the largest citadels in Europe to secure the northern boundary of the growing French state. The city's location on the southern end of the Flanders plain provided a sound basis for further challenging the Habsburg domination of the productive lands to the north, now modern Belgium.

Except for the Paris region, the area around Lille had the densest railway system in France. Five main lines into France from Belgium and Germany passed through Lille and the nearby towns of Valenciennes, Tourcoing, and Roubaix. Lille itself had three large marshaling yards: near the industrial complex of Fives to the east, La Délivrance to the west, and La Madeleine to the north. Because of the nearby coal mines, the French constructed the track lines in this region to carry heavier loads, twenty tons per axle rather than the standard sixteen as was common in the remainder of the country. Given the proximity to other rail centers in Brussels, Mons, and Ghent, Lille had the characteristics of a railway tunnel, with massive traffic moving through a narrow corridor. Used heavily by the Germans in both world wars, this concentration of industry, raw materials, and rail made this region an obvious Allied target.[85]

Located four kilometers west of the ancient Vauban citadel, the suburb of Lomme had a population in 1936 of more than 21,000 citizens. The triage yard, called Lille-La Délivrance, contained a large coaling station, locomotive sheds and repair shops, carriage repair facilities, and a large marshaling area. A full moon illuminated Lille on a cloudless night shortly after midnight on April 10, 1944. Approaching from the northwest, 166 Halifaxes, 40 Lancasters, 22 Stirlings and 11 Mosquitoes—239 aircraft in all—approached the city in two waves at 16,000 feet. At 0130 the Mosquitoes began dropping their flares to mark the target. The official report indicated that they marked them accurately, and the bombers were able to see the bomb zone. At 0137, the lead planes began to drop their explosives. Within twenty minutes the crews dropped 3,335 500-pound bombs on the western side of Lille. The next day the after-action report indicated that "good timing and adequate marking led to a well-centered attack which achieved the required density of bombing in the target area." Even this report, however, indicated that the raid had mostly missed the main buildings, destroying only half of four locomotive repair shops and only 10 percent of the main engine shed. Only 49 bombs had hit the target. The post-damage reports confirm the massive damage to the rail yard and its facilities. The British Air Staff's weekly report to Churchill indicated that intelligence sources had determined that the bombers had killed 50 to 120 civilians, with 50 of those being railroad employees. It also noted that the German and French sources had announced that the attack had killed between 500 and 600 civilians. The Axis reports, discounted at the time, were much closer to the truth.[86]

The French perspective, again, was different. April 9 was Easter Sunday, a cherished holiday in a Catholic country celebrating Jesus' resurrection after his crucifixion. Father Lucien Detrez was a priest at the cathedral and observed the raid and its aftermath. Recording his comments soon after the event, he noted that the city was quiet following the Easter Sunday celebrations. It had been a joyous day of celebration and family dinners following the somber period of Lent. No one was expecting an attack. Their first indication of trouble was the roar of explosions around 1245 in the morning. The flares illuminated the machine depot at the rail yard, and they could see the waves of bombers approaching from the southwest. Paralyzed by the speed and violence of the attack, the citizens living next to the rail yard had nowhere to run and could not make it to the local shelters. The charming homes of the railroad workers, constructed with wood, exploded into fire. The attack destroyed all the local utilities, and the district was without water. Seventy years later, a survivor, Michael Jean-Bart, commented, "I remember it. Like it was yesterday. It was then that the house exploded into pieces, the window smashed into pieces. We saw the glows from the bombs, the dust, everything, everything was swept away. For three quarters of an hour. Horror. Horror. Horror. Horror."[87]

Once the bombing stopped, the local citizens worked by the light of the full moon and burning buildings to find their friends and family members. Within the hour, members of the passive defense and Red Cross from all parts of Lille made their way through the ruins to join in the rescue. French and German vehicles moved to provide illumination from their headlights. Nurses and doctors established aid stations to treat the hundreds of wounded rescuers pulled from the wreckage. Long past dawn, the rescue work continued. There were some small victories as rescuers discovered twenty people still alive in a basement at ten in the morning. But the situation was tragic, as they pulled more than five hundred charred corpses from the ruins. Many would never be identified, and others were never located. Detrez praised the rescuers who without any apparent fatigue cleared the rubble and examined shelter and basement entrances and vents. Often encountering little more than shreds of flesh or formless and bloody human remains, they did their best to deliver them to makeshift morgues. There they lay the remains out so that their bereaved families could identify them. The Red Cross and passive defense workers, "with the most utter contempt of danger and fatigue," were the real heroes on that day.[88]

In the small pavilion adjacent to the railway line where she lived, Marcelle Tassart, sixteen and a half, sat close to her mother in one of the rooms on the ground floor where the family gathered during the bombing. None of the rail workers' homes, built in 1921, had a basement, so each family hid the best they could. "We were petrified," she testified. Everybody was crying and praying. Then a bomb blew out the house's windows, and dust was everywhere. Then it was quiet, and everyone was stunned by what had just happened. "Outside, wounded people trapped in their homes call for help."[89]

Twenty-eight bombs hit the Loos prison, south of the rail yard. According to Jean Canoit, who lived in Lambersart to the northeast, "The prisoners, some who were members of the Resistance, were in a panic but could do nothing but cover their heads. The bombs opened four holes in the wall, and German soldiers opened the gates to the prisoners screaming under the influence of a more or less simulated terror. Then the guards and other soldiers try to restore order. When it was over, two hundred and four prisoners got away."[90] Canoit noted that "rescuers, equipped with stretchers, traveled the ravaged streets, such as Dunkerque Avenue where the tram rails were crushed as straws, and tried to avoid the giant craters fifteen to twenty meters wide to remove the rubble, taking advantage of the moonlight and car headlights." Detachments of German soldiers worked alongside the French mobile reserve police. One group discovered "a house collapsed on a family: parents and their five girls, the oldest of thirteen years. Other rescuers found a young couple, dead in each other's arms."[91]

The suburb of Lomme suffered terribly that night as the attack killed approximately 450 civilians and wounded another 620. It destroyed the "Cité des Cheminots" where the rail workers and their families lived. In total the attackers destroyed or damaged more than five thousand homes and buildings outside the rail yard. That same evening, the RAF struck at Villeneuve-Saint-Georges outside of Paris. The next night they repeated the effort against rail yards at Tours, Laon, Tergnier, Aulnoye, and Ghent in Belgium. In two days more than 1,600 heavy bombers attacked these rail centers and the associated towns, killing more than a thousand French and Belgian civilians.[92]

The Eighth Air Force had bombed the industrial complex at Lille Fives in the last three months of 1942. In addition to being a major producer of iron bridges and locomotives, Lille Fives was also a major rail center located on the east side of the city. The factory and rail yard employed more than 8,000 people in the 1920s. Planners estimated that more than 29,000 civilians were at risk and that a bombing could kill as many as 1,460.[93] On the evening of May 10, Bomber Command launched eighty-nine heavy bombers toward the Lille Fives complex. Among the hundreds of 500-pound bombs was at least one 4,000-pound bomb. On this run they planned on testing a targeting procedure called “offset” bombing. The intent was to drop the target markers at one point and then, by entering an adjusted setting into their bombsight, have the crews aim for a different point. The goal was to avoid missing the target because of obscuration or because later bombs would move the markers. The Mosquitos dropped the first flares at 0026 as planned. Unfortunately the plan did not work as the wind on the ground caused smoke to cover the target and caused most of the planes in the first wave to miss the objective zone completely. The master bomber suspended the mission until he could recalculate and remark the target. This recalculation took about twenty minutes, and the mission resumed with a greater effect on the rail yard. This lull, however, allowed Luftwaffe night fighters to arrive on the scene and engage the British raiders, destroying twelve of the attacking aircraft, a high loss rate (13 percent) for a raid over France in May. In return, Bomber Command had cut the tracks and damaged some the key facilities.[94] But it was not a clean strike, as they also destroyed more than 400 homes and severely damaged another 1,600. In Lille and its suburbs, the raid killed 150 civilians and wounded another 124.[95]

Angers

Located near the intersections of the Mayenne, Sarthe, Oudon, and Loire Rivers, Angers is an ancient city with roots dating back to the pre-Roman Celts. Its location has always made it a natural transportation hub. Along with Nantes in the west and Tours in the east, it was one of the principal traffic routes from the south to the invasion area. Its population in 1936 was 87,988, but it may have had as many as 15,000 more as a result of dislocations farther north. A relatively peaceful place in a beautiful river valley, it had avoided the physical destruction so common to northern France during the Great War and the recent German invasion. That changed on May 29, when 118 Lancaster bombers assembled in the British skies before midnight and headed for the city.[96]

Sixty years later, Henri Joubert remembers that until then his community of Angers had not received the intense Allied bombing that nearby cities, such as Saint-Nazaire, Tours, and Lorient had. Day and night he watched the massive fleets of bombers heading across the sky and toward other cities in France, destroying entire neighborhoods and burying families under tons of rubble. A young child, Henri lived close to the train station with his parents. Although many of his friends had moved away from the town center since the Allies began bombing, his family remained. Their peaceful existence changed shortly after midnight on May 29. Eight Mosquito bombers broke the silence by marking the rail yard with flares and incendiary bombs. Accustomed to a night world of darkness because of the blackouts, he was shocked by the intense amount of red light. An experienced railway worker, who had been through these attacks before, yelled that it was time to leave since the bombers were directly behind. He was right; the Lancasters began dropping their 529 tons of bombs on the rail yard and its locomotive works. Henri ran back into the house just as the bombs began to fall, and his mother herded the family under the staircase. Soon all the windows shattered and the house shook in all directions. Henri tried to look outside, but his mother pulled him back just before a piece of metal penetrated the wall against which he was leaning. His brother was screaming, and things looked bad. His mother decided to run for it and leave their disintegrating home and take their chances. They were lucky, as the bombardment was over. Their house was shattered, but they were alive.

His uncle Marcel's family nearby was not as fortunate. Marcel had worked with glass in Lorient earlier in the war and witnessed the constant bombardment of the submarine pens. He was happy to be transferred back to Angers where he, his wife, and five children lived in one of the family's buildings on the rue Jacques-Grannau, a block north of the train station. Unfortunately, bombs demolished the building they and another family took shelter in, and all of them, about fifteen people, were gone. His mother and brother went to identify the bodies.

That day, in addition to the rail yard, Bomber Command destroyed 800 civilian homes and structures, killed more than 254 French civilians and wounded at least 220 others. The official records call it a "good concentrated attack with tracks and rolling stock seriously damaged." Sixty years later, Henri's testimony still reflected his bitterness.[97]

There are many more examples, and each city has its story. While these details are from operations in the north, the Fifteenth Air Force was also at work striking rail centers near the Mediterranean. Its attack against the yards at Saint-Charles and Le Blancard near Marseille on May 27 was especially damaging, killing more than 1,700 civilians and wounding another 2,700.[98]

Across France the lists of civilian deaths and injuries may be extensive or mercifully limited. The damage to individual rail centers may be extensive or practically unnoticeable. Just like the infantry battalions that stormed ashore on the beaches or dropped from the sky, each rail center has a history of combat. Unfortunately, the story of those who endured the power of Allied air power is generally unknown. What we do know is that when American troops raced across France later in July and August, those rail yards were of little help. The official history of the US Army's logistics effort is clear that the destruction of the rail centers was a severe handicap to supporting ground units breaking out of the bridgehead in August. "Destruction (of rail centers and rail tracks) by the Allied air forces in fact threatened to have a more disastrous effect on the Allied logistic capabilities than on the enemy's operations."[99] Repairing the centers and track lines was a problem that absorbed an unanticipated amount of construction resources. In the short term, the destruction was so complete that a makeshift truck supply system, the so-called "Red Ball Express," had to serve in place of railroad cars loaded with petrol and ammunition well into September.[100] We also know that many of those impressive rail depots never recovered and, seventy years later, still show the effects of the destructive power of Allied bombers.

As Eisenhower hoped, the destruction of the rail yards contributed to the delay of enemy reinforcements into the invasion area. How significant this bombing was to Neptune's success is an open question. At the time most Allied leaders believed destroying French rail centers had contributed to keeping German tanks off the invasion beaches. Hitler's hesitancy to transfer forces to Normandy soon after the invasion, however, may have been just as critical. Once the High Command decided to intervene, German units were able to negotiate the damaged rail system reasonably well. The 9th and 10th Panzer Divisions are good examples. Alerted for movement from Poland on June 12, they entered the battle near Caen on June 25. Given the Allied dominance of the air, which made daylight movement difficult, two weeks is not an excessive amount of time to move a division from one theater to another.[101] Could the Allies have achieved the same delay by a more targeted operation against fewer lines? Or could they have employed an array of bombers, fighter-bombers, and Resistance sabotage to achieve a comparable delay without killing more than 16,000 civilians, wounding at least as many, and destroying at least 25,000 buildings?[102] Perhaps Eisenhower's determination to employ the heavy bombers in support of the invasion precluded operations of such finesse. Possibly, given the many problems of equipping and directing the French insurgents on the continent, planners simply ruled out alternate means of disrupting rail traffic. It was not only rail centers, though, but also bridges over the Seine and Loire that experienced the fury of the Allied air forces.

CHAPTER NINE

THE BRIDGES

In April 1944 twenty-one-year-old Genevieve Cotty was living with her mother in a small apartment on the Avenue du Miroir in the town of Athis-Mons, south of Paris. Her father had passed away before the war and her brother had perished during the Battle of France in June 1940. Located where the small Orge River flowed into the Seine, the town occupied a strategic location south of Orly Airport and east of the large rail center at Juvisy. It was also a site of a major rail bridge across the Seine. It was a natural target for Allied bombers, and everyone knew it. During the nightly alerts, Genevieve and her mom had varied their routine between hiding in their home and moving to a shelter in a nearby park, which could accommodate about fifty people. As a young woman in a busy community, she was able to obtain a job with the town's commissioner of police. One of her colleagues, the public works contractor, had built a shelter in his garden and invited Genevieve and her mother to join him during the next alert. As she was leaving work on the evening of April 18, her boss pulled her aside. While she did not realize it at the time, he was one of the region's Resistance leaders, and he had received word that the area would be a target that evening. He bluntly told her, "If there is an alert tonight, do not stay home, go to a shelter." Shaken, she returned home and warned her mother. After dinner, they prepared a bag with things they could carry: money, identity papers, and some clothing. They decided to run to her colleague's shelter when the alert sounded, which it did at around 2300 hours. Neither of the women had completely undressed, so they were quickly up and heading toward the door, her mother remembering to shut off the gas before they departed. Just as they arrived in their neighbor's yard, the bombs started falling, and they got undercover and joined some friends cowering under the explosions.

Juvisy firefighter plaque commemorating those firefighters who perished suppressing the fires caused by the bombardment of April 18, 1944. *Photograph by author*

That evening Bomber Command sent 202 Lancaster heavy bombers and several Mosquito light bombers to destroy the rail yard and the large iron rail bridge across the Seine that intelligence analysts had determined was an important route for German rail traffic.[1] When the bombing was over, she emerged to a wasteland of destruction. Most of the houses were gone or burning, as was her church. Her apartment was gone, and they had nothing left. The bombs had destroyed the shelter in the nearby park, killing everyone inside. Firefighters, local officials, and members of the community's passive defense organization were immediately out on the smoldering streets looking for survivors. Like terrorists, Bomber Command had dropped some of their munitions with delayed-action fuses, and the bombs continued to explode well into the early morning. They moved away from the explosions and ran into her boss, who was relieved that she had survived but who scolded her for not reporting immediately for work after she had emerged from the shelter, as was the standard procedure for city employees. Shortly after that, she learned that two of her coworkers were dead. Apparently the police department's secretary and a guard had been searching for Genevieve when a delayed explosion killed them both near her home. The secretary's story was especially moving because he had previously fled Alsace with his family, determined not to live under German domination.

More than sixty years later, with the passage of time, Genevieve realized how horrible it was for her mother, who had lost everything: her husband, her son, and all of her possessions. Only Genevieve remained to remind her of her once comfortable life. She never forgot the horror of the evening. "The bombing lasted for an hour, in waves. Never, never shall I forget that infernal noise of planes, bombs, explosions. . . . Everyone was praying in the shelter. . . . And yet, there were surely among us unbelievers. But you have to have experienced it to understand. Since that day, I cannot hear a siren, whether for tests, on TV, in a movie or documentary. I saw this terrible moment, and I still have this noise in my ears."[2] Bomber Command believed this raid was an outstanding success. In its report to Prime Minister Churchill in the middle of May, the AEAF Air Staff report estimated that the attack killed about 960 French civilians, which was less than they had anticipated.[3] Surprisingly, the revised figures are lower; French authorities believed the bombing killed 125 civilians in Juvisy and 230 in Genevieve's hometown of Athis-Mons.[4]

The Athis-Mons raid reflects another, lesser-known aspect of the Transportation Plan, the destruction of the main bridges over rivers leading into the anticipated battle area. Few nations have had so much of their military history defined by rivers as France. For the Romans, the Rhine was the most important defensible barrier between Gaul and the barbarian German tribes to the north. Descendants of the invading tribes, especially the Franks, established their armed camps along the major rivers, especially the Seine, the Loire, and the Rhône. The castles that emerged on these prominent locations became military objectives throughout the Middle Ages and the early modern era. It was the desire to regain France's natural boundaries, especially along the Rhine, that motivated some of King Louis XIV's wars. During the French Revolution some armies took the name of a prominent river, such as the Armée de Sambre-et-Meuse, or Armée de Moselle. Rivers often defined the Great War's battlefields. The First and Second Battles of the Marne, the Battle of the Somme, the Aisne-Marne Offensive, and the Meuse-Argonne Offensive are just some of the most prominent. Finally, it was the German army's crossing of the Meuse, and the French army's inability to defend it, that led within weeks to France's defeat in 1940. By 1944 hundreds of bridges crossed France's rich river infrastructure. Some were ancient, such as the sturdy stone bridge at Pontaubault, probably constructed by Anne of Brittany around 1500. Many others were of a more recent vintage, less durable, metal bridges intended to carry railway traffic. Those that lay on the route of German reinforcements were natural targets and, from the Allied planner's perspective, needed to be destroyed.

Between April 19 and May 29, Allied air forces attacked the Athis-Mons rail bridge five times with heavy bombers, medium bombers, and fighter-bombers, reflecting its importance in Eisenhower's operational design. Historians ignore the details of the bridge operation because of the target's relationship to a more prominent bombing objective, in this case the large rail yard at Juvisy, which became the focus of much poststrike analysis and discussion. In other instances the bridge became part of a larger target group, such as the chokepoints this book discusses later. The destruction of France's bridges, especially those over the Seine and the Loire and those near Paris, was part of Operation Neptune from the beginning. Like the air bombardment of rail, the offensive against bridges had its origins in "COSSAC Staff Study 6, Delay of Enemy Reserves" (December 30, 1943). Morgan's staff believed that "the most effective method of blocking rail movement is to destroy bridges, whether across rivers or roads." For the mission of disrupting German rail traffic, they were fourth in priority, behind destroying railway centers, cutting tracks, and destroying railheads. The staff also agreed that destroying road bridges was critical in slowing German movement. The planners cautioned that in both cases this bombing, if it were to achieve its goals, would require a large amount of ordnance and would waste much of it.[5] The final edition of the staff study, published several days later on January 4, identified some priorities but was not specific concerning bridge targets.[6]

The Plan

While the attacks on the rail centers were primarily the concern of Tedder, Leigh-Mallory, Spaatz, and Harris, destroying the bridges was most important for Montgomery and his army commanders: lieutenant generals Harry Crerar (Canadian army), Miles Dempsey (British army), and Omar Bradley (US Army). The planners considered bridge dropping to be tactical missions, while attacks on rail centers were strategic tasks. In modern military parlance, the bombing of most of these bridges were operational functions, as they affected the success of the campaign as a whole and were well beyond the ability of any of the army commanders to direct or control. The planners identified three lines of interdiction: One moved down the Seine toward Paris, then south toward the Loire, and along the river west to Nantes. The second line of interdiction was the collection of bridges east of Paris and north to the Pas-de-Calais. The Allies never attacked the third line of bridge interdiction, which ran across Belgium and then along the Meuse, in any systematic manner.[7]

This section examines the first line of interdiction, which also consisted of three groups of bridges. The first seven bridges stretched along the Seine between Rouen in the west and Mantes-Gassicourt in the east, and they carried traffic between Normandy and the Pas-de-Calais. This sector received most of the pre-invasion bombardment, which destroyed all these bridges, at least temporarily, before D-Day. The planners identified ten bridges in a second section, the so-called Paris-Orleans gap between the Seine and Loire, through which rail lines ran from Paris to either the Neptune or Fortitude areas. This high-speed rail avenue of approach allowed for the movement of reinforcements from the Frankfurt-Mannheim, Germany, region. The third section was the ten bridges on the Loire from Blois to the sea, which allowed for the passage of German units from southern France and Italy into the Normandy region. Major bridges near Nantes, Saumur, and Tours were essential for German operations and communications. The Allies were always concerned about security, so the bombing of targets of bridges and rail junctions along the Seine and in the Paris-Orleans Gap would commence on D-20, or around May 16. The planners did not believe these raids, along with others in the Pas-de-Calais, would disclose Neptune's location to the Germans. After the landings most of the aircraft from the Second and Ninth Tactical Air Forces would operate in support of the invasion forces, while the heavy bombers attacked the bridges on the Loire and narrow routes at key locations on the German route to Normandy. Toward the end of May, planners at the Twenty-First Army Group became nervous about the movement of enemy reinforcements from the south and directed the AEAF to take out the rail bridges over the Loire before D-Day. Appendix C lists the bridges that the various air forces actually attacked between May 15 and June 8. As in the case of the rail centers, some of the bridges are in Belgium, especially across the Meuse River.[8]

As in all operations, Leigh-Mallory faced problems as his planners addressed how to attack these bridges. Zuckerman, Tedder's advisor, did not believe it was viable to use bombers in this role: too many bombs for one small target. As discussed in the previous chapter, Harris and Spaatz were not supporters of using bombers to go after French bridges or anything that took their aircraft away from their primary mission of bombing Germany. While the bombers could do the job, they were easily the least effective means of destroying a precise target such as a bridge. Brereton's Ninth Air Force demonstrated how it could be done on May 7, when eight Thunderbolts from the 365th Fighter Group attacked the bridge at Vernon, between Paris and Rouen. It was a brilliant strike, and the bridge was in the water with no collateral damage. This raid, however, was carried out not by a standard fighter group but by one specially trained for the mission.[9] In reality, the Ninth had not trained its fighter units to conduct such missions. For the previous few months their primary role had been flying escort for the Eighth Air Force's bombers in demanding missions over Germany. They were an integral part of the raids resulting in "Big Week" at the end of February, which destroyed much of the Luftwaffe's fighter strength. These missions would do much to ensure that the sky over the invasion beaches was free from enemy interference, but the trade-off was a lack of training for ground support. While these aircraft could attack targets at lower altitudes, ostensibly with greater accuracy than large and medium bombers, this role was quite challenging and different from air-to-air combat. At a low level, smoke and ground-based anti-aircraft guns made finding and hitting the target tough.[10] Therefore, all kinds of aircraft would participate in the bombing of French bridges: heavy bombers, medium bombers, fighter-bombers, and even air-to-air fighters.

Rouen: Red Week

A classic example of the bridge attacks that spring took place at Rouen. As mentioned earlier in this book, the Allies had bombed the nearby rail center at Sotteville several times during the war. From a bridge perspective, the city had two major road bridges that crossed the Seine at this point: the Pont Jeanne d'Arc on the west and the Pont Boieldieu to the east. It also had a rail bridge, the Viaduc d'Eauplet, also called the Pont-aux-Anglais, on the Paris-Le Havre line. The French army had destroyed another bridge, the Pont Pierre-Corneille, crossing the river at the Ile Lacroix, on June 9, 1940, when defending against the German army.[11] In 1944 these bridges were the westernmost on the river between Paris and the coast and the most direct route between Boulogne and Caen.[12] On May 24 Leigh-Mallory directed his air units to begin destroying the river bridges along the Seine and Loire rivers. For Rouen the priority was the Viaduc d'Eauplet, the iron bridge on the east side of the city that crosses the Seine and links Paris with the region's rail stations. The two road bridges were secondary targets since they would require bombs heavier than those available to the smaller aircraft.

The first notable raid was at midday on Thursday, May 25, when thirty-four P-47 Thunderbolt fighter-bombers from the 405th Fighter Group, flying a raid down the Seine River, attacked the city's bridges. The pilots' poor training was evident as the local gendarme station recorded that only one 500-pound bomb struck a bridge while others went wide of the target, hitting the rail station and some other buildings and killing at least three civilians. The Germans quickly repaired all the damage. German air defense guns destroyed one of the American fighter-bombers and captured the American flyer. The American fighters killed two German soldiers. Gontran Pailhès, a journalist living in Rouen who maintained a diary throughout the occupation, noted that these attacks were not effective. One of its subordinate units got lost and bombed the wrong bridge further east.[13]

The Ninth Air Force's attack against Rouen's bridges and transportation complex continued on May 27. At 1430 hours, twenty-nine P-47 Thunderbolts from the 373rd Fighter Group dive-bombed the Viaduc d'Eauplet.[14] When the alert sounded, the train from Paris was on the inside of a tunnel just north of the rail bridge. Feeling safe, the engineer decided to halt the train and wait until the air raid sirens stopped wailing. When he thought it was

Bombing of Rouen bridges, May 1944. Note burning fires on north side of river (bottom of image).
NARA RG 342 US Air Force Photo Collection

all clear, he pulled the throttle back and the train moved forward across the bridge. At precisely that moment, the Thunderbolts dove from the sky and began dropping their 500-pound bombs. Hidden from the pilot's view was the effect of their attack. One of the passenger cars received a direct hit from bombs and machine guns and burst into flames. Forty-eight travelers were immediately, in the words of local observers, "carbonized" and another thirty were wounded and burned. The bombing dislocated the rail tracks but did not destroy the bridge. Other bombs missed the area completely and fell in the suburb of Bon Secours, 1,500 meters southeast.[15] At 2100 hours, the same fighter group returned and repeated the assault and attacked the still-burning bridge, still covered with workers from the passive defense agency working to recover bodies and wounded. Cumulatively, these aircraft dropped approximately forty-three 1,000-pound bombs on and around the bridge sites.[16]

On Pentecost Sunday, May 28, the dive-bombing continued in the late afternoon. On the ground, Pailhès thought this group were Royal Air Force Mosquito bombers and was impressed how they followed each other into their precise dives. The attackers were, however, American P-47 Thunderbolts from the Ninth Air Force. These fifty-one aircraft from the 48th Fighter Group proceeded to attack the bridges, with forty-six 1,000-pound bombs and another twenty 500-pound bombs. This attack seriously damaged the viaduct, and one of its spans tumbled into the river.[17] With this mission, the Ninth Fighter Command had accomplished its task of cutting the rail line across the Seine at Rouen.[18]

Rouen commemorates May 30, 1944, as the beginning of La Semaine Rouge, or Red Week, an event remembered far more than the invasion a week later. Shortly after 1040 hours, UK time, Capt. (Bert) Hale pulled back the throttle on his B-26 Marauder, number K9 S and headed down the runway at Stansted, north of London. Soon thirty-seven other aircraft formed up into two groups and headed toward the English Channel. Crossing over the French coast south of Fécamp, they headed toward the village of Quittebeuf, northwest of Évreux, and then turned to the northeast. Near Pont-de-l'Arche they turned left and headed for Rouen. At 1115, Central European Time, the 344th Bomb Group was over the city at 11,000 feet. They flew in two groups, called boxes, carrying a total load of 143,000 pounds of explosives. Each box had three flights, arranged in an inverted V, of six aircraft each. The first six aircraft dropped their bombs near the bridge, damaging it. The remainder of the bombers missed their target, and according to the official report, many bombs fell on residential property.[19]

Fifteen minutes later, another thirty-five B-26 bombers, this time from the 322nd Bombardment Group, with Capt. A. W. Bouquet in the lead aircraft of the first box, began their attack from 11,500 feet. This time, the targets were the two road bridges, and they let loose their 134,000 pounds of bombs on the undamaged structures. The crews could see smoke in the city coming from the previous attack and light anti-aircraft guns shooting back. The smoke obscured the target for many of the bombers. Out of the sixty-seven 2,000-pound bombs, perhaps four may have hit either of the targets. Some bombs hit the water between the bridges while many other bombs, by the pilots' admission, landed in residential areas west and south of the bridges as well as the train station to the north.[20] On the ground, Pailhès believed that dive-bombers conducted these first two attacks rather than the B-26 Marauder bombers.[21] None of these bombers broke formation, however, and all attacked in a prescribed manner.

Finally, fifteen minutes later, the third flight of B-26s, this time from the 394th Bomber Group, arrived above the city. By now smoke filled the sky and identifying targets was difficult. The bombers attacked the road bridges and the port area to the west, but they were not accurate, as bombs hit the nearby residential areas and structures in the city along the river's edge. Some of the bombs hit nine hundred yards south of the bridges, causing fires in the residential and industrial areas, while other bombs were so far off target the target analysts could not find them.[22] Pailhès believed these bombers were B-17 Flying Fortresses flying at high altitude, but they were actually the two-engine Marauders, flying at 12,000 feet above the city. The poststrike intelligence report indicated that both of the road bridges were unserviceable but not beyond repair. The official Allied press release cited the heavy anti-aircraft fire near the bridges and the accuracy of the bombing. The report cited one bombardier as saying, "Our first box of bombs hit one of the bridges and the others I saw struck close enough to be called good bombing." Neither the intelligence report nor the press release made any comment concerning damage to the city.[23]

With the bombers gone, the citizens began to assess the damage. The intensity of the attack, greater in some accounts than the Bomber Command attack on April 19, caused some observers again to believe this was the work of Eighth Air Force B-17 Flying Fortresses. But no, it was only the medium bombers from the Ninth Air Force.[24] Even though they flew much lower than the heavy bombers, they were just as inaccurate. The Palais des Consuls, designed by the famous architect Jean-François Blondel and finished in 1734, was gone, as was the historic Bourse, or the stock market. The customs house, designed by the renowned architect Charles Isabelle and completed in 1836, was almost entirely destroyed. At the entrance, the bombers damaged a beautiful bas-relief by sculptor Nicolas Coustou dating to 1726. By the end of the day, the casualties were adding up, though there was not yet an accurate count.[25] That night fire broke out across many of the nearby residential areas. Citizens scurried to move their belongings out into the public squares to protect them from the blaze and water the fire crews would dump on the blaze. Early the next morning a heavy rain began to fall, destroying the treasures the residents had tried to save.[26]

All night the fires in Rouen's center burned. The next morning, May 31, while firefighting and rescue efforts continued throughout the city, the passive defense members watched the horizon. Shortly after 1209 hours, the watch officer's log noted that the sky was quiet.[27] Above the city, at almost that exact moment, forty-one B-26 Marauder medium bombers from the 394th Bombing Group, which had attacked the day before, approached from the southeast. The observation from the air was good, with a visibility of eight to ten miles. No German aircraft took off to intercept the attackers, and antiaircraft fire was noisy but inaccurate. From an altitude of 9,500 to 12,800 feet, approximately two miles (3.2 kilometers) above the city, the bombardiers began dropping their sixty-eight 2,000-pound bombs. The bomber crews reported "excellent results."[28]

Fifteen minutes later, the 397th Bomb Group appeared over the burning city. Lt. Col. Frank L. Wood was the senior officer on this mission, but lieutenants commanded most of the forty B-26 Marauders. Altogether these aircraft carried about 240 American airmen. The crews from the first two flights of six bombers each reported hitting and damaging the south side of Pont Boieldieu. The other crews, however, admitted that they probably missed the target. The third group's munitions landed nowhere near the bridges and destroyed buildings on the west end of Ile Lacroix. The next flight reported excellent results but attributed this to hitting buildings in the city on the north side of the river, in the location of the stock exchange and the Performance Theater (Théatre des Arts). The fifth group missed Rouen entirely and dropped its 2,000-pound bombs in an open field. The last group probably did the most damage as it hit the city 6,000 feet (1.8 kilometers) north of the bridge, in what the crews believed to be an industrial area.[29] Bombing through smoke, from two miles in the sky, how precise can a crew be?

The 397th Group had just departed Rouen when the 386th Bombardment Group appeared overhead. By now fire from the anti-aircraft batteries was becoming more intense, and the bridges, with smoke blowing across them from the fires north of the river, were difficult to locate. The flight leaders reported the results as "fair," but it is hard to determine the basis of this assessment. The first flight missed the bridge and hit the area near the Halle aux Toiles, or cloth market, part of the port structure begun by Louis IX in 1256. The second flight of six got lost, but the third followed the first into bombing the north side of the bridge, as did the fourth. The next group steered to the west of the smoke and hit the city in the Bourse area. The final six aircraft went a little farther and bombed the area near the Vieux-Marché. None of the thirty-six aircraft had dropped a bomb on the target; all scattered their 106,000 pounds of bombs in the city.[30]

Now, at 1300 hours, the last group of B-26 bombers from the 322nd Bombardment Group joined the attack. By now the riverfront was ablaze and the wind, blowing from the northwest to southeast, had covered the bridges with smoke. These thirty-six aircraft, unable to see the actual aiming point, scattered their ordnance across the city. According to the official report, the bombs fell in all directions. As usual, the squadron organized itself into two groups of three flights each. The first flight hit 1,300 feet north of the bridges, the second 750 feet east, and the third flight of six bombed the city 1,700 feet to the northwest. The second group did no better, with the fourth flight hitting buildings 1,700 feet to the southwest, the fifth scattering its bombs from 1,000 feet southeast of the target to 1,000 feet north, and the last dropping most of its thirty-six 2,000-pound bombs 1,800 feet south-southeast of the target. The navigator from this group did observe one aircraft drop a bomb 1,800 feet north of the bridge. The medium bombers were supposed to be more precise than the larger B-24s and B-17s. When attacking from these high altitudes, though, with the target obscured by smoke and light from the anti-aircraft fire, they were both inaccurate and ineffective.[31]

The aircraft departed after fifteen minutes. One hundred fifty-four American medium bombers, dropping 253 2,000-pound bombs, had been able to hit the two bridges only a few times. Both bridges were damaged but not destroyed. Among other buildings, the attackers wiped out the Eden Cinéma and the impressive sixteenth-century church, Saint-Vincent, containing the finest stained-glass windows in Rouen. Authorities discovered more than fifty people dead in the shelter near the Catherine Graindor School.[32] The customs house and much of the area near the bridges were in flames. At the Crédit Lyonnais, a bank near the river, a bomb penetrated a shelter and rescuers discovered more than a dozen bodies of employees and customers in the wreckage. The Vieux-Marché (Old Market), where the English had executed Joan of Arc in 1431, was in shambles with most buildings either burning or severely damaged. That was the scene in much of the old city. More than forty fire units from Rouen and the suburbs spent the afternoon and evening fighting fires, trying to save the city's center.[33]

The next morning, June 1, the city's center still burned. The AEAF daily event log noted that the day before, "181 medium bombers, escorted by 120 fighters, bombed road bridges in the PARIS-ROUEN area, dropping 319 tons with good results."[34] Other than two Lancasters, which dropped mines in the Rouen harbor area, the Anglo-Americans did not target the city's bridges on Thursday.[35] Nevertheless, at 0940 hours the police sounded the air raid alert. Panic ensued as citizens scurried around seeking shelter. But the bombers did not come, and the city called "all clear." That afternoon around 1530 hours, the authorities called another alert, this time without the siren, and the nervous inhabitants once again rushed to their shelters. At 1730 the alarms went off yet again, and people rushed to cover. Again the bombers did not come. Suddenly the twelfth-century Cathédrale Notre-Dame burst into flames. Most evidence indicates that the heat of nearby fires set off an unexploded bomb. The roof on the front tower (Saint-Romain) went up in flames, which spread through the entirety of the building, full of ancient treasures. All night the citizens, helped by German soldiers, fought to save the cathedral.[36]

The fire fighting continued in the afternoon. When the fire was out, the cathedral was full of holes and missing its belfry, but it was still standing.[37] It was a small victory. The bombers damaged the bridge but also managed to destroy Rue des Charettes, its "cafes, taverns, bars, and brothels" so familiar to Flaubert,[38] and the Tour Saint-André, a relic of a fifteenth-century church, and the fountain of Joan of Arc at Place de la Purcelle.[39]

Allied bombing across France became more intensive as the projected date of the invasion, June 5, approached. For the bridges across the Seine River, the Ninth Air Force's task was to finish off any bridges that were still standing, such as Rouen's rail bridge. The best way to accomplish this, according to the planners, was to use fighter-bombers to deliver their ordnance directly on the target. That evening, thirty P-51 Mustang fighters from the 363rd Fighter Group attacked the Viaduc d'Eauplet, dropping twenty-nine 500-pound bombs with the intent of keeping the rail line closed.[40] The reconnaissance mission that evening reported that the attacks had cut the road bridge to the east (Pont Boieldieu), and its approaches were severely damaged. The western bridge (Pont Jeanne D'Arc) had suffered only minor damage. The railroad bridge remained cut and unusable. The report's accounting of the attack's effects on the city was brutally honest: "Gare d'Orleans demolished and wide areas surrounding devastated."[41]

On Saturday morning, June 3, the American aircraft returned. Fifty-four P-47 Thunderbolt fighter-bombers from the 366th Fighter Group attacked the highway bridges with sixty-nine 1,000-pound bombs. Their reports indicated that their results were "excellent." Several hours later, however, a reconnaissance aircraft took pictures of Rouen and its bridges. Its report noted that "No new damage to either bridge since 2 June." And the western bridge was impaired but "partially serviceable."[42] By contrast there can be no question as to what happened as bombs hit and severely damaged the sixteenth-century Gothic Église Saint-Maclou. From the citizen's perspective, the Allied pilots were seeking to destroy each of their ancient places.[43] The bombs also ripped through Boulevard des Belges, a shopping district on the west side of the city, destroying the central post office.[44] The next day, June 4, Allied forces began moving out of their ports and into staging areas in preparation for the landing the next day. Although the weather forecast would delay the invasion by one day, many of the planned air missions went ahead as scheduled.[45] For Rouen this meant another mission to ensure that the Germans would be unable to use the road bridges across the Seine. The last thing the Allied planners wanted was the movement of enemy reinforcements from the north side of the river into the battle zone. At 1600 hours forty-six P-47 Thunderbolts from the 50th Fighter Group attacked the remains of the road bridges with eighty-three 1,000-pound bombs. The pilots, as usual, reported the results as "good."[46] Aerial reconnaissance the next day, however, noted that there was no change over the previous few days and the eastern bridge was still usable.[47] The long Red Week had finally ended. Nine days worth of constant bombardment and the progressive destruction of their *patrimoine* had scarred the city and its citizens. Two of the three bridges were now in the river and all, for the time being, were useless. As in other cities along the Seine, the Ninth Air Force had done its job of slowing the movement of German reinforcements.

There is no agreement among officials and historians as to the civilian casualty list for Red Week. Bomber Command had already destroyed much of the targeted area, so most inhabitants were living in other parts of the city. Nevertheless, between 160 and 400 residents of Rouen perished in the week's bombardment, and countless hundreds more were wounded. As the Allies landed on the Normandy beaches to the west, the air attacks shifted to preventing German reinforcements from reaching the coast.[48] For Rouen's civilians, the war did not end on June 6. For more than two months, the city continued to see both the movement of German forces to the front and the continuation of attacks by fighter-bombers. Finally, in late July, the Allies emerged from their enclave on the Norman coast. In mid-August the Germans began to withdraw across the Seine. Thousands of trucks, tanks, and other vehicles converged on the destroyed bridge sites and were ferried across the river. The retreating Germans piled up unusable and less essential equipment on the riverbank and left it behind. The Wehrmacht continued to defend the crossing sites, and its 559th Grenadier Regiment fought a sharp battle with the Canadian 2nd Infantry Division just west of the city at the Forêt de La Londe. But the 3rd and 4th Canadian Divisions crossed the Seine near Elbeuf and enveloped Rouen from the east. After destroying the train station on August 30, the Germans departed, and the Canadians moved into the city, thus ending Rouen's long nightmare.

Mantes-Gassicourt

A second example of the bridge-bombing operation is Mantes-Gassicourt, renamed Mantes-la-Jolie after the war. Located on the Seine approximately halfway between Rouen and Paris, it occupied an important intersection for both north-south and east-west traffic. Two road and two rail bridges connected it with the town of Limay on the north side of the river.[49] As in the case of many of these bridge locations, such as Athis-Mons, a large rail center was nearby to handle the sorting and rearranging of railcars. During the 1940 invasion, German aircraft bombed the city and killed approximately thirty-eight civilians. The main road along the Seine, Route Nationale 13, was the most direct way to travel between Paris and Caen. When going between his headquarters at La Roche Guyon and Paris, Rommel could cross the Mantes bridge to catch the main road. That spring, the Allies began attacking the rail line, with the first attack on April 20. Gaston Marin, who lived in the city during the war, captured the details of the spring bombing in his article published in a local journal in 1962.[50]

Between that first mission and May 6, most of the raids were relatively accurate strikes. Waves of fighter-bombers attacked the rail yard and created considerable damage around the facility, with only a handful of civilians killed or wounded. The nature of these attacks changed on Sunday morning, May 7, when Bomber Command struck the city with 77 Halifaxes, 64 Lancasters, and 8 Mosquitoes, 149 aircraft in all, primarily from the 4th Group. The Mosquitoes arrived at 0200 and began marking the targets. Then came the steady stream of heavy bombers, dropping 610 tons of bombs on the once-sleeping city. The raid caught the citizens by surprise and, with little time to run to a shelter, most hid in their homes the best they could. For twenty minutes the bombing continued, the explosions following one another without interruption as the bombers streamed over the target. No night interceptors rose to meet them, as they would have in Germany, and little anti-aircraft fire interfered with this mechanical process. As was the case with most raids by these kinds of aircraft, few bombs hit the target, with most exploding among homes and fields far from the target. In this case, they hit the small town of Dennemont, more than two miles from the rail yard, killing fourteen civilians and destroying its historic old mill.[51]

In the morning Mantes' citizens surveyed the results. They discovered that more than 128 buildings in the small town, including the historic city hall, were gone, and another 260 other were partially destroyed and uninhabitable. Rescuers and citizens combed the streets looking for survivors and searched basements for those buried under the rubble. The final accounting showed that this attack had killed forty Mantais in addition to about twenty victims from outside the city.[52]

Rouen after May and June bombardments. *Archives Départmentals de la Seine-Maritime*

With Bomber Command's destruction of the rail depot, the US Ninth Air Force began concentrating on the rail and road bridges connecting the city with the north river bank. On May 10 the town's citizens were holding the funeral for the victims of the British bombing when the alert sounded. The people stayed put and continued to mourn and remember their families and friends. Then American fighters arrived and began raking the bridges with machine-gun fire and 500-pound bombs, and the citizens stayed in their benches. The church organ and survivors' voices competed with the racket of explosions and the shattering of windows, but the residents remained. The *préfect*, who was also present at this event, invited the citizens to go to the shelters while the public officials and workers continued their duty. The people remained in the church, and for more than an hour they continued to honor their dead. Meanwhile, four citizens in Limay, across the river, perished in this raid.[53]

Most bridge raids consisted of twenty to thirty fighter-bombers, primarily P-47 Thunderbolts, doing relatively little collateral damage but not destroying the bridges. On May 27 seventy B-26 Marauder medium bombers hit the bridge, creating some damage but no casualties. The next day, the bombardment continued as sixty-eight medium bombers returned in the early afternoon and attacked the bridges again. While some bombs landed on the target, most fell among the nearby homes and shops. That evening another thirty-six Marauders returned to continue the assault, but they missed their target. When it was over, five more civilians had perished in the Air Force's vain attempt to drop two generally undefended bridges into the river.[54]

Monday, May 29, was quiet as the community continued to pick up the pieces from the month's damaging attacks. The AEAF reconnaissance reports clearly indicated that the attacks had severely damaged the rail bridges, with the western span in the water and the other apparently not useable. Certainly there was no need to attack them again.[55] But they did. A little after 1130 hours the next day, thirty-five B-26 Marauders from the 386th Bomb Group arrived at the town and began dropping sixty-nine 2,000-pound bombs. As was standard practice, the group attacked in two "boxes," each made up of three flights of generally six aircraft each. At least one aircraft in each flight had cameras to record the effectiveness of the attack. The first flight's bombs hit the bridge, and the photographs indicated that the center span was collapsing. The bombs from the second flight missed the target completely and, according to the mission summary, "Bursts occurred on the river's edge and in a built-up area 3100 feet north of the desired M.P.I. [main point of impact]."[56]

The successive waves reportedly dropped their munitions near the aiming point and "possibly" hitting the bridge. An hour later, thirty-eight bombers from the 391st Bomb Group attacked the same target. Again, attacking in two groups of three waves each, the first six bombers missed the mark completely, dropping their 2,000-pound bombs 1,200 feet west of the bridges, again in the city area. The last two waves from the second group were not sure where their projectiles landed. The bombardiers in both cases reported hitting the bridge, but these visual reports were notoriously undependable. At 1300 hours bombers from the 397th Group attacked the smoke-obscured targets. To make matters worse, they were lost and were searching for the bridge at Meulan, fifteen miles east of Mantes. Seeing the smoke, they decided to drop twenty-four 2,000-pound bombs on this bridge instead. The reports from these three flights indicate that the first two missed their targets completely. Cumulatively these aircraft expended a total of 161 bombs and may have hit the two bridges six or seven times. By any measure, this was an unimpressive display of bombing proficiency.[57]

From the French perspective, once the siren went off everyone headed for his or her shelters, hoping there would be no further attacks. Little did the citizens realize that this was industrial war and once the planners issued the air tasking order, the raids would continue even if the target was no longer there. Those on the ground, who could observe the attacks, watched in horror as aircraft missed the intended objective completely and struck at the heart of the old town. Once the attacking stopped, the town's inhabitants began emerging from the protection of the shelters just as the lost 397th Group appeared and dropped its bombs, missing the bridges completely. When it was over, their picturesque old city was in ruins. The Hôtel de Ville became the center of the destruction. Most buildings in the town center had old underground rooms, often used for storage or as wine cellars, which provided some protection from the bombing effects. But these apparently secure structures also became graves, as rescuers could not remove the rubble in time to prevent the inhabitants from suffocating. Conversely, shallow cellars provided an illusion of safety, such as when a bomb had a direct hit on a winery's basement near the town hall, killing seven people, including a teacher and a city councilor.[58]

In Limay across the river, the bombers destroyed much of the town near the river, killing twenty-five civilians. Among the dead were six children aged three through twelve years old, killed while taking shelter with their mother and grandmother. The attackers hit the town's main church, and the bombs pulverized its cemetery, disinterring human remains from the graves and spreading them around the area. Most tragic that day was the destruction of the local prison, only a hundred meters from the old bridge. Thanks to broadcasts from London, everyone knew that anything within five hundred meters of a bridge was in danger, yet the local authorities packed the facility mostly with people guilty of minor offenses. In addition to the guards and administrators, the building held 80 detainees from Mantes and another 125 from nearby Poissy. The Allies had damaged both of these facilities in previous strikes, and the authorities still were clearing the rubble. It was a catastrophe waiting to happen as three or four bombs hit the building and destroyed it and the weakly constructed shelters. As Gaston Marin, who provides us the details of this attack, noted, at least 200 people perished in this instance. Many of the bodies were unidentifiable because they were incomplete. For hours rescuers heard calls for help and groans from those severely wounded but trapped under the rubble. Without equipment to move the heavy timber and boulders, there was often little they could do. "For a few hours at the jail, we heard calls, groans, then gradually there was silence, the heavy silence of death."[59]

When the citizens left their shelters, they were shocked by the destruction. The air was thick with dust and smoke and the smell of exploded bombs. The city was in turmoil as people ran through the damaged streets of both Mantes and Limay looking for their family members. Rescuers raced against the clock, without heavy machinery, to move the piles of stone that blocked access to those in shelters below. The destruction of this town, generally not reported in the historical literature, was significant. For example gone was the ancient bridge, too small to carry modern traffic, so beautifully captured on canvas by the painter Jean-Baptiste-Camille Corot in 1870. The city hall, reconstructed in 1838, was a pile of ruins, and its old bell lay in the street. The old shops and buildings in the town square that made up life in traditional French villages along the river were in ruin. A beautiful Renaissance-era fountain was gone forever, as were many ancient structures dating back to the sixteenth century. The church, Our Lady of Mantes (Collégiale Notre-Dame de Mantes), built between 1155 and 1350, somehow survived the carnage, with everything around it a pile of rubble. At least 317 civilians, including those in the prison and in Limay, died that day. The actual number, because of transients in town and those not counted in the suburbs, is probably higher.[60] Official histories and reports say little about the destruction of this old city. In most accounts, it was simply another bridge.

For the citizens of Mantes-Gassicourt, the war did not end with the landings on June 6, any more than it had for the citizens of Rouen. Six major raids occurred in June, seven more in July, and several more in early August. A bombing on July 19 was especially vicious and resulted in forty-five civilian deaths.[61] Finally, following the breakout from the Norman beachhead and the Battle of the Falaise Pocket, the US 79th Infantry Division, XV Corps, moved into Mantes.[62] Three days later, a dozen German aircraft launched an unusual night raid on the city, attacking the American troops repairing the road bridge.[63] With the war over, the city quickly repaired the damage or rebuilt whole sections of the most devastated districts. The provincial town grew into an urban environment. The northwestern part of the city, Le Val Fourré, has become an industrial center and one of France's greatest concentrations of immigrants. Few who live there today remember the events of that summer.

Tours

While the primary bridge-destroying operation was along the Seine, the Loire River Valley was never far from the planners' minds. Nantes, Angers, Tours, Blois, and Orleans all possessed extensive rail yards and bridges that spanned the wide river. Any significant movement of German reinforcements from the south of France or Italy, by rail or road, would have to pass through these areas. Of most concern was the 17th Panzer Grenadiers located southeast of Angers, and the 2nd SS Panzer Division near Toulouse, both of which could be extremely useful in an enemy attempt to throw the invasion back. Therefore the planners identified ten bridges along their potential lines of march. The Allies had already bombed most of these relatively large urban areas since they also contained factories, airfields, rail centers, or, in the case of Nantes, a port. But, fearful that focusing attacks on the river's bridges too early would permit German intelligence analysts to bracket the invasion area, they held off while the Ninth Air Force demolished the Seine bridges. On May 26 General Montgomery believed it was time to take the risk and notified AEAF planners that he wanted the Loire's rail bridges and rail yards shut down before June 5, the anticipated invasion day. Prominent on the list were Saumur, Orleans, Nantes, and Tours.[64] Most of these targets were beyond the effective range of medium bombers, so they were the responsibility of Bomber Command and the Eighth Air Force. Remember, neither Harris nor Spaatz wanted anything to do with these missions and considered them ineffective and a wasteful diversion from their primary task of destroying Germany cities and factories.[65] The heavy bombers struck Nantes eight times between May 31 and June 15, Angers five times between May 29 and June 28, Saumur three times in June, and Orleans nine times in May and June. Tours was the winner in this game of death, with heavy bombers striking this key city a dozen times in three months.[66]

Tours is one of France's great cities, with a history that extends from long before the Roman presence. Bounded by the small Cher River to the south and the Loire to the north, it was a natural trading and communications center. Not too far south, in 732, a hodgepodge Christian army stopped a large Muslim Umayyad force plundering its way north from Spain. Most eighteenth- and nineteenth-century historians considered the Battle of Tours to be a major turning point in European history. The American Expeditionary Force made it the headquarters for its service of supply during the Great War. By 1936, almost 84,000 citizens called it home. Traditionally a center of silk manufacturing, it had also diversified during the Great War. Most of the region's manufacturing plants were in the suburb of Saint-Pierre-des-Corps, just to the east, where, for example, Société Liotard produced aircraft engines. Until the summer of 1941, the Luftwaffe based a bomber group at the airport for operations against Britain. Soon after Germany invaded Russia, however, this unit headed east and was never replaced. In fact, the Wehrmacht had no air or ground units anywhere near Tours after 1942. With the Germans gone, it seemed logical to most citizens that the war had passed them by and their biggest problem would be with other aspects of the occupation.[67] That, of course, was not to be. Bomber Command attacked the rail yard and manufacturing area with Mosquitoes at least five times in 1943. These raids consisted of flights of ten to twenty-six aircraft, which because of their nature were relatively precise with little collateral damage. The Eighth Air Force increased the bombing intensity, and concern among the citizens, with massive raids against the airfield in January, February, and March of 1944. Each of these attacks consisted of between seventy-four and ninety B-17 bombers. These were all during daylight, the citizens had time to reach shelters, and the target was outside the urban area.[68]

This precision and isolation changed on April 11, when Bomber Command sent 180 Lancaster bombers to destroy the rail yard once and for all. Since the attack took place in the middle of the night without warning, most residents were unable to get under cover. Those on the ground believed the rail yard was unusable and out of action. Those who emerged from their shelters saw nothing but destruction. Eighteen civilians died that night. Delayed-action munitions killed another nine several days later.[69] A memorandum issued by Eisenhower's headquarters on May 5 urged his air commanders to take into account the casualties French cities had already suffered when selecting targets. The attached appendix indicated that 690 citizens from Tours had already perished under Allied attack.[70] But the worst was yet to come. On May 20, 113 Lancasters and a handful of Mosquitoes appeared over the city a little after midnight. The target was the public rail station in the center of the city, surrounded by civilian homes and shops. Although the attackers were ordered to be careful about the marking and bombing of the target, that was almost impossible, and the raid destroyed more than three hundred homes and killed 137 civilians. In one tragic case, an extended family group named Audenet—André (forty-eight years old), Alice (forty-six), Renee (fifty), Roger (fifty-five) and Michelle (sixteen)—were home when the sirens announced the approaching bombers. Other members of the family, mostly women and young children, were twenty kilometers away visiting other relatives. The group left their home and ran to the safety of the nearby bomb shelter. It turned out to be a wrong decision as their home emerged untouched but the shelter took a direct hit. Thirty-four people died instantly.[71]

After putting the airfield and the rail complex out of action, the Allied air forces now focused on the bridges, which were somehow still standing after all this carnage. The day after the D-Day landings, 180 Eighth Air Force B-17s headed for the Tours bridges. Amazingly, given the presence of navigation radar, none of them found their assigned targets, and they bombed "other" locations. The report does not account for all the places this group attacked.[72] The next day, the air planners sent another 216 bombers to take out the bridges. This time, they found their target, and at least fifty civilians

Destroyed bridges in Rouen. Note damage to cathedral and north side of river. *Archives Départmentals de la Seine-Maritime*

perished in this attack. One young witness named Jacqueline, who was apparently attending a religious school, wrote to her brother and sister that she taken shelter in the basement of a bell tower and had survived. Among the dead, she learned, were two of her friends and their parents, who had not taken cover in the best location.[73] The raids continued for several more weeks, the last major attack occurring on August 1, when 100 B-17 bombers attacked the city one more time.[74] By the beginning of September, the Germans had departed, and the citizens began rebuilding.

Craven and Cate, in the official Air Force history of the Second World War, mention Tours, Mantes, and Rouen among the other dozen or so bridges attacked that May. None get a special mention or any discussion of the cost suffered by the city's citizens. In fact there is no mention of French casualties in regards to bombing the bridges at all.[75] The Ninth Air Force's published report on its role in the invasion describes the attacks on the bridges, but there is no mention of any collateral damage, no mention of how inaccurate the bombings were, or any indication the air groups may have destroyed much of the city in pursuit of this objective.[76] The best book on the operations of the Ninth Air Force, Thomas Hughes' *Over Lord* (1995), describes the bombing of the Seine's bridges and mentions Rouen as one of the targets. The tone is positive about the success of these missions with the author saying nothing about how inaccurate the bombings were. As in the official histories, it makes no mention of collateral damage or the fate of the Frenchmen who lived near these bridges.[77]

There is no doubt that the destruction of the Seine bridges severely hindered the mobility of German reinforcements. The June 10 intelligence report indicated, "So far no Division has made the difficult journey round the useless bridges from N of the SEINE."[78] Today we know that some of this delay was because of the High Command's decision not to commit all of its forces to Normandy with an Allied threat against the Pas-de-Calais still possible. While some reinforcements could still cross the Seine by ferry in June and July, units often grouped on the north side of the river waiting for transport. These became excellent targets for the ever-present fighter-bombers. The absence of bridges directly contributed to German ammunition shortages in the combat area.[79]

In most cases reconstruction hides the evidence of this destruction from the current generation. Rouen, for example, is a thriving, vibrant city, with a beautiful riverfront, great shopping, and excellent cafés and restaurants. Tourists, following the trail of Joan of Arc, head for the famous Vieux Marché and the site of her execution. From there, they can wander up Rue du Gros Horloge, now a pedestrian way, past the shops to the restored Cathédrale Notre Dame that still dominates the city. If they take the time to observe the buildings as they walk the narrow streets, however, evidence of the wartime destruction is evident: damage to the front of the Palace de Justice, the remains of burned-out buildings, and the noticeable differences in the architecture of buildings constructed before and after the war. Periodically they will see monuments and plaques that commemorate events that provide a narrative different from the Anglo-American story of the European campaign. In 2007 more than six decades later, the city erected a monument at the end of the Halle aux Toiles on the Place de Gaillardbois. The memorial is simple, with just the numerals 1940 and 1944 placed in the center of the original medieval fabric market's entrance. A small inscription honors those from Rouen and its suburbs who died during the bombardments. Tour guides often fail to identify these monuments to visitors. Nevertheless the presence and recent construction of such monuments reinforce the impression of a different narrative that underscores modern French society.

CHAPTER TEN

THE LANDINGS

Like thousands of French families up and down the coast, the 120 or so citizens that remained in the villages of Saint-Marcouf and Fontenay-sur-Mer went to bed on the night of June 5 knowing that the Allied invasion was going to happen soon. Everyone knew it was coming; the only questions were when and where? Many years later Yvette Moreau remembered that "everyone in Normandy shared the hope that the landings would take place elsewhere. Farther north, in the Nord, of course!"[1] The weather was terrible, so few expected it would be that night.[2] For two years they had lived in the shadow of the German naval artillery battery at Crisbecq, less than a mile away from where many people had lived, farmed, and worked for generations. And veterans of the previous war probably had some foreboding of the danger they were in if the invasion took place on the eastern beaches of the Cotentin Peninsula. At 0130 hours the ubiquitous Mosquito bombers arrived above the German artillery and dropped their target markers.[3] Behind them came a stream of heavy bombers, ninety-two in all, with 534 tons of munitions. There was no warning, and the sleepy villagers had to make an immediate choice between staying put in their homes or running to the shelter. In Saint-Marcouf the air raid shelter was in the church, about three hundred meters east of the village center. Many never made it. Rene Millét, the mayor of the small town, remembered fifty years later the wounded crying for help and the sight of the dead, those who could not reach the shelter, lying in the road. Over the next few days, in the midst of the fighting going on around them, they would search the shattered homes and recover the dead. The Bazin family (Claude, Georges, Louis, Marie, Valentine), the Carré family (Alexander Gustave, Alexander Louis, Juliette, René, Renée, and Thérèse) all perished in the attack. The Tixier family (Armandine, Etienne, Gertrude, and Michael) also died, and the list goes on. Forty-five French civilians, approximately a third of the population of these two villages, died that morning in the opening rounds of the invasion.[4]

If there is an air narrative to Operation Neptune, it revolves around the airborne assault, popularized by Cornelius Ryan and Stephen Ambrose.[5] Three gliders from the 6th British Airborne Division circled the village of Bénouville and crash-landed along the Caen Canal. Major John Howard's troops stormed the bridge, soon to be called Pegasus, and secured the invasion's left flank. Simultaneously in the gap between Omaha and Utah beaches, American paratroopers from the 82nd and 101st Airborne Divisions dropped into the countryside, creating havoc among German defenders. Today a parachute with a mannequin of Pvt. John Steele still hangs from the steeple of the church of Sainte-Mère-Église, celebrating the fight in that city's square. Nearby, the site of the artillery battery at Brécourt Manor that threatened Utah Beach has become a shrine to Dick Winters and his "Band of Brothers," whose story has profoundly affected the invasion's American narrative. Missing in both of these accounts are the heavy bombers, medium bombers, and fighter-bombers that got into the fight before any ground troops arrived in France. Yet this was the greatest air assault in history. Nothing before or after can compare with the scale, sophistication, and complexity of the American and British air forces on June 5 and 6. Surprisingly, historians of the invasion have virtually ignored its details.

The standard invasion narrative acknowledges that the Allies bombed the beaches. Every historical account mentions the bombing, but none of them goes into any detail. Stephen Ambrose writes in grand generalities with no specifics on what the Air Force bombed, except for the location around the Utah Beach museum, and one German officer who lost his guns during the bombardment.[6] Rick Atkinson writes in a similar general manner with no details of what was the object of the attack.[7] Anthony Beevor gives us no details of the bombing but repeats the often-told lament that none of the bombs directed at Omaha actually hit the targets. Quoting one American officer, he notes, "The Air Corps might just as well have stayed home in bed for all the good that their bombing concentration did."[8] Canadian historian Terry Copp points out that assessment teams found no bomb craters at strongpoints and resistance nests in the Anglo-Canadian sectors.[9] In another example Carlos D'Este notes that the British aircraft dropped five thousand tons of bombs on the German coastal defense in the British landing sector, followed by the guns of the British fleet. He then goes on to note that the American beaches experienced the same. That is all![10] Most standard, allegedly comprehensive histories ignore any details about the preliminary air bombardment.

Reflecting the attitude of Harris and Spaatz, the air historians have also minimized the particulars of that morning's events. Operation Flashlamp, of which the attack on the Crisbecq battery was one part, receives minimal coverage in most British accounts. This operation used more than 1,130 heavy bombers and Mosquito markers, yet it seldom gets a sentence.[11] The American official history provides us a much more comprehensive summary, but with little detail.[12] This chapter intends to fill in some of the details missing from the standard accounts by explaining what the targets were and why the air forces attacked them. It will describe what happened to some of the inhabitants of these bombing objectives, French civilians who found themselves terrorized for hours, days, and, especially in the case of Caen, weeks. Finally, it will consider the effectiveness of this massive assault and its consequences for both the German defenders and the Allied attacking force. The next chapter will describe another lesser-known aspect of the Neptune assault.

The Plan

After surveying all the beaches from Belgium to the Bay of Biscay, the COSSAC planners selected the sector north of Caen as the landing zone. Excellent beaches, weakly held by the Germans, and close to Allied air bases in the United Kingdom made it the best of the available options. The original plan consisted of a three-division amphibious invasion, and an airborne assault to seize Caen. Montgomery recommended from the beginning an enlargement of the landing area. Under the final concept, five reinforced divisions would land, complemented by three airborne divisions on the flanks.[13] The landings took place in Basse Normandie (lower Normandy), consisting of the departments of Calvados and La Manche. The region's eastern edge rests on the Seine and the ancient fishing port of Honfleur. A string of fishing villages and beach resorts, the most important being Cabourg, extend to the Orne River and its adjacent canal. The Orne is a serious obstacle to east-west traffic, and the planners made securing the bridges and a nearby artillery battery a high priority for the British 6th Airborne Division. Along the coast the port-resort complex of Ouistreham-Riva-Bella was a gateway to Caen, ten miles south. Caen was the largest city in the region and the invasion force's primary objective.

Between Ouistreham and Longues-sur-Mer, small fishing villages dot the coast, with Courseulles-sur-Mer and Arromanches-les-Bains being the most important. This part of the coast was the sector for the three Commonwealth beaches: Sword, Juno, and Gold. Longues itself is steep terrain, and one can view the entire invasion area from its elevated promontory. Between Longues and Grandcamp, the coastline is rugged and extremely defensible. It was here that the planners identified the first American beach: Omaha. The second American invasion beach was Utah, across the Banc du Grand Vey, formed by the mouths of the converging Douvre and Vireo Rivers. The large fishing village of Carentan lay between these two invasion sectors, and the Allies wanted to capture them early in the assault. The attackers needed to seize two more urban areas early in the invasion. The ancient city of Bayeux, eight miles beyond the coast, dominated east-west traffic on Route Nationale 13 and was a major road network into the heart of the countryside. The other was the port of Cherbourg, the largest between Le Havre and Brest and capable of serving as a supply support facility. Behind the beaches, the terrain was classic medieval farmland: hundreds of small stone villages surrounded by farmers' fields. Ancient hedges with extensive root systems, complemented by discarded stones, the famous bocage, bordered most farmers' fields. In 1936 almost 1.2 million French men and women lived in the region, most making their living by farming, fishing, and maritime trade.

The Wehrmacht had developed this portion of the Atlantic Wall much less than the area around Boulogne. The Allies attacked the seam between the Fifteenth and Seventh German Armies. To avoid using a stream or river as a boundary between units is a fundamental tactical principle, and General Salmuth's Fifteenth Army was responsible for both sides of the Seine. His zone of action was immense, as he was also the commander of coastal defenses all the way to the Dutch border. Between the Seine and the Dive River, just west of Cabourg, he placed one static infantry division, the 711th Infantry

Division. With only two regiments to cover twenty-five miles of coastline, Lieutenant General Josef Reichert did not have sufficient combat forces stop a serious advance.[14]

The main landings took place in General Dollmann's Seventh Army area. Lieutenant General Wilhelm Richter's 716th Infantry Division was responsible for defending the sector between Merville and Ver-sur-Mer, a front of more than twenty miles. He organized his eight thousand or so second-class soldiers into about three dozen resistance nests, structured around mortars, machine guns, and light antitank guns. He also deployed six batteries of artillery that could range the coast.[15] Lieutenant General Dietrich Kraiss commanded the 352nd Infantry Division on Richter's left flank, which was opposite Omaha Beach. It was ironic that Dollmann placed his best infantry unit in the most defensible terrain. Kraiss arrayed his three regiments along the coast in four dozen defensive locations supported by twelve batteries of artillery.[16] Lieutenant General Karl-William von Schlieben deployed part of his 709th Infantry Division, made up of many defectors from eastern European states, along the sands of Utah Beach. He also built a series of strongpoints and had at least two artillery batteries, including the one at Crisbecq.[17] Almost all these positions included concrete bunkers, pillboxes, fighting positions, and artillery casements. But few contained many soldiers. Only about a dozen German soldiers manned Widerstandsnest 61 (Resistance Nest 61), and another thirty-five at nearby Widerstandsnest 62 on Omaha Beach, for example.[18] Crucially, however, the German forces constructed many of these facilities, especially near the Orne at Ouistreham, in or near French homes and other buildings, where civilians lived and worked. All of them came under attack on the morning of June 6.

The Joint Fire Plan issued on April 8 and signed by the chiefs of staff of each of the component commanders, provided the guidelines for air and naval gunfire support during the invasion. Montgomery's Twenty-First Army Group staff took the lead in identifying the enemy positions they wanted destroyed or neutralized to protect the landing force, while Ramsey and Leigh-Mallory's planners determined the facilities or installations they needed to attack to support the forces in the sea and air. The first group of targets was the artillery batteries, such as Crisbecq, that could interfere with the approaching invasion fleet. Bomber Command hit them first, just after midnight. The plan next focused on attacking the prepared German positions:

"The importance of neutralizing the beach defenses requires their engagement by air attack, though owing to their nature complete destruction is only likely to be achieved in a very small proportion of cases." In separate appendices, the planners identified which enemy positions they wanted bombed and when:

A. Batteries for air attack prior to D-Day
B. Cover Plan targets for air attack immediately prior to D-Day (the Fortitude targets not included in this list).
C. Targets for air attack on D-1.
D. Batteries for attack by bombers prior to H-hour.
E. Targets for naval bombardment.
F. Beach targets for daylight bombing during the assault.
G. Targets specially suitable for fighter bombers.[19]

The air forces attacked most of these fifty or so targets more than once. Meanwhile, they continued to attack bridges, transportation centers, airfields, ports, Fortitude installations, and vengeance weapon sites. This list does not include the missions that turned the surrounding towns into chokepoints, which we will discuss in the next chapter.

Of course, even though the senior commanders and staff officers had an agreement, the Joint Fire Plan was a long way from implementation and now became the intellectual property of junior planners at all secondary levels. They had to allocate the hundreds of targets across France, Belgium, and into the Atlantic to more than 678 air squadrons and 12,600 aircraft of all kinds except transports. They had to plan the routes so that returning aircraft would not fly into other units heading toward the coast.[20] Naval planners had similar problems of planning and sequencing 7 battleships, 2 monitors, 23 cruisers, and 108 destroyers and other vessels in the assault zone, and many others on the flanks and into the Atlantic. Their problems were, in many ways, even more complicated, since more than 4,000 other vessels, sailing in darkness without lights, would be hauling troops and supplies to and from the invasion beaches. And, before the landing craft could drop their troops, mine sweepers, caught under fire between friendly vessels and enemy artillery, had to remove mines and obstacles in the lanes to the coast.[21] Air and naval planners had to analyze each target, determine the kind of munitions that were appropriate, and then match them with the potential ships and squadrons that could execute the mission. Finally, they needed to sequence these missions so they took place at the right time and in the right order of priority. All this had to happen in such a way that the landing forces would not mistakenly be hit by the massive firepower landing on the French coast. In the end, incredibly detailed targeting schedules found their way down to both ships and air squadrons. The prime planning consideration in the assault was continuity of bombardment so that the enemy forces would not have time to recover and reinforce. For the air attack, Leigh-Mallory's planners prepared a detailed Neptune air plan that spelled out the responsibilities for all of the air units.[22] As a precaution, bombing had to be complete ten minutes before the landing craft arrived on French soil.[23]

On the eve of the landings, many leaders remained concerned about using the heavy bombers during the assault. For example, at the second air commanders meeting on May 26, less than two weeks before the anticipated landings on June 5, Professor Solly Zuckerman, Tedder's scientific advisor, gave an evaluation of attacks on the coastal batteries. He explained that Allied bombers had already dropped a total of 8,700 tons of bombs on these types of fortified targets in the Neptune and Fortitude area. Of the 51 guns attacked in the Neptune area, they had partially damaged only 18, and out of 101 in the Fortitude area, only 26. The bombers had destroyed none of them. He estimated that it took ninety-seven sorties and 420 tons of bombs to hit one gun. Simply to have one bomb fall within five yards of a target, the air forces would need to drop 2,500 bombs. Zuckerman was not reassuring to the Army and Navy leaders who wanted these targets neutralized before they arrived. The weather forecast continued to be a problem for the air commanders, and Tedder wondered if the attack could go forward if the bombers could not find the target.[24]

At the same meeting, General Doolittle made it clear that if the weather conditions allowed his bombers to take off, and provided Army leaders would accept a bombing accuracy of a half mile from the target, "he was prepared to undertake any task allotted to the Eighth Air Force." He also noted that he was grounding all H2X aircraft for two days before D-Day to ensure that every plane equipped with this aid would be available to operate when the time came. He said that the Eighth Air Force had been practicing bombing with H2X along the coast a hundred miles north of the Neptune landing zone, using four groups of eighteen bombers to determine how effective his force could be in hitting coastal targets. In his tests, the average error in range was four hundred yards, and the average deflection eight hundred yards. From these trials he deduced that, excluding gross error, the Eighth Air Force could bomb within an accuracy of one-half-mile and one-mile deflection, provided there were certain definite physical features such as a coastline and a river by which to guide the pilots.[25]

Doolittle was promising a relatively high degree of accuracy for his bombers. Most likely, if he had been allowed to proceed the way he briefed his peers and senior airmen, the Eighth Air Force would have put many of the German positions in the target area out of action. While protected casements may have survived, the attack would have damaged trenches, supply dumps, and exposed artillery batteries, and it would have certainly stunned the defenders. But that was not to be; and a debate continued among leaders and planners concerning the dangers of hitting the soldiers in their landing craft heading for the coast. Some time after June 1, someone modified Doolittle's concept. According to the Eighth Air Force's analysis of the D-Day bombing:

> When it became apparent that weather conditions would necessitate use of the latter, which involved navigating by GEE fixes and bombing on H2X Pathfinder instruments, it was deemed advisable to adopt further precautionary measures to prevent bombs from falling on friendly troops. (The time interval between the cessation of bombing of the immediate beach areas and the touchdown of the initial assault waves had been already increased from five minutes under the visual bombing plan to ten minutes under the revised overcast bombing plan.) Accordingly, in conjunction with Headquarters AEAF, it was decided that if cloud cover should prevent visual synchronization, bombs would be dropped on Pathfinder indications in the normal manner except that the release would be delayed so that the Mean Point of Impact would be no less than 1,000 yards from the forward wave of the water borne assault forces."[26]

With the revised plan the H2X operator in the lead aircraft, who sat at a console behind the pilot, was to delay the actual drop. He did this by telling the bombardier, who controlled the bomb's release, to execute from five to thirty seconds, depending on the target, after he had identified it. Since none of the trailing aircraft had these machines, the actual drop by these crews would be several seconds later.[27] The intent of this delay was supposedly to limit casualties among the friendly landing forces. But it also limited the damage it could do to the German defenders, as a five-second delay resulted in missing Doolittle's bombing box by almost a thousand feet; a thirty-second delay would move that target zone a mile south of where the defenders waited. Craven and Cate point out that the air planners directed this delay "in the interest of greater safety and with Eisenhower's approval."[28] Exactly who recommended this critical change, why, and when they briefed Eisenhower is not evident. The authors provide no citation in this otherwise well-documented series. Eisenhower was deliberate about his decision making, and so far this author has discovered no evidence that he was aware of the change and approved it in advance.

Flashlamp

Shortly after midnight Bomber Command commenced the formal invasion by executing Operation Flashlamp, the initial raids on the most dangerous artillery batteries overlooking the invasion sector. After some refinement of the original target list from the previous April, they settled on ten artillery batteries, seven in Calvados (St. Pierre du Mont, Mont-Fleury, Ouistreham, Longues-sur-Mer, Maisy, Houlgate, and Merville) and three in the Manche (Crisbecq, Saint-Martain-de-Varreville, and La Pernelle). Flying during a full moon but between 6,000 and 12,000 feet above the generally thick clouds below, they had little chance of accurately finding or hitting their targets. More than 1,300 bombers took part, with each battery, occupying between one and two football fields in space, receiving the full attention of between 100 and 131 Lancasters or Halifaxes.[29] The purpose of these raids was not to destroy the batteries but to "send the gun crews into their shelters" and "disorganize the batteries by damaging buildings, communications, dumps, and ancillary installations."[30]

Widerstandnest 83 was a strong German defensive position southwest of Grandcamp-Maisy, with six 155-mm howitzers that could range the landings on Omaha Beach. Nearby were two other batteries comprising eight additional artillery pieces that could affect the landing on Omaha. Bomber Command sent 112 aircraft from No. 4 Group, including 16 Halifax bombers from the RAF 346 Squadron as the morning's first attack on the complex. The 346th was a Free French force that had fought earlier in North Africa,

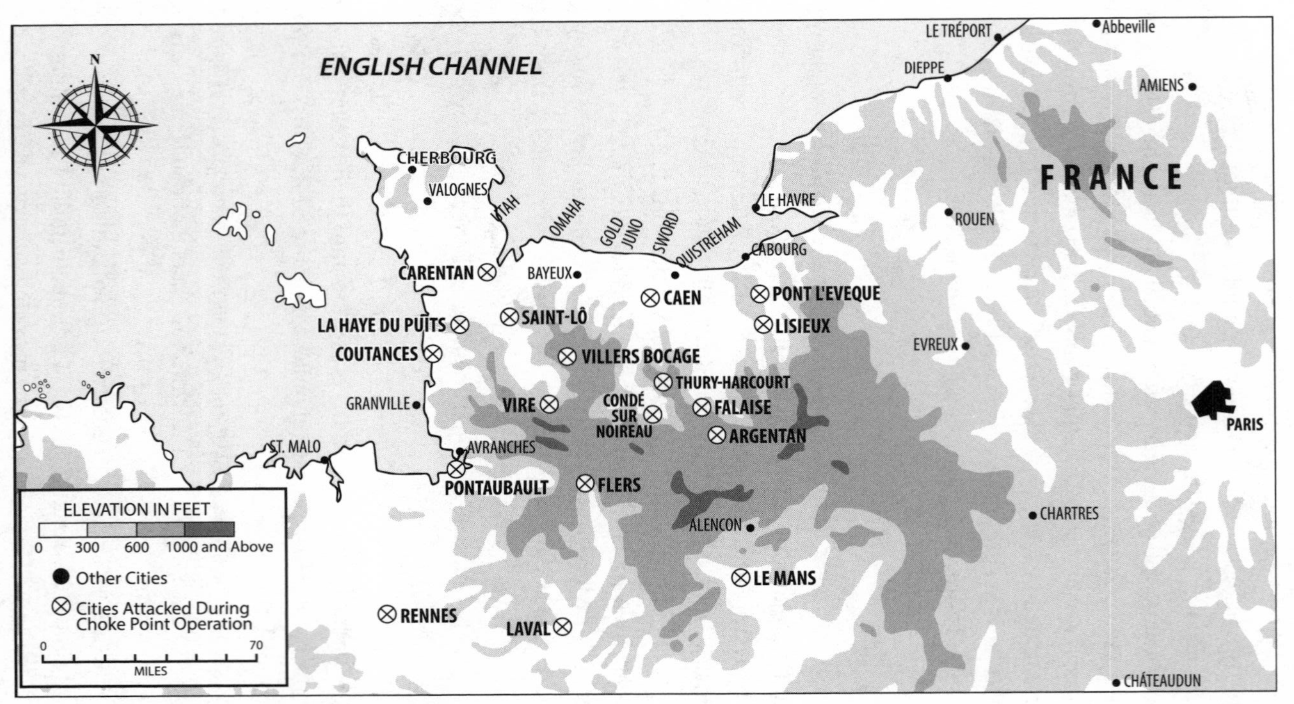

Map 3. Bombing targets, June 6–8, 1944

and now they were conducting bombing operations against their homeland, certainly not something that prewar air theorists had considered.[31]

Marcel Destores and his family lived in Maisy, where he was a prosperous farmer and leader of the local civil defense unit. Soon after 0315 on June 6, he heard the bombers approaching the complex. It was a familiar sound, as the Allies had bombed this battery before, as recently as the previous morning. Unlike the previous night, the bombs did not fall on the target but on the town itself. His wife noted in her diary, "We thought it [the bombing] was coming from behind the house, but in fact it's coming from the other side, very near to us! Windows exploded, the floor trembles like a tree shaken by a storm; the dust falls everywhere and an odor of gunpowder tugs at our throats." Marcel rescued the children from their bedrooms and together they ran to a nearby trench that served as their shelter. The family had two live-in servants, and Marcel went out again to find them, fortunately returning with both unharmed. Cowering under a large umbrella, they waited out the horrible experience, holding each other "tighter and tighter." In his role as civil defense leader, Marcel headed to town after the bombing stopped for a quick inspection, returning two hours later: "Its a disaster," he told his wife. "The entire center of the town is wiped out! The Sehier family is under the rubble, as are Mauret's wife and their son, as the entire Clément family! . . . Give me some sheets so I can bury their bodies. I just brought two to the city hall. Mauret's wife is in pieces, disemboweled. It's horrible!"[32] Indeed, the grandfather Albert Clement (sixty-two) and his daughter-in-law Alice Avonde Clement (thirty-four) perished during this raid, along with Alice's two young children Albert (six) and Alice (four). The Sehier family lost three of its children: André (five), Jean (six), and Andrée (twelve). Mauret's wife was most likely Amanda Deschamps Coquet, who perished three days short of her eighty-third birthday. Another dozen villagers perished hiding in a local trench to escape the attack. In the nearby village of Géfosse-Fontenay, a bomb hit the Boudier home, wiping out eight members of this farming family.[33]

By all accounts the bombing did little damage to any of the guns in these batteries, especially to those protected by concrete casements. But the attack did have an effect on those French civilians living nearby. As mentioned at the beginning of this chapter, we do know about the damage done to Saint-Marcouf and Fontenay during the attack on the Crisbecq battery. During the assault on Merville, bombs hit the town of Cabourg five miles away, killing firefighter Marcel Bérand and his fourteen-year-old son Roland, as well as twenty-six other civilians. Bombers hit the town of Isigny, seven miles inland from the battery. Rescuers later discovered a home with five dead bodies, mostly children six months to twelve years old. They found two people wounded and a trembling dog still chained to a shattered stove. In the middle of the sector at Ver-sur-Mer, near the Mont-Fleury battery, another twelve citizens died under the bombs. British bombs apparently killed another forty civilians near Ouistreham before a single paratrooper or Allied infantryman touched French soil.[34]

The US Air Force

As the British aircraft departed the French coast, American bombers took their place. Units from the Ninth Air Force attacked installations on Utah Beach while the heavy bombers of the Eighth Air Force struck the targets on Omaha and the Commonwealth landing areas. The air units had to complete their bombing runs and fly the aircraft out of the area five minutes before H-Hour, the time when the landing craft reached the coast. The timing was different in each sector, with American infantry touching down at 0730 and the Commonwealth forces landing at 0825, CET.[35] Army group planners identified forty-seven specific defensive positions for the Fortresses and Liberators to attack. In most cases the actual positions took up no more than a thousand square feet, and usually much less. Since the Eighth Air Force attacked with squadrons consisting of six aircraft flying in two rows of three each, the distance between the two outer planes' bomb doors was much greater than the space occupied by the German defenders. Therefore, even if the lead aircraft hit the target, it was almost a given that the wingmen would not. Considering the bombing altitude of between 14,000 and 18,000 feet and the dense clouds below that, finding the small target was nearly impossible. With the H2X delay, is no wonder that almost none of the targets suffered any serious damage.[36]

Shortly after 0650, the 450 B-24 Liberators from Maj. Gen. James P. Hodges' 2nd Bomb Division arrived at Omaha Beach. Unlike the general accounts of the bombing, the Eighth Air Force operation orders spelled out the names of the specific towns that became the bombardiers' aiming points. Planners and commanders selected these small beachside French villages, which have since become famous in the traditional narratives, for destruction.

Ninth Air Force on bombing mission somewhere in Normandy, June 1944. Note cloud cover. *NARA RG 342 US Air Force Photo Collection*

Considering the time delay, it is not surprising that the actual impact point was not on the German position. From east to west, 24 B-24s attacked the small fishing village of Port-en-Bessin, which housed two German fighting positions. At the same time, 74 bombers attacked several resistance nests on the beaches outside of Colleville-sur-Mer, and another 130 the four German positions at Saint-Laurent-sur-Mer. The fishing village at Vierville-sur-Mer, again the home of a prominent Widerstandsnest, felt the power of 84 heavy bombers. Finally, 24 aircraft attacked the fighting positions at a prominent location called La Percée, northwest of Vierville-sur-Mer, which had an excellent view of most of Omaha Beach. When it was over, the 2nd Division dropped 587.5 tons of high explosives and another 307.5 tons of fragmentation bombs specifically designed to kill the defending troops.[37] But while the bombing had an effect on the defenses, it did not destroy them. By some accounts, less than 2 percent of the bombs hit the targets and destroyed German positions. Warnings about fratricide had produced an overcautious attitude. American infantry believed that the Air Force wasted thousands of tons of ordnance and gave them no help.[38] When the bombs landed south of the enemy defenders, however, they fell right onto the homes and farms of the French people.

Given the intensity of the air attacks, sea bombardment, and subsequent assault, it is hard to assess the precise cause of each French civilian casualty during this period. Port-en-Bessin on Omaha Beach lost twenty-five citizens, many from aerial bombardment and others from the intense ground battle. The Delain family report, for example, indicates air bombardment as the cause of the death of Blanche (forty-nine), Gustave (fifty-six), and Raymond (twenty-two), and that Èdouard (fifty-one) was killed by a grenade. Forty-one-year-old André died from a mine explosion, while two other family members, Alice (fifty-two) and Jean (eleven) perished during the air attack on Isigny-sur-Mer. Some reports indicate the day of death as June 6, others much later, indicating they had fought to stay alive in the hospital.[39]

Maj. Gen. Robert B. Williams' 1st Bomb Division picked up the middle sector of the raid that morning, attacking the towns and villages near Gold Beach, the objective of the 50th British Division, and the western portion of Juno, where the 3rd Canadian Division would land. He matched his 450 B-17 Flying Fortresses against fifteen identified targets. Against the artillery battery at Longues, made famous in Cornelius Ryan's *The Longest Day*, he allocated only 36 aircraft. The fishing village of Arromanches, future home of the British Mulberry Harbor, had one improved resistance nest, several smaller defensive points, and an artillery battery. Against this location, he sent 103 Flying Fortresses. Nearby defenses at Le Hamel and Meuvaines merited another 63. Twenty squadrons, 125 aircraft in all, attacked the strongpoints and artillery units near Ver-sur-Mer that dominated the British division's sector. The fishing and prewar tourist village of Courseulles-sur-Mer and its resistance nests merited 60 bombers.[40] Because these villages were on the coast, most of the bombers missed the defenses, the ruins of which one can still see along the coast today. The picturesque Courseulles suffered the most with fourteen dead, including George (thirty-eight) and Bernadette Labreque (thirty-four) and their three-month-old daughter Èlizabeth.[41]

The main effort, if there was one in this massive expenditure of firepower, belonged to Maj. Gen. Curtis E. LeMay's 3rd Bomb Division. LeMay's task was to suppress and destroy German military emplacements on the eastern portion of the invasion beaches, half of Juno Beach, where the Canadians landed, and Sword Beach, opposite the approaches to Caen. He allocated sixty-nine squadrons, 354 B-17s in all, to destroying the critical beach targets. In the 3rd Canadian Infantry Division sector, these included the machine-gun and light artillery positions at Bernières-sur-Mer and Saint-Aubin-sur-Mer, both major complexes the Canadians needed to capture to secure Juno. It also hit a battalion headquarters at Tailleville.[42] The British 3rd Infantry Division sector, Sword Beach, was the most developed and built up in the entire invasion area. Before the war it was a resort for Parisians and those farther inland to escape to the coast, and it consisted of summer homes, shops, and a casino opposite the Riva-Bella beach in Ouistreham. The developed nature of the region, with structures built of brick, stone, and concrete right up to the water's edge, made it a more dangerous sector. LeMay's air division attacked strongpoints at Petit Enfer, Lion-sur-Mer, and two in Ouistreham. It also struck artillery batteries at Périers-sur-le-Dan, Molineaux, Colleville-sur-Orne, and Ouistreham. LeMay also sent 72 B-17s against the artillery battery and defensive complex at Merville-Franceville across the Orne, which the British 6th Airborne Division would assault in its effort to protect the eastern approach to the invasion zone.[43]

The Ninth Air Force had responsibility for bombing the German installations in the Utah Beach area, and it began its attack against the village of La Madeline. Just east of this small hamlet was Widerstandsnest 5, consisting of several bunkers, an 88-mm gun, machine guns, and several artillery tubes. It blocked the main route past the swampy lowlands, and the 4th Division had to seize it immediately to get off the beach. In sequence, six squadrons of 18 B-26 medium bombers, 108 aircraft in all, attacked this position, which was not much larger than a standard football field. Each aircraft carried sixteen 250-pound general-purpose bombs and wreaked havoc on the relatively weak position. The bombardiers reported that some bombs hit the fortifications, while others missed and scattered in the surrounding fields. The soldiers had been hiding in their bunkers under orders from a battle-hardened young German officer. When they emerged, there was nothing left of their defenses.[44] Unlike the Eighth Air Force's and Bomber Command's operations, the Ninth's squadrons were extremely efficient.[45] All morning B-26 Marauders attacked German installations up and down the coast. Defensive positions grouped around Saint-Martin-de-Varreville and St. Marie-du-Mont received most of the attention. In all, the Ninth sent 423 aircraft out that morning, with 330 able to bomb their designated targets; given the overcast weather, this was an excellent performance. Because most installations were away from the built-up area, the civilian casualties were relatively light.[46]

Naval Bombardment

The naval bombardment was part of the Joint Fire Plan and, for those in the invasion area, part of a seamless web of munitions exploding all around them. By dawn it was obvious the war had come to the lower Norman coast. Around 0600, once the bombers had departed, the almost 140 warships that had moved into position began engaging the surviving German artillery batteries. Often these were older ships. For example, USS *Nevada*, initially launched in 1912 and rebuilt after being severely damaged at Pearl Harbor on December 7, used its 14-inch guns to destroy artillery positions near Azeville. In another case, HMS *Warspite*, commissioned in 1915 and a veteran of the Battle of Jutland, attacked German defenses near Villerville. Moving among the larger ships and trying to avoid the landing craft were more than one hundred destroyers and small ships, who contributed their guns to destroying or suppressing reinforced enemy firing positions, in some cases grounding on the sand to provide accurate fire.[47] By the time the naval forces arrived off the coast, most Frenchmen on the beaches had already experienced the worst that the air and sea could deliver. Now they had to remain in hiding as landing Allies fought it out with the defending German forces, who hoped their reinforcements were on the way.

Memories of these days never went away for those who survived. In 1993 a lady named Bernadette, who was six at the time of the invasion and lived in Vierville on the western portion of Omaha Beach, remembered her father's death. She remembered that her mother could not sleep that night and continued to pester her husband, who was a veteran of the Great War. "I cannot sleep, something is wrong," she would say. "Sleep, leave me alone" was his reply. She remembered nothing about the bombardment but does remember her dad going out into the garden that overlooked the sea early in the morning. In the faint light, he saw the ships and began yelling at his wife, "Dress the kids! We have to get out of the house! I'll wake all the neighbors," which he did. He wanted them to hide in a nearby ditch, but his wife would not leave the house. He persisted and tried to improve the shelter for her. Just as she was about to join him a shell, probably from one of the three or four ships bombarding the German positions at Verville, cut open her father's stomach.

Obviously it was a sight Bernadette would never forget.[48] Certainly, other civilians perished during the final bombardment phase. Neither the Allies nor the Germans, however, had any option other than to fight it out on the beaches. Those who have lived in a battle zone, from time immemorial, have had few options other than to hide.

Given the intensity of the air attacks, sea bombardment, and subsequent assault, it is hard to assess the precise cause of each French civilian casualty during this period. Ouistreham, the largest town along the coast, suffered ninety-seven dead on June 6 and 7, thirty of them hit by a naval gun while hiding from the bombardment. Port-en-Bessin on Omaha Beach lost twenty-five citizens, while Saint-Aubin-sur-Mer on Juno suffered twenty-five dead. The list continues and blends with those who died because of ground combat during the landings. The fighting destroyed all the villages on the invasion beaches, leaving survivors homeless and dazed in the wake of the assault.[49] Civilians in the landing zone were the unfortunate ones, though, and most French men and women had no illusions that, as the invasion approached, those in the assault area would not suffer. Most were well aware of the fate of those caught between the opposing armies during the Great War of 1914, and most were aware of what had happened to those in the path of the German forces in the 1940 invasion. One suspects that many who remained in the invasion area knew they were taking a gamble and hoped it would happen somewhere else, such as the coast near Dieppe, where the Allies had landed before, or the Pas-de-Calais, which they knew the Germans were watching carefully. Of course most simply had no choice but to remain and hope for the best. Yvette Moreau, mentioned at the beginning of this chapter, was wrong. She was in the invasion's path.

Caen

What was different, and unexpected to most Normans, was the aerial assault on Caen. Sitting six miles south of Sword Beach on the banks of the beautiful Orne River, Caen's central location has long made it a traveler's haven and regional crossroads. First mentioned in reports around the first century, it was a regular objective of Viking raiders into the ninth century. Soon after that, it became one of the great settlements of the new Norman dukedom. In the eleventh century, it was Duke William's favorite city. William the Conqueror, as he was known after launching his own cross-channel invasion in 1066 and becoming William I of England, began work on a castle on the hill dominating the town in 1060. By 1800 it also had a dozen churches and abbeys, most dating back to the eleventh through the fifteenth centuries. It had always been a market town, and since 1840 farmers from the south displayed their wares with coastal fishermen next to the Bassin Saint-Pierre. Ferries from Portsmouth routinely docked at the nearby port of Ouistreham, and passengers would catch the train to Paris from the city's station. Caen has had a university since the fifteenth century. By 1940 this prosperous market town of 62,000 dominated the main east-west road and rail routes between the port at Cherbourg and Paris. Its bridges over the Orne River and the adjacent canal provided direct access to the invasion beaches. This critical transportation hub was Operation Neptune's primary initial objective.[50]

All the targets that the air and naval forces bombarded that morning contained German troops. But Caen contained few enemy soldiers. What the Twenty-First Army Group wanted was to prevent German reinforcements from moving through it to the front. It was the first of twenty-six towns and small cities that the Army planners wanted Leigh-Mallory's air forces to destroy because they contained so-called chokepoints. These were critical crossroads, usually characterized by a bridge crossing a stream or small river, where rubble from buildings could prevent German troops from using that route. The next chapter will discuss the details of that operation, but since the initial assault order, Eighth Air Force's Field Order 727, specified that the bombers were to attack Caen on the morning mission, it is appropriate to discuss the first raids here.[51]

The field order is specific about the routes, times, and altitude the aircraft would take to the city and how they would return. Given the thousands of aircraft in the sky that day and the absence of sophisticated air traffic control, this was an absolute requirement for the air staff. Mistakes in this regard, especially during the horrible flying weather that existed on June 6, could have been catastrophic. The actual targeting information, however, is relatively primitive. On a simple sketch map portraying only roads, rail lines, and main waterways, the planners identified four chokepoints. The most prominent terrain feature in the city, Duke William's historic castle, was unmarked. Two of these, chokepoints three and four, were relatively straightforward to understand. Target three was a road bridge across the Orne River. Just to the northeast was point four, which consisted of two bridges, one road, and the other rail. More troubling was target two, a road intersection on the northwest side of town. No river or terrain feature is apparent, just two main roads coming together inside the city, near the famous botanical garden called le Jardin des Plantes and its great institute, founded in 1689. Even more troubling was chokepoint number one, southwest of the castle. The planners had drawn a circle on the intersection of two main roads. Not marked on the sketch map were two ancient churches on either side of the intersection. William himself had founded the Abbey of Saint-Étienne south of the target area in 1063; it was a historical and impressive example of Romanesque architecture. Its crypt contained the remains of England's last conqueror. Across the street is the Church of Saint-Nicolas, begun by monks in 1083. Supporting these churches, and surrounding the intersection, were a host of shops, a hospital, schools, and other old and classic stone structures. As those in the Eighth Air Force plans section knew, the Army planners wanted the bombers to destroy these historic treasures and cause the rubble to spill into the streets, blocking German movement.[52]

The Eighth Air Force headquarters assigned both Williams' 1st Bomb Division and LeMay's 3rd to targets in Caen that morning to coincide with the bombings on the beach. Chokepoints three and four, the river bridges, were the assigned targets for the 1st Division, and Williams sent eleven squadrons, sixty-six B-17s, against them at 0825 that morning. The weather for the bombing was terrible, and they navigated using GEE and H2X navigation radar, with the intent of using the "overcast bombing technique," which was little more than an educated guess and was, in the case of small cities, inaccurate. Although forty-seven crews claimed to have bombed the bridges, French citizens reported neither bombs nor damage and, most likely, the bombers destroyed something else outside of Caen. LeMay sent sixteen squadrons of B-24 bombers, ninety-six aircraft, to attack the road intersections at targets one and two. Arriving near the city at 0906, they were also unable to find any bombing markers, apparently because of a problem with the pathfinder aircraft. This effort would be one of LeMay's least successful missions, as his B-17s dropped no ordnance on Caen that morning and returned to England.[53]

Throughout the morning, Caen's citizens had heard the commotion on the coast fifteen kilometers away. Following the ineffective earlier raid, the 1st Bomb Division returned with another eighty aircraft around 1030 hours. Cloud cover was, as the report reads "10/10," meaning they could see nothing, could not find the target, and did not drop any bombs.[54] By noon word was coming in from the communities to the north that the coast was in British hands and that the fighting had moved inland. Few remember German troops traveling through the city toward the front, yet the citizens could hear the combat in the distance and tried to guess where it was taking place. The situation was relatively calm as afternoon arrived, and after several days of bad weather, the sun was peeking through the clouds, encouraging people to come outside. Many were on the streets visiting markets, gathering provisions, and moving food and other supplies into their cellars so they could stay out of sight during the battle. Around 1230 the word spread that General Eisenhower had broadcast his message to the French confirming that the Allies had invaded France.[55]

By midmorning Army commanders were concerned that in spite of all their preparations, the Germans were managing to reinforce the defenders. The Twenty-First Panzer Division was on the move and heading for the landing areas. The situation was tense on Omaha Beach as the American V Corps was stuck on the beach and the British and Canadians were having trouble forcing their way to Caen. The only way for German panzer units to get to landing beaches from the southeast was through Caen's winding streets and across the Orne on its bridges. The bombers must destroy these bridges, chokepoints three and four, and the Twenty-First Army Group told the Eighth Air Force to do it again. Its planners gave the mission to the Hodges B-24-equipped 2nd Bomb Division, which had attacked Omaha that morning. Execution of a "hasty attack" was not a task described by the strategic bombing doctrine of the period, and one can only imagine the atmosphere as the ground crews scrambled to get the aircraft ready and air crews struggled to understand the nature of their target. Mostly, they repeated the target approach used that morning, although none of these aircraft or crews had participated earlier and it was new to them. The division had fifteen bomber groups available for this mission, such as the 453rd Bombardment Group based in Buckenham, England. Like the crews in other units, they reported for the mission's prebriefing. The group's operations officer, newly promoted Maj. James Stewart, briefed the airmen on the situation, their objective, bombing altitude, and ingress and egress routes. With few questions, the crews headed for their machines; they had bombed France many times and looked forward to what would be another easy mission.[56]

Starting their engines at 1130, they were soon in the air, and for the next hour and a half the bombers from the 453rd continued to circle over central England as they waited for aircraft from eight other squadrons, seventy-three aircraft in all, to join them. It was evident to those in the plane's front seats that it was not the best-planned mission, as the various groups, generally consisting of twelve aircraft, had difficulty in joining their assigned formations. One pilot noted at about 1245 that "ships scattered all over the sky" and "milling like a bunch of sheep."[57] Finally the assembled mission headed south, crossing the English coast at 1400 hours, French time. The weather was still horrible, and only fifty-six aircraft arrived over their target thirty minutes later. They flew in an arrow formation with one group of three bombers in front, and a group of three more on either side, slightly to the rear. Behind the lead group flew the fourth group, twelve bombers in all. The formation crossed the English Channel near Quettehou, southeast of Cherbourg, and then made a ninety-degree left turn, approaching the city from the northwest. The cloud cover was still thick and dense, and most likely the only terrain feature they could make out, since this was all done visually, was William the Conqueror's castle. This towering structure stood about a half mile from the Orne and, most likely, became the navigator's trigger point. From 20,000 feet, with little ability to see what they were aiming at, the bombardiers dropped their loads on the city below. More than 155 tons of high-explosive munitions hit the ancient city, turning it into an inferno as the old wooden buildings burst into flames. After ten minutes the Liberators had finished their work and headed for home. The bridges, however, remained open because few of the bombs hit their targets.[58]

The passive defense committee had established its posts throughout the city and had begun implementing duty schedules to allow members to rotate back to their homes. Thirty-nine-year-old Bernard Goupil, a member of the post on the Rue Du Carmes, came back home to relax after his tour ended at 1300. He remembered sitting in his garden and hearing one of his neighbors cry, "The bombers are coming for us!" and "Those are bombs, true?" Suddenly everything began blowing up around him. Running back into his house, he and his family hid under a kitchen table until it was over.[59] When the bombing stopped, Goupil went outside and found the old town a hellscape of fire and stone. Most of the bombs had fallen east of the castle and into the old town, far from the bridges. The small fire department was unable to stop the blaze that was feeding on ancient timber, and it continued to consume much of the city center. The bridges themselves were mostly undamaged and German troops kept crossing without interference. Among the smoldering ruins lay four hundred dead civilians and a much greater number of wounded.[60]

In spite of the protestations found in various after-action reports that the Allies had dropped leaflets, the citizens of Caen were surprised and shocked by this sudden attack. Many survivors now began packing their belongings and heading to, they hoped, safer locations in the countryside.[61] In combat with the Canadian forces, the infamous commander of the Hitler Youth, Hubert Meyer, witnessed the assault from a distance. "I was already searching for cover under the wall of a house in the village ahead of us when I saw the explosions. Distance, 20KM to the southeast, that could only be Caen. The black column of smoke was growing ever larger, lit by flames. Then we could also hear the boom of the explosions! What a terrible spectacle, what a drama when one thought of the many people in this town. Only hours ago we drove through it, or was it days ago?"[62]

Observations on D-Day's Fire Support

The Joint Fire Plan's authors wanted this preparatory air assault to be both violent and sustained. To overpower the German defenders, the operational planners sequenced a string of supporting tactical actions: Bomber Command's attack, the subsequent bombings by the Eighth and Ninth Air Forces, the naval bombardment, the airborne assaults, and the actual landings. Unfortunately, except in the Ninth Air Force sector, the inaccurate air attack had done little other than alert German troops to the invasion force's arrival. It is doubtful that more precise bombing would have permitted the seizure of Caen as planned. The bombing did, however, have an effect on French civilians and the American troops attacking Omaha Beach, which was the toughest objective of all.[63]

How many civilians died in the initial bombardment? For many reasons it is doubtful that there will ever be a fully accurate accounting with positive identification of all victims. It is also doubtful that, for many, there will ever be a definitive cause of death in each case. Was it a British bomb, an American warship, or an infantryman's hand grenade that caused the civilian's demise? Did the unfortunate farmer or shopkeeper perish under the initial assault or the next day's attack? Professors and students at the University of Caen have done a significant amount of detective work in the last few decades, and what they have determined is that in the coastal towns attacked that first morning almost six hundred civilians perished under the combined onslaught of the world's largest invasion force, and another four hundred in Caen. Given what we know about the Eighth Air Force's adjustment of the bombing times, it is reasonable to assume that many of those perished because the bombs did not hit the intended German defenders but hit homes and farms a few hundred meters behind the target.[64] These citizens lived in the wrong place, and their demise is unfortunately part of the war. Assigning specific responsibility is a fruitless and needless exercise after so many years. But it is proper to recognize that those civilians that remained on the beach were part of that day's drama. It was not, as depicted in most movies, a sterile battlefield consisting only of combatants.

A second aspect of the bombardment concerns its effectiveness. The Army commanders wanted the beach targets put out of action during the assault: "The importance of neutralizing the beach defenses requires their engagement by air attack," reads the guidance in the Joint Fire Plan.[65] For seventy years, participants and historians have complained about the inaccuracy of the heavy bombers and how they destroyed so few of the German defensive positions before the landings. Official histories have acknowledged this ineffectiveness but have sought to mitigate the criticism. The RAF draft narrative, written soon after the war and classified and unavailable for public use until the mid-1970s, acknowledges that Bomber Command missed their targets but notes, "The effectiveness or otherwise of this bombing has remained a question which has never been finally answered." On the next page, the official historian notes, "Nevertheless it does seem likely that the disheartening effect upon the enemy and the encouragement to our own troops of such a tremendous show of air power was of immense moral significance during the first critical hours of the assault."[66] This was not the result either Montgomery or Bradley wanted. For those in the landing craft, the Air Force and Navy had to neutralize the defenders, not scare them and encourage our troops.

The official US Army Air Force account notes that everyone was concerned with inaccurate bombing and hitting friendly troops, so, "with

Eisenhower's approval the pathfinder bombardiers were ordered to delay up to thirty seconds after the release point showed on their scopes before dropping."[67] After bombing occupied Europe for more than two years, the air commanders acknowledged how inaccurate their weapons were, something the French, Belgians, and Italians already knew. The agreement to deliberately miss these targets is a critical decision that seventy years later seems a bit perplexing. The time adjustment ensured that the heavy bombers would leave the enemy positions untouched, and ground commanders must have known they would pay a price. Was the plan so inflexible that they could not have the bombers arrive a few minutes earlier? Could they not delay the assault wave by five minutes? Could they alter the flying formation? Did they consider other options? No matter, planning meetings had evolved into an atmosphere where commanders and staffs often expressed concern for bombers hitting friendly troops. Therefore, for right or wrong, someone at Eighth Air Force headquarters decided to add a time delay as insurance. Neither Doolittle, Spaatz, nor Leigh-Mallory asked for concurrence at either of the supreme commander's meetings on May 29 or June 2.[68] The war's records are clear that Eisenhower did not make snap decisions without all the evidence before him. A decision to intentionally miss all the desired targets was certainly not the kind one made without any serious analysis of the costs and benefits. Such a critical delay was also not the kind of decision he would make without informing his subordinate commanders. So far, this author has no evidence that Eisenhower ever made such a decision. Bradley, commanding American forces during the invasion, summed it up in his memoirs: "Not until later did we learn that most of the 13,000 bombs dropped by these heavies had cascaded harmlessly into the hedgerows, three miles behind the coast."[69] In fact, someone at Eighth Air Force published a volume soon after the landings praising the accuracy of the radar-assisted D-Day bombings. This important source says nothing about time delays and praises the bombardment's accuracy.[70] Apparently not until the ground commanders' reports worked their way back to London were the air commanders aware of their error.

The Eighth Air Force's evaluation report, written weeks later, confirms that "the damage to physical installations on the beaches was slight." The same report argued that it had a psychological effect on the German defenders, which is probably true.[71] British reports noted Bomber Command was just as ineffective during Operation Flashlamp. At one point bombers over Merville were wide of their target with "bombs falling uncomfortably close to the position taken up by the 6th Airborne Division advanced party."[72] Readers should remember how close these missions were to the United Kingdom, that the air forces had the use of the full array of electronic navigational aids that they had been developing for years, they bombed with ineffective antiaircraft fire, and flew to and from their targets without any interception by German fighter aircraft. Yet the best the bombers could do, in this totally permissive environment, was drop bombs close to their cloud-covered targets and cause some disorientation and psychological damage. Craven and Cate recognized that the commanders on Omaha Beach were disappointed with the air component's inability to neutralize the German defensive positions, but they suggest "accurate assessment of the effectiveness of these attacks is impossible."[73] This evaluation is not entirely correct, and in most instances it is relatively easy to evaluate the results of this bombing assault.

For example, a little after 0730, Central European Time, thirty-five German soldiers from the 352nd and 716th Infantry Divisions manned their positions at Widerstandsnest 62. They had been on alert since 0200 hours and had taken cover as heavy bombers and ships tore up the terrain all around them. Other than filling the air with dust and causing their ears to ring, the bombardment had done little damage, and no one was hurt. One of the most powerful German fighting positions on Omaha Beach was intact and ready to fight as several companies from the US 16th Infantry Regiment, 1st Infantry Division, approached the beach in their landing craft. Lieutenant Bernard Frerking, the supporting artillery forward observer, picked up his telephone and was pleasantly surprised to hear the voice of his battery commander, a couple of kilometers away. In spite of the massive bombardment, the line to the artillery unit was intact, and all the battalion's 105-mm guns were untouched and ready to fire. Within moments the strongpoint's machine guns, small arms, and light artillery began raking the Americans with direct fire. Mortars within the strongpoint dropped high-explosive shells at the water's edge. The field artillery, thousands of meters behind the strongpoints, began bombarding landing craft as they reached the coast. The firepower from this relatively small number of defenders was devastating. According to historian John C. McManus, by the end of the day, US 16th Infantry lost one-third of its manpower, 820 soldiers killed, wounded, or missing in action.[74]

Widerstandsnest 62 was labeled target 43 in the field order, and it was the US 2nd Bomb Division's responsibility to attack it. They sent thirty-six B-24 Liberators, carrying fifty-two fragmentary or high-explosive 100-pound bombs. Because of the time delay, they all missed their targets.[75] As Bradley pointed out in his autobiography, "This margin for safety had undermined the effectiveness of the heavy air mission. To seasick infantry, bailing their craft as they wallowed through the surf, this failure in air bombing was to mean many more casualties upon Omaha Beach."[76] The inaccuracy of that morning's air assault, and much of this book is about inaccurate bombing, had consequences beyond the toll it took on French civilians. It allowed the German defenders in this one strongpoint, and almost every other one along the invasion beach, to do their job unhindered, and it directly contributed to some of the white headstones in the US military cemetery in the bluffs overlooking this position. It is probable that the adjustment to the bombing times had the opposite effect of what planners intended and caused more Allied and French casualties than it prevented. No wonder few air enthusiasts have wanted to realistically discuss the details of this assault, since the largest single air attack in history failed to accomplish its mission. It is certainly an operation that requires much more critical analysis than it has received in the seven decades since that day in June.

Finally, with the bombing of Caen, the nature of the combat took a different turn. For the first time during the war, American bombers purposefully attacked French homes. These raids would continue as the heavy bombers switched their fires from attacking German positions along the beach to the calculated destruction of twenty-six cities, towns, and villages. For the French, it is the bombings that began in the early afternoon, the subject of the next chapter, that evoke some of the greatest and most emotional response.

CHAPTER ELEVEN

THE TOWNS

Seventy miles to the southwest of Caen is one of the oldest cities in Normandy, Avranches. As early as 511 it was a Christian bishopric and figured prominently in medieval politics. In 1944 it was a major road and rail crossroads for traffic arriving from Brittany and the south. That June, Louis Adam was a student at the Lycée Émile-Littré. Since German troops occupied the college itself, the students and teachers moved to the abandoned Ursulines convent. Students had just taken their examinations, and many had gone home to finish their final essays. Louis noted in his diary that he had "nothing to report" on Sunday and Monday, just some lesson reviews and playing ball in the yard that bordered the garden and overlooked the bay of Mont Saint-Michel. On Tuesday, June 6, he learned that the main invasion had taken place, but "here, it does not concern us, since it is in the north of the department. However, the staff had made up the beds and moved all the furniture to the dormitory downstairs to keep everyone together. All of this was happening in good spirits since the war had passed this city by."[1] All that would change on June 7. Brereton's Ninth Air Force had the task of blocking the routes out of Avranches, and thirty-six B-26 Marauders attacked the rail yard a little before 1430.[2] Louis watched the bombs fall, each ending in an unimaginable crash, just below the garden. "What a fright! Without losing his cool, the principal gathers us and tells us that we will leave for the country."[3] At 1515 hours, fifteen P-47 Thunderbolt fighters returned to attack traffic on the bridges headed north.[4]

> My friend went to the police station where he has friends. I accompany him there, not knowing what to do. Then, I go back to college. Everything is demolished, and rescuers are on site. The wounded are evacuated by ambulance. I learned that the "boss" [probably the director] is dead. He had lost his arm, and his son, "Little Louis," which he held by the hand, was also killed. I help carry corpses to the courtyard of a school near the church of Notre-Dame. Lack of stretchers, a wheelbarrow, is used. . . . I was asked the identity of the dead I know. . . . A priest comes to collect the body and to my dismay, took me with him to the rectory.[5]

Today Americans remember this city as the place where Patton's Third Army began its breakout in July. Those in Avranches remember June 7 as the day the war came to their sleepy town and killed sixty-four of their fellow citizens.[6]

The Plan and Execution

Although the bombing of the rail centers has received most of the attention in traditional D-Day narratives, the bombing of the towns surrounding the invasion area are, in this author's view, the most troubling. Away from the coast, agriculture and horse breeding characterized the Norman economy, with farmers and their families living near streams or rivers, where water provided power for the community grain mill. Next to the stone bridges that crossed these waterways, citizens set up their shops, the town hall, and religious schools. Homes of varying size and quality circled the community. Before the war, walking, bicycles, and horses were the primary means of getting from the village to the field or barn in the surrounding higher ground. Over the centuries the dirt paths became improved roads leading to market towns, of which the most important were Caen, Lisieux, and Saint-Lô. Frederick Morgan's original concept of stopping the enemy reserves identified the bridges in these three small cities for destruction.[7] Although it was modified and revised, this requirement, generally referred to as creating "chokepoints," remained part of the Neptune plan.[8]

By the end of April, planners at Twenty-First Army Group identified twenty-six towns they wanted "heavily bombed on D-Day and D-Day plus one to create road blocks."[9] In other words, the Army wanted the air forces to pulverize French homes to slow the German movement.[10] Neither Harris nor Spaatz wanted anything to do with this. But on May 20 Montgomery got involved and made it clear that after the bridge bombings on the Seine and Loire, stopping the movement of panzers within the "inner zone close to the bridgehead," should be a high priority. Two days later Leigh-Mallory met with the Eighth Air Force commander. Doolittle was adamant that "heavy bombers were not tactical weapons."[11] This aversion to using the bombers as flying artillery was also Harris' position: "the heavy bomber is a first-class strategic weapon and one of the least effective tactical weapons."[12] Tedder agreed with his bomber commanders and argued that bombing the road centers would, since planners had based it only on map reconnaissance, be a wasteful use of airplanes and would result in excessive civilian casualties.

That afternoon Montgomery got word that the air staffs were challenging his demand to bomb the towns. At 1500 he called Leigh-Mallory and asked him if there had been any changes. The AEAF commander assured him and replied that "he stood by the plan absolutely and would resign rather than abandon it."[13] Apparently, no one wanted to confront the ground force commander, whom they all knew Eisenhower would support. That would be the end of the debate, either regarding the utility of bombing towns or the likely effects on French civilians. On June 5 Leigh-Mallory approved the final target list, which had not changed since May 10. Air operations officers scheduled twenty-six towns, with their churches, shops, and homes, for destruction. Under protest, Spaatz and Doolittle agreed to obey orders to bomb towns that had little German military presence, but they got the concession to drop leaflets warning the inhabitant of the impending attacks.[14] To the French survivors, these towns came to be called the "Villes martyres de Basse-Normandie," the martyred cities of lower Normandy.[15]

Caen Again

If there were a competition among these unfortunate cities for the most damaged, Caen would have to take the lead. Starting with that first mission on the afternoon of June 6, the city was under fire every day until Canadians cleared German forces out of the hills south of town on August 10. As defined by the Twenty-First Army Group, the goal of the bombing attacks on Caen was clear: "Maximum disruption of town and communications."[16] What strikes the modern reader is the absence of any consideration of the cultural and historical aspects of destroying this ancient city. Was it permissible for the Allies to destroy the Abbaye-aux-Hommes, built between 1066 and 1077, or the Abbaye-aux-Dames, founded by Queen Matilda in 1062? Was it lawful for bombers to wreck the Château, dating back to 1060, and inflict on it the same fate as Monte Casino in Italy? Did "military necessity," an often used but poorly defined term, justify the destruction of any of the more than half dozen medieval-era churches scattered across the city? How would the destruction of these historic, religious, and cultural edifices contribute to the Allied invasion's success? What would be the long-term effects of these bombing operations? And, from a military perspective, how would the destruction of this city contribute to Allied military operations? Between June 1 and June 10, there was little discussion among Allied leaders about the cost of these events.[17]

Following the bombing earlier that afternoon, some of Caen's citizens began to leave, hoping to get out of the city before dark, when Britain's night bombers might join in the bombing. They dared not get caught in anything that looked like a convoy, as the fighter-bombers machine-gunned first, and then inspected the target.[18]

The Ninth Air Force's medium bombers played a significant role in assaulting these towns. A little after 1630, only two hours after the Eighth Air Force's 2nd Bomb Division's attack, the Ninth's 323rd Bomb Group arrived over the city with thirty-six B-26 Marauders, heading for one of the road junctions. The group's bombs went everywhere, and their after-action comments reflect this inaccuracy. The bombers attacked in a box formation of twelve aircraft each. The report read:

- Box I—First 4. POOR. In a fair concentration the bombs centered 1200 feet North of the desired M.P.I, among houses on a road "Y."
- Second 4. GROSS. The center of impact occurred 1 mile southeast of the desired M.P.I., bombs of two a/c scoring direct hits on the primary target of 391 BG, a highway bridge. At the time of impact, it was estimated there was a German armored vehicle on the bridge. (Clouds interfered with bombardier's aim).
- Third 4: FAIR. Bursts centered 600 feet north of the desired M.P.I., a fairly well concentrated pattern hitting in streets and houses.

Subsequent attacks by the next two formations were not any better. As the 323rd Group tried to bomb specific streets, the 391st Group sought to do the same with two of the bridges across the Orne River. Again it was a useless endeavor as bombs went everywhere except on the bridges.[19] This time the bombers destroyed different parts of the city, as they hit south of the Orne, near the Église Saint-Michel de Vaucelles, begun in the twelfth century. Along the Rue de Falaise, the main road south, several blocks of homes collapsed, burying the inhabitants hiding in their cellars. Rather than a German armored vehicle, mentioned in the report above, the bomb hit a French Red Cross ambulance, knocking it into the river. Citizens found the body of the driver, twenty-seven-year-old Teresa Hérilier, in the water several weeks later.[20] Bombs also destroyed the section of town on the other side of the river, near the secluded harbor called Bassin Saint-Pierre. Firefighters and city officials struggled to put out the flames. Most of the old city was not made of brick or stone but highly flammable lath and timber. Late-exploding incendiary bombs interrupted their work, as did the constant discovery of wounded survivors and victims, or sometimes parts of victims.[21] During the bombing thirty-nine-year-old Bernard Goupil was supervising an aid station on the Rue des Carmes, near the fifteenth-century Church of Saint-Jean. He kept a passionate and illuminating journal of his experiences, and most French researchers cite him when investigating the Caen bombings. His exclamation in the middle of the diary that afternoon represents the feelings of many that day: "I feel a sense of outrage at the massacre of which I do not understand the military purpose."[22]

By that evening, in the words of the official RAF narrative, "anxiety at Headquarters, Twenty-one Army Group regarding the chances of blocking the routes through Caen and the towns south and east of the Assault Area had reached an acute stage."[23] One battalion of panzer-grenadiers from the 21st Panzer Division had split the British and Canadian forces, reaching the coast at Lion-sur-Mer. Had following German panzer forces not been diverted to attack other objectives, the tactical situation on the ground on the eastern portion of the invasion area would have become much more challenging. To the west, on Omaha Beach, the US V Corps had finally secured the landing beaches and was holding onto a relatively small perimeter south of Route Nationale 12, the main road connecting Carentan with Bayeux and Caen. German forces moving from the south could threaten its precarious hold on this little piece of France. The chokepoints, starting with Caen, needed to be blocked. It was time for Bomber Command, which already had a reputation for destroying cities, to join the fight.[24] Around 0230 in the morning, it hit Caen in a violent attack, carried out using the standard format the command had perfected over the previous year. First came the Mosquitos dropping their incendiaries, flaming torches suspended under parachutes designed to illuminate where the master bomber should start the attack. Then, one after another, in single file, 125 Halifax and Lancaster bombers, built to destroy German factories and cities, began dropping their almost 500 tons of bombs on civilians they intended to liberate. For thirty minutes, bomber after bomber followed each other in a fruitless attempt to destroy several small stone bridges. What they did do was turn the city into a pile of smoking rubble.[25]

Like others, Bernard Goupil hid wherever he could find some semblance of shelter from this thirty-minute-long earthquake with accompanying thunder. In his case, he was on duty at the aid station. He noted in his diary:

> Here is a deafening explosion louder than others. But, this time, the bomb did not fall directly on us, and the patients of this aid station they will not be buried or killed, as many poor Caennais must be around us. The blow is struck with a terrible crash, the walls flickering, silently the building seems to rise on its foundations for a few seconds, then the structure slips back to the ground. Does this mean these few seconds are not the last of our life? Instinctively electric lights are on. One of us, occupying the recess of the door of the station control room, views with concern the stones crack. However, the room's roof and the staircase arches are intact. It is not yet time for our lives to come to an end. These regular and repeated waves of aircraft do not stop. The minutes are long! Many pray during these tragic moments when death touches us.[26]

At around 0300 hours the bombing finally ended. When the passive defense workers, the police, and firefighters could get back out onto the burning streets, they recovered two hundred bodies. Many dozens of wounded found their way to aid stations and the hospital; many of these would not survive the next few days. Destroyed buildings and burning remains filled street after street. Rescuers encountered the typical horrible scenes, such as on 214 Rue Saint-Jean where a building collapsed, smothering to death eighteen people, including ten belonging to the same family. They discovered another twenty corpses, including several police officers, crushed in a trench on the Place de la République, where they had taken refuge. Other searchers found more than thirty bodies in the rubble of a nearby medical clinic. The bombs spared no one: nuns, the sick, the wounded, doctors, and nurses.[27]

The entire center of Caen was in flames, a mass of fallen stone and smoldering timber. The reconnaissance flight the next day, however, showed all bridges intact! Of course rubble had filled the streets, and bombs with delayed fuses continued to explode, making movement through any open corridors dangerous and slow.[28] Therefore, as the day came to a close, at around 1800 the Ninth Air Force's 391st Bomb Group returned to Caen and added another sixty-eight 2,000-pound bombs to the burning wreckage of the historic city in an attempt to block the crossings over the Orne.[29]

Unfortunately the Anglo-Canadian forces did not liberate Caen the next day, as planned. German forces moved north of the city and blocked any further Allied advance. On June 26 the British began Operation Epsom and employed Bomber Command again as a tactical weapon providing direct support for advancing British tanks and infantry. On the city's northern suburbs, an area that bombing had not yet entirely destroyed, Harris, at Montgomery's request, launched 467 Lancasters, Halifaxes, and Mosquitoes. More than five million pounds of bombs wrecked the area near where the Mémorial de Caen now stands. Incredibly, the bombing, while massive and shaking up the defenders, killed few Germans.[30] As the attacking troops inched their way south, artillery replaced the bomber as the liberator's means of destruction. German defenders used the city's rubble to reinforce fighting positions and block movement. By the end of the day on July 9, the British I Corps had reached the bridges over the Orne in Caen. Amazingly, while damaged and blocked by German troops on the other side, some were still standing and usable. The Germans still held the southern portion of the city.[31]

The British launched Operation Goodwood on July 18 to secure the high terrain south of the city and clear German units from the southern suburbs. Again a massive air bombardment, this time with more than 4,500 aircraft from all the Allied air forces, opened the assault. Farms and hamlets caught between German and Commonwealth forces virtually ceased to exist. The bombing demolished the city's eastern region. Two days later, Canadian forces moved through the city, finally bringing it under Allied control and ending its hellish existence. It would remain, however, under enemy artillery fire for another three weeks.[32]

A summary of activity at the small hospital Bon Sauveur, north of the river on the southwest side of the city, reflects this intensity. From June 6 until the departure of the last German, its six surgical teams operated around the clock on a total of 1,693 wounded citizens, an average rate of 34 per day. They had only three operating rooms, but doctors, nurses, and members of the Red Cross from other facilities and towns aided them. In spite of their best efforts, 233 of their patients did not survive.[33] Because of the transient nature of much of the population during the war, it is almost impossible to categorically report an exact number of civilians who perished in Caen during this period. Based on their permanent addresses, however, it appears that the best guess is 1,741, mostly on June 6 and 7, and many thousands more wounded.[34] Of the original population of 62,000, only about 17,000 remained and almost all the city's center and its ancient buildings and historical treasures had vanished. Today much of the city's construction reflects the hasty effort in the 1950s and 1960s to rebuild with exterior walls of an almost prefabricated motif. Occasionally one finds a restored timber building in the old Norman style, surrounded by the newer architecture. And one can still find in the new city remains dating back to the bombing, such as remains of the Church of Saint-Gilles on the high ground in the center of the town. Its origins go back to the middle of the eighth century but, after it was destroyed during the bombing of June 6 and 7, the citizens chose not to rebuild it. It remains as silent testimony to the events of that summer.[35]

Saint-Lô

Montgomery wanted Saint-Lô blocked, along with Caen.[36] Since before the sixth century, Saint-Lô had been an important Gallic market town and crossroads. The ancient part of the city, the Enclos, or enclosure, rested atop a rocky perch that dominated the slow-moving Vire. All traffic had to pass below its mighty ramparts, begun in the eighth century. In addition to the old Église Notre-Dame, started in the thirteenth century, the ancient city was rich in historical and architectural treasures extending back more than five hundred years to the beginning of the Middle Ages. Because of the war, the population had dropped from 16,000 citizens in 1936 to 12,800 by 1944. Unlisted on the official rolls were a large number of refugees from the coastal areas and places under more intense German occupation.[37] With a regional road network almost as important as Caen's, the city's central location made it a logical target for bombers creating chokepoints. The Allied planners identified three objectives in the city: Target C1 was the main bridge crossing the river just below the Enclos. Target C2 was a crossroads just south of the escarpment. The planners identified a third target (C3) in the written order but had not marked it on the map, and there was probably some confusion as to the bombers' exact aiming point. There was no question about the fourth target. On the map was a big "X" in the middle of the old city and the order only labeled as a "chokepoint." The army wanted the bombers to destroy the ancient city.[38]

Saint-Lô's citizens went to bed as normal on the evening of June 5. Although rumors of the impending invasion had been in the air for weeks, they apparently had no particular concerns. Suddenly, around 2330 hours, an anti-aircraft gun opened up on a cargo aircraft, probably one that had just carried American airborne forces to their drop zone, and it burst into flames. Now everyone was awake, and by early morning, news of the landings had spread throughout the city. The French Resistance, alerted by the coded Allied broadcast that the invasion was under way, had begun cutting telephone lines. As the word of the landings spread, the citizens had little thought of returning to sleep. By dawn they were able to hear the fighting along the coast, thirty-five kilometers away. An American aircraft dropped leaflets on the city, urging the citizens to evacuate. Most did not, especially since the pamphlets did not specifically indicate which towns the Allies intended to destroy. No one on the ground realized that shortly before 0900 hours, seventy-eight American bombers from seven B-17 squadrons had approached Saint-Lô, intent on destroying it. None of the units were able to locate the city, and they turned back toward England without dropping a bomb.[39] During the day, those citizens, realizing they might be caught in intense fighting when the Americans arrived, took precautions, such as hiding their valuables and stocking up on food and water. All day they heard the sounds of the fighting in the distance and watched as German vehicles moved through the town toward the front lines.[40] A few Allied aircraft attacked the central electric plant around 1000 hours, without any serious result. Fifteen minutes later, the aircraft returned again, knocking out the city's power. These minor raids, entertaining and mostly painless, probably deceived some citizens as to the nature of the fighting that would come. Throughout the day, those on the edge of the city watched as American fighter-bombers from the Ninth Air Force attacked German units moving toward the coast.

One can only imagine what was going through the minds of those in Saint-Lô, who had avoided the destruction that much of France and Europe had already experienced. For example, Jean Roger, a twenty-three-year-old who worked with the local Resistance, found the day exciting. Planes in the sky, agitated Germans, American prisoners, the sense of imminent liberation, kept him and his fellow citizens on edge. For him, the day was "full of joy, curiosity, anxiety, waiting, impatience and a gut feeling that perhaps the invasion may have failed."[41] But the Allies were still coming, and at 1330 hours the BBC broadcast an appeal to evacuate the city and get at least three kilometers away. Unfortunately for the French, the Germans had confiscated most radios, and few heard this appeal, and even fewer understood the consequences for not complying. The Germans posted signs at street intersections prohibiting the citizens from traveling on public roads, so movement would have been difficult. Even the local Resistance leader was unaware of the impending attack.[42] Most buildings used by the occupiers were closed, indicating that the soldiers were leaving for the front. The first real indication that the war was getting closer was a strike of about fourteen Mustang fighters that strafed and bombed railcars and troops near the train station. Citizens with any understanding of what was happening rushed to gather water and provisions for what could be a difficult time and began to move valuable objects to places of safekeeping. By the end of the day, they learned that the Allies had liberated Carentan, and many of the most optimistic remained in their homes anticipating a liberation celebration.[43]

By late afternoon, fighting was heavy, and the situation at Omaha and Utah Beaches, and among the airborne units, were unusually tense, as battalion after battalion of German troops moved forward to join the fight. Other than Caen, none of the chokepoints that the Twenty-First Army Group wanted to be blocked had been closed. Early that evening, the Eighth Air Force sent another 736 heavy bombers to ten of the most critical towns, including Saint-Lô. Allied reconnaissance determined that the German 84th Corps' reserve, the 30th Mobile Brigade, and other units were moving through the city past the Enclos. The 2nd Bomb Division sent out seventy-two B-24s to Saint-Lô. Only thirty-six found the city and aimed directly at the church and ramparts in the city's center, dropping 128 tons of 500- and 300-pound bombs.[44]

As the bombers arrived, Jean-Roger and his mother were sitting outside her house. He saw the approaching American aircraft and marveled at how fantastic they looked. Suddenly a sensation came over him that "directly changed his life. They are bombing!" They ran downstairs to find his father and look for shelter. Along with about twenty other people, they found a cellar and took cover.[45] The policeman Louis Duprey remembered many years later that after his work shift was over at 1900 hours, he headed to his aunt's home for dinner at the Bascule crossroads, arriving at around 2000. They began discussing the day's events when they could hear humming in the distance. It was a beautiful evening, and they could see the bombers approaching. As they marveled at the light reflecting off the aircraft, they noticed the bombs beginning to fall. Once the bombing stopped, Duprey headed back to the city and stayed there for more than twenty-three hours rescuing victims, some of whom he knew personally. He remembered pulling children from beneath a tangle of beams and rubble. The police station was a mangled mess, with many victims buried underneath. He noted, "The scenes are heartbreaking: The mother seeking her child (. . .), the wife recovering her wounded husband." He goes on: "The horror reached its peak. The rooms, hallways are filled with injured people, screaming, calling their relatives; a wounded mother arrived carrying her dead child at the station. The dying and wounded together in makeshift stall."[46]

Concerned that the Americans had not accomplished the mission, the planners directed RAF Bomber Command to destroy the city. At 0200 hours (June 7), it arrived with 110 Lancaster and Halifax bombers, each capable of carrying 14,000 pounds of bombs. With possibly seven hundred tons of bombs aimed at the Enclos, there was no pretending that this was a precision mission, and, guided by the flames from the earlier Eighth Air Force strike, they dropped their bomb load in the heart of the old city.[47] Michelle Chapron and her grandmother were outside as the next wave of bombers arrived, and she watched as the city was bombed even more heavily than before. She remembers watching large waves of aircraft passing very low over her house. The bombs themselves made a howling sound as they headed toward the ground, followed by the explosive's crashing sounds and bright flashes. Terrorized, she hid with her grandmother and aunt in what they hoped was a safe room in the house. One of the neighbors, who had "a veau Verdun" (a Verdun leg, referring to a wound from the Great War), led them to a place that would be safer. It was for them "la nuit du grand cauchemar," the night of the great nightmare.[48] There was nothing left. The local prison contained about two hundred civilians the security services had rounded up in the previous few weeks. The British attack demolished this compound, killing seventy-six of the inhabitants.[49]

The next day an American photo reconnaissance mission took pictures of Saint-Lô's bombed area. The photographs showed that most of the buildings in the Enclos were destroyed or severely damaged. The photos show large concentrations of craters in the center, south, and east of the city center. The raid had partially destroyed the railway station, but the primary target, the main bridge across the Vire River, had been hit directly only once. What the airborne photographers could not report or comment on was the human cost of this attack.[50] It is almost impossible to count the number of deaths within and around Saint-Lô with any accuracy. In addition to its citizens, many refugees from the countryside and the coast had found shelter with family and friends. Of course, in the confusion of regional combat and the intense burning in the city, many bodies were simply never recovered. Estimates and casualty reports extend from a minimum of 300 dead to more than 3,000. Boivin and Garnier, the most authoritative source, established that 326 residents of this city perished from the bombings on June 6 and 7, and thousands more were physically and psychologically injured.[51]

The horror for the survivors of this city was not over. Fighters and bombers from the Ninth Air Force visited Saint-Lô many times over the next six weeks and bombed the center on at least four more occasions. As the Americans approached, the rubble ironically facilitated the German infantry's defenses, allowing them to create stronger and harder-to-find firing positions, as they had in Caen. Finally, after an intense two-week battle that cost more than five thousand American casualties, German troops left Saint-Lô for good on July 19.[52] By the time the Americans moved in, the city was little more than "a heap of smoking rubble."[53] A week later the US VII Corps lined up along a section of the highway northwest of the ruined city. After some delays and missteps, 1,500 B-17 and B-24 heavy bombers dropped more than three thousand tons of bombs in an imaginary box two miles wide by four miles long occupied by the German Panzer Lehr Division. Within forty-eight hours, the breakout from Normandy was in full force.[54]

Rather than the invasion or liberation, the citizens remember the bombing. Michelle Chapron, who recorded her thoughts many years later, had some profound memories of the next day. Once the embers had cooled, she made her way back to the Gravey home, where she lived while attending school. Nothing was left. The madame, who ran the house, and her four children, ranging in age from two to nine, were dead. Madame Barbier and her daughter also died. One of her classmates, who lived there, was also found in the ruins. Michelle's race across town the previous afternoon had saved her life.[55] Today a large plaque rests on the side of the Enclos. It commemorates the 500 civilian residents who perished during the invasion, 352 who died within twenty-four hours on June 6–7. Among them were Geneviève, Georgette, Jean, Yves, and Simone Gravey on Rue Verrier.[56]

Saint-Lô monument to the victims of the June 6, 1944, bombardment. *Photograph by author*

Lisieux

Readers encountered Lisieux, home of six-year-old J. P. Cordier, in chapter 1. It is a small city on the main route from Paris, sixty-five kilometers east of Caen. It rests on the east bank of the Touques River, a narrow waterway a little more than a hundred kilometers in length, with two bridges for motor vehicles and another railway bridge connecting the town with the rest of the region. By 1939 it was best known as the home of Saint-Thérèse, a devout young lady who died in 1897, only twenty-four years old, and was canonized by popular demand in 1925. In 1944 one of the helicopter's early inventors, Paul Cornu, the first to achieve free flight while carrying a passenger in 1907, still lived there. Its most important historical site was the old Cathédrale Saint-Pierre, which its citizens began constructing in 1170 and finished in the thirteenth century. On the eve of the German invasion, it had approximately 15,000 citizens.[57] The most direct route for German units moving to Normandy from the north or from Paris was through Lisieux, making it a natural place to interdict replacements and supplies. In April the 12th SS Panzer Grenadiers, the Hitler Youth Division, had moved into the area. The city's central location and developed road network allowed the division to consolidate rapidly and move either toward the Norman beaches or, more likely in the view of the senior German commanders, north toward the Pas-de-Calais region, where they expected the main invasion. Only a few hours from the beaches, this unit could cause havoc if it arrived before the Allied forces were ready to receive it.[58] To prevent this movement, Allied army planners identified three chokepoints in the city, bridges and stone buildings, on the west side of the Touques River and directed the Air Force to destroy them to "delay road movement from East to West."[59]

Since the beginning of 1944, Lisieux's citizens had been anticipating the invasion. Few suspected that their city would immediately become part of the drama.[60] As in Caen and Saint-Lô, the Lexoviens, as they call themselves, knew before dawn on June 6 that the invasion was taking place nearby; they had been awakened in the middle of the night by an intense, distant cannonade coming from the direction of the coast. The dawn sky was full of aircraft, and sounds of the fighting increased in intensity. Before the sun came up, reconnaissance units from the 12th SS Panzer Division passed through the center of the city, heading west toward the sounds of the fighting. German unit commanders noted the residents' apparent calm, and in spite of the distinct sounds of war, they appeared to be beginning the day as if it were just like any other.[61] The rumble of battle continued all morning, and Allied aircraft seemed to be everywhere above the clouds. No one on the ground realized that at 0900 eighty-one B-17 Flying Fortress aircraft were overhead and preparing to drop their bombs on the city. The bombardiers, however, could not locate their targets through the cloud cover and returned to England with loads intact. As the day went on, people poured into the streets looking for details. Rumors, such as false reports that the Allies had already captured both Honfleur and Caen, circulated among the crowd. Few had radios, since the Germans had confiscated them earlier, and there was no way to verify the news. As the morning turned into afternoon, civilians heard less from the beaches, and the firing was not quite as loud and more intermittent. Allied aircraft, primarily fighter-bombers, flew over the town and sometimes machine-gunned the German convoys along Route 13. Watching these events, everyone waited in fear that the cannonade would surely come their way.[62]

Staff officers at the Twenty-First Army Group command post were not happy that the main east-west highway was still open on the afternoon of June 6. Caen, the original Allied landing objective, had not been captured and German units from throughout the area were passing, almost unopposed, to the beaches. Most importantly, they knew that the 12th SS Panzer, concentrated near Lisieux, was on the move and that Hitler had ordered SS general Joseph (Sepp) Dietrich, commander of the I SS Panzer Corps, to throw the invaders "back into the sea."[63] Determined to stop German units from heading to the front, the Army Group planners contacted AEAF headquarters and demanded another bombing mission, before sunset, against the principal towns surrounding the beaches, including Lisieux. Around 2000 hours, seventy-two B-24 Liberator bombers crossed the English Channel and flew toward the city. This time, since the leaders expected that the cloud cover would prohibit any precision, they ordered the crews to use "overcast bombing techniques," a euphemism for area bombing without regard to either accuracy or civilian casualties. To make accuracy more problematic, increasingly severe weather forced the aircraft to fly higher than anticipated, up to 23,000 or 24,000 feet. Still, many aircraft were unable to find either this or any target and headed back to England. Twenty-five B-24s, though, fought through the weather and headed for Lisieux intent on dropping their seventy-three tons of explosives on their assigned objective.

At 2020 hours the Liberators appeared over the city center and began dropping their munitions, just as the residents sat down for their evening meals and young children went to bed.[64] Twenty-year-old Gérard Hanocque, a university student, like many others was just getting ready for bed as the bombers approached. In spite of the excitement far away near the coast, everyone was following the curfew from sunset to sunrise, so the early evening was quiet and the streets were empty. Suddenly he heard the sounds of aircraft engines humming in the sky. That did not worry him since he recognized the bombers as American. Many times they had flown overhead, always heading for targets further to the east. But this was different, as the bombers opened their bellies and began dropping their bombs. Many fell close to his home, and Gérard momentarily passed out from the explosion. He was unhurt and moved to the window to see what was happening. He saw the nearby hospital covered by a huge cloud of smoke. But the bombing was not over, and a new string of bombs fell just in front of his house. He found himself hiding from flying glass as the walls shook violently. The explosions broke all the windows in his father's house. Amazingly, he was alive.[65]

At least forty people died in the attack that hit the center of the city.[66] Those on the edge of town, generally on higher ground than Lisieux itself, watched in horror at the explosions, smoke, and fire in the heart of their district. Just across the Touques, in the small suburb of Saint-Désir, Madame Yvonne Petit managed a café. It was in her home on the main road to Caen. All day she had watched German reinforcements move toward the battle zone and watched as the American bombers attacked the city in the early evening. Living with her was a sister who had been handicapped since birth, a two-year-old son Christian, and her seven-year-old daughter, Ginette. In addition, a young lady helped her as a waitress in the café. Right after the bombing that afternoon, she had many discussions with people from the town about what to do next. Some of her neighbors, and everyone in that small community was a neighbor, were brandishing the leaflets dropped by the Eighth Air Force. She remembers many people asking her for advice. What should they do? Should they stay? Leave? Given her circumstances, and with most of the city still standing, she decided to remain. So did many civilians that night and, with much of the city still standing, most hoped the danger had passed. Rather than leave the city, many returned to their beds.[67]

As in the case of Saint-Lô, Montgomery and his planners had begun to lose faith in the Americans' ability to block the routes across the Touques and called on Bomber Command to finish the job. Arriving above the city at 0120 hours, 102 Lancasters began systematically dispensing their ordnance around the region. The bulk of their bombs fell on the western portion of the target, especially the village of Saint-Désir. When she awoke after the attack, Yvonne had her wounded two-year-old son Christian in her arms. Apparently the explosions had thrown her out onto a balcony just outside her house. Then, as she began to move, another explosion threw her back inside. She was able to move her son to safety, and then started looking to see how everyone else was. The last bomb shattered the lower part of the house where the café operated, immediately killing her disabled sister. The explosion trapped her daughter and the young waitress in the debris. She was able to free her assistant, but not Ginette, who was too badly injured for her to pull from the rubble. The crying child exclaimed, "Mama, I will die, but the war will be finished." As Yvonne, who was also severely injured in the head and legs, tried to comfort her, Ginette died. "Sometime before, she had told my mother that she would like to die young to be an angel. This wish is my only comfort." Her testimony, written in 1981 in beautiful cursive prose, is an emotional reminder that there is another, nonheroic, narrative of this campaign. She concluded her letter with: "I hope no one ever has to see this again."[68]

Gérard Hanocque remembers hearing the bombers approach. He saw the light from the Mosquito pathfinders, and then the bombs began falling. French survivors often use the word *chapelet*, literally defined as a rosary, to describe the appearance of the bombs falling from the aircraft. In his testimony he describes uninterrupted strings of *chapelets* hitting the ground. There were infernal noises and unseen shock waves that shook his bed and walls, causing windows and shingles to fall into the street. Then more flashes, wind, and shock waves. According to him, it was a constant rumble, like a drum roll, shaking and overturning everything. He smelled the burnt explosives as Lisieux disappeared under a cloud of dust. The bombardment lasted for seventeen minutes that, to him, seemed like hours. Then it was done, and only the smell of burnt explosives remained. His father moved outside and could see Saint-Désir in flames, with the church burning like a torch. Aircraft were still circulating overhead. Around 0500 Gérard, alive and uninjured, fell asleep.[69]

He woke up at around 0800 to a burning city. The sky was empty of aircraft. A great silence fell over the city, punctuated at times by the bursting of a bomb, the crackle of the fire, or a collapsing house. He remembered that it was raining, and the clouds seemed close and dark. Gérard's family decided to evacuate the city so they would never have to live through that experience again. Many of his neighbors had already departed. As he left, he discovered that the bombing had destroyed Saint-Désir, still engulfed by fire and smoke. The church was no more. High winds moved clouds of smoke up toward his family and burnt paper fluttered in the sky. Bombs, probably with delayed-action fuses, continued to explode. He remembered, "In the street in front, nobody, silence, silence and desolation all this monotonous and low gray skies and drizzle. Nothing can ever erase that vision." As he moved out of the city, he started to learn some of the tragic stories that were part of the horror. About Dr. Prévost, who dismantled his house on Rue Pont Mortain brick by brick, to find his buried wife and daughter. And Madame Cornu, wife of the great inventor, who died with their six children. And many other horrible stories he would learn about later.[70]

The next morning, the ground force's operations staff was still not satisfied with the progress the air forces were making in blocking German movement. Again they demanded more attacks on several key chokepoint locations, including Lisieux. Six squadrons, twelve aircraft each, from the B-24-equipped 2nd Bomb Division flew from the United Kingdom back to Lisieux. The bombers attacked at 20,000 feet, flying in a formation with nine aircraft wide and with three more trailing the lead center group. They planned for a two-minute interval between each wave of attackers. Given standard formations of the time, each squadron created a 1,000-foot wide path of devastation, dropping 120 500-pound bombs in the target zone, an extremely broad interpretation of "precision bombing." In fact, because of the thick cloud cover, they employed the "overcast bombing technique," which provided limited accuracy for targets of this nature. When the raid was over 180 tons of bombs finished the city off.[71] The next day the weather cleared enough for a photographic reconnaissance mission. The photo shows the fires still burning and, in the words of the analyst who examined the photos, "much destruction in the town."[72]

These three attacks killed at least 781 Lisieux citizens and probably more refugees from the coast. Of course many more were wounded and suffered from the memories of those forty-eight hours.[73] The bombers damaged the town's two main highway bridges, but the Germans replaced one of them almost immediately. While the demolished buildings slowed some traffic, they had little effect on German movement to the battle area.[74] In fact the ruined nature of the city, providing natural machine-gun emplacements, contributed to the Germans' stubborn defense against the British 51st (Highland) Division, which lasted for four days during the so-called pursuit to the Seine. The Highlanders finally drove the Germans out of the city on August 23, after fighting that resulted in even more civilian casualties.[75] The first stage of Lisieux's agony came to an end on that summer day. Now its remaining citizens tried to put the pieces of their lives back together, rebuild their city, and reconcile their relationship with the arriving British forces. Above the rebuilt suburb of Saint-Désir is the municipal cemetery, with row after row of family sarcophagi, identifying the inhabitants as having perished during the bombardment of June 1944. Resting on one of those old large marble slabs is a small newer stone rectangle, one with the simple inscription: J-P Cordier, 1938–1992, the young man mentioned at the beginning of this book. Forty-eight years after losing his family, he returned to their company.

This chapter has discussed only three of the fourteen towns marked for destruction. Caen, Saint-Lô, and Lisieux accounted for 2,844 civilian deaths on June 6 and 7 alone. While these were three of the largest examples of civilian losses as a result of this operation, they were not unique. Most of the cities on the original bombing list took casualties as the air forces attempted to convert their sleepy towns and villages into piles of stone for military purposes. Falaise, to the west, is best known as the scene of the German retreat and near-encirclement in August. Yet the Americans and British turned it into a pile of ruins by massive bombings on June 7, resulting in 151 dead. The village of Condé-sur-Noireau, south of Caen, sacrificed 246 of its citizens, 5 percent of its population, for the goal of delaying German troops, as did Coutances, which lost another 500. Bombers killed 214 civilians in Valognes, and Aunay-sur-Oden contributed 8.6 percent of its population, 145 civilians, to the same cause. Neither of these were on the original list but were added later. The bombing wiped out both of these villages as the photographs of each show to striking effect. Photos of all these towns the Allies attacked on June 6–8 tell the same story. While it is impossible to get accurate casualty numbers as to when and how the Norman civilians perished, Boivin, Bourdin, and Quellien, the experts in this regard, have calculated that 14,000 died during the invasion, most of them during the period between June 6 and 15 and by far the most ("et de très loin") as a result of aerial bombardment.[76] Thousands more found themselves wounded or maimed for life. Thousands more suffered the heartbreak of painful loss. The issue, in this author's opinion, is not that the French absorbed these casualties, comparable with Allied battle losses of 4,413 killed on June 6 (2,499 American), with the losses increasing as more Allied and German forces arrived in the battle area, but why is this information not part of the operation's narrative?[77]

Headstone of the Faucon family killed by the June 7, 1944, Allied bombing of Lisieux. *Photograph by author*

The US Army Air Force published a report soon after the end of the war discussing the use of their heavy bombers in the invasion. It explains in some detail, using several pages with maps, the attacks on beach targets. There are no details about the missions against "road choke-points in Caen and several smaller Normandy towns."[78] Craven and Cate devote one paragraph to attacks on these so-called chokepoints, noting only that they had dropped "warning leaflets for the benefit of the French population." They provide us no details on the effectiveness of the leaflet drop.[79] Harris does not mention Bomber Command's missions against any of these targets in his after-action report.[80] Ambrose mentions that after the morning attacks on the beaches, the Eighth Air Force "were in the air again, bombing Saint-Lô and other inland targets."[81] He provides no details, nor do D'Este or Hastings, who discusses ground operations in masterful detail without mentioning the intense bombing fifty kilometers south of the beaches.[82] While newer campaign narratives, such as those by Beevor and Atkinson, do acknowledge that the Allies bombed French cities beyond the beaches, none provide details even remotely comparable to the dramatic accounts of the infantry landings and airborne drops.[83] In general, therefore, historians have ignored the fate and drama of these towns that were beyond the beach and not in most cases observed by journalists accompanying the invading armies, Caen and Saint-Lô being the most important exceptions.

A second issue concerns the effectiveness of these attacks. How important were these missions in delaying the arrival of German panzer units into the battle zone? Certainly, as the Eighth Air Force's after-action report notes, the Germans did encounter problems moving to the front.[84] Later, however, what its Operational Research Section discovered was not so reassuring. It noted the widespread destruction of houses, churches, and all other kinds of property. The investigators also acknowledged the high civilian casualties, usually caused by inferior shelters. It found, however, that bombing had not "uniformly covered the streets with debris." Also, especially in the larger towns, "bombing failed to block all routes but caused scattered areas of destruction."[85] According to Major General Fritz Krämer, commander of the I SS Panzer Corps, when German units arrived at a destroyed area, such as Falaise, their military police directed the tanks and trucks around the rubbled town with little delay, although supply vehicles had difficulty bypassing the blocked chokepoints.[86] General Fritz Bayerlein, the commander of the Panzer Lehr Division, had little problem with roads leading to the beaches but complained about Allied fighters catching his units during the day, which is a common lament among Wehrmacht officers.[87] Could these air attacks have been as effective if the Allies had not destroyed these towns?

Finally, more than anywhere else in this book, these air strikes reflect an American (and British) rejection and violation of the laws of war. A guide published in 1917 for infantry leaders, such as Eisenhower and Bradley, reprints the Hague Convention's rules of land warfare, which include: "The attack, or bombardment, by whatever means, of towns, villages, dwellings, or buildings which are undefended is prohibited."[88] In the 1920s a postwar conference at the Hague amplified these rules: "Article 24: Aerial bombardment is legitimate only when directed at a military objective, that is to say, an object of which the destruction or injury would constitute a distinct military advantage to the belligerent."[89] Everyone in positions of responsibility understood these rules, although none of the belligerents had ratified them but acquiesced in their violation against Germany and later Japan. Spaatz and Doolittle believed it was the wrong thing to do and all of them, Harris included, believed it was a waste of a powerful weapon. Eisenhower, supporting Montgomery, overruled them. After June 6 the bomber leaders did as the ground commanders wished, with little protest.

Eisenhower, learning from his experiences in North Africa, Sicily, and Italy, had gained control of all aircraft in his theater of operations. He had no intention of releasing the bombers back to Operation Pointblank until he was certain his lodgment in France was secure. Montgomery, fearful of Rommel and German counterattack doctrine, believed in firepower-centric operations. Using heavy bombers to block roads to slow the panzers' arrival was a part of his way of war. How effective the attacks on chokepoints were is understandably a matter for historical debate. What is not debatable is that historians outside France have failed to include details of these towns' destruction in most published accounts. Like the casualties on Omaha Beach, the destruction of Norman cities is part of Operation Overlord's narrative, and French civilian deaths were part of the human sacrifice that contributed to the Allied victory on June 6.

CONCLUSIONS AND OBSERVATIONS

Once ashore, the Allies continued to consolidate and expand their lodgment. To a significant degree, Operation Fortitude had worked, and the deception had affected the German High Command's decision-making process. Rather than stage a dramatic buildup and counterattack, the Germans continued to dribble reinforcements into Normandy, most not released by Hitler until the end of July, when it was too late. Those German units that traveled by rail felt the effect of the Transportation Plan, as they had a slow and painful journey through severely damaged rail yards or moved around slowly on secondary routes. Once near Normandy, most had to detrain and move by road, always threatened by the ever-present Allied Typhoons and Thunderbolts. Since the Allies had damaged or destroyed almost all the river bridges, the need to ferry equipment to the other side or traverse makeshift crossings further slowed the progress of reinforcements to the front. As one German, captured by the US 4th Infantry Division near Carentan in the middle of June, reported, "I crossed the German border into France through Metz two weeks ago. My journey to Périers-Carentan took me twelve days. Railway lines are completely broken up by air attacks. Lines of communication are completely disorganized. Troops on furlough had to be transported by wood-burning trucks."[1] The bombing did not cause all the delays, as the US VII Corps historian at the time noted:

> From reports received it was now clear that the French resistance movement had made a considerable contribution to the invasion plan, having

> fostered wide-spread sabotage, including the cutting of rail and other communications. Telephone and cable wires were disrupted, rails and bridges rendered un-serviceable, canals and barges sabotaged as were war plants, and in one specific incident 46 locomotives were destroyed by the Maquis. Resistance activities had good results, not only in tying down the enemy's forces, but also in hindering to some extent the movement of both troops and supplies into the Normandy battle area.[2]

More German infantry and armor did arrive, however, and by the end of July General Günther von Kluge, who had replaced Rommel after his wounding on July 17, still had about twenty-five divisions in contact, with most of his armor arrayed against the British near Caen. By then the US VII Corps had captured Cherbourg and moved to the outskirts of Saint-Lô. Eisenhower called the heavy bombers back to support the ground commanders again at the end of July. First, more than two thousand heavy and medium bombers attacked villages southeast of Caen in support of Operation Goodwood on July 18–20. This massive air strike did little to the German defenders but managed to destroy a dozen French villages. Fortunately civilian casualties were light since most had already evacuated the area. Following the massive bombing of the German lines outside of Saint-Lô on July 25, starting Operation Cobra, Lt. Gen. Omar Bradley's newly formed Twelfth Army Group took command of all American forces in the bridgehead, and his divisions poured out of the beachhead and into the French countryside.[3]

Hitler finally realized that Normandy was the main Allied effort and ordered his armor to drive the Americans back into the sea. It was too late as Bradley's new command stopped the German counterattack at Mortain on August 7. By August 13 Commonwealth forces were attacking south away from Caen and came close to joining the Americans near Falaise, almost capturing most of the German army in western France. By August 25 American and Commonwealth forces were approaching the Seine, as the 2nd French Armored Division and 4th US Infantry Division moved to Paris. General Alexander Patch's US-French Seventh Army landed on the Riviera on August 15 and linked up with Eisenhower's forces near Dijon on September 11. While Bradley's armies continued to drive across France to the German border, Montgomery, now commanding only his Twenty-First Army Group, drove his forces across Belgium. Along the way, they overran the remains of the permanent vengeance weapon launch sites, all destroyed by Allied bombardment before they could fire a shot. Of course the mobile V-1 and V-2 launchers continued to fire until almost the end of the war. Eisenhower's forces, slowed by a lack of supplies and increasing enemy resistance, continued to push toward the German border. The operation in Lorraine had been especially difficult as combat around Metz, Strasbourg, and Colmar consumed the attention of nine Allied army corps, including two from the newly reconstituted French First Army. By December 15 most of France was free of German forces with the major exceptions of eastern Lorraine, some mountainous terrain along the Italian border, and five fortress-ports, including Royan and Dunkerque. The German offensive in the Ardennes took place primarily in Belgium, and the French First Army under General Jean de Lattre de Tassigny drove the Germans out of Colmar Pocket in early February. Hard fighting continued until the German general Alfred Jodl signed the instrument of surrender at Reims, France, on the night of May 6. The last of the fortress ports, Saint-Nazaire, capitulated on May 11, 1945.

As the Allies advanced, they continued to use their overwhelming air advantage. Once ashore, the Second and Ninth Tactical Air Forces supported Montgomery's and Bradley's army groups. Behind the lines, they took over abandoned airfields or constructed new, temporary ones. As the ground troops advanced, so did the airfields, to maintain faster aviation response to Army needs. This direct support continued until the end of the war, with thousands of missions against German-defended targets in France. Air operations in the Falaise pocket are some of the best examples of the power of these units in destroying the German forces. Less well known is the participation of the heavy bombers during the advance. Eisenhower retained control of Spaatz' and Harris' commands until June 17. Bomber Command attacked Flers, Le Mans, Laval, Rennes, Étampes, Achères, Dreux, Orléans, and a host of other cities before the middle of the month. Rail centers and airfields continued to be the primary targets.[4] The same was true of the Eighth Air Force, which attacked Orleans, Rennes, Angers, Nantes, St. Denis, Dreux, Bordeaux, Le Mans, and much more.[5]

While the heavy bombers turned their attention to missions in Germany, they continued to bomb targets across France. More than 56 percent of all Allied bombs dropped on France were dropped during the months of June, July, and August 1944.[6] Ahead of advancing troops, they continued to hit airfields and rail yards in August and September. Earlier sections of this book described attacks on Boulogne, Le Havre, and Royan that took place well after the Allied landings. Now that the Germans were using temporary launch facilities, they concentrated on destroying V-1 and V-2 storage sites, many located north of Paris. As late as September 28, Bomber Command was still hammering German positions, and the French countryside, in the Pas-de-Calais. These were not small raids, as this last one consisted of almost five hundred aircraft. Other than the attack against Royan in January, the strike against Calais was the last Bomber Command mission against a target in France.[7] The Eighth and Fifteenth Air Forces, the latter flying out of Italy, provided similar support across France. The Eighth's last missions in France were in support of American ground troops against Metz on November 9, when it sent more than eight hundred bombers to support Patton's Third Army in the seizure of the city, and finally the attacks against Royan on April 15, 1945.[8]

Was Eisenhower's air operation successful? Historians and analysts have long debated the value of the bombing campaign against France. Indeed, the air forces, although neither of them had wanted to do it, pointed with pride to their record, in particular against rail yards and bridges. There is no question that the Transportation Plan, and its associated attacks on bridges, hindered the Germans in using their interior lines of communications to move forces rapidly from distant theaters of operations into the invasion zone. Others point out that bombing cities and rail yards was counterproductive and that the primary reason the Germans could not reinforce the landing area was because Hitler would not release the reinforcements or because of poor operational and tactical decisions.[9] Most German accounts credit Allied fighter-bombers, rather than bombers, with delaying their movement.[10] They also point out the ability of their forces to use the bombed-out villages as defensive positions. Some Allied accounts note the problems American and Commonwealth troops had in moving and supplying themselves along damaged roads, bridges, and rail lines. Nevertheless, the fact is that in June, Canadian, British, and American infantrymen landed on the French beaches and stayed there. Exactly what operations contributed the most is in the realm of conjecture. Cumulatively the air attacks against France directly contributed to Eisenhower's goal of "stopping the panzers" and keeping them away from the beaches.[11] Decisive German reinforcements never arrived at the beach.

What is apparent in reviewing the records of bombing missions is that until January 1944, the air operations against targets in France were destructive but not devastating. Faced with catastrophic losses during the Battle of the Atlantic, Churchill and his cabinet demanded massive air strikes at the ports housing the U-boats. Generally, against their will, the British and American bomber commanders destroyed several ports in a futile effort to destroy the submarine pens. For self-preservation, they attacked airfields the Luftwaffe could use. In missions related to Operation Pointblank, they struck selected factories that produced trucks, engines, and tires. Also under intense political pressure and against their will, Spaatz and Harris went after the Noball launcher sites. The strategic air forces conducted these missions in the only way they knew how, by the massive bombardment of the targeted area. Again, the bomber leaders wanted nothing to do with it, as their real desire was to continue city destruction, in the case of Harris, or precision bombing, in the case of Spaatz, against Germany. Bombing France and Belgium, unless it was a factory producing material supporting the German air war, was not on their agenda. Those kinds of missions would not validate strategic bombing doctrine or verify their right to be an independent military service.

All that changed with Eisenhower's arrival. In the tradition of Scott, Grant, and Pershing, he took command. He forced the political authorities to acknowledge that he was the supreme Allied commander, a dramatically imposing title if there ever was one. Then he forced the bomber barons, Spaatz and Harris, to bend to his will. Tedder acted as his go-between, but the fact was the air commanders worked as part of a combined arms team, not independently. Then, through Tedder and Leigh-Mallory, who does not get the credit he deserves, SHAEF developed a series of operations to achieve Eisenhower's first objective: gain and retain a lodgment on the European continent. He incorporated operations against airfields and ports into his scheme. He continued and coordinated operations against factories and vengeance weapon sites. He embraced Morgan's deception plan and ensured the air forces were in support of Operation Fortitude. He adjudicated battles between senior leaders and made the decision that bombing rail yards was the best use of his heavy bombers. He supported his ground force commander and ordered the destruction of all the bridges German troops could cross into the invasion area. Finally, in what this author believes is his most controversial decisions, Eisenhower supported Montgomery in destroying a ring of French towns beyond the landing area and, later, his use of heavy bombers in direct support of his tactical forces, such as at Le Havre and Royan. It was Dwight David Eisenhower who harnessed the air combat power to his will.

No one in Washington, in London, or at SHAEF wanted to kill French civilians or destroy their property. After all, de Gaulle was on the Allied side, and the governments would have to work with him or his successor in the postwar era. Unfortunately killing citizens and destroying their homes was unavoidable given the decisions that ground and air force leaders made on the use of air power in the campaign. One reason for the destructive nature of these air operations is that, at its most fundamental level, the Allied airmen were still learning the art and science of air warfare. The American and British air forces represented a new dimension of war, and they had not developed doctrine, process, or technology for conducting operations over enemy-occupied territory. The scale of this effort, with thousands of aircraft flying missions around the clock, only increased the probability of killing civilians. Military doctrine is usually the product of experience and military theory. Douhet, Trenchard, Mitchell, and their advocates in Bomber Command and the Tactical School developed bombing doctrine in the absence of extensive historical experience. All believed that air power was a way to avoid the horrific casualties of the Great War. All of them envisioned the heavy bomber, used against enemy economic targets, as the key to victory. Many, echoing the writings of Douhet and Trenchard, also believed that bombing would significantly affect the enemy's morale and will to fight.

None of these early theorists explained how their military forces could use these powerful weapons when the enemy occupied a friendly state. American air leaders presented their fighting doctrine in several documents, and the fundamental strategic statement, AWPD-1, discussed earlier, explicitly argues that the Army Air Force's role was to fight a strategic bombing war against German military power. While it does discuss supporting ground forces, there are no details in this regard and the document says nothing about using air power against objectives in an occupied state. When the report describes attacks on transportation installations, they are all in Germany.[12] The authors of the general aviation doctrinal manual, Field Manual 1–5, make no mention of problems conducting operations against forces in friendly countries.[13] Without a doctrine on how to carry out operations over occupied states, it is no wonder Spaatz and Harris were hesitant to support the Army's needs.

A second issue that contributed to French (and Belgian, Dutch, and Italian) civilian casualties is the problem of process. Exactly what should they bomb? Targeting was, and is, not an exact science, and in 1944 it was still in its infancy. The reason for the intensity of the debate in March among the senior leaders concerning the relative value of bombing rail centers, bridges, oil targets, and the like is that no one had the answer. The best "science" anyone could produce at the time was by Solly Zuckerman, a zoologist, who evaluated operations in Italy. His conclusion was that bombing French and Belgian rail centers was the best way to proceed. But was it? What about the political effect of civilian casualties or the secondary effects of having a destroyed French rail system? Would a concentration of power against several key nodes just before the landing be more efficient than a four-month process that destroyed everything? Was it possible to develop an approach combining rail, road, and bridge attacks that would give better results with less damage? Would blocking town centers significantly delay enemy movement, or would it create more destruction than it was worth? If the air leaders assumed that bombing would break German civilian morale, would it not do so also to the French? Most of those involved in determining what to bomb were young men with relatively little experience. Most had little planning experience before the war and learned on the job. There were no perfect answers, and they did the best they could to achieve Eisenhower's goal of keeping enemy tanks off the beach. As Robert S. Ehlers points out, the Allies had enough aircraft to target bridges, rail yards, and oil production simultaneously, all of them contributing to their commander's objective.[14] There was no reason to make a firm decision.

Additionally, the technology available at the time ensured that it was almost impossible to conduct air operations with any degree of precision. The heavy bomber's ability to find the correct general target continued to improve throughout the war as technicians perfected GEE and H2X navigation radar. But these systems were only marginally useful in actually identifying the target. Spaatz himself admitted in March 1944 that these devices were best used against "area objectives." He continued to be annoyed with his radar and argued in April that these systems were not "satisfactory enough for precision bombing of high priority strategic targets."[15] It is no wonder

Spaatz had no confidence in his ability to destroy German defenses on the Normandy beaches on June 6, and it explains why the Eighth Air Force had to abort so many missions later that day and why these commands continued to hit wrong locations often throughout the war. Anyone who believes that the US Air Force conducted precision bombing in the Second World War should carefully study what happened in Normandy from June 6–8.

The overcast bombing technique was, at best, a guess and not a precise calculation. Even when aircraft found the right city or town, hitting the right spot and creating the desired effect, as predicted by the staff that wrote AWPD-1 before the war, was problematic. The physical arrangement of aircraft in formation, while moving with a human releasing the bomb load in the lead aircraft followed by others executing at later times, ensured that the munitions would hit in an extended pattern. While it was possible to manipulate the bombing pattern to some degree, crews could not control the bombs once they left the aircraft. Some might hit the desired target, but most would not. Of course the problem was worse when ground commanders asked for these blunt weapons to provide them tactical support, such as on the Normandy beaches or at Le Havre. These heavy bombers were simply not capable of this kind of precision. Fighter-bombers often produced more accurate results, but dive-bombing and close air support were skills most Ninth Air Force pilots lacked in the middle of May. By D-Day they had much more practice and the Ninth's fighter and medium bombers did their jobs well.

Finally there is the issue of the intensity of the bombing effort. This air assault, as measured by the number of aircraft, took place on a scale never witnessed before or since. On June 6 the Allies had at their disposal almost 13,000 aircraft of all types, including 5,146 heavy bombers. Because their bases in the United Kingdom were so close to France, it was possible for aircraft to fly more than one sortie per day. In this precomputer era, all computations for mission requests, target allocation, planning for assembly in the air, deconfliction of fight ingress and egress routes, bomb configuration, and the list goes on, were done by humans with charts and manual devices. It was not unusual to have almost 4,000 aircraft flying across French airspace on any single day in May, and even more during invasion week. This constant effort, especially during the intense period of the weeks before and after the landing, exhausted everyone involved in this endeavor. Fatigue by air and ground planners, flight leaders, and individual pilots and navigators translated to mistakes in planning and execution. In some cases these errors created mishaps in the air when aircraft flew into each other. In others, bombs landed where they should not. In others, aircraft attacked objectives that other groups had already destroyed. It is also important to remember that because of the number of planners, pilots, and crews, these were often inexperienced young men. After flight training most learned their tactics, techniques, and procedures on the job. Since the ultimate goal was to bomb Germany, leaders often considered operations in France practice runs. Cumulatively, therefore, an absence of tested doctrine, problems with the process, limitations of the technology available, and the simple scale of the operation ensured that civilians would often suffer from these attacks.

Unfortunately the French paid the price for this centralization of power. According to the historians working at the Centre de Recherche d'Histoire Quantitative, the three principal departments in the invasion zone—Calvados, Manche and Orne—suffered 12,476 civilian deaths during the battle of Normandy. Most of these were from June 6–8, and air bombardment caused more than 60 percent of the deaths, almost 7,500 civilians who lived in these departments. The casualty figures for those killed during this period who had lived in other places before the war, but had become refugees in this previously tranquil part of France, are incomplete. And there is little information available concerning those injured during the attacks.[16] Not considered in this toll are the thousands of civilians killed across France, from Boulogne-sur-Mer to Marseille, who perished because the Allies targeted their cities in support of the invasion or the landings in the south. When it was over, cities and infrastructure across France were in ruin, and between 60,000 and 70,000 French civilians were dead resulting from this air offensive.[17] No one in the government during the postwar world wanted to discuss it. Exposing and explaining the demise of so many friendly civilians, and this includes those in Italy, Belgium, and the Netherlands, was not in any of the military service's best interests. There was no independent reporting of these incidents, and the public could find few details in war-era newspapers and magazines. Finally, the complexity of French society trying to recover and rebuild in the postwar era militated against any serious discussion of these events, except at the local level.

This book started out with a discussion of narrative. The American national narrative remembers being bombed at Pearl Harbor and landing on the Normandy beaches. Celebrating these events has become a national ritual, often accompanied by reading the names of those who perished. The French remembrance is more complex than the Allies', and, as noted many times in these pages, the memories of these events never left those who experienced them. For them, the Allied liberation of France did not take place only in June on the sands of Normandy, but beyond the beaches from Calais to Clermont-Ferrand to Metz. It took place along inland rivers, near isolated German installations, and at rail yards. They learned to fear aircraft overhead in the same way they avoided German military patrols or panicked when they heard a knock on the door. For several months in early 1944, the Americans, British, and Canadians were not liberators, but the enemy. Perhaps that is all forgotten today. But in an age when modern military forces routinely commit acts of collateral damage, a euphemism for killing friendly civilians by mistake, perhaps it is appropriate to consider the effects of those events more than seventy years ago. How did the surviving citizens of these

Vichy propaganda poster after bombing of Rouen. Reads, "Assassins always return to the scene of the crime." *Archives Départmentals de la Seine-Maritime*

destroyed villages and damaged cities interact with Anglo-Americans in the decades after 1945? Was de Gaulle's alleged comment that the United States would defend Europe until the last European a not-so-subtle reminder of these early events? Were the "Yankee go home!" slogans painted on walls in the early Cold War the work of communists, as alleged? Or was it the work of survivors who truly wanted the Americans out? How did a mature J. P. Cordier, Jean Roger, Michelle Chapron, and the hundreds of thousands of other survivors react to visiting American and British tourists in the 1950s and 1960s?

APPENDIX A

Targeted Factories (Selected)

City	Company	Purpose
Arras	Various	Rail factories
Asnières-Seine	Various	Industrial area
Beaumont-sur-Oise	Hispano-Suiza	Aviation
Blanc-Misseron	ANF	Locomotive
Bois-Colombes (Paris)	Hispano-Suiza	Engines
Boulogne-Billancourt (Paris)	Renault	Trucks, autos, weapons
Châteauroux	Breguet	Aero engines
Clermont-Ferrand	Michelin	Tires
Gennevilliers	Gnome et Rhône	Aero engines
Issy-Les-Moulineaux	(Paris) Renault	Trucks
Ivry-sur-Seine	(CAM)	Aviation
Javel (Paris)	Citroën	Trucks, autos
La Ricamarie	Nadella	Bearings
Le Creusot	Schneider	Artillery, armored vehicles
Le Creusot	Breuil	Steel manufacturing
Le Mans	Renault	Trucks, autos, weapons
Le Mans	Gnome et Rhône	Aero engines
Le Trait	ACMS	Boats and ships
Les Mureaux	SNCA	ME 108 Liaison plane
Lille	Compagnie de Fives	Locomotive
Lille	Atelier d'hellemmes	Locomotive
Limoges	Gnome et Rhône	Aero engines
Méaulte	Avions Potez	Aircraft

Mérignac (Bordeaux)	SNCA	Aviation
Montbéliard	Peugot	Trucks, autos
Poissy	Ford	Light trucks
Strasbourg/Meinau	Mathis (Junkers)	Engines
Toulouse	Bréguet	Aircraft and aircraft repair
Villacoublay	Bréguet	Aircraft repair

ANF: Ateliers de Construction du Nord de la France

CAM: Compagnie d'Applications Mécaniques

CMS: Ateliers et Chantiers Maritime de la Seine

SNCA: Société Nationale des Constructions Aéronautiques

Sources for bombing overview: Roger A. Freeman, Alan Crouchman, and Vic Maslen, *Mighty Eighth War Diary*, London: Arms and Armour Press, 1990; Martin Middlebrook and Chris Everitt, *The Bomber Command War Diaries: An Operational Reference Book*, New York: Viking, 1985.

APPENDIX B

Rail Centers Attacked in 1944

Community	Nation	Target #
Aarschot	Be	ZB.925
Abancourt	Fr	
Alencon	Fr	
Amberieu	Fr	Z.238
Amiens-Longueau	Fr	Z.446
Amiens-St. Roch	Fr	
Angers	Fr	
Angoulleme	Fr	
Antwerp-Dam	Be	ZB.926
Argentan	Fr	
Arras	Fr	Z.436
Aulnoye	Fr	Z.599
Avignon	Fr	Z.806
Baden Givors	Fr	Z.629
Beaumont	Fr	
Beauvais	Fr	
Belfort	Fr	Z.822
Béthune	Fr	Z.823
Blainville-sur-l'Eau	Be	ZB.807
Boulogne-sur-Mer	Fr	Z.805
Brussels/Midi	Be	ZB.928
Brussels/Shaerbeck	Be	ZB.40
Busigny	Fr	Z.824
Calais	Fr	Z.825

Community	Nation	Target #
Cambrai	Fr	Z.600
Carnoules	Fr	Z.808
Chalons sur Marne	Fr	Z.809
Chambery	Fr	Z.810
Chambly	Fr	Z.836
Charleroi/Monceau	Be	ZB.906
Charleroi/Montigny	Be	ZB.115
Charleroi/St. Martin	Be	ZB.116
Chaumont	Fr	Z.826
Conflans-Saint-Honorine	Fr	
Courcelles-sur-Seine	Fr	
Courtrai (Kortrijk)	Be	ZB.886
Creil	Fr	Z.601
Culmont-Chalindrey	Fr	
Dijon	Fr	
Douai	Fr	Z.830
Dreux	Fr	
Epinal	Fr	Z.831
Etampes	Fr	
Évreux	Fr	
Fougeres	Fr	
Ghent-Meirelnbeck (Gand)	Be	ZB.884
Gournay-en-Bray	Fr	
Grenoble	Fr	Z.811
Haine-Saint-Pierre	Be	ZB.876
Hasselt	Be	ZB.889
Hazebrouk	Fr	
Hirson	Fr	Z.603
Joigny La Roche	Fr	
Laon	Fr	Z.604
LeMans	Fr	Z.444
Lens	Fr	Z.798
Liege (Luik)	Be	ZB.819
Lille (Fives)	Fr	Z.183

Community	Nation	Target #
Lille/Deliverance	Fr	Z.571
Limoges	Fr	
Louvain (Leuven)	Be	ZB.917
Luxembourg	Lux	ZL.124
Lyon/Berliet	Fr	
Lyons /Venissieux	Fr	Z.640
Lyons/La Mouche	Fr	Z.812
Malines	Be	ZB.918
Mantes/Gassicourt	Fr	Z.804
Marsailles La Blancarde	Fr	Z.630
Marsailles/St. Charles	Fr	Z.630
Mayenne	Fr	
Metz	Fr	Z.642
Miramas	Fr	Z.631
Mohon	Fr	Z.643
Mons	Be	ZB.910
Montdidier	Fr	
Montzen	Be	ZB.907
Mulhouse	Fr	Z.813
Namur Ronet	Be	ZB.892
Nantes	Fr	
Nice	Fr	Z.815
Nîmes	Fr	Z.626
Orleans/Les-Aubrais	Fr	
Ottignies	Be	ZB.893
Paris-Achères	Fr	Z.442
Paris-Juvisy	Fr	Z.605
Paris/La Chappelle	Fr	Z.799
Paris/Noisy le Sec	Fr	Z.800
Poitiers	Fr	
Reims (Rheims)	Fr	Z.802
Rouen/Sotteville	Fr	Z.435
Saargeumines	Fr	Z.817
Saint-Etienne	Fr	Z816

Community	Nation	Target #
Saint-Ghislain	Be	ZB.909
Saint-Pierre-des-Corps	Fr	Z.434
Saintes	Fr	
Samur	Fr	
Somain	Fr	Z.834
St. Etienne	Fr	Z.816
Strasbourg	Fr	Z.298
Terginer	Fr	Z.572
Thionville	Fr	Z.615
Tourcoing	Fr	Z.835
Tournai	Be	ZB.908
Trappes	Fr	Z.431
Troyes	Fr	Z.803
Vaires-sur-Marne	Fr	Z.606
Valenciennes	Fr	Z.610
Versailles	Fr	
Vierzon	Fr	
Villeneuve St. Georges	Fr	Z.801
Vitry-Le-François	Fr	

Note: Targets with numbers reflect original target list. It includes targets attacked after the initial Transportation Plan and reflects the continued bombing of these facilities. It also lists rail centers in Belgium, which were an integral part of the plan.

Sources include:
Air Ministry, "War Room Monthly Summary of Bomber Command Operations, January–August 1944," RG 243 United States Strategic Bombing Survey, College Park, MD, NARA; Headquarters, Eighth Air Force, "Monthly Summary of Operations: January–August 1944," RG 243, NARA; Headquarters, Ninth Air Force, "Operations Report Form 34, April–June 1944," AFHRA; Air Ministry, "Bombing Policy Occupied Countries Part 3," AIR 20/2799, UKNA.

APPENDIX C

Bridges Attacked May 15–June 8, 1944

Seine River Valley

Achères (Paris)
Acquigny
Andé
Athis-Mons (Paris-Juvisy)
Bennecourt
Conflans-Sainte-Honorine
Courcelles-sur-Seine
Elbeuf
Étaples
Heudebnouville
Le Manoir
Maisons-Laffitte
Meulan
Oissel
Orival
Pont-de-l'Arche
Rangiport
Rouen
St. Germain-en-Laye
Vernon

Loire River Valley

Angers
Blois/St. Denis
Cinq-Mars (Tours)
La Frillière (Tours)
La Possonière
La Riche (Tours)
Le Port-Boulet
Mantes-Gassicourt
Nantes
Orléans
Saumur
Saint-Pierre-des-Corps (Tours)

Meuse River

Lumes (Charleville-Mézières)
Mohon (Charleville-Mézières)
Namur (Be)
Renory (Leige) (Be)
Seraing (Leige) (Be)
Val Benoit (Leige) (Be)

Other

Abbeville
Aire
Anthéor
Avranches
Beaumont-Sur-Oise
Blain
Évreux
Gisors
Hasselt (Be)
Hennebont
L'Aigle
La Loupe
Le Mans
Lessay
Le Vicomté-sur-Rance
Mohon
Poix
Pontaubault
Pontoise
Rambouillet
Rennes
St. Laurent-di-Var
Vicomté-sur-Rance

Source: Units from all air forces attacked bridge targets, and planning tasks priorities changed daily. The best details of what the Allies actually attacked are found in "Allied Expeditionary Air Force, 'Daily Int/Ops Summary'" prepared each day for the AEAF commander and staff (Papers of Air Vice-Marshal E-J Kingston-McCloughry, London: Imperial War Museum).

NOTES

Preface

1. Eddy Florentin, *Quand les Alliés bombardaient la France* (Paris: Perrin, 1997).
2. Eric Alary, Bénédicte Vergez-Chaignon, and Gilles Gauvin, *Les Français Au Quotidien, 1939–1949* (Paris: Perrin, 2006), 497–529; Claudia Baldoli and Andrew Knapp, *Forgotten Blitzes: France and Italy under Allied Air Attack, 1940–1945* (New York: Continuum International Publishing Group, 2012), 260–62.

Chapter 1. A Missing Narrative

1. Michelle Chapron, "Mémoires De L'été 1944," *Témoignages écrits* (Caen: Mémorial de Caen (MC), 1984); Michael Boivin and Bernard Garnier, *Les Victimes Civiles De La Manche Dans La Bataille De Normandie: 1er Avril-30 Septembre 1944* (Caen: Centre de recherche d'historie quantitative, 1994), 176.
2. J. P. Cordier, "Souvenirs Personnels-Lisieux Bombardement De Juin 1944," MC, 1984.
3. Gontran Pailhès, *Rouen Et Sa Région Pendant La Guerre, 1939–1945* (Rouen): H. Defontaine, 1949, repr., Luneray (France): Editions Bertout "La Mémoire Normande," 1993), 218–20.
4. The United States Strategic Bombing Survey (USSBS), "Statistical Appendix to Over-All Report (European War)" (Washington, DC: Government Printing Office, 1947), charts 4 and 5.
5. Office of Statistical Control, "Army Air Forces Statistical Digest" (Washington, DC: U.S. Army Air Forces 1945), table 141.
6. Jeffrey J. Kubiak, *War Narratives and the American National Will in War* (New York: Palgrave Macmillan, 2014), 27.
7. "Dunkerque" is the French spelling for the more familiar English version "Dunkirk." When given a choice, I have adopted the French spellings.
8. William H. McNeill, "The Care and Repair of Public Myth," *Foreign Affairs* 61, no. 1 (1982); Benedict Anderson, *Imagined Communities* (New York, Verso, 1983); Edward W. Wood Jr., *Worshipping the Myths of World War II: Reflections on America's Dedication to War* (Washington, DC: Potomac Books, 2006).
9. Michael R. Dolski, "'Portal of Liberation': D-Day Myth as American Self-Affirmation," in *D-Day in History and Memory: The Normandy Landings in*

International Remembrance and Commemoration, ed. Michael Dolski, Sam Edwards, and John Buckley (Denton: University of North Texas Press, 2014), 43–84.

10. Quoted in Douglas Brinkley, *The Boys of Pointe Du Hoc: Ronald Reagan, D-Day, and the U.S. Army 2nd Ranger Battalion* (New York: Harper Perennial, 2006), 226.
11. Ibid., 234.
12. Paul Fussell, *Wartime: Understanding and Behavior in the Second World War* (New York: Oxford University Press, 1989), ix.
13. Baldoli and Knapp, *Forgotten Blitzes*; Joris Adrianus Cornelis Van Esch, "Restrained Policy and Careless Execution: Allied Strategic Bombing on the Netherlands in the Second World War" (MA thesis, United States Army Command and General Staff College, 2011); Giovanni Corrado, "Tactical Enthusiasm, Operational Blindness, and Civilian Casualties: Questioning the Allied Air Campaign against Italy during the Second World War" (United States Army Command and General Staff College, 2015).
14. Norman Davies, *No Simple Victory* (New York: Penguin Books, 2006), 482.
15. For the greatest generation discussion, see Tom Brokaw, *The Greatest Generation* (New York: Random House, 1998).
16. See especially Gordon A. Harrison, *The European Theater of Operations: Cross-Channel Attack*, United States Army in World War II (USAWWII) (Washington, DC: Office of the Chief of Military History, 1951), 222–23; Forrest C. Pogue, *The European Theater of Operations: The Supreme Command*, USAWWII (Washington, DC: Office of the Chief of Military History, 1954), 123–37; Martin Blumenson, *The European Theater of Operations: Breakout and Pursuit*, USAWWII (Washington, DC: Office of the Chief of Military History, 1960).
17. C. P. Stacey, *The Victory Campaign: Operations in North-West Europe 1944–1945*, vol. 3, *Official History of the Canadian Army in the Second World War* (Ottawa: Queen's Printer and Controller of Stationery, 1960); L. F. Ellis, *Victory in the West*, vol. 1. *The Battle of Normandy* (London: HMSO, 1962).
18. Stephen E. Ambrose, *D-Day: June 6, 1944* (New York: Simon & Schuster, 1994); Stephen E. Ambrose, *Band of Brothers* (New York: Simon & Schuster, 1992); Terry Copp, *Fields of Fire: The Canadians in Normandy* (Toronto: University of Toronto Press, 2003); Carlo D'Este, *Decision in Normandy* (New York: HarperPerennial, 1994).
19. Cornelius Ryan, *The Longest Day* (New York: Simon & Schuster, 1959).
20. Brinkley, *The Boys of Pointe Du Hoc*; John C. McManus, *The Dead and Those About to Die. D-Day: The Big Red One at Omaha Beach* (New York: NAL Caliber, 2014).
21. McManus, *The Dead and Those About to Die*, 5.
22. Ryan, *The Longest Day*, 75–92, 252–53, 79.
23. D'Este, *Decision in Normandy.*

24. Max Hastings, *Overlord: D-Day and the Battle for Normandy* (New York: Simon & Schuster, 1984), 39–45, 198–200.
25. Ambrose, *D-Day: June 6, 1944*, 90–99, 239–53.
26. Antony Beevor, *D-Day: The Battle for Normandy* (New York: Viking, 2009); Rick Atkinson, *The Guns at Last Light: The War in Western Europe, 1944–1945*, The Liberation Trilogy (New York: Henry Holt, 2013).
27. Robert F. Futrell, "The U. S. Army Air Corps and the United States Air Force, 1909–1973," in *A Guide to the Sources of United States Military History*, ed. Robin Higham (Hamden, CT: Archon Books, 1975), 409–10.
28. Wesley Frank Craven and James Lea Cate, *Volume I: Plans and Early Operations, January 1942 to August 1942, The Army Air Forces in World War II* (Chicago: University of Chicago Press, 1948), 666.
29. Wesley Frank Craven and James Lea Cate, *Volume II: Europe, Torch to Pointblank, August 1942 to December 1943, The Army Air Forces in World War II* (Chicago: University of Chicago Press, 1948), 687.
30. Ibid., 667, 841–52.
31. USSBS, "Statistical Appendix," Charts 4–5 (26,728 vs 21,740).
32. Wesley Frank Craven and James Lea Cate, *Volume III: Europe, Argument to V-E Day, January 1944 to May 1945, The Army Air Forces in World War II* (Chicago: University of Chicago Press, 1948), 138–86.
33. Ibid., 193.
34. Craven and Cate, *Torch to Pointblank*, 149–62.
35. Conrad C. Crane, *American Airpower Strategy in World War II: Bombs, Cities, Civilians, and Oil* (Lawrence: University Press of Kansas, 2016), 189.
36. Air Ministry, Air Historical Branch, "RAF Narrative (First Draft): The Liberation of North West Europe; Volume I: The Planning and Preparation of the Allied Expeditionary Air Force for the Landings in Normandy" (Northholt: Air Historical Branch (AHB), 1946); "RAF Narrative (First Draft): The Liberation of North West Europe; Volume II: Administrative Preparations" (AHB, 1946); Air Historical Branch Air Ministry, "RAF Narrative (First Draft): The Liberation of North West Europe; Volume III: The Landings in Normandy" (AHB, 1945).
37. Hilary St. George Saunders, *Royal Air Force: Vol III, The Fight Is Won* (London: Her Majesty's Stationery Office, 1954).
38. Charles Webster and Noble Frankland, *The Strategic Air Offensive against Germany, 1939–1945. Volume III, Victory* (London: Her Majesty's Stationery Office, 1961).
39. Brereton Greenhous et al., *The Crucible of War, 1939–1945: The Official History of the Royal Canadian Air Force, Volume III* (Toronto: University of Toronto Press, 1994), 790–828.
40. Donald L. Miller, *Masters of the Air: America's Bomber Boys Who Fought the Air War against Nazi Germany* (New York: Simon & Schuster, 2006).
41. Max Hastings, *Bomber Command* (New York: Penguin, 1979).

42. Stephen Darlow, *D-Day Bombers: The Veterans' Story: RAF Bomber Command and the US Eighth Air Force Support to the Normandy Invasion 1944* (London: Grub Street, 2004; repr., Mechanicsburg, PA: Stackpole Books, 2010), 79–82.
43. Baldoli and Knapp, *Forgotten Blitzes*; Richard Overy, *The Bombing War: Europe 1939–1945* (London: Allen Lane, 2013). Note: The shorter American edition to this work is *The Bombers and the Bombed: Allied Air War over Europe, 1940–1945* (New York: Viking, 2013).
44. Personal visits by author. See also Kate C. Lemay, "Gratitude, Trauma, and Repression: D-Day in French Memory," in *D-Day in History and Memory: The Normandy Landings in International Remembrance and Commemoration*, ed. Michael Dolski, Sam Edwards, and John Buckley, 159–87 (Denton: University of North Texas Press, 2014); and Mary Louise Roberts, *D-Day through French Eyes, Normandy 1944* (Chicago: University of Chicago Press, 2014).
45. Office of Statistical Control, "Army Air Forces Statistical Digest," Table 141; Arthur T. Harris, *Despatch on War Operations, 23 February 1942 to 8th May 1945* (London: Frank Cass, 1995), 44 (as refined by Andrew Knapp).
46. Jean Quellien and Bernard Garnier, *Les Victimes Civiles Du Calvados Dans La Bataille De Normandie: 1er Mars 1944–31 Décembre 1945* (Caen: Editions-diffusion du Lys, 1995), 14; Boivin and Garnier, *Les Victimes Civiles*, 7; Gérard Bourdin and Bernard Garnier, *Les Victimes Civiles De L'orne Dans La Bataille De Normandie: 1 Avril–30 September 1944* (Caen: Éditions-Diffusion du Lys, 1994), 15–16.
47. Michèle Battesti and Patrick Facon, eds., *Les Bombardements Alliés Sur La France Durant La Seconde Guerre Mondialle: Stratégies, Bilans Materériels Et Humains*, Cahiers Du Centre D' Études D'histoire De La Défense, No 37 (Vincennes: Ministère de la Defense, 2009), 7–9.
48. Lindsey Dodd and Andrew Knapp, "'How Many Frenchmen Did You Kill?' British Bombing Policy Towards France (1940–1945)," *French Historical Studies* 22, no. 4 (Spring 2008): 469–70; Alary, Vergez-Chaignon, and Gauvin, *Les Français Au Quotidien*, 504; Olivier Wieviorka, *Normandy: The Landings to the Liberation of Paris*, trans. M. B. DeBevoise (Cambridge, MA: Harvard University Press, 2008), 323–24.
49. A good illustration of the Allied, indeed the American, narrative is found in Brinkley, *The Boys of Pointe Du Hoc*.
50. See Robert O. Paxton, *Vichy France: Old Guard and New Order, 1940–1944* (New York: Columbia University Press, 2001). The same applies to the memory of the millions of French civilians that fled the advancing Germans in 1940. See Hanna Diamond, *Fleeing Hitler: France 1940* (Oxford: Oxford University Press, 2007), 203–10.
51. Olivier Wieviorka, *Divided Memory: French Recollections of World War II from the Liberation to the Present*, trans. George Holoch (Stanford, CA: Stanford University Press, 2012). Wieviorka's discussion of official memory says very little about memorializing the Allied bombing.
52. Florentin, *Quand Les Alliés Bombardaient La France.*

53. John Barzman, Corinne Bouillot, and Andrew Knapp, eds., *Bombardements 1944: Le Havre, Normandie, France, Europe* (Mont-Saint-Aignan: Presses Universitaires de Rouen et du Havre, 2016). Based on a conference held in September 2014.
54. This has been a common theme after this author's presentation at many seminars and conferences. It is also the title of an article, William I. Hitchcock, "The Price of Liberation," *MHQ: The Quarterly Journal of Military History* 21, no. 3 (Spring 2009).
55. Overy, *The Bombing War: Europe 1939–1945*, xxiv–xxv.

Chapter 2. The Operational Environment

1. Richard G. Davis, *Carl A. Spaatz and the Air War in Europe* (Washington, DC: Center for Air Force History, 1993), 98; Craven and Cate, *Plans and Early Operations*, 661; Paul Le Trevier, *Objectif Rouen: 1er Raid Américain Sur L'europe* (Le Mesnil-Esnard, France: Comever- De Rameau, 2005), chronologie.
2. Craven and Cate, *Plans and Early Operations*, 662–63; Le Trevier, *Objectif Rouen*, chronologie.
3. Kit Carter and Robert Mueller, eds., *The Army Air Forces in World War II: Combat Chronology* (Washington, DC: Air Force Historical Studies, 1973), 33; Craven and Cate, *Plans and Early Operations*, 655–88; Florentin, *Quand Les Alliés Bombardaient La France*, 64.
4. Le Trevier, *Objectif Rouen*, 90.
5. Office of Statistical Control, "Army Air Forces Statistical Digest" (Washington, DC: U.S. Army Air Forces), 1945, table 141; Dodd and Knapp, "How Many Frenchmen Did You Kill?," 471–72, note 1.
6. Population statistics from http://www.annuaire-mairie.fr (accessed January 2015).
7. William G. Sinnigen and Arthur E. R. Boak, *A History of Rome to A.D. 565*, 6th ed. (New York: Macmillan, 1977), 214; Julius Caesar, *The Conquest of Gaul*, trans. S. A. Handford, Penguin Classics (New York: Penguin Books, 1982), 107. Exactly where he debarked, *Portus Itus*, is in dispute, but probably Boulogne-sur-Mer or the smaller port of Wissant to the north.
8. David Hackett Fischer, *Champlain's Dream: The European Founding of North America* (New York: Simon & Schuster, 2008), 120.
9. Office of Strategic Services, "Civil Affairs Handbook on France: Section Eleven Transportation Systems (Preliminary Draft)," in William J. Donovan Papers, AHEC.
10. AAF Evaluation Board in the European Theater of Operations, "Effectiveness of Air Attack against Rail Transportation in the Battle of France," AFHRC, 1945, 1–5; G-2 Office of Assistant Chief of Staff, "Weekly Intelligence Summary #1: For Week Ending 26 March 1944," box 30, Smith Papers 1941–1945, Supreme Headquarters Allied Expeditionary Force, Weekly Intelligence Summaries, I [March 26–July 15, 1944], DDEPL.

11. Air Ministry, Air Historical Branch, "RAF Narrative (First Draft): The Campaign in France and the Low Countries," AHB, map: Order of Battle: British and French Forces in France, May 9th, 1940.
12. Elizabeth Greenhalgh, *The French Army and the First World War*, Armies of the Great War (Cambridge: Cambridge University Press, 2014), 305, 86–92.
13. Gordon Wright, *France in Modern Times* (New York: W. W. Norton, 1995), 300.
14. The best military history of France in World War I is Robert A. Doughty, *Pyrrhic Victory: French Strategy and Operations in the Great War* (Boston: Belknap Press, 2005). Also important is Greenhalgh, *The French Army and the First World War.*
15. Wright, *France in Modern Times*, 305–6.
16. Ibid., 307–8.
17. Leonard V. Smith, *France and the Great War, 1914–1918*, ed. William Beik and T. C. W. Blanning, New Approaches to European History (New York: Cambridge University Press, 2003), 146–47; Jay Winter, *Sites of Memory, Sites of Mourning: The Great War in European Cultural History* (Cambridge: Cambridge Press Syndicate of the University of Cambridge, 1998), 15–35.
18. Robert Allan Doughty, *The Breaking Point: Sedan and the Fall of France, 1940* (Hamden, CT: Archon, 1990); Julian Jackson, *The Fall of France: The Nazi Invasion of 1940* (New York: Oxford University Press, 2003); Karl-Heinz Frieser and John T. Greenwood, *The Blitzkrieg Legend: The 1940 Campaign in the West* (Annapolis, MD: Naval Institute Press, 2005).
19. Jackson, *The Fall of France*, 27–30; Alistair Horne, *To Lose a Battle: France 1940* (New York: Penguin Books, 1990), 170–71, 73, 73–75.
20. Frieser and Greenwood, *The Blitzkrieg Legend*, 197.
21. Jackson, *The Fall of France*, 56–57.
22. William L. Shirer, *The Collapse of the Third Republic: An Inquiry into the Fall of France 1940* (New York: Simon and Schuster, 1969), 655.
23. André Corvisier, *Histoire Militaire De La France, 3: De 1871 Á 1940* (Paris: Presses Univ. France, 1992), 397–98.
24. Horne, *To Lose a Battle*, 597.
25. Étienne Dejonghe and Yves le Maner, *Le Nord-Pas-De-Calais Dans La Main Allemande* (Lille: La Voix du Nord, 1999), 50–52.
26. Jackson, *The Fall of France*, 94–97; Frieser and Greenwood, *The Blitzkrieg Legend*, 318.
27. Shirer, *The Collapse of the Third Republic*, 752.
28. Ibid., 751.
29. Alary, Vergez-Chaignon, and Gauvin, *Les Français Au Quotidien*, 77; Helen McPhail, *The Long Silence: Civilian Life under the German Occupation of Northern France, 1914–1918* (New York: I. B. Tauris, 1999); John Horne and Alan Kramer, "German 'Atrocities' and Franco-German Opinion, 1914: The Evidence of German Soldiers' Diaries," *Journal of Modern History* 66, no. 1 (1994).

30. Jackson, *The Fall of France*, 174.
31. Hanna Diamond, *Fleeing Hitler: France 1940* (Oxford: Oxford University Press, 2007), 203–10; Alary, Vergez-Chaignon, and Gauvin, *Les Français Au Quotidien*, 77–95; Jackson, *The Fall of France*, 174–78; Richard Vinen, *The Unfree French: Life under the Occupation* (New Haven, CT: Yale University Press, 2006), 38; Jean-Luc Leleu et al., eds., *La France Pendant La Seconde Guerre Mondiale, Atlas Historique* (Paris: Editions Fayard, 2010), 46–47.
32. Shirer, *The Collapse of the Third Republic*, 757–79.
33. Paxton, *Vichy France*, 8.
34. Shirer, *The Collapse of the Third Republic*, 878–87.
35. Dodd and Knapp, "How Many Frenchmen Did You Kill?," 474.
36. Paul Auphan and Jacques Mordal, *The French Navy in World War II* (Annapolis, MD: Naval Institute Press, 2016); Roger A. Freeman, Alan Crouchman, and Vic Maslen, *Mighty Eighth War Diary* (London: Arms and Armour Press, 1990), 255–71; Douglas Porch, *The Path to Victory: The Mediterranean Theater in World War II* (Old Saybrook, CT: Konecky & Konecky, 2004), 365.
37. G-2 Office of Assistant Chief of Staff, "Weekly Intelligence Summary #7: For Week Ending 6 May 1944," box 30, Smith Papers 1941–1945, Supreme Headquarters Allied Expeditionary Force, Weekly Intelligence Summaries, I [March 26–July 15, 1944], DDEPL; Earl F. Ziemke, "Rundstedt," in *Hitler's Generals*, ed. Correlli Barnett (New York: Grove Weidenfeld, 1989), 185–98.
38. Ziemke, "Rundstedt," 199.
39. Harrison, *Cross-Channel Attack*, 231–67; Beevor, *D-Day*, 31–43.
40. G-2 Office of Assistant Chief of Staff, "Weekly Intelligence Summary #4: For Week Ending 15 April 1944," box 30, Smith Papers 1941–1945, DDEPL; United States War Department, "Handbook on German Military Forces (Tm-E 30–451)," *War Department Technical Manual* (Washington, DC: United States Government Printing Office, 1945), 88–89.
41. Alan F. Wilt, *The Atlantic Wall: Hitler's Defense in the West, 1941–1944* (New York: Enigma Books, 1975), 27; H. R. Trevor-Roper, *Blitzkrieg to Defeat: Hitler's War Directives 1939–1945* (New York: Holt, Rinehart, and Winston, 1971), 111–16.
42. Trevor-Roper, *Blitzkrieg to Defeat*, 148–53; Harrison, *Cross-Channel Attack*, 132–33.
43. Leleu et al., *La France Pendant La Seconde Guerre Mondiale*, 227; "Weekly Intelligence Summary #7: For Week Ending 6 May 1944," box 30, Smith Papers 1941–1945, DDEPL.
44. Wilt, *The Atlantic Wall*, 45–51, 108–9; "Weekly Intelligence Summary #11: For Week Ending 3 June 1944," box 30, Smith Papers 1941–1945, DDEPL; SHAEF Historical Division, "German Report Series: Atlantic Wall to the Siegfried Line, a Study in Command," CARL Digital Library (CARL), 60–61; "Weekly Intelligence Summary #10: For Week Ending 27 May 1944," box 30, Smith Papers 1941–1945, DDEPL.

45. Wilt, *The Atlantic Wall*, 40–41; Historical Division, "Atlantic Wall to the Siegfried Line," 61–62; "Weekly Intelligence Summary #3: For Week Ending 8 April 1944," box 30, Smith Papers 1941–1945, DDEPL.
46. Harrison, *Cross-Channel Attack*, 257–58; United States War Department, "Handbook on German Military Forces," 88–89; Russell F. Weigley, *Eisenhower's Lieutenants, the Campaign of France and Germany, 1944–1945* (Bloomington: Indiana University Press, 1981), 30–31.
47. Combined Commanders Planning Staff, "Review of Certain Factors Affecting Preparations for a Return to the Continent," Barker, Ray W. Papers, 1942–1946, Combined Commanders Planning Staff, DDEPL.
48. Stephen Brooks, ed. *Montgomery and the Battle of Normandy: A Selection from the Diaries, Correspondence and Other Papers of Field Marshal the Viscount Montgomery of Alamein, January to August, 1944* (London: History Press for the Army Records Society, 2008), Montgomery's notes for "Brief Summary of Operation 'OVERLORD' as affecting the Army, 7 April."
49. "Weekly Intelligence Summary #6: For Week Ending 29 April 1944," box 30, Smith Papers 1941–1945, DDEPL.
50. Leleu et al., *La France Pendant La Seconde Guerre Mondiale*, 56–67.
51. Vinen, *The Unfree French*, 116–17; Leleu et al., *La France Pendant La Seconde Guerre Mondiale*, 234–35; Théo Lippe, *La Bosse De Beton* (Brussels: Private, 1973); Mark Mazower, *Hitler's Empire: How the Nazis Ruled Europe* (New York: Penguin Press, 2008), 316.
52. Doughty, *The Breaking Point*, 8–10; Leleu et al., *La France Pendant La Seconde Guerre Mondiale*, 17–25.
53. Leleu et al., *La France Pendant La Seconde Guerre Mondiale*, 52–53; Alary, Vergez-Chaignon, and Gauvin, *Les Français Au Quotidien*, 127–35.
54. Leleu et al., *La France Pendant La Seconde Guerre Mondiale*, 54–55. Dejonghe and Maner, *Le Nord-Pas-De-Calais*, 80–93; Robert Gildea, *Marianne in Chains: Daily Life in the Heart of France during German Occupation* (New York: Metropolitan Books, 2003), 70–71.
55. Dejonghe and Maner, *Le Nord-Pas-De-Calais*, 129–30. Leleu et al., *La France Pendant La Seconde Guerre Mondiale*, 54–55.
56. Leleu et al., *La France Pendant La Seconde Guerre Mondiale*, 68–69; Paxton, *Vichy France*, 81–80, 182–83.
57. Paxton, *Vichy France*, 18–19. Leleu et al., *La France Pendant La Seconde Guerre Mondiale*, 74–75.
58. Mazower, *Hitler's Empire*, 432–41; Gildea, *Marianne in Chains*, 256–61. Leleu et al., *La France Pendant La Seconde Guerre Mondiale*, 76–77, 84–85, 204–5.
59. Thierry Chion, *Pompiers sous les bombes: Rouen 1940–1944* (Louviers, France: Ysec Médias, 2013), 5–16; Antoine Hardy, "La Défense Passive À Rouen Et Dans Son Agglomération" (MA thesis, Université de Rouen, 2005), 38; Antoine Hardy, "La Défense Passive À Rouen," *Études normandes*, no. 1 (2008); Baldoli and Knapp, *Forgotten Blitzes*, 53, 73–74.

60. Ian Ousby, *Occupation: The Ordeal of France, 1940–1944* (New York: Cooper Square Press, 2000), 55.
61. Gildea, *Marianne in Chains*, 64–66.
62. Leleu et al., *La France Pendant La Seconde Guerre Mondiale*, 44–45. According to the French Ministry of Defense, 55,000 confirmed dead, with possibly another 6,300 unconfirmed, between May 10 and June 30. As the authors point out, published casualty figures have ranged between 90,000 and 123,000 dead.
63. Jackson, *The Fall of France*, 126; Leleu et al., *La France Pendant La Seconde Guerre Mondiale*, 100–101; Gildea, *Marianne in Chains*, 72–79.
64. Gildea, *Marianne in Chains*, 277–90; Leleu et al., *La France Pendant La Seconde Guerre Mondiale*, 119–21; Pieter Lagrou, *The Legacy of Nazi Occupation: Patriotic Memory and National Recovery in Western Europe, 1945–1965* (New York: Cambridge University Press, 2000), 138–43.
65. Vinen, *The Unfree French*, 142–44; Julian Jackson, *France: The Dark Years 1940–1944* (New York: Oxford University Press, 2001), 217–19; Leleu et al., *La France Pendant La Seconde Guerre Mondiale*, 204–7; Wieviorka, *Divided Memory*.
66. Paxton, *Vichy France*, 14.
67. Ibid., 45–69; Ousby, *Occupation*, 55.
68. Moshik Temkin, "'Avec un certain malaise': The Paxtonian Trauma in France, 1973–1974," *Journal of Contemporary History* 38, no. 2 (April 2003): 391–406; Ousby, *Occupation*, 38; Vinen, *The Unfree French*, 77–78.
69. Olivier Wieviorka, *The French Resistance*, trans. Jane Marie Todd (Cambridge, MA: Belknap Press, 2016), 2.
70. Gildea, *Marianne in Chains*, 185–90.
71. The best recent accounts of this complex phenomenon are found in Wieviorka, *The French Resistance*; Robert Gildea, *Fighters in the Shadows: A New History of the French Resistance* (Cambridge, MA: Belknap Press, 2015); Benjamin F. Jones, *Eisenhower's Guerrillas: The Jedburghs, the Maquis, & the Liberation of France* (New York: Oxford University Press, 2016).
72. Gildea, *Marianne in Chains*, 16.

Chapter 3. Eisenhower's Command

1. Michel Boivin, Gérard Bourdin, Jean Quellien, *Villes Normandes Sous Les Bombes* (Juin, 1944) (Caen: Universitaires de Caen, 1994), 103–7; Quellien and Garnier, *Les Victimes Civiles Du Calvados*, 47–48.
2. Quellien and Garnier, *Les Victimes Civiles Du Calvados*, 17, 51.
3. Richard Overy, *The Air War, 1939–1945* (New York: Stein and Day, 1980), 11.
4. Carl Von Clausewitz, *On War*, trans. Michael Howard and Peter Paret, Indexed ed. (Princeton, NJ: Princeton University Press, 1984), 81; Clausewitz, *Vom Kriege* (Frankfurt / M, GE: Ullstein GmbH, 1991), 25.

5. Paul Alkon, *Finest Hour: Churchill on Clemenceau: His Best Student? Part I* (http://www.winstonchurchill.org/publications/finest-hour/finest-hour-150/churchill-on-clemenceau-his-best-student-part-I) (accessed July 26, 2015).
6. John Gooch, "Churchill as War Leader," in *The Oxford Companion to World War II*, ed. C. B. Dear and M. R. D. Foot (New York: Oxford University Press, 1995), 235–42; Eliot A. Cohen, *Supreme Command: Soldiers, Statesmen and Leadership in Wartime* (New York: Free Press, 2002), 110–53.
7. Robert Dallek, "Roosevelt as War Leader," in *The Oxford Companion to World War II*, ed. C. B. Dear and M. R. D. Foot (New York: Oxford University Press, 1995), 960–66; Eric Larrabee, *Commander in Chief: Franklin Delano Roosevelt, His Lieutenants & Their War* (New York: Harper & Row, 1987), 623–47; Leo J. Meyer, "The Decision to Invade North Africa (Torch)," in *Command Decisions*, ed. Kent Roberts Greenfield (Washington, DC: Office of the Chief of Military History, 1960), 173–98; Maurice Matloff and Edwin M. Snell, *The War Department: Strategic Planning for Coalition Warfare, 1941–1942*, USAWWII (Washington, DC: Office of the Chief of Military History, 1953), 282–84.
8. Beatrice Heuser, *The Evolution of Strategy: Thinking War from Antiquity to the Present* (New York: Cambridge University Press, 2010), 3; Lawrence Freedman, *Strategy: A History* (New York: Oxford University Press, 2013), x–xi.
9. Clausewitz, *On War*, 177.
10. Gordon A. Craig, "The Political Leader as Strategist," in *Makers of Modern Strategy from Machiavelli to the Nuclear Age*, ed. Peter Paret (Princeton, NJ: Princeton University Press, 1986), 482.
11. David Rigby, *Allied Master Strategists: The Combined Chiefs of Staff in World War II* (Annapolis, MD: Naval Institute Press, 2012), 2–46.
12. Hastings, *Bomber Command*, 41, 57; Winston S. Churchill, *Their Finest Hour*, vol. 2, *The Second World War*, vol. 2, *Their Finest Hour* (Boston: Houghton Mifflin Company, 1949), 20.
13. Allan R. Millett, Peter Maslowski, and William B. Feis, *For the Common Defense: A Military History of the United States from 1607–2012*, rev. and exp. ed. (New York: Free Press, 2012), 379–80; Rigby, *Allied Master Strategists*, 2–46; John F. Shortal, *Organizational Development of the Joint Chiefs of Staff* (Washington, DC: Joint History Office, Office of the Chairman of the Joint Chiefs of Staff, 2013), 1–10.
14. Shortal, *Organizational Development of the Joint Chiefs of Staff*, 2–4; Richard M. Leighton and Robert W. Coakley, *The War Department: Global Logistics and Strategy, 1940–1943*, USAWWII (Washington, DC: Office of the Chief of Military History, 1984), 144.
15. Pogue, *The Supreme Command*, 39–40; Rigby, *Allied Master Strategists*, 24–27.
16. Maurice Matloff, *The War Department: Strategic Planning for Coalition Warfare, 1943–1944*, USAWWII (Washington, DC: Office of the Chief of Military History, 1959), 346–69.
17. Ibid., 378–83; Forrest C. Pogue, *George C. Marshall: Organizer of Victory, 1944–1945* (New York: Viking Press, 1973), 318–22; Pogue, *The Supreme Command*,

32; Davis, *Carl A. Spaatz*, 271–72; Alfred D. Chandler Jr. and Stephen E. Ambrose, eds., *The Papers of Dwight David Eisenhower*, vol. 3, *The War Years* (Baltimore: Johns Hopkins Press, 1970), 1588.

18. Matthew F. Holland, *Eisenhower between the Wars: The Making of a General and Statesman* (Westport, CT: Praeger, 2001), 1–22; American Battle Monuments Commission, *American Armies and Battlefields in Europe*, 1938 (rpt. Washington, DC: US Army Center of Military History, 1992); Mark C. Bender, "Watershed at Leavenworth: Dwight D. Eisenhower and the Command and General Staff School" (MMAS, US Army Command and General Staff College, 1988).
19. Christopher R. Gabel, *The U.S. Army GHQ Maneuvers of 1941* (Washington, DC: US Army Center of Military History, 1991), 187; Carlo D'Este, *Eisenhower: A Soldier's Life* (New York: Henry Holt, 2002), 277–83.
20. Matloff and Snell, *The War Department: Strategic Planning for Coalition Warfare, 1941–1942*, 87, 183–87.
21. Harrison, *Cross-Channel Attack*, 172.
22. Chandler and Ambrose, *The War Years*, vol. 3, 1648.
23. Pogue, *The Supreme Command*, 53–55.
24. Ibid., 42–45.
25. U.S. Department of War, *Field Manual, 100–15, Field Service Regulations: Larger Units* (Washington, DC: Government Printing Office, 1942), 10–11; Joint Chiefs of Staff, *Joint Publication 5.0, Joint Operation Planning* (Washington, DC: U.S. Department of Defense, 2011), GL12. Appointing officers to senior commands was a complex event involving chiefs of staff and political leaders.
26. Pogue, *The Supreme Command*, 73–97.
27. Alex Danchev and Daniel Todman, eds., *War Diaries, 1939–1945: Field Marshal Lord Alanbrooke* (Berkeley: University of California Press, 2001), 496–500.
28. An excellent one-volume narrative of these relationships is found in Alistair Horne and David Montgomery, *The Lonely Leader: Monty, 1944–1945* (London: Pan Books, 1995).
29. Stephen Ashley Hart, *Montgomery and "Colossal Cracks": The 21st Army Group in Northwest Europe, 1944–45* (Westport, CT: Prager, 2000), 23–28.
30. Bernard Montgomery, *The Memoirs of Field-Marshal Viscount Montgomery of Alamein, K.G.* (London: Collins, 1958), 220.
31. Winston S. Churchill, *Closing the Ring*, vol. 5, *The Second World War*, vol. 5, *Closing the Ring* (Boston: Houghton Mifflin Company, 1951), 619; Pogue, *The Supreme Command*, 46–47; Christopher D. Yung, *Gators of Neptune: Naval Amphibious Planning for the Normandy Invasion* (Annapolis, MD: Naval Institute Press, 2006), 1–4; Craig L. Symonds, *Neptune: The Allied Invasion of Europe and the D-Day Landings* (New York: Oxford University Press, 2014), 174–75.
32. W. B. Smith, "Neptune: Joint Fire Plan," box 66, RG 331, Records of Allied Operational and Occupation Headquarters, World War II, NARA; Symonds, *Neptune*, 210–18.

33. One of the best, most concise explanations this development is David MacIsaac, "Voices from the Central Blue: The Air Power Theorists," in *Makers of Modern Strategy: From Machiavelli to the Nuclear Age*, ed. Peter Paret (Princeton, NJ: Princeton University Press, 1986), 624–48.
34. Giulio Douhet, *Command of the Air*, trans. Dino Ferrari (New York: Coward-McCann, 1942; repr., Washington, DC: Air Force History and Museums Program, 1998), 125–42; MacIsaac, "Voices from the Central Blue," 630–31.
35. Douhet, *Command of the Air*, 128; MacIsaac, "Voices from the Central Blue," 625.
36. Overy, *The Bombing War*, 24–25.
37. John Buckley, *Air Power in the Age of Total War* (Bloomington: Indiana University Press, 1999), 78; Heuser, *The Evolution of Strategy*, 303.
38. Richard Overy, "Strategic Bombardment before 1939: Doctrine, Planning, and Operations," in *Case Studies in Strategic Bombardment*, ed. R. Cargill Hall (Washington, DC: Air Force History and Museums Program, 1998), 40–41; Tami Davis Biddle, *Rhetoric and Reality in Air Warfare: The Evolution of British and American Ideas about Strategic Bombing, 1914–1945*, Princeton Studies in International History and Politics (Princeton, NJ: Princeton University Press, 2002), 114–15.
39. Robert Frank Futrell, *Ideas, Concepts, Doctrine: Basic Thinking in the United States Air Force, 1907–1960*, vol. 1 (Maxwell Air Force Base, AL: Air University Press, 1989), 38–39; Ronald Schaffer, *Wings of Judgment: American Bombing in World War II* (New York: Oxford University Press, 1985), 26–27. Mitchell routinely antagonized his superiors, and, on orders of President Calvin Coolidge, the War Department court-martialed him for insubordination in 1925 after he accused the Navy Department of incompetence. The expected guilty verdict led to his retirement from the service.
40. Overy, "Strategic Bombardment before 1939," 42–43; Biddle, *Rhetoric and Reality*, 162–63; Crane, *American Airpower Strategy*, 21–30.
41. Chief of the Army Air Forces, "AWPD/1 Munitions Requirements of the Army Air Forces," Air Force History Research Center (AFHRC), IRIS: 00118161, 1.
42. Ibid., 10.
43. Mark Skinner Watson, *The War Department: Chief of Staff: Prewar Plans and Preparations*, USAWWII (Washington, DC: Office of the Chief of Military History, 1950), 374–78; Chief of the Army Air Forces, "AWPD/1: Munitions Requirements of the Army Air Forces" (Maxwell Air Force Base, AL: Air Force Historical Research Center, 1941), 10–11; The United States Strategic Bombing Survey, "Statistical Appendix to Over-All Report (European War)" (Washington, DC: Government Printing Office, 1947), 2–7.
44. United States War Department, *Field Manual 100–15, Larger Units* (Washington, DC: Government Printing Office, 1942) esp. chap. 7, "Air Forces."
45. Montgomery, *The Memoirs of Field-Marshal the Viscount Montgomery*, 141.
46. Ibid., 1220.

47. Chandler and Ambrose, *The War Years*, vol. 3, 1312.
48. Martin Blumenson, *The Mediterranean Theater of Operations: Salerno to Cassino*, USAWWII (Washington, DC: Office of the Chief of Military History, 1969), 120–21; Chandler and Ambrose, *The War Years*, vol. 3, 1457; Dwight D. Eisenhower, *Crusade in Europe* (Garden City, NY: Garden City Books, 1948), 222.
49. Air Ministry, Air Historical Branch, "Planning and Preparation," 40.
50. Air Ministry, Air Historical Branch, "The Landings in Normandy," 3–4.
51. Ibid.
52. E. J. Kingston-McCloughry, *The Direction of War* (New York: Frederick A. Praeger, 1958), 116–17.
53. Air Ministry, Air Historical Branch, "Planning and Preparation," 53.
54. Overy, *The Bombing War: Europe 1939–1945*, 285–90; Hastings, *Bomber Command*, 133–40.
55. Arthur William Tedder, *With Prejudice: The War Memoirs of Marshal of the Royal Air Force Lord Tedder, G. C. B.* (Boston: Little, Brown, 1966), 504.
56. Arthur T. Harris, "The Employment of the Night Bomber Force in Connection with the Invasion of the Continent from the United Kingdom," Appendices to Part VI of Notes of the Planning & Preparation of the Allied Expeditionary Air Force for the Invasion of Northwest France, Air Ministry, Air Historical Branch, 1944; Dudley Saward, *Bomber Harris* (Garden City, NY: Doubleday & Company, 1985), 246–48.
57. Davis, *Carl A. Spaatz*, 3–35.
58. Carl Spaatz, "Notes from a Meeting between Gen Spaatz and Gen Vandenburg, 10 April 1944," in Papers of Carl Spaatz, Diaries (Washington, DC: Manuscript Division, Library of Congress (LC), 1944).
59. Air Ministry, Air Historical Branch, "Planning and Preparation," 42–44; Overy, *The Bombing War*, 44–55; MacIsaac, "Voices from the Central Blue," 629–39; R. Cargill Hall, ed. *Case Studies in Strategic Bombardment* (Washington, DC: Air Force History and Museums Program, 1998), 38–62; Davis, *Carl A. Spaatz*, 29–30.
60. Churchill, *The Second World War*, vol. 5, *Closing the Ring*, 424; Tedder, *With Prejudice*, 490.
61. Chandler and Ambrose, *The War Years*, vol. 3, 649.
62. Pogue, *The Supreme Command*, 124; Dwight D. Eisenhower, "Memo to Tedder, Re Overlord Air Plan, 9 March 1944." In Dwight D. Eisenhower: Papers, Pre-Presidential, 1916–1952, box 115, principal file (Abilene, KS: Dwight David Eisenhower Presidential Library (DDEPL), 1944).
63. Air Ministry, Air Historical Branch, "Planning and Preparation," 44–46.
64. Chandler and Ambrose, *The War Years*, vol. 3, 1601.
65. Charles Portal, "Bombing Policy—France and Occupied Countries: March & April 1944," Air 19/218 (National Archives (UKNA)); Combined Chiefs of

Staff, "Memorandum: Control of Strategic Bombing for Overlord," Air 8/1185, UKNA.

66. W. B. Smith, "Direction of Operations of Allied Air Forces against Transportation Targets (April 15, 1944)," box 66, RG 331, NARA.
67. Air Ministry, Air Historical Branch, "The Landings in Normandy," app. I.
68. Humphrey Wynn and Susan Young, *Prelude to Overlord* (Novato, CA: Presidio, 1983), 88–89; Vincent Orange, "Coningham, Air Marshal Sir Arthur," in *The Oxford Companion to World War II*, edited by I. C. B. Dear and M. R. D. Foot (New York: Oxford University Press, 1995), 262–63.
69. Roger G. Miller, "A 'Pretty Damn Able Commander'—Lewis Hyde Brereton: Part II," *Air Power History* 48, no. 1 (2000); Kathryn Gaetke, "Joint by Design: The Western Desert Campaign" (Monograph, US Army Command and General Staff College, 2015); Lewis H. Brereton, *The Brereton Diaries: The War in the Air in the Pacific, Middle East, and Europe, 3 October 1941–8 May 1945* (New York: William Morrow, 1946), 217–20.
70. Air Ministry, Air Historical Branch, "The Landings in Normandy," app. I.
71. Most aircraft comments and statistics are from Paul Eden, ed., *The Encyclopedia of Aircraft of World War II* (London: Amber Books, 2004).
72. Air Ministry, Air Historical Branch, "The Landings in Normandy," app. I.
73. Martin Middlebrook and Chris Everitt, *The Bomber Command War Diaries: An Operational Reference Book* (New York: Viking, 1985), 22.
74. Biddle, *Rhetoric and Reality*, 7–9.
75. Arthur T. Harris, *Despatch on War Operations, 23 February 1942 to 8th May 1945* (London: Frank Cass, 1995), xii–xiii; Overy, *The Bombing War*, 284–93.
76. Middlebrook and Everitt, *The Bomber Command War Diaries*, 222–37.
77. Harris, *Despatch on War Operations*, 14–22.
78. Air Ministry, Air Historical Branch, "The Landings in Normandy," app. I.
79. Davis, *Carl A. Spaatz*, 267–83.
80. Ibid. AF Statistical Digest indicates that 3,100 heavy bombers were in theater at the time. Table 89.
81. Kevin Mahoney, *Fifteenth Air Force against the Axis: Combat Missions over Europe during World War II* (Lanham, MD: Scarecrow Press, 2013), 103–35. 1,300 in the theater. Table 90.
82. Craven and Cate, *Torch to Pointblank*, 370–76; Overy, *The Bombing War*, 308–27.
83. For example, R. D. Hughes, "Conference Held at A.E.A.F. Headquarters, Stanmore, 15 February 1944," in Papers of Carl Spaatz, LC.
84. Carl Spaatz, "Letter to Eisenhower Use of 8th Air Force Against Transportation Targets," in ibid.; Harris, "The Employment of the Night Bomber Force"; Randal T. Wakelam, *The Science of Bombing* (Toronto: University of Toronto Press, 2009), 185.
85. Overy, *The Bombing War*, 296; Chief of the Army Air Forces, "AWPD/1," Tab 2b.

86. Overy, *The Bombing War*, 296, 346, 86.
87. Matloff, *Strategic Planning for Coalition Warfare, 1943–1944*, 18–42; Pogue, *The Supreme Command*, 23–25; Pogue, *George C. Marshall*, 20–37; Winston S. Churchill, *The Hinge of Fate*, vol. 4, *The Second World War* (Boston: Houghton Mifflin Company, 1950), 674–95; Historical Sub-Section, "History of COSSAC (Chief of Staff to Supreme Allied Commander), 1943–1944," General Staff Office of the Secretary (London: Supreme Headquarters, Allied Expeditionary Force, 1944); F. E. Morgan, "COSSAC Directive (43), 28, 14 July 1943, Operation 'Overlord,'" Historical Reference Collection, CMH.
88. Howard L. Oleck, Henry J. Webb, and Vernon W. Hoover, "Outline Chronology of Notes on the History of Planning of Continental Operations, E. T. O., Volume 2. Outline by Title," Headquarters U.S.F.E.T. (Rear) Historical Reference Collection, CMH, 50; Pogue, *The Supreme Command*, 23–25, 58–59, 106; Historical Sub-Section, "History of COSSAC, 1943–1944"; Morgan, "COSSAC Directive (43)."
89. Historical Sub-Section, "History of COSSAC," 28.
90. Morgan, "COSSAC Directive (43)," 28.
91. Smith, "Neptune: Joint Fire Plan."
92. Trafford Leigh-Mallory, "Operation Neptune, Allied Expeditionary Air Force Overall Air Plan" (April 15, 1944) box 29, Smith Papers, DDEPL.
93. Overy, *The Bombing War*, xxiv.
94. Dodd and Knapp, "How Many Frenchmen Did You Kill?," 481–86; Pogue, *The Supreme Command*, 123–37.

Chapter 4. Airfields and Ports

1. Churchill, *Their Finest Hour*, 99–118.
2. Dejonghe and Le Maner, *Le Nord-Pas-De-Calais*, 54–71.
3. Churchill, *Their Finest Hour*, 225–26.
4. Ibid., 281–83.
5. Middlebrook and Everitt, *The Bomber Command War Diaries*, 57–58.
6. Trevor-Roper, *Blitzkrieg to Defeat*, 34–37.
7. Ibid., 37–38.
8. Baldoli and Knapp, *Forgotten Blitzes*, 26.
9. André Itsweire, "Douanier À Dunkerque, Et Observateur Privilége," in *Chronoiques D' Un Port En Guerre: Dunkerque, 1939–1945*, ed. Patrick Oddone and Catherine Lesage (Dunkerque: Musée portuaire, 2010), 138–39.
10. Leleu et al., *La France Pendant La Seconde Guerre Mondiale*, 240–41.
11. Air Ministry, Air Historical Branch, "The Campaign in France and the Low Countries."
12. Denis Richards, *Royal Air Force*, vol. 1, *The Fight at Odds* (London: Her Majesty's Stationery Office, 1953), 107–32.
13. Dejonghe and Maner, *Le Nord-Pas-De-Calais*, 111; Richards, *The Fight at Odds*, 160–61.

14. Leleu et al., *La France Pendant La Seconde Guerre Mondiale*, 228–31.
15. Eden, *The Encyclopedia of Aircraft*, 76–77; Florentin, *Quand Les Alliés Bombardaient La France*, 13.
16. Middlebrook and Everitt, *The Bomber Command War Diaries*, 56–91; Préfecture de Pas de Calais, "Bombardements Et Chutes D'avions : Messages Et Rapports De Police Et De Gendarmerie, Rapports Du Préfet, États Statistiques (1940–1942)," in Archives Départmentals du Pas-de-Calais, M 5247, Arch62.
17. Overy, *The Bombing War*, 255–65.
18. Craven and Cate, *Argument to V-E Day*, 46–47.
19. Freeman, Crouchman, and Maslen, *Mighty Eighth War Diary*, 209; Florentin, *Quand Les Alliés Bombardaient La France,* 236; http://www.biarritz-bombardement.com/Us/USa011.html (accessed December 3, 2016).
20. "Neptune: Joint Fire Plan;" Leigh-Mallory, "Overall Air Plan" box 66, RG 331, NARA.
21. "Neptune, Overall Air Plan," para. 14, box 104, RG 331, NARA.
22. Air Ministry, Air Historical Branch, "Planning and Preparation," 11, 32–34; "Neptune, Overall Air Plan," Para. 55, 60.
23. Andrew Knapp, *Les Français Sous Les Bombes Alliées, 1940–1945* (Paris: Tallandier, 2012), 133, Middlebrook and Everitt, *The Bomber Command War Diaries*, 508.
24. Middlebrook and Everitt, *The Bomber Command War Diaries*, 506–9.
25. Compaignie du Pas-de-Calais à Arras Gendarmerie Nationale, "Registres De Correspondance Confidentielle Au Départ (R/2), 1er Au 23 Mai 1944," in *Gendarmerie Nationale,* ed. Legion des Flandres Gendarme, Compaignie du Pas-de-Calais (Château de Vincennes: Service Historique de la Défense, 1944), SHD, 47; Richard G. Davis, *Bombing the European Powers: A Historical Digest of the Combined Bomber Offensive, 1939–1945* (Maxwell AFB: Air University Press, 2006), database.
26. Freeman, Crouchman, and Maslen, *Mighty Eighth War Diary*, 248.
27. Allied Expeditionary Air Force (AEAF), "Daily Int/Ops Summary No 117, 29 May 1944," in Kingston-McCloughry Papers, IWM.
28. Daily Int/Ops Summary No 119, 30 May 1944, in Kingston-McCloughry Papers, IWM.
29. Operations, Deputy Chief of Staff, "Eighth Air Force Tactical Operations in Support of Allied Landings in Normandy, 2 June–17 June 1944," IRIS# 00221391, AFHRC, Field Order (FO) 710; Daily Int/Ops Summary No 124, 1 June 1944; Daily Int/Ops Summary No 125, 2 June 1944, in Kingston-McCloughry Papers, IWM, 1944.
30. Daily Int/Ops Summary No 133, 7 June 1944; Daily Int/Ops Summary No 135, 8 June 1944, in Kingston-McCloughry Papers, IWM, 1944; Field Order #737, "Eighth Air Force Tactical Operations in Support of Allied Landings in Normandy, 2 June–17 June 1944," AFHRC.
31. United States Strategic Bombing Survey, Statistical Appendix, 27.

32. Paul Kennedy, *Engineers of Victory: The Problem Solvers Who Turned the Tide in the Second World War* (New York: Random House, 2013), 253.
33. Ryan, *The Longest Day*, 246–48.
34. Daily Int/Ops Summary No 131, 6 June 1944; Daily Int/Ops Summary No 134, 7 June 1944, in Kingston-McCloughry Papers, IWM.
35. Préfecture de Pas de Calais, "Bombardements Et Chutes D'avions: États Statistiques (Juin 1944)," M 5394 2, Archives départementales du Pas-de-Calais (Arras) (Arch62), "Bombardements Et Chutes D'avions: États Statistiques (May 1944)," M 5393 2, Arch62.
36. Auphan and Mordal, *The French Navy*, 255–71.
37. Trevor-Roper, *Hitler's War Directives*, 34–37.
38. Churchill, *Their Finest Hour*, 283.
39. Ibid., 292.
40. Shirer, *The Rise and Fall of the Third Reich*, 764.
41. Ibid., 768–73.
42. Leleu et al., *La France Pendant La Seconde Guerre Mondiale*, 240–41.
43. Du Nord Préfect, "Bombardment Dunkerque 10 Février 1941," *1486 Bombardements des communes du Nord*, Lille: Archives Départmentals du Nord (Arch59); Middlebrook and Everitt, *The Bomber Command War Diaries*, 122.
44. Patrick Oddone, "L'arrondissement De Dunkerque À L'épreuve Des Bombes Alliées (16 June 1941–29 Novembre 1943)," *Revue Historique de Dunkerque et du Littoral*, no. 5 (2005); Middlebrook and Everitt, *The Bomber Command War Diaries*, 279.
45. Terry Copp, *Cinderella Army: The Canadians in Northwest Europe, 1944–1945* (Toronto: University of Toronto Press, 2006), 55–56; Rémy Desquesnes, *Les Poches De Résistance Allemandes Sur Le Littoral Français, Août 1944–Mai 1945* (Rennes: Editions Ouest-France, 2011), 18–20.
46. Desquesnes, *Les Poches De Résistance Allemandes*, 54–58; Émile Dubuisson, "Un Porte Mutilé—18 Juin 1940–9 Mai 1945," in *Chronoiques D' Un Port En Guerre: Dunkerque, 1939–1945*, ed. Patrick Oddone and Catherine Lesage (Dunkerque: Musée portuaire, 2010), 203–13; Jean-Claude Lantenois and Michel Chaubiron, *Dunkerque, 1940–1945: Guide Historique & Touristique* (Paris: Ysec, 2007).
47. Hugh Clout, "Place Annihilation and Urban Reconstruction: The Experience of Four Towns in Brittany, 1940–1960," *Geografiska Annaler. Series B, Human Geography* 82, no. 3 (2000): 168; Florentin, *Quand Les Alliés Bombardaient*, 178–79.
48. Craven and Cate, *Torch to Pointblank*, 720.
49. Gildea, *Marianne in Chains*, 88–89.
50. Churchill, *Their Finest Hour*, 598.
51. David Porter, *The Kreigsmarine, 1939–1945: The Essential Facts and Figures for the German Navy* (London: Amber Books, 2010), 113–49.

52. Ibid., 149–51; Winston S. Churchill, *The Grand Alliance,* vol. 3, *The Second World War* (Boston: Houghton Mifflin, 1950), 121–22; Dan Van Der Vat, *The Atlantic Campaign* (Edinburgh: Birlinn, 1988), 235–38.
53. Porter, *The Kreigsmarine*, 151–59; Churchill, *The Grand Alliance*, 308–9. This event obviously affected Churchill as he devotes fifteen pages of his history to sinking the *Bismarck*.
54. Middlebrook and Everitt, *The Bomber Command War Diaries*, 115.
55. Ibid., 139, 41; Jeremiah S. Heathman, "The Bombing of Brittany: Failing to Solve the Problem" (monograph, United States Army Command and General Staff College, 2010), 9–10.
56. Correlli Barnett, *Engage the Enemy More Closely: The Royal Navy in the Second World War* (New York: W. W. Norton, 1991), 445–55; Porter, *The Kreigsmarine, 1939–1945*, 160–61; Heathman, "The Bombing of Brittany," 10–11.
57. Knapp, *Les Français Sous Les Bombes Alliées*, 77–79; Jean-Yves Besselièvre, "Les Bombardements De Brest (1940–1944)," in *Les Bombardements Alliés Sur La France Durant La Seconde Guerre Mondiale: Stratégies, Bilans Materériels Et Humains, Cahiers Du Centre D'Études D'histoire De La Défense, No 37*, ed. Michèle Battesti and Patrick Facon (Vincennes: Ministère de la Defense, 2009), 111–14.
58. Besselièvre, "Les Bombardements De Brest (1940–1944)."
59. Van Der Vat, *The Atlantic Campaign*, 190–91, 292–93.
60. Baldoli and Knapp, *Forgotten Blitzes*, 26.
61. Van Der Vat, *The Atlantic Campaign*, 524–25.
62. Davis, *Bombing the European Powers*, database.
63. Heathman, "The Bombing of Brittany," 15–17; Clout, "Place Annihilation," 167; Desquesnes, *Les Poches De Résistance*, 105.
64. Timothy P. Mulligan, *Records of the German Navy: Operational Commands in World War II,* Guide to Microfilmed Records of the German Navy, 1850–1945, no. 4, NARA; Porter, *The Kreigsmarine*, 175–78.
65. Dwight D. Eisenhower, "Letter to Marshall: Censorship and Slapton Sands," in Dwight D. Eisenhower: Papers, Pre-Presidential, 1916–52, principal file, DDEPL; Rick Atkinson, *The Guns at Last Light: The War in Western Europe, 1944–1945.* The Liberation Trilogy (New York: Henry Holt, 2013), 16–17; Barnett, *Engage the Enemy More Closely*, 798.
66. Wilt, *The Atlantic Wall*, 107–11; Desquesnes, *Les Poches De Résistance*, 11–15.
67. John T. McGrath, *The French in Early Florida* (Gainesville: University Press of Florida, 2000), 13–14.
68. Leleu et al., *La France Pendant La Seconde Guerre Mondiale*, 22–23.
69. Stacey, *The Victory Campaign*, 331–32.
70. Hart, *Montgomery and "Colossal Cracks,"* 92–95.
71. Stacey, *The Victory Campaign*, 331–36; Andrew Knapp, "The Destruction and Liberation of Le Havre in Modern Memory," *War in History* 14, no. 4 (2007): 478–80.

72. Copp, *Cinderella Army*, 59.
73. Stacey, *The Victory Campaign*, 331.
74. S. Zuckerman and E. S. D. Drury, "B. A. U. Report No 27. The Effects of Air Bombardment of German Defenses at Le Havre," AIR 37/1263, UKNA, 3–4; Middlebrook and Everitt, *The Bomber Command War Diaries*, 528; Seine Inferieur Préfect, "Arrondissement Du Havre," 271 W279 Rapports, Sectional Départmental de la Défense Passive, Rouen: Archives Départmentals de la Seine-Maritime (Arch76), 1944.
75. Middlebrook and Everitt, *The Bomber Command War Diaries*, 554; Seine Inferieur Préfect, "Arrondissement Du Havre."
76. Canadian Special Interrogation Branch, "Colonel Eberhard Wildermuth Interrogation Report," CAB 146/473, UKNA, 7–8.
77. Zuckerman and Drury, "B. A. U. Report No 27," 10.
78. Middlebrook and Everitt, *The Bomber Command War Diaries*, 554; Seine Inferieur Préfect, "Arrondissement Du Havre."
79. Zuckerman and Drury, "B. A. U. Report No 27," 9.
80. Ibid., vii; "Colonel Eberhard Wildermuth Interrogation Report," 9.
81. Canadian Special Interrogation Branch, "Colonel Eberhard Wildermuth Interrogation Report," 11.
82. Hart, *Montgomery and "Colossal Cracks,"* 49–61, 92–97.
83. Ibid., 155–59.
84. Douglas E. Delaney, *Corps Commanders: Five British and Canadian Generals at War, 1939–45*, ed. Dean F. Oliver, Studies in Canadian Military History (Vancouver: UBC Press, 2011), 160–67; John Buckley, *Monty's Men: The British Army and the Liberation of Europe, 1944–1945* (New Haven, CT: Yale University Press, 2013), 192–95.
85. M. Dandel et al., *Les Victimes Civiles Des Bombardements En Haute-Normandie: 1er Janvier 1944–12 Septembre 1944* (Cormelles-le-Royal: Mandragore, 1997), 73–86; Knapp, "The Destruction and Liberation of Le Havre," 477.
86. Knapp, "The Destruction and Liberation of Le Havre," 489.
87. Translated: They did not have twenty years. Author's visit, September 2014.
88. Desquesnes, *Les Poches De Résistance*; Dominique Lormier, *Les Poches De L Atlantic: Médoc-Royan-Ile D'oléron-La Rochelle-Ile De Ré, 1944–1945* (Saint Paul, France: Lucien Souny, 2008), 108–16; Marie-Catherine Villatoux, "Les Bombardements De Royan (Janvier Et Avril, 1945)," in *Les Bombardements Alliés Sur La France Durant La Seconde Guerre Mondialle: Stratégies, Bilans Materériels Et Humains, Cahiers Du Centre D' Études D'histoire De La Défense, No 37*, ed. Michèle Battesti and Patrick Facon (Vincennes: Ministère de la Defense, 2009).
89. Statement by Maj. Gen. Ralph Royce, WO 219.241, UKNA.
90. Statement by Brig. Gen. D. M. Schlatter, WO 219.241, UKNA.
91. Middlebrook and Everitt, *The Bomber Command War Diaries*, 647–48.

92. Letter Gen. Alphonse Juin to Gen. Dwight D. Eisenhower, 24 January 1945, WO 219.241, UKNA.
93. Memo Air Marshal J. M. Robb to Lt. Gen. Walter B. Smith, 5 February 1945, WO 219.241, UKNA.
94. Letter Lt. Gen. Walter B. Smith to Gen. Alphonse Juin, 7 February 1945, WO 219.241, UKNA.
95. Freeman, Crouchman, and Maslen, *Mighty Eighth War Diary*, 488; Desquesnes, *Les Poches De Résistance*, 80–83; Lormier, *Les Poches De L'atlantic*, 123–38.
96. Howard Zinn, *The Bomb* (San Francisco: City Light Books, 2010), 86.
97. Ibid., 80.

Chapter 5. Industry

1. Overy, *The Bombing War*, 45; Biddle, *Rhetoric and Reality*, 94–95, 205–7; Futrell, *Ideas, Concepts, Doctrine*, 109–11; Chief of the Army Air Forces, "AWPD/1," 5–7.
2. Combined Chiefs of Staff, "ANFA Conference Directive: The Bomber Offensive from the United Kingdom," Smith Papers 1941–1945, Combined Chiefs of Staff, ANFA Conference [Casablanca, January 14–23 1943] (DDLPL), series 1, box 1.
3. Matloff, *Strategic Planning for Coalition Warfare, 1943–1944*, 29.
4. Denis Richards, *The Hardest Victory: RAF Bomber Command in the Second World War* (New York: W. W. Norton, 1994), 30.
5. Charles Portal, "Bomber Command: Night Photograph Analysis (Butt Report)." AIR 8/1356, UKNA, 1941; Overy, *The Bombing War*, 266–69.
6. Wakelam, *The Science of Bombing*, 22–23.
7. Crane, *American Airpower Strategy in World War II*, 21–30.
8. Baldoli and Knapp, *Forgotten Blitzes*, 18.
9. Churchill, *The Hinge of Fate*, 678–80; Craven and Cate, *Torch to Pointblank*, 370–76.
10. Overy, *The Bombing War*, 91.
11. Greenhalgh, *The French Army*, 304–6, 86–90.
12. Gordon Craig, *Europe since 1914* (New York: Holt, Rinehart, and Winston, 1966), 682–85; Maddison Historical GDP Data, http://www.worldeconomics.com/Data/MadisonHistoricalGDP/Madison%20Historical%20GDP%20Data.efp (accessed August 2016); Leleu et al., *La France Pendant La Seconde Guerre Mondiale*, 22–23; Adam Tooze, *The Wages of Destruction: The Making and Breaking of the Nazi Economy* (New York: Penguin Books, 2006), 405.
13. Talbot Imlay and Martin Horn, *The Politics of Collaboration during World War II: Ford France, Vichy, and Nazi Germany* (New York: Cambridge University Press, 2014), 1–18.
14. Peter Jackson, "Recent Journeys along the Road Back to France, 1940," *The Historical Journal* 39, no. 2 (June 1996): 12–21; Eugenia C. Kiesling, *Arming*

against Hitler: France & the Limits of Military Planning (Lawrence: University of Kansas Press, 1996), 62–84.

15. I. C. B. Dear and M. R. D. Foot, *The Oxford Companion to World War II* (New York: Oxford University Press, 1995), 1059–63; Jackson, "Recent Journeys along the Road Back to France," 12–21; Tooze, *The Wages of Destruction*, 371–72.
16. Annie Lacroix-Riz, *Industriels Et Banquiers: Français Sous L'Occupation*, nouvelle édition (Paris: Armand Colin, 2013), 151–53, 57; Alan S. Milward, *The New Order and the French Economy* (Oxford: The Clarendon Press, 1970), 36.
17. Richard Vinen, *The Politics of French Business, 1936–1945* (New York: Cambridge University Press, 1991), 152–53.
18. Lacroix-Riz, *Industriels Et Banquiers*, 88–89; Paxton, *Vichy France*, 144.
19. Daniel Uziel, *Arming the Luftwaffe: The German Aviation Industry in World War II* (London: McFarland, 2012), 41.
20. Imlay and Horn, *The Politics of Collaboration*, 137.
21. Ibid., 1.
22. Baldoli and Knapp, *Forgotten Blitzes*, 23–24; Uziel, *Arming the Luftwaffe, 42–44.*
23. Hein Klemann and Sergei Kudryashov, *Occupied Economies: An Economic History of Nazi-Occupied Europe, 1939–1945* (New York: Berg Publishers Limited, 2012), 83.
24. Harris, *Despatch*, 14.
25. Dodd and Knapp, "How Many Frenchmen Did You Kill?," 476–77.
26. http://media.renault.com/global/en-gb/renaultgroup/Media/PressRelease.aspx?mediaid=33291 (accessed January 2016).
27. Lacroix-Riz, *Industriels Et Banquiers*, 33.
28. Headquarters, 15th Air Force, "Renault Raid 3 and 4 March 1943," AFHRC, IRIS: 00248940.
29. Barnett, *Engage the Enemy More Closely*, 445–55; Porter, *The Kreigsmarine*, 160–61.
30. Overy, *The Bombing War*, 276–80; Middlebrook and Everitt, *The Bomber Command War Diaries*, 240.
31. Saward, *Bomber Harris*, 118; Middlebrook and Everitt, *The Bomber Command War Diaries*, 241, 44–45.
32. Baldoli and Knapp, *Forgotten Blitzes*, 107.
33. Lacroix-Riz, *Industriels Et Banquiers*, 1533.
34. Saward, *Bomber Harris*, 118–19.
35. Alary, Vergez-Chaignon, and Gauvin, *Les Français Au Quotidien*, 506.
36. Simon Kitson, "Criminals or Liberators? French Public Opinion and the Allied Bombing of France, 1940–1945," in *Bombing, States and Peoples in Western Europe 1940–1945*, ed. Claudia Baldoli, Andrew Knapp, and Richard Overy (London: Continuum International Publishing Group, 2011), 280.
37. Knapp, *Les Français Sous Les Bombes Alliées*, 243; Lindsey Dodd, "'It Did Not Traumatize Me at All': Childhood 'Trauma' in French Oral Narratives of Wartime Bombing," *Oral History* 41, no. 2 (Autumn 2013): 43.

38. David G. Herrmann, *The Arming of Europe and the Making of the First World War* (Princeton, NJ: Princeton University Press, 1996), 107, 24, 34–35, 38, 205.
39. Florentin, *Quand Les Alliés Bombardaient La France*, 453 note 2.
40. Ministère de la Culture, "Fonderie Henri-Paul," http://www.culture.gouv.fr/documentation/merimee/PDF/sri26/IA71000109.PDF.
41. Harris, *Despatch*, 12.
42. Richards, *The Hardest Victory*, 292–93.
43. Middlebrook and Everitt, *The Bomber Command War Diaries*, 317; Florentin, *Quand Les Alliés Bombardaient La France*, 78–86.
44. Richards, *The Hardest Victory*, 163–70.
45. Direction de La Défense Passsive, Etat Français Ministere de l'Interieur, "Bulletin De Renseignement No. 10, June 1943," 502/W3, Rennes: Archives Départmentals et du Patrimoine; Middlebrook and Everitt, *The Bomber Command War Diaries*, 398–99. Florentin, *Quand Les Alliés Bombardaient La France*, 86–87.
46. USSBS, Physical Damage Division, "Gnome Et Rhone Aero Engine Factory, Limoges, France," 9; "Tactical Targets: Area 4800 (Le Mans)," box 26, RG 243, NARA.
47. Lacroix-Riz, *Industriels Et Banquiers*, 150–51.
48. SHAEF, "Tactical Targets: Area 4800 (Le Mans)," box 26, RG 243, NARA.
49. USSBS, Physical Damage Division, "Gnome Et Rhone Aero Engine Factory, Limoges," 10–11.
50. Ibid., 15; Freeman, Crouchman, and Maslen, *Mighty Eighth War Diary*, 72–74.
51. Ibid.; http://www.91stbombgroup.com/Dailies/324th1943-2.html (accessed February 12, 2014); http://www.303rdbg.com/missionreports/048.pdf (accessed February 12, 2014); http://www.ouest-france.fr/4-juillet-1943-violent-independance-day-au-mans-701004 (accessed February 12, 2014).
52. http://www.ouest-france.fr/pays-de-la-loire/le-mans-72000/4-juillet-1943-violent-independance-day-au-mans-701004;http://www.genealogie.com/v4/forums/recherches-genealogiques-recherche-victimes-ou-temoins-bombardement-4/7/1943-au-mans-t1160975-p1.html; http://www.lemans.maville.com/actu/actudet_-Qui-se-souvient-des-victimes-du-4-juillet-1943-_-1016917_actu.Htm (all accessed January 7, 2016).
53. Florence Goger, "Research Bombing Victims or Witnesses 04/07/1943 at Le Mans," http://www.genealogie.com/v4/forums/recherches-genealogiques-recherche-victimes-ou-temoins-bombardement-4/7/1943-au-manst1160975-p1.html.
54. Freeman, Crouchman, and Maslen, *Mighty Eighth War Diary*, 72–74; "Gnome Et Rhone Aero Engine Factory, Le Mans, France," USSBS, 15; "Target Damage File: Le Mans"; "AWPD/1," Tab 2b.
55. Craven and Cate, *Argument to V-E Day*, 30–48; Overy, *The Bombing War*, 369; Davis, *Bombing the European Powers*, 292.
56. Smith, *France and the Great War*, 36.

57. Porch, *The Path to Victory*; USSBS, Physical Damage Division, "Gnome Et Rhone Aero Engine Factory, Limoges, France," 1–5.
58. Middlebrook and Everitt, *The Bomber Command War Diaries*, 471; Knapp, *Les Français*, 101.
59. http://www.historyofwar.org/air/units/RAF/617_wwII.html (accessed February 11, 2014).
60. Lacroix-Riz, *Industriels Et Banquiers*, 117–18; Free French Government, "French Public Opinion," 3AG2 333, Paris: Archives nationales (AN), 1945, 92; USSBS, Physical Damage Division, "Gnome Et Rhone Aero Engine Factory, Limoges, France."
61. Middlebrook and Everitt, *The Bomber Command War Diaries*, 480.
62. USSBS, Physical Damage Division, "Gnome Et Rhone Aero Engine Factory, Limoges, France"; http://www.raf.mod.uk/rafcms/mediafiles/262EB144_5056_A318_A8947809CAD08895.pdf.
63. http://www.regardsetviedauvergne.fr/2014/08/clermont-ferrand-bombardements-de.html (Feb 2016); http://www.lamontagne.fr/auvergne/actualite/departement/puy-de-dome/clermont-ferrand/2014/05/17/la-capitale-auvergnate-subit-deux-raids-aeriens-en-mars-et-avril-1944_11007139.html (accessed February 2016).
64. Middlebrook and Everitt, *The Bomber Command War Diaries*, 480.
65. Tooze, *The Wages of Destruction*, 648–50; USSBS, "Statistical Appendix," 13.
66. Schaffer, *Wings of Judgment*, 106; Crane, *American Airpower Strategy in World War II*; Alexander B. Downes, *Targeting Civilians in War* (Ithaca, NY: Cornell University Press, 2008); John Tirman, *The Deaths of Others: The Fate of Civilians in America's Wars* (New York: Oxford University Press, 2011); Dietmar Süss, *Death from the Skies: How the British and Germans Endured Aerial Destruction in World War II* (Oxford: Oxford University Press, 2014), 521.

Chapter 6. Crossbow

1. Winston S. Churchill, *The Second World War*, vol. 6, *Triumph and Tragedy* (Boston: Houghton Mifflin, 1953), 40–41; Norman Longmate, *The Doodlebugs: The Story of the Flying-Bombs* (London: Hutchinson, 1981), 125; Atkinson, *The Guns at Last Light*, 108–9.
2. Air Historical Branch, Air Ministry, "Raf Narrative (First Draft): Air Defense of Great Britain, the Flying Bomb and Rocket Campaigns, 1944–1945," AHB (1945), 2–4.
3. Ibid.
4. Dear and Foot, *The Oxford Companion to World War II*, 1251–53; Tracy D. Dungan, *V-2 Combat History of the First Ballistic Missile* (Yardley, PA: Westholme, 2005), 169.
5. USSBS, Military Analysis Division, V-Weapons (Crossbow) Campaign, ed. European Division, 2nd ed., United States Strategic Bombing Survey (Washington, DC: Government Printing Office, 1947), 3.

6. Hugues Chevalier, *Bombes Et V1 Sur Le Pas-De-Calais 1944: Raids Alliés, Crashes, Destructions . . .* (Vottem, BE: Snel Grafics à Vottem, 2009), 116. Official passive defense figures have 3,670 deaths from bombing in Pas-de-Calais, 3,713 for Nord, and 1,077 for Somme, August 1943 through August 1944 inclusive. Note from Andrew Knapp to author, November 2016.
7. Walter Dornberger, *V-2* (New York: Viking, 1954), pers. hist.; Dungan, *V-2 Combat History of the First Ballistic Missile*; Steven J. Zaloga, *German V-Weapon Sites 1943–1945* (Oxford: Osprey, 2007); Steven J. Zaloga and Jim Laurier, *V-1 Flying Bomb 1942–1952: Hitler's Infamous "Doodlebug"* (Oxford: Osprey, 2005); Roland Hautefeuille, *Constructions Speciales: Histoire De La Construction Par "L'organizaton Todt," Dan Le Pas De Calais Et Le Cotentin, Des Neufs Gránds Sites Protégés Pur Le Tir Des V1, V2, V3 Et La Production D'oxygène Liquide (1943–1944)* (Tourcoing, France: Jean-Bernard, 1985); Philip Henshall, *Hitler's Rocket Sites* (New York: St. Martin's Press, 1985); Dungan, *V-2 Combat History of the First Ballistic Missile*; Benjamin King and Timothy J. Kutta, *Impact: The History of Germany's V-Weapons in World War II* (Rockville Centre, NY: Sarpedon, 1998).
8. Norman Longmate, *Hitler's Rockets: The Story of the V-2s* (Yorkshire, UK: Frontline Books, 2009).
9. Craven and Cate, *Plans and Early Operations*; Charles Webster and Noble Frankland, *The Strategic Air Offensive against Germany, 1939–1945,* vol. 2, *Endeavor* (London: Her Majesty's Stationery Office, 1961); Webster and Frankland, *The Strategic Air Offensive against Germany, 1939–1945,* vol. 3, *Victory*; Pogue, *The Supreme Command*; Sebastian Cox, ed. *The Strategic Air War against Germany, 1939–1945: Report of the British Bombing Survey Unit* (London: Frank Cass, 1993).
10. Maud Jarry, "Le Bombardement Des Sites V En France (Été 1943-Été 1944)," in *Les Bombardements Alliés Sur La France Durant La Seconde Guerre Mondiale: Stratégies, Bilans Matérials Et Humains*, ed. Michèle Battesti and Patrick Facon (Vincennes: Cahiers du Center D'études D'historie de la Défense, 2009); Florentin, *Quand Les Alliés Bombardaient La France*; Baldoli and Knapp, *Forgotten Blitzes*; Chevalier, *Bombes Et V1 Sur Le Pas-De-Calais 1944*; Laurent Bailleul, *Les Sites V1 En Flandres Et En Artois* (Hazebrouck: S. A. Presse Flamande, 2000); Dejonghe and le Maner, *Le Nord-Pas-De-Calais Dans La Main Allemande.*
11. James Aulich, "Memory, What Is It Good For? Forced Labour, Blockhouses and Museums in Nord-Pas De Calais, Northern France," in *Contested Spaces: Sites, Representations and Histories of Conflict*, ed. Louise Purbrick, James Aulich, and Graham Dawson (New York: Palgrave Macmillan, 2007); Jarry, "Le Bombardement Des Sites V En France."
12. Henshall, *Hitler's Rocket Sites*, 56–57; Aulich, "Memory, What Is It Good For?"
13. *Flakzielgerat* translates as an anti-aircraft target device and was so named to deceive the British as to its real purpose. The German propaganda ministry

referred to it as the Vergeltunswaffe-1. The British preferred to call it the V-1 "flying bomb" to distinguish it from the V-2 rocket. Zaloga and Laurier, *V-1 Flying Bomb*, 6–9; USSBS, Crossbow, 9; Air Ministry, Air Historical Branch, "The Flying Bomb and Rocket Campaigns," 16–24.

14. *Aggregat-4* translates to prototype or model number 4.
15. Dungan, *V-2 Combat History of the First Ballistic Missile*, 2–3, 205; http://www.v2rocket.com/start/makeup/design.html (accessed March 14, 2016); Tooze, *The Wages of Destruction*, 619–20.
16. Air Ministry, Air Historical Branch, "The Flying Bomb and Rocket Campaigns," 2–10. Longmate, *The Doodlebugs*, 30–31; Cox, *The Strategic Air War against Germany*, 20; Longmate, *Hitler's Rockets*, 47.
17. War Office, "Bodyline: Intelligence Meeting Shell Mex House 30 Sep. 1943," WO 199/549, UKNA; Churchill, *Closing the Ring*, 226–33; Air Ministry, Air Historical Branch, "The Flying Bomb and Rocket Campaigns," 4, 15–17. Longmate, *Hitler's Rockets*, 73–78.
18. Office of the Secretary General Staff, "Letter: C. R. Price to Ltg F. E. Morgan, 'Crossbow' (16 December 1943)," box 71, RG 331, NARA; COSSAC, "Interim Report by COSSAC on the Effect of "Crossbow" on "Overlord" (20 December 1943)," box 71, RG 331, NARA.
19. Chiefs of Air Staff War Cabinet, "Crossbow" Report by the Chiefs of Air Staff, December 17, 1943, box 71, RG 331, NARA; USSBS, Crossbow: 2.
20. "Memorandum: Eisenhower to Tedder. Re: Crossbow Priorities, 18 June 1944," box 71, RG 331, NARA.
21. Joint Planning Staff, "Chemical Warfare in Connection with CROSSBOW: Report by the Joint Planning Staff," box 71, RG 331, NARA.
22. Longmate, *The Doodlebugs*, 442–43; USSBS Crossbow: 6–7, app. 10.
23. AG SHAEF, "Security of BIGBEN," box 71, RG 331, NARA; Dungan, *V-2 Combat History of the First Ballistic Missile*, 115–87; Air Ministry, Air Historical Branch, "The Flying Bomb and Rocket Campaigns," 228–302.
24. Duncan Sandys, "Investigation of the 'Heavy' Crossbow Installations in Northern France, Volume 1," CAB 80/92, UKNA; Harrison, *Cross-Channel Attack*, 416–19, map XXIII.
25. Florentin, *Quand les Alliés bombardaient la France*, 217.
26. Sandys, "Investigation," app. D, 1–4; Copp, *Cinderella Army*, 44–54; Stacey, *The Victory Campaign*, 354–56.
27. Sandys, "Investigation," 5–9.
28. Ibid., app. C.
29. Henshall, *Hitler's Rocket Sites*, 55.
30. Hautefeuille, *Constructions Speciales*, 190; Henshall, *Hitler's Rocket Sites*, 32–33, 69–77.
31. Longmate, *Hitler's Rockets*, 6, 58–59, 103; USSBS, Crossbow, 10–11; Sandys, "Investigation," 7–11; Anti-Aircraft Artillery Section, "V2 Rocket Attacks and

Defense," in Reports of the General Board, United States Forces, European Theater, ed. United States Forces General Board, Europe, CARL, 1945, 9–10, appendix.

32. Office, "Bodyline: Intelligence Meeting Shell Mex House 30 Sep. 1943"; Sandys, "Investigation," 7, A1–A4; Hautefeuille, *Constructions Speciales*, 14–15.
33. War Office, "Bodyline Intelligence, 17 December 1943," WO 199/549, UKNA; Zaloga, *German V-Weapon Sites*, 24–25; R(eginald) V. Jones, *Most Secret War: British Scientific Intelligence 1939–1945* (London: Hamish Hamilton, 1978), 458–63; Robert G. Dancy, *Flying Bomb Launching Sites: A Description of What Was Still to Be Seen of Some of the 1944 V1 Launching Sites in Northern France About 60 Years Later* (Self-published, 2009), http://www.christianch.ch/history/V1_sites_rgd.pdf. 110–14 (accessed March 10, 2015).
34. Longmate, *The Doodlebugs*, 79–80; Air Ministry, Air Historical Branch, "The Flying Bomb and Rocket Campaigns," 72–75, 187; Zaloga and Laurier, *V-1 Flying Bomb*, 16–17.
35. Dungan, *V-2: Combat History of the First Ballistic Missile*, 115.
36. Air Ministry, Air Historical Branch, "The Flying Bomb and Rocket Campaigns," 223; Zaloga, *German V-Weapon Sites*, 50–52.
37. Air Ministry, Air Historical Branch, "The Flying Bomb and Rocket Campaigns," 57–58.
38. Survey, USBBS, Crossbow, 3, 27; Chevalier, *Bombes Et V1 Sur Le Pas-De-Calais 1944*. A sortie is one aircraft on one mission.
39. Préfecture de Pas de Calais, "Bombardements Et Chutes D'avions : Messages Et Rapports De Police Et De Gendarmerie, Rapports Du Préfet, États Statistiques (Feb 1944)," M 5393 2, Arch62. This report by the Préfecture de Pas-de-Calais lists every known air strike in the department. Often the annotation "dans les champs" (in the field) is recorded as the result
40. Survey, USSBS, Crossbow, exh. 6.
41. Sebastian Cox, "Raids on Mimoyecques V3 Site 1943–1944," AHB, 1985; Hautefeuille, *Constructions Speciales*, 199.
42. "AWPD/1," Tab 2b.
43. Préfecture de Pas de Calais, "Bombardements Et Chutes D'avions : Messages Et Rapports De Police Et De Gendarmerie, Rapports Du Préfet, États Statistiques (Jan 1944)," in M 5393 2, Arch62. Entry for January 31, 1944; Florentin, *Quand Les Alliés Bombardaient La France*, 217.
44. Duane Heath and Wesley R. Williams, "Diary of T/Sgt William Heath, 492nd Bomb Group (H)," www.492ndbombgroup.com/stories/HeathWarDiary (accessed March 2015).
45. Chevalier, *Bombes Et V1 Sur Le Pas-De-Calais 1944*, 186–87.
46. Carter and Mueller, *Combat Chronology*, 180; Air Ministry, Air Historical Branch, "The Flying Bomb and Rocket Campaigns," 12.
47. Freeman, Crouchman, and Maslen, *Mighty Eighth War Diary*, 313–14; Hautefeuille, *Constructions Speciales*, 188–90; Henshall, *Hitler's Rocket Sites*, 59–61.

48. The Tallboy was a 12,000-pound bomb, generally used by the 617 Squadron of the Royal Air Force. It was designed to penetrate and destroy thick concrete targets.
49. Longmate, *Hitler's Rockets*, 147; Stacey, *The Victory Campaign*, 325.
50. 416th Bomb Group, "416th Bomb Group (L) Combat Missions," http://416th.com/missions/combat_missions.html; 387th Bombardment Group, "387th Bombardment Group (Medium): The Tiger-Striped Marauders," http://387bg.com; Jenns Robertson, "Project Thor," AHB, 2013; Dancy, *Flying Bomb Launching Sites*.
51. AEAF, "Daily Int/Ops Summary No 125, 2 June 1944"; Robertson, "Project Thor."
52. W. McArthur Charles, *Operations Analysis in the United States Army Eighth Air Force in World War II, History of Mathematics* (New York: American Mathematical Society, 1991), 111–15; Baldoli and Knapp, *Forgotten Blitzes*, 34.
53. Préfecture de Pas de Calais, "Bombardements Et Chutes D'avions: Messages Et Rapports De Police Et De Gendarmerie, Rapports Du Préfet, États Statistiques. (April 1944)," M 5394 1, Arch62; Sous-préfecture de St. Omer, "Lettre À Prefect Du Pas-De-Calais: 24 Avril 1944, Bombardment St. Omer 22–23 April," M 5394 1, Arch62; Chevalier, *Bombes Et V1 Sur Le Pas-De-Calais 1944*, 50, 273.
54. Chevalier, *Bombes Et V1 Sur Le Pas-De-Calais 1944*, 142–43.
55. Sous-Prefecture de Béthune, "Rapport À Préfet Du Pas-De-Calais: Bombardement Aérian (20, 21, 22, 23, & 27 Avril)," M 5394 2, Arch62.
56. Préfecture de Pas de Calais, "Bombardements Et Chutes D'avions : Messages Et Rapports De Police Et De Gendarmerie, Rapports Du Préfet, États Statistiques (April 1944)," M 5394 1, Arch62; "Bombardements Et Chutes D'avions: États Statistiques (May1944)" M 5394 1, Arch62.
57. Stephen Darlow, *Sledgehammers for Tintacks: Bomber Command Confronts the V-1 Menace, 1943–1944* (London: Grub Street, 2002; repr.), 150–51.
58. Calais, "Bombardements Et Chutes D'avions: Messages Et Rapports De Police Et De Gendarmerie, Rapports Du Préfet, États Statistiques (April 1944)," "Bombardements Et Chutes D'avions: États Statistiques (Juin1944)," M 5394 2, Arch62.
59. Isbergues Commissaire du Police, "Rapport À Sous Préfet Du Bethune: Bombardement Ville De Saint Venat, 12 Mai 1944," M 5394 2, Arch62.
60. Arras Commissaire du Police, "Rapport À Préfet Du Pas-De-Calais: Bombardement Aérian 30 Avril (1 Mai 1944)," M 5394 1, Arch62.
61. Chevalier, *Bombes Et V1 Sur Le Pas-De-Calais 1944*, 264.
62. Aulich, "Memory, What Is It Good For?," 194.
63. Jarry, "Le Bombardement Des Sites V En France," 45.
64. Aulich, "Memory, What Is It Good For?" With the help a Polish doctor who worked in the camp, his father was able to escape to work with the local Maquis as a courier. When the Canadians arrived, they sent him to Scotland for training with the Polish 1st Armored Division, and within a few weeks he was back

in France in a reconnaissance unit. It is ironic that he was wounded when an American air attack hit the Polish division by mistake.

65. Ibid. Electronic mail between Aulich and author.
66. Among the best are Chevalier, *Bombes Et V1 Sur Le Pas-De-Calais 1944*; Laurent Bailleul, *Les Sites V1 En Flandres Et En Artois*; Dejonghe and le Maner, *Le Nord-Pas-De-Calais Dans La Main Allemande.*

Chapter 7. Fortitude

1. Chandler and Ambrose, *The Papers of Dwight David Eisenhower*; Message, Eisenhower to Marshall, April 29, 1944, 1657–58.
2. David Eisenhower, *Eisenhower: At War 1943–1945* (New York: Random House, 1986), 218–22; Chandler and Ambrose, *The War Years*, Letter, Eisenhower to Patton, May 3, 1944, 1846–47; Anthony Cave Brown, *Bodyguard of Lies: The Extraordinary True Story behind D-Day* (Guilford, CT: Lyons Press, 1975), 467–78.
3. Kennedy, *Engineers of Victory*, 256–57; Hastings, *Overlord*, 36; Mary Kathryn Barbier, *D-Day Deception: Operation Fortitude and the Normandy Invasion*, Stackpole Military History Series (Mechanicsburg, PA: Stackpole Books, 2009), 85.
4. Rémy Desquesnes, *Le Mur De L'atlantique, De Dunkerque Au Tréport* (Lille: Editions Ouest-France, 2014), 6, 52–55; Steven J. Zaloga, *The Atlantic Wall (1): France (Fortress)* (Oxford: Osprey, 2007), 14–15.
5. Alain Chazette et al., *Forteresse Boulogne-Sur-Mer 1939–1944: Occupation-Fortifications-Libération* (Paris: Éditions Histoire et Fortifications, 2007), 44–49; Desquesnes, *Le Mur De L'atlantique*, 67–69.
6. Desquesnes, *Le Mur De L'atlantique*, 56–59; Wilt, *The Atlantic Wall*, photos following page 69; Dejonghe and le Maner, *Le Nord-Pas-De-Calais*, 119.
7. Roger Hesketh, *Fortitude: The D-Day Deception Campaign* (New York: Overlook Press, 2002), 63–69; Barbier, *D-Day Deception*, 11–20, 41–62.
8. Hesketh, *Fortitude*, 80–130; Barbier, *D-Day Deception*, 63–73.
9. SHAEF, "Plan Fortitude," AIR 37, UKNA.
10. Hesketh, *Fortitude*, 87–93, 125–48, 382–87; Barbier, *D-Day Deception*, 63–84, 94–95; Brown, *Bodyguard of Lies*, 460–62.
11. Almost every book on the invasion mentions Fortitude in passing: Beevor, *D-Day*, 3–5; Hastings, *Overlord*, 38–36; Eisenhower, *Eisenhower: At War*, 108; D'Este, *Decision in Normandy*, 107; Richard Overy, *Why the Allies Won* (New York: W. W. Norton, 1995), 151–52; and most recently, Kennedy, *Engineers of Victory*, 256–57.
12. Brown, *Bodyguard of Lies*, 522–23.
13. Deputy Chief of Staff Operations, "Eighth Air Force Tactical Operations in Support of Allied Landings in Normandy, 2 June–17 June 1944," 4.
14. Julius Caesar, *The Conquest of Gaul*, trans. S. A. Handford, Penguin Classics (New York: Penguin, 1982), note 28.

15. Middlebrook and Everitt, *The Bomber Command War Diaries*, 52.
16. Chazette et al., *Forteresse Boulogne-Sur-Mer 1939–1944*, 21–38.
17. Ibid., 25; Dejonghe and Maner, *Le Nord-Pas-De-Calais*, 114–23.
18. Alary, Vergez-Chaignon, and Gauvin, *Les Français Au Quotidien*, 504; Guy Bataille, *Boulogne Sur Mer: 1939–1945* (Dunkerque: Westhoek-éditions, 1984), 65.
19. Middlebrook and Everitt, *The Bomber Command War Diaries*, 511–12.
20. Préfecture de Pas de Calais, "Bombardements Et Chutes D'avions: États Statistiques (May 1944)," M 5394 2, Arch62; Bataille, *Boulogne Sur Mer*, 70; Compaignie du Pas-de-Calais à Arras Gendarmerie Nationale, "Registres De Correspondance Confidentielle Au Départ (R/2), 1er Au 23 Mai 1944," in Gendarmerie Nationale, ed. Legion des Flandres Gendarme, Compaignie du Pas-de-Calais, SHD, 48. It is impossible to determine with any accuracy the number of civilians in the city by June 1944. Numbers range from a high of 30,000 to only 6,000.
21. Dejonghe and le Maner, *Le Nord-Pas-De-Calais*, 337; Middlebrook and Everitt, *The Bomber Command War Diaries*, 430; Freeman, Crouchman, and Maslen, *Mighty Eighth War Diary*, 108; Craven and Cate, *Europe, Torch to Pointblank*, 688–89.
22. "Daily Int/Ops Summary No 108, 24–25 May 1944," Kingston-McCloughry Papers, IWM; Bataille, *Boulogne Sur Mer*, 73.
23. Bataille, *Boulogne Sur Mer*, 73.
24. "Daily Int/Ops Summary No 125, 2 June 1944," Kingston-McCloughry Papers, IWM.
25. Commissaire Central-Boulogne, "Bombardment Aèrien," in Archives Départmentals du Pas-de-Calais, M 5394 2, Arch62; ibid.
26. Préfecture de Pas de Calais, "Bombardements Et Chutes D'avions: États Statistiques (Juin 1944)," M 5394 2, Arch62.
27. "Eighth Air Force, Normandy," FO 719, "Eighth Air Force Tactical Operations in Support of Allied Landings in Normandy, 2 June–17 June 1944."
28. Ibid., FO 725.
29. Préfecture de Pas de Calais, "Bombardements Et Chutes D'avions: États Statistiques (Juin 1944)."
30. Thierry Capillier, *Boulogne, 40–44: Une Exposition Basée Sur Les Témoignages De Six Boulonnais* (Boulogne-sur-mer: Archives Municipales, 2005), 72; Middlebrook and Everitt, *The Bomber Command War Diaries*, 529; Préfecture de Pas de Calais, "Bombardements Et Chutes D'avions: États Statistiques (Juin 1944)."
31. Capillier, *Boulogne, 40–44*, 72–73.
32. Scott Simon Gerald LeBlanc, "Breaching the Ramparts: The 3rd Canadian Infantry Division's Capture of Boulogne in World War Two" (Monograph, US Army Command and General Staff College, 2016); Copp, *Cinderella Army*, 63–77; Chazette et al., *Forteresse Boulogne-Sur-Mer*, 166–69.

33. Capillier, *Boulogne, 40–44*, 70–72; "Annuaire Des Mairies Et Villes De France," http://www.annuaire-mairie.fr (accessed April 2016).
34. "Annuaire Des Mairies Et Villes De France." http://berckbrel.ecole.free.fr/la.htm (accessed March 16, 2014).
35. Leleu et al., eds., *La France Pendant La Seconde Guerre Mondial*, 227; Dejonghe and Maner, *Le Nord-Pas-De-Calais*, 116–19.
36. Overy, *The Bombing War*, 346–47, 386–87; Wakelam, *The Science of Bombing*, 119; Davis, *Carl A. Spaatz*, 346; Crane, *American Airpower Strategy in World War II*, 104–13.
37. "Eighth Air Force, Normandy," FO 715.
38. http://berckbrel.ecole.free.fr/la.htm (accessed March 16, 2014). Other reports indicate fifty-eight killed, seven missing, and eighty-three wounded.
39. Maeve O'Brien, "'Something in Me Said, Now, You Must See This': Reconciliation of Death and 'the Empty Beaches of Memory' in Sylvia Plath's 'Berck-Plage,'" *Plath Profiles: An Interdisciplinary Journal for Sylvia Plath Studies* 6 (2013); Sylvia Plath, "Berck-Plage," in *Ariel* (London: Faber and Faber, 1965), 22–27.
40. James Clarke, *A Topographical and Historical Description of Boulogne and Its Vicinity* (London: J. S. Hodson, 1835), 43–49.
41. Chazette et al., *Forteresse Boulogne-Sur-Mer*, 44–49; Desquesnes, *Le Mur De L'atlantique*, 67–69.
42. "Eighth Air Force, Normandy," FO 709.
43. Préfecture de Pas de Calais, "Bombardements Et Chutes D'avions: États Statistiques (Juin 1944)."
44. Middlebrook and Everitt, *The Bomber Command War Diaries*, 518–20; Air Staff Intelligence Headquarters Bomber Command, "Interceptions/Tactics No. 126/44, Night 2nd/3rd June 1944," RG 243, RAF Bomber Command, Tactics Apr–May 1944, box 18, NARA; Compaignie du Pas-de-Calais à Arras Gendarmerie Nationale, "Registres De Correspondance Confidentielle Au Départ (R/2), 24 Mai Au 12 Juin 1944," in *Gendarmerie Nationale*, ed. Legion des Flandres Gendarme, Compaignie du Pas-de-Calais, SHD, 81; "Eighth Air Force, Normandy," FO 715, 19; Préfecture de Pas de Calais, "Bombardements Et Chutes D'avions: États Statistiques (Juin 1944)."
45. Le Sous-Préfet de Boulogne, "À Monsieur Le Préfet Du Pas-De-Calais," M 5394 2, Arch62.
46. Préfecture de Pas de Calais, "Bombardements Et Chutes D'avions: États Statistiques (Juin 1944)."
47. Discussion with a local farmer in Boulogne in August 2014.
48. Barbier, *D-Day Deception*, 192–95.

Chapter 8. The Rail Centers

1. Air Ministry, Air Historical Branch, "Planning and Preparation," chaps. 7 and 8; F. H. Hinsley et al., *British Intelligence in the Second World War, Its Influence*

on Strategy and Operations, vol. 3, part 2 (New York: Cambridge University Press, 1988), 107.

2. Joint Chiefs of Staff, *Joint Publication 1-02, Department of Defense Dictionary of Military and Associated Terms*, 125.
3. United States War Department, *Field Manual 1–5, Employment of Aviation of the Army* (Washington, DC: Government Printing Office, 1940), 23.
4. Eisenhower, *Crusade in Europe*, 231.
5. Futrell, *Ideas, Concepts, Doctrine*, 22–26; Jenns Robertson, THOR (Theater History of Operations Reports) (Maxwell Air Force Base, AL: Air Force Historical Research Institute, 2013).
6. United States War Department, *Employment of Aviation of the Army*, 32.
7. Gaetke, "Joint by Design"; Christopher M. Rein, *The North African Air Campaign* (Lawrence: University Press of Kansas, 2012), 40–66.
8. Corrado, "Tactical Enthusiasm," 29–30.
9. Tedder, *With Prejudice*, 442.
10. "Weekly Intelligence Summary #6: For Week Ending 29 April 1944," box 30, Smith Papers, DDEPL; Richard Dinardo, *Germany and the Axis Powers: From Coalition to Collapse* (Lawrence: University of Kansas Press, 2005), 189.
11. John Merriman, *A History of Modern Europe: From the Renaissance to the Present*, 2nd ed. (New York: W. W. Norton, 2004), 559–64; Hajo Holborn, *A History of Modern Germany: 1840–1945* (New York: Alfred A. Knopf, 1975), 378.
12. Hajo Holborn, "The Prusso-German School: Moltke and the Rise of the General Staff," in *Makers of Modern Strategy from Machiavelli to the Nuclear Age*, ed. Peter Paret (Princeton, NJ: Princeton University Press, 1986), 287–88; Holborn, *A History of Modern Germany: 1840–1945*, 375; Arthur Banks, *A Military Atlas of the First World War* (Barnsley, UK: Pen and Sword, 1989), atlas, 21. Union and Confederate forces also moved troops by rail during the American Civil War.
13. "Weekly Intelligence Summary #1: For Week Ending 26 March 1944," box 30, Smith Papers, DDEPL; Martin Van Creveld, *Supplying War: Logistics from Wallenstein to Patton* (Cambridge, MA: Harvard University Press, 1977), 77–80.
14. AAF Evaluation Board in the European Theater of Operations, "Effectiveness of Air Attack against Rail Transportation in the Battle of France," AFHRC, 1945, 1–5; "Weekly Intelligence Summary #1: For Week Ending 26 March 1944," box 30, Smith Papers, DDEPL.
15. AAF Evaluation Board, "Effectiveness of Air Attack against Rail," 15; Paul Le Trevier and Daniel Rose, *Ce Qui S'est Vraiment Passé Le 19 Avril 1944* (Le Mesnil-Esnard, France: Comever-De Rameau, 2004), 14–19; AC of S Intelligence Analysis Division, "Evaluation of Transportation as an Air Target," AFHRC, 1944, 8–9.

16. Photographs from the period clearly show the proximity of civilian life to the rail infrastructure.
17. Joint Planning Staff, "Study No. 6, Delay of Enemy Reserves (First Draft)," ed. COSSAC, AHB, 1943, 11.
18. Forrest C. Pogue devotes an entire chapter of his *The Supreme Command* to "SHAEF's Air Problems." See Pogue, *The Supreme Command*, 125–37.
19. Combined Commanders Planning Staff, "Review of Certain Factors Affecting Preparations for a Return to the Continent," in Barker Papers, DDEPL; Hinsley et al., *British Intelligence in the Second World War*, 106.
20. "Study No. 6, Delay of Enemy Reserves (Final), AHB, 1944.
21. Ibid.
22. Hinsley et al., *British Intelligence in the Second World War*, 106.
23. Air Ministry, Air Historical Branch, "Planning and Preparation," 142; Solly Zuckerman, "Air Attacks on Rail and Road Communications," AHB, 1943.
24. Zuckerman and his ideas were controversial and remained so after the war. See Henry D. Lytton, "Bombing Policy in the Rome and Pre-Normandy Invasion Aerial Campaigns of World War II," *Military Affairs* (April 1983): 53–58; W. W. Rostow, *Pre-Invasion Bombing Strategy: General Eisenhower's Decision of March 25, 1944*, Ideas and Action (Austin: University of Texas Press, 1981).
25. Air Vice-Marshal E-J Kingston-McCloughry, "The Transportation Plan," in Papers of Air Vice-Marshal E-J Kingston-McCloughry, IWM, 1946, 3.
26. Air Ministry, Air Historical Branch, "Planning and Preparation," 146–47; Davis, *Carl A. Spaatz*, 336–37; General Carl A. Spaatz, interview by Noel F. Parrish and Alfred Goldberg, February 21, 1962, AFHRA.
27. Kingston-McCloughry, "The Transportation Plan," 8; Charles P. Cabell Jr., *A Man of Intelligence: Memoirs of War, Peace, and the CIA* (Colorado Springs, CO: Impavide Publications, 1997), 119; AHB, "Planning and Preparation," 153–54.
28. Chiefs of Staff Committee, "Attacks on Rail Targets in Enemy Occupied Territories, 19 March 1944," UK War Cabinet, AHB.
29. Combined Chiefs of Staff, "Memorandum: Control of Strategic Bombing for Overlord," AIR 8/1185, UKNA, 1944; Air Ministry, Air Historical Branch, "Planning and Preparation," 155.
30. Kingston-McCloughry, "The Transportation Plan," 10.
31. Trafford Leigh-Mallory, "Letter to Air Ministry: Targets Outside of Germany," AHB, 1944.
32. Ibid.
33. Committee, "Attacks on Rail Targets in Enemy Occupied Territories, 19 March 1944"; Air Ministry, Air Historical Branch, "The Landings in Normandy," 160; Tedder, *With Prejudice*, 520–21.
34. Charles Portal, "Bombing Policy—France and Occupied Countries: March & April 1944," AIR 19/218, UKNA, note 29, March 1944.

35. Winston S. Churchill, "Letter to Eisenhower Re: French Casualties, April 3, 1944." Dwight D. Eisenhower: Papers, Pre-Presidential, 1916–1952, principal file, DDEPL.
36. Winston S. Churchill, "Letter to Eisenhower Re: Concern over French Civilian Casualties, April 29, 1944," box 66, RG 331, NARA.
37. Dwight D. Eisenhower, "Letter to Churchill, Reply to Previous Letter, 2 May 1944," box 66, RG 331, NARA.
38. French Committee of National Liberation, "Memorandum: Re Allied Bombing of France," May 1944, box 66, RG 331, NARA.
39. Warren F. Kimball, ed., *Churchill & Roosevelt: The Complete Correspondence*, vol. 3, *Alliance Declining, February 1944–April 1945* (Princeton, NJ: Princeton University Press, 1984), 122.
40. Roosevelt, "Telegram to Churchill, Reply to Previous Telegram in Regards to French Casualties," May 1944, box 66, RG 331, NARA.
41. Jacques Garnier, ed. *Dictionnaire Perrin: Des Guerres Et Des Batailles De L'historie De France* (Paris: Perrin, 2004), 147–50; Porch, *The Path to Victory*, 270–73; Charles de Gaulle, *The Complete War Memoirs of Charles de Gaulle*, trans. Jonathan Griffin and Richard Howard (New York: Carroll & Graff, 1998), 291–300.
42. Jones, *Eisenhower's Guerrillas*, 116–17.
43. Chapin, "FCNL Invites . . .," SHAEF SGS 1943–1945, French Committee of National Liberation, 373.24, vol. 2, Military Objectives for Aerial Bombardment, DDEPL.
44. Walter Bedell Smith, "Msg: Smith to George C. Marshall, May 171055b, "Eyes Only," Smith Papers 1941–1945, DDEPL.
45. "Bombing Policy Occupied Countries Part 3" AIR 20/2799, UKNA. https://liberationroute.com/belgium/historical-location/kortrijk-bombing-poi208 (accessed December 2016).
46. Charles Portal, "Final Minutes of a Meeting Held on Saturday, March 25th to Discuss the Bombing Policy in the Period before 'Overlord,'" AIR 19/218, UKNA.
47. Ibid.
48. Ibid.
49. Air Ministry, Air Historical Branch, "Planning and Preparation," 162; Air Ministry, Air Historical Branch, "The Landings in Normandy," 25.
50. Middlebrook and Everitt, *The Bomber Command War Diaries*, 495–96; Florentin, *Quand Les Alliés Bombardaient La France*, 287–92.
51. Craven and Cate, *Plans and Early Operations*, 661–68; Le Trevier, *Objectif Rouen*.
52. Guy Pessiot, *Histoire De Rouen 1939–1958: La Guerre 39/45 Et La Reconstruction En 900 Photographies* (Rouen: Editions PTC, 2004), 108; Sandrine Folliot, "Sotteville-Les-Rouen Pendant La Seconde Guerre Mondiale Et La Periode De Reconstruction (1939–1965)" (MA thesis, University de Rouen, 1990), 43–46.

53. Le Trevier and Rose, *Ce Qui S'est Vraiment Passé Le 19 Avril 1944*, 8–19; Hardy, "La Défense Passive À Rouen Et Dans Son Agglomération," 10.
54. SHAEF, "Tactical Targets: Area 4901e (Rouen)," box 28, RG 243, NARA.
55. Hardy, "La Défense Passive À Rouen Et Dans Son Agglomération," 108.
56. G2 SHAEF, "Target Damage File: Lille," box 97/98, RG 243, NARA.
57. United States Strategic Bombing Survey, "Immediate Interpretation Report No. K.2044: Rouen/Sotteville M/Y," box 139, RG 243, NARA.
58. M.F.A. & A Specialist Officer, "Report on Monuments of Rouen," in *Papers of Ronald Edmona Balfour*, ed. 1st Canadian Army SACO, Kings College, 1944.
59. Seine Inferieur Préfect, "Compte Rendu Du Bombardement De L'agglomération Rouennaise Du 19 Avril 1944," in 271 W283 Rapports, Arch76; Hardy, "La Défense Passive À Rouen Et Dans Son Agglomération," 108–9.
60. Préfect, "Compte Rendu Du Bombardement De L'agglomération Rouennaise Du 19 Avril 1944"; Hardy, "La Défense Passive À Rouen Et Dans Son Agglomération," 109; Pailhès, *Rouen Et Sa Région Pendant La Guerre*, 198–204; André Maurois, *Rouen Dévasté* (Paris: Les Editions Nagel, 1948), 52–58.
61. "4,000 Tons Dropped at Night," *Times* (London), April 20, 1944.
62. "Allies Step Up Record Bombing, Dropping 8,000 Tons in 36 Hours," *New York Times*, April 20, 1944.
63. Whitehall Air Ministry, "Reactions to Allied Raids on W. Seaboard of Europe, 29 April 1944," box 66, RG 331, NARA.
64. Seine Inferieur Préfect, "Bombardment De L'agglomeration Rouen 19 Avril 1944," 271 W282 Rapports, Arch76.
65. Operational Research Section, "Technique of Raid Analysis and Forward Planning: Attacks on Specific Towns in France and Belgium," AIR 14/4587, UKNA, 1945; Harris, *Despatch on War Operations, 23 February, 1942 to 8th May, 1945*, 24; Middlebrook and Everitt, *The Bomber Command War Diaries*, 492.
66. Martin Gilbert, *The First World War: A Complete History* (New York: Henry Holt, 1994), 409–12; Doughty, *Pyrrhic Victory*, 477–78.
67. Horne, *To Lose a Battle: France 1940*, 559–60.
68. Middlebrook and Everitt, *The Bomber Command War Diaries*, 53; Natacha Fromentin, "La Gare D'amiens Et Le Réseau Amiénois (1939–1957)" (MA thesis, Université de Picardie Jules Verne, 1999).
69. Carter and Mueller, *Combat Chronology*, 34; Freeman, Crouchman, and Maslen, *Mighty Eighth War Diary*, 12.
70. G2 SHAEF, "Target Damage File: Amiens," RG 243, box 3, NARA.
71. Freeman, Crouchman, and Maslen, *Mighty Eighth War Diary*, 45; "Target Damage File: Amiens," RG 243, box 3, NARA.
72. 391 Bomb Group (391) Headquarters, "Mission Report-Amiens 2 March 1944," IRIS 00088338, AHRA; 387 Bomb Group (387) Headquarters, "Mission Report-Amiens 2 March 1944," IRIS 00087854, AHRA.

73. Middlebrook and Everitt, *The Bomber Command War Diaries*, 480–81.
74. Ibid., 512. J. M. Robb, "Summary of Results of Attacks on Rail Transportation Targets, 25 May 1944," WO 205, UKNA.
75. Florentin, *Quand Les Alliés Bombardaient La France*, 357.
76. "Daily Int/Ops Summary No 113, 27 May 1944, Kingston-McCloughry Papers, IWM; Jean-Pierre Ducellier and Raymonde Gilmann, "Les 60 Ans Des Bombardements D'amiens," Les 60 ans des bombardements d'Amiens, http://fresques.ina.fr/picardie/fiche-media/Picard00422/les-60-ans-des-bombardements-d-amiens.html (accessed December 2014); Florentin, *Quand Les Alliés Bombardaient*, 368.
77. 344 Bomb Group (344) Headquarters, "Mission Report-Amiens 28 May 1944," IRIS 00084102, AHRA.
78. Ibid.
79. Florentin, *Quand Les Alliés Bombardaient la France*, 368.
80. "Daily Int/Ops Summary No 115, 28 May 1944," Kingston-McCloughry Papers, IWM; "Daily Int/Ops Summary No 117, 29 May 1944"; "Daily Int/Ops Summary No 129, 4 June 1944"; IX Bomber Command (IXBC) Headquarters, "Intelligence Report to Combat Crews of Operations: 26 May to 1 June," IRIS 002346, AHRA.
81. "Daily Int/Ops Summary No 117, 29 May 1944."
82. Florentin, *Quand Les Alliés Bombardaient La France*, 368.
83. Fromentin, "La Gare D'Amiens et Le Réseau Amiénois (1939–1957)."
84. Ellis, *Victory in the West*, 469–70.
85. SHAEF, "Tactical Targets: Area 5003e (Lille Area)," in box 26, RG 243, NARA.
86. Robb, "Summary of Results of Attacks on Rail Transportation Targets, 25 May 1944, WO 205, UKNA; Lindsey Dodd, *French Children under the Allied Bombs, 1940–1945, An Oral History* (Manchester: Manchester University Press, 2016), 19.
87. Dodd, *French Children under the Allied Bombs*, 97.
88. Chanoine L. Detrez, *Quand Lille Avait Faim* (Lille: S. I. L. I. C., 1945), 168–70.
89. Florentin, *Quand Les Alliés Bombardaient La France*, 281–82.
90. Ibid., 282.
91. Ibid.
92. Middlebrook and Everitt, *The Bomber Command War Diaries*, 492–93; Knapp, *Les Français Sous Les Bombes Alliées*, 118; Dejonghe and le Maner, *Le Nord-Pas-De-Calais Dans La Main Allemande*, 342; Florentin, *Quand Les Alliés Bombardaient La France*, 283.
93. Chiefs of Staff Committee, "Attacks on Rail Targets in Enemy Occupied Territories, 19 March 1944."
94. "Attacks on Specific Towns in France and Belgium," AIR 14/4587, UKNA, 1945; Robb, "Summary of Results of Attacks on Rail Transportation Targets, 25 May 1944"; 97 Squadron Association, "97 Squadron Operations Record Book

1944," http://www.97squadronassociation.co.uk/history/operations/97-squadron-operations-record-book-jan-june-1944/; Daniel Carville, "France-Crashes 39–45," Frencecrashes39-45.net (accessed January 2016).

95. http://lhistoireenrafale.blogs.lunion.com/2014/05/10/10-mai-1944-loffset-marking-pour-lille/ (accessed February 15, 2015).
96. "Daily Int/Ops Summary No 116, 28/29 May 1944"; Davis, *Bombing the European Powers*, database; Middlebrook and Everitt, *The Bomber Command War Diaries*, 516–17.
97. http://www.jaillard.net/58-angers.php (accessed December 2015).
98. Knapp, *Les Français Sous Les Bombes Alliées*, 120; Florentin, *Quand Les Alliés Bombardaient La France*, 393; Mahoney, *Fifteenth Air Force against the Axis*, 125–26.
99. Roland G. Ruppenthal, *The European Theater of Operations: Logistical Support of the Armies*, vol. 1: *May 1941—September 1944*, USAWWII (Washington, DC: Office of the Chief of Military History, 1953), 550.
100. Ibid., 544–59; Roland G. Ruppenthal, *The European Theater of Operations: Logistical Support of the Armies*, vol. 2: *September 1944—May 1945*, USAWWII (Washington, DC: Office of the Chief of Military History, 1959), 134–35.
101. Jean-Charles Foucrier, "Le Transportaton Plan, Aspects Et Représentations Une Histoire Des Bombardements Aériens Alliés Sur La France En 1944" (MA thesis, Université Paris-Sorbonne, 2015), 409.
102. Baldoli and Knapp, *Forgotten Blitzes*, 30.

Chapter 9. The Bridges

1. Middlebrook and Everitt, *The Bomber Command War Diaries*, 495.
2. http://dandylan.over-blog.com/article-6050567.html (accessed May 2016).
3. Office of the Secretary General Staff, "Summary of Results of Attacks on Rail Transportation Targets, 19 May 1944," box 67, RG 331, NARA; Tobin Jones, *617 Squadron, the Operational Record Book, 1943–1945* (Bicester (UK), Binx Publishing, 2002), 194–95.
4. http://www.aerosteles.net/stelefr-juvisy-bomb (accessed May 2016).
5. "Study No. 6, Delay of Enemy Reserves (First Draft), AHB, 1943.
6. "Study No. 6, Delay of Enemy Reserves (Final), AHB, 1944.
7. Office of the Secretary General Staff, "Effectiveness of Air Attack against Rail Transportation in the Battle of France," 24–26.
8. Air Ministry, Air Historical Branch, "Planning and Preparation," 177–80.
9. Ibid., 179–80; Rostow, *Pre-Invasion Bombing Strategy*, 60–61; Thomas Alexandar Hughes, *Over Lord: General Pete Quesada and the Triumph of Tactical Air Power in World War II* (New York: Free Press, 1995), 129.
10. Craven and Cate, *Argument to V-E Day*, 30–47; "Ninth Air Force Invasion Activities: April–June 1944," 9, Smith Papers 1941–1945, DDEPL, 1944; Hughes, *Over Lord*, 128–31.

11. R.-G. Nobécourt, *Rouen Désollé* (Paris: Éditions Médicis, 1948), 82–85.
12. Le Trevier and Rose, *Ce Qui S'est Vraiment Passé Le 19 Avril 1944*, 8–19; Hardy, "La Défense Passive À Rouen," 10.
13. 81st Fighter Squadron (81) Headquarters, "Historical Data: Eighty-First Fighter Squadron, Fiftieth Fighter Group (Se) May 1944," IRIS 57457, AFHRC; Fighter Group (50) Headquarters, "Historical Data: AAF Headquarters Group Fighter, Fiftieth Fighter Group (Se)M 1 May to 1 June 1944," IRIS 80123, AFHRC; Legion de Normandie Gendarmerie Nationale, Compaignie de la Seine-Inférieure, Section de Rouen, "Registres De Correspondance Confidentielle Au Départ (R/4), 20 Septembre 1940 Au 21 Décembre 1946," SHD; Pailhès, *Rouen Et Sa Région Pendant La Guerre*, 207; "Daily Int/Ops Summary No 109, 25 May 1944," Kingston-McCloughry Papers, IWM; Stan D. Bishop and John A. Hey, *Losses of the US 8th & 9th Air Forces: Aircraft and Men, 1st April 1944–30th June 1944* ([London]: Bishop Book Productions, 2009), 529.
14. "Daily Int/Ops Summary No 113, 27 May 1944"; Ninth Air Force (9AF) Headquarters, "Operations Report Form 34, 1–31 May 1944," IRIS 236149, AFHRC.
15. Pailhès, *Rouen Et Sa Région*, 208; Dandel et al., *Les Victimes Civiles Des Bombardements En Haute-Normandie*, 61; Legion de Normandie Gendarmerie Nationale, Compaignie de la Seine-Inferieure, Section de Rouen, "Registres De Correspondance Courante Au Départ (R/2), 24 Janvier Au 28 Août 1944," SHD, 271. Florentin, *Quand Les Alliés Bombardaient La France*, 321; Nobécourt, *Rouen Désollé*, 229.
16. "Daily Int/Ops Summary No 113, 27 May 1944"; (9AF) Headquarters, "Operations Report Form 34, 1–31 May 1944"; "Daily Int/Ops Summary No 114, 27/28 May 1944"; "Registres De Correspondance Courante Au Départ (R/2), 24 Janvier Au 28 Août 1944," SHD, 271; Florentin, *Quand Les Alliés Bombardaient La France*, 321.
17. Pailhès, *Rouen Et Sa Région*, 208; (9AF) Headquarters, "Operations Report Form 34, 1–31 May 1944"; "Daily Int/Ops Summary No 115, 28 May 1944."
18. Headquarters IX Fighter Command (IX FC), "Unit History IX Fighter Command and IX Tactical Air Command Covering Period 1 May 1944 to 31 May 1944," IRIS 0237286, AFHRC.
19. 344 Bomb Group (344) Headquarters, "Mission Report-Rouen 30 May 1944," B0290, AFHRC; "Daily Int/Ops Summary No 119, 30 May 1944"; (9AF) Headquarters, "Operations Report Form 34, 1–31 May 1944"; IX Bomber Command Headquarters, "Mission Summary 30 May 1944, Ninth Air Force, AFHRC.
20. 322 Bomb Group (322) Headquarters, "Mission Report-Rouen 30 May 1944" IRIS 82815, AFHRC; "Daily Int/Ops Summary No 119, 30 May 1944"; (9AF) Headquarters, "Operations Report Form 34, 1–31 May 1944"; IX Bomber Command Headquarters, "Mission Summary 30 May 1944."

21. 394 Bomb Group (394) Headquarters, "Mission Report-Rouen 30 May 1944," B0449, AFHRC.
22. Ibid.; "Daily Int/Ops Summary No 119, 30 May 1944"; (9AF) Headquarters, "Operations Report Form 34, 1–31 May 1944"; IX Bomber Command (IXBC) Headquarters, "Mission Summary 30 May 1944."
23. "Daily Int/Ops Summary No 119, 30 May 1944."
24. Dandel et al., *Les Victimes Civiles Des Bombardements En Haute-Normandie*; Hardy, "La Défense Passive À Rouen," 119; Pailhès, *Rouen Et Sa Région*, 209.
25. Pailhès, *Rouen Et Sa Région*, 209–10.
26. Ibid., 211.
27. Florentin, *Quand Les Alliés Bombardaient La France*, 330.
28. 394 Bomb Group (394) Headquarters, "Mission Report-Rouen 31 May 1944," B0449, AFHRC; "Daily Int/Ops Summary No 121, 31 May 1944"; IX Bomber Command (IXBC) Headquarters, "Mission Summary 31 May 1944," IRIS 236146, AFHRC.
29. 397 Bomb Group (397) Headquarters, "Mission Report-Rouen 31 May 1944," B0459, AFHRC; Pessiot, *Histoire De Rouen 1939–1958*, 305; (IXBC) Headquarters, "Mission Summary 31 May 1944."
30. 386 Bomb Group (386) Headquarters, "Mission Report-Rouen 31 May 1944," B0393, AFHRC)"; (IXBC) Headquarters, "Mission Summary 31 May 1944."
31. 322 Bomb Group (322) Headquarters, "Mission Report-Rouen 31 May 1944," IRIS 82816, AFHRC; (IXBC) Headquarters, "Mission Summary 31 May 1944."
32. "Daily Int/Ops Summary No 119, 30 May 1944"; M.F.A. & A Specialist Officer, "Report on Monuments of Rouen," in Papers of Ronald Edmona Balfour, KC; Pailhès, *Rouen Et Sa Région*, 211–13.
33. Hardy, "La Défense Passive À Rouen," 118–22.
34. SHAEF, "Incoming Cable Logs 1944," Smith Papers 1941–1945, DDEPL, entry for June 1, 1944.
35. "Daily Int/Ops Summary No 123, 1 June 1944."
36. Florentin, *Quand Les Alliés Bombardaient La France*, 331; Pessiot, *Histoire De Rouen 1939–1958*, 214–15; M.F.A. & A Specialist Officer, "Report on Monuments of Rouen."
37. Pailhès, *Rouen Et Sa Région*, 214–15; Florentin, *Quand Les Alliés Bombardaient La France*, 331; Pessiot, *Histoire De Rouen 1939–1958*, 315; M.F.A. & A Specialist Officer, "Report on Monuments of Rouen."
38. Gustave Flaubert, *Madame Bovary* (Paris: Michel Lévy frès, 1856; repr., 1994, Hertfordshire, Wordsworth Editions Limited), 171–72.
39. Florentin, *Quand Les Alliés Bombardaient La France*, 331; Pessiot, *Histoire De Rouen 1939–1958*, 315; "Daily Int/Ops Summary No 127, 3 June 1944," Kingston-McCloughry Papers, IWM; Pailhès, *Rouen Et Sa Région*, 214–16.
40. "Daily Int/Ops Summary No 125, 2 June 1944," Kingston-McCloughry Papers, IWM; Craven and Cate, *Argument to V-E Day*, 159; "Ninth Air Force Invasion Activities," 9–10.

41. “Daily Int/Ops Summary No 125, 2 June 1944,” Kingston-McCloughry Papers, IWM.
42. “Daily Int/Ops Summary No 125, 3 June 1944,” Kingston-McCloughry Papers, IWM.
43. Allied records (to date) list no attacks on Rouen on Sunday, but the French on the ground are confident they took place.
44. Pessiot, *Histoire De Rouen 1939–1958*, 315; “Daily Int/Ops Summary No 113, 27 May 1944”; Florentin, *Quand Les Alliés Bombardaient La France*, 332.
45. Harrison, *Cross-Channel Attack*, 272–73; “Eighth Air Force Tactical Operations in Support of Allied Landings in Normandy, 2 June–17 June 1944,” Field Order 719, Deputy Chief of Staff, Operations. “Eighth Air Force Tactical Operations in Support of Allied Landings in Normandy, 2 June–17 June 1944,” AFHRC.
46. “Daily Int/Ops Summary No 129, 4 June 1944,” Kingston-McCloughry Papers, IWM.
47. “Daily Int/Ops Summary No 130, 5 June 1944,” Kingston-McCloughry Papers, IWM.
48. Henri Amouroux, *La Grande Histoire Des Français Sous L’occupation, Un Printemps De Mort Et D’espoir Joies Et Douleurs Du Peuple Libéré, September 1943–6 Août 1944* (Paris: Éditions Robert Laffont, 1999), 321; M.F.A. & A Specialist Officer, “Report on Monuments of Rouen.”
49. Ninth Air Force (9AF) Headquarters, “Fighter-Bomber Attacks on the Seine River Bridges (Report No. 90),” IRIS 232843, AFHRC; “An Analysis of Weapon Effectiveness of Seine River Bridge Operations (Report No. 77),” IRIS: 232841, AFHRC.
50. Gaston Marin, “Les Bombardements De L’agglomération Mantaise Pendant La Duxième Guerre Mondiale,” *Le Mantois 13: Bulletin de la Société “Les Amis du Mantois”* no. 13 (1962).
51. Middlebrook and Everitt, *The Bomber Command War Diaries*; J. M. Robb, “Summary of Results of Attacks on Rail Transportation Targets, 25 May 1944,” in WO 205, UKNA. Marin, “Les Bombardements De L’agglomération Mantais,” 39–40.
52. Middlebrook and Everitt, *The Bomber Command War Diaries*; “Summary of Results of Attacks on Rail Transportation Targets, 25 May 1944”; Marin, “Les Bombardements De L’agglomération Mantais,” 39–40; Florentin, *Quand Les Alliés Bombardaient La France*, 341.
53. Marin, “Les Bombardements De L’agglomération Mantais,” 25, 40.
54. “Daily Int/Ops Summary No 115, 28 May 1944,” Kingston-McCloughry Papers, IWM; Marin, “Les Bombardements De L’agglomération Mantais,” 40.
55. “Daily Int/Ops Summary No 117, 29 May 1944,” Kingston-McCloughry Papers, IWM; “An Analysis of Weapon Effectiveness of Seine River Bridge Operations (Report No. 77), IRIS: 232841, AFHRC.”
56. “Daily Int/Ops Summary No 119, 30 May 1944, Kingston-McCloughry Papers, IWM.”

57. "An Analysis of Weapon Effectiveness of Seine River Bridge Operations (Report No. 77), IRIS: 232841, AFHRC."
58. Ibid.
59. Marin, "Les Bombardements De L'agglomération Mantais," 26–31–40; Florentin, *Quand Les Alliés Bombardaient La France*, 328–29.
60. Marin, "Les Bombardements De L'agglomération Mantais," 26–31–40; Florentin, *Quand Les Alliés Bombardaient La France*, 328–29.
61. Marin, "Les Bombardements De L'agglomération Mantais," 41.
62. Blumenson, *Breakout and Pursuit*, 577–78.
63. Marin, "Les Bombardements De L'agglomération Mantais," 42.
64. Air Ministry, Air Historical Branch, "Planning and Preparation," 180–81.
65. Davis, *Carl A. Spaatz*, 406; E-J Kingston-McCloughry, "The Transportation Plan," in *Papers of Air Vice-Marshal E-J Kingston-McCloughry*, ed. Allied Expeditionary Air Force (AEAF) (IWM, 1946), 14–16.
66. Gildea, *Marianne in Chains*, 291–98.
67. Leleu et al., eds., *La France Pendant La Seconde Guerre Mondiale*, 227–31; Gildea, *Marianne in Chains*, 297–98.
68. Middlebrook and Everitt, *The Bomber Command War Diaries*; Freeman, Crouchman, and Maslen, *Mighty Eighth War Diary*, chronology.
69. Gildea, *Marianne in Chains*, 298.
70. Secretary Office of the Chief of Staff, General Staff, "Military Objectives for Aerial Bombardment Vol 2," box 66, RG 331, NARA.
71. Middlebrook and Everitt, *The Bomber Command War Diaries*, 512; J. M. Robb, "Summary of Results of Attacks on Rail Transportation Targets, 25 May 1944," in RG 331, NARA; http://mesancetres-40generations.over-blog.com/2015/02/fatalite-ou-destin-les-bombardements-allies-sur-tours-en-1944. (accessed May 2016).
72. Deputy Chief of Staff, "Eighth Air Force, Normandy," FO 735.
73. http://www.clauderioland.com/histoire/bombardements_1944_tours.htm (accessed May 2016). Deputy Chief of Staff, "Eighth Air Force, Normandy," FO 737.
74. Freeman, Crouchman, and Maslen, *Mighty Eighth War Diary*, 308.
75. Craven and Cate, *Argument to V-E Day*, 158–62, 215.
76. Headquarters, "Ninth Air Force Invasion Activities," 9–10.
77. Hughes, *Over Lord*, 130–31.
78. "Weekly Intelligence Summary #12: For Week Ending 10 June 1944."
79. "Effectiveness of Air Attack against Rail," 41; Intelligence Assistant Chief of Air Staff, "Tab B Overlord—the Interdiction Campaign," AFHRC.

Chapter 10. The Landings

1. Roberts, *D-Day through French Eyes*, 21.
2. Ibid., 11–12.

3. All times are Central European Time (CET), which is what French and German authorities used to record the events. The Americans and British used Greenwich Mean Time (GMT), which was one hour earlier and was so recorded in their orders and reports.
4. Boivin and Garnier, *Les Victimes Civiles De La Manche*, 45–46, 301.
5. These and other famous stories are popularized in books and subsequent movies. Ryan, *The Longest Day*; Ambrose, *Band of Brothers*, 78–84.
6. Ambrose, *D-Day*, 239–53.
7. Atkinson, *The Guns at Last Light*, 53–56.
8. Beevor, *D-Day*, 91.
9. Copp, *Fields of Fire*, 43.
10. D'Este, *Decision in Normandy*, 112–13.
11. Webster and Frankland, *Victory*; Richards, *The Hardest Victory.*
12. Craven and Cate, *Argument to V-E Day*, 190–94.
13. Morgan, "COSSAC Directive (43) 28, 14 July 1943," Historical Reference Collection, CMH; Historical Sub-Section, "History of COSSAC," 121–22; Pogue, *The Supreme Command.*
14. David C. Isby, ed., *Fighting the Invasion: The German Army at D-Day*, Kindle ed. (New York: Skyhorse Publishing, 2000), loc. 2762.
15. Harrison, *Cross-Channel Attack*, map XII.
16. Ibid., maps X, XII.
17. Isby, *Fighting the Invasion*, loc. 2080.
18. McManus, *The Dead and Those About to Die*, 59.
19. "Neptune: Joint Fire Plan," box 66, RG 331, NARA.
20. Air Ministry, Air Historical Branch, "The Landings in Normandy," app. I.
21. Yung, *Gators of Neptune*, 76–82; Barnett, *Engage the Enemy More Closely*, 753–809.
22. Air Ministry, Air Historical Branch, "The Landings in Normandy," 439–42; Trafford Leigh-Mallory, "Operation Neptune, Allied Expeditionary Air Force Overall Air Plan," Smith Papers 1941–1945, DDEPL.
23. Craven and Cate, *Argument to V-E Day*, 190.
24. Allied Expeditionary Air Force (AEAF), "Minutes of Second Allied Air Commander's Conference Held at 1100 Hours, 26 May 1944," in Air 37/563: Minutes of Allied Air Commanders Conferences, UKNA, 1944.
25. Ibid.
26. Deputy Chief of Staff, Operations, Field Order 727, in "Eighth Air Force Tactical Operations in Support of Allied Landings in Normandy, 2 June–17 June 1944," 5.
27. Deputy Chief of Staff, Operations, "Survey of Effectiveness of Bombing of Invasion Coast Defenses, 7 July 1944," in "Eighth Air Force Tactical Operations in Support of Allied Landings in Normandy, 2 June–17 June 1944," AFHRC, 2.
28. Craven and Cate, *Argument to V-E Day*, 190.

29. Air Staff Intelligence Headquarters Bomber Command, "Interceptions/Tactics No. 129/44, Night 5th/6th June 1944," box 18, RG 243, NARA.
30. Air Ministry, Air Historical Branch, "The Landings in Normandy," 64.
31. Tonie Holt and Valmai Holt, *Major & Mrs Holt's Battlefield Guide to the Normandy Landing Beaches* (Barnsley, South Yorkshire: Leo Cooper, 2000), 97; Air Historical Branch, Air Ministry, "The Landings in Normandy," 121, app. 2B. https://www.landmarkscout.com/lost-and-found-the-missing-maisy-battery-near-grandcamp-maisy-in-normandy-france/ (accessed January 2017).
32. Roberts, *D-Day through French Eyes*, 71–72.
33. Boivin and Garnier, *Les Victimes Civiles De La Manche*, 29, 212, 14, 406.
34. The attack did little other than alert German defenders that something might be happening on this portion of the French coast. Quellien and Garnier, *Les Victimes Civiles Du Calvados*, 29, 453; Air Historical Branch, Air Ministry, "The Landings in Normandy," 119–22.
35. Air Historical Branch, Air Ministry, "The Landings in Normandy," 41–42.
36. Deputy Chief of Staff, Operations, "Eighth Air Force Tactical Operations in Support of Allied Landings in Normandy, 2 June–17 June 1944"; Air Historical Branch, Air Ministry, "The Landings in Normandy," 206.
37. "Eighth Air Force, Normandy," FO 727.
38. Atkinson, *The Guns at Last Light*, 56; Richard Hargreaves, *The Germans in Normandy* (Barnsley, South Yorkshire: Pen & Sword, 2006), 44.
39. Quellien and Garnier, *Les Victimes Civiles Du Calvados*, 224.
40. "Eighth Air Force, Normandy," FO 727.
41. Quellien and Garnier, *Les Victimes Civiles Du Calvados*, 299.
42. "Eighth Air Force, Normandy," FO 727; Marc Milner, *Stopping the Panzers: The Untold Story of D-Day* (Lawrence: University Press of Kansas, 2014), 65.
43. "Eighth Air Force, Normandy," FO 727.
44. Hargreaves, *The Germans in Normandy*, 47–48; Paul Carell, *Invasion! They're Coming! The German Account of the D-Day Landings and the 80 Days Battle for France*, trans. David Johnston (Atglen, PA: Schiffer Military History, 1995), 58–62.
45. Ambrose, *D-Day*, 242–48; Atkinson, *The Guns at Last Light*, 55.
46. IX Bomber Command Headquarters, "Mission Summary, Field Order 348-S, 6 June 1944," box 42, RG 243, NARA.
47. Barnett, *Engage the Enemy More Closely*, 814–26; Yung, *Gators of Neptune*, 177–89.
48. Quellien and Garnier, *Les Victimes Civiles Du Calvados*, 30; "Eighth Air Force, Normandy," FO 727.
49. Quellien and Garnier, *Les Victimes Civiles Du Calvados*, 34–35; Roberts, *D-Day through French Eyes*, 69–74; Amouroux, *Des Français Des Français Sous L'occupation*, 447.
50. Montgomery, *The Memoirs*, 254
51. "Operation 'Overlord'—Preparatory Air Operations," in WO 205, UKNA.

52. "Eighth Air Force, Normandy," 10, FO 727, target maps.
53. "Eighth Air Force, Normandy," FO 727.
54. "Eighth Air Force, Normandy," FO 727-1, FO 737-2.
55. Christopher Beaudufe, *Le Sacrifice Des Normands: L'été 1944* (Paris: Perrin, 2004), 58–59.
56. Capt. Ray L. Sears, "Flight Plan/Record, 453 Bombardment Group, 6 June 1944," IRIS 00093671, AFHRA; "Eighth Air Force, Normandy," 729; Andrew S. Low and Lloyd W. Prang, eds., *The Liberator Men of Old Buc: The Story of the 453rd Bombardment Group in World War II, 29 June 1943–15 September 1945*, rev. ed. (Tuleta, TX: 453rd Bomb Group Association, 1999).
57. Sears, "Flight Plan/Record, 453 Bombardment Group, 6 June 1944," AFHRA. Log is in GMT.
58. Ibid.; "Eighth Air Force, Normandy," 729; Low and Prang, *Liberator Men of Old Buc.*
59. M. Bernard Goupil, "Caen Et Ses Ruines," MC.
60. André Gosset and Paule Lecomte, *Caen Pendant La Bataille* (Paris: Carrefour des Lettres, 1974), 20–21; Quellien and Garnier, *Les Victimes Civiles Du Calvados*, 38–43.
61. Gosset and Lecomte, *Caen Pendant La Bataille*, 20–21; Quellien and Garnier, *Les Victimes Civiles Du Calvados Dans La Bataille*, 38–43.
62. Hubert Meyer and Harri H. Henschler, *The History of the 12. SS-Panzerdivision "Hitlerjugend"* (Winnipeg: J. J. Fedorowicz, 1994), 29, 31.
63. See Adrian R. Lewis, *Omaha Beach: A Flawed Victory* (Chapel Hill: University of North Carolina Press, 2001).
64. Quellien and Garnier, *Les Victimes Civiles Du Calvados*, 429–88; Boivin and Garnier, *Les Victimes Civiles De La Manche*, 271–310.
65. "Neptune: Joint Fire Plan."
66. Air Ministry, Air Historical Branch, "The Landings in Normandy," 206–7.
67. Craven and Cate, *Argument to V-E Day*, 190.
68. "Supreme Commander Allied Expeditionary Force 20th Meeting, 29 May 1944," WO 205, UKNA; SHAEF—Supreme Commander, "Minutes of Supreme Commander's Conference No. 21, 1000 Hours, 2 June 1944," in WO 205: Headquarters Papers, 21st Army Group, ed. Office of the Secretary General Staff, UKNA, 1944.
69. Omar N. Bradley, *A Soldier's Story* (New York: Holt, Rinehart and Winston, 1951), 268.
70. Headquarters, Eighth Air Force, "The Role of H2X on D-Day," Hoover Institution Archives and Library (HIAL), Frederick L. Anderson Papers, 1944.
71. Deputy Chief of Staff, Operations, "Survey of Effectiveness of Bombing of Invasion Coast Defenses," 2.
72. Air Ministry, Air Historical Branch, "The Landings in Normandy," 120–22.

73. Craven and Cate, *Argument to V-E Day*, 193.
74. McManus, *The Dead and Those About to Die*, 74, 292.
75. "Eighth Air Force, Normandy," FO 727.
76. Bradley, *A Soldier's Story*, 268.

Chapter 11. The Towns

1. Louis Adam, "Avranches Bombing June 7," Témoignages écrits, MC.
2. "Daily Int/Ops Summary No 135, 8 June 1944," Kingston-McCloughry Papers, IWM.
3. Adam, "Avranches," MC.
4. "Daily Int/Ops Summary No 135, 8 June 1944."
5. Adam, "Avranches," MC.
6. Boivin and Garnier, *Les Victimes Civiles De La Manche*, 100.
7. "Study No. 6, Delay of Enemy Reserves (Final)," AHB, 1944.
8. Dwight D. Eisenhower, "Supreme Commander's Conference, Meeting, No. 1, 21 January 1944," AIR 37/559, UKNA.
9. Air Ministry, Air Historical Branch, "Planning and Preparation," 181.
10. Deputy Chief of Staff, Operations, "Eighth Air Force Tactical Operations in Support of Allied Landings in Normandy, 2 June–17 June 1944," 10.
11. Air Ministry, Air Historical Branch, "Planning and Preparation," 182.
12. Henry Probert, *Bomber Harris: His Life and Times* (London, Greenhill Books, 2001), 293.
13. Charles P. Cabel, "Notes Taken by General Cabell at Air Commander's Meeting at Stanmore, 3 June," Papers of Carl Spaatz; Air Ministry, Air Historical Branch, "Planning and Preparation," 184.
14. Trafford Leigh-Mallory, "Minutes of Allied Air Commanders Conferences, June 3, 1944," AIR 37/563, UKNA; "Operation 'Overlord'—Preparatory Air Operations," WO 205, UKNA; Air Ministry, Air Historical Branch, "The Landings in Normandy," 216.
15. Alary, Vergez-Chaignon, and Gauvin, *Les Français Au Quotidien*, 522.
16. "Operation 'Overlord'—Preparatory Air Operations" UKNA.
17. Dodd and Knapp, "How Many Frenchmen Did You Kill?," 484–85.
18. Beaudufe, *Le Sacrifice Des Normands*, 79–81.
19. IX Bomber Command Headquarters, "Mission Summary, Field Order 349, 350, 351, 6 June 1944," in RG 243 United States Strategic Bombing Survey, NARA.
20. Quellien and Garnier, *Les Victimes Civiles Du Calvados*, 42, 279.
21. Gosset and Lecomte, *Caen Pendant La Bataille*, 22.
22. Boivin, Bourdin, and Quellien, *Villes Normandes Sous Les Bombes*, 92.
23. "Eighth Air Force," Field Order 730, "Eighth Air Force Tactical Operations in Support of Allied Landings in Normandy, 2 June–17 June 1944," AFHRC.

24. Harrison, *Cross-Channel Attack*, map XIV; Carell, *Invasion!*, 108–9; Air Ministry, Air Historical Branch, "The Landings in Normandy," 217.
25. Quellien and Garnier, *Les Victimes Civiles Du Calvados*, 61–66; Middlebrook and Everitt, *The Bomber Command War Diaries*, 523.
26. M. Bernard, Goupil, "Caen et Ses Ruines," Témoignages écrits, MC, 1944; Boivin, Bourdin, and Quellien, *Villes Normandes Sous Les Bombes*, 87–102.
27. Quellien and Garnier, *Les Victimes Civiles Du Calvados*, 62.
28. Allied Expeditionary Air Force (AEAF), "Daily Int/Ops Summary No 133, 7 June 1944," in Papers of Air Vice-Marshal E-J Kingston-McCloughry, London Imperial War Museum.
29. "Daily Int/Ops Summary No 134, 7 June 1944," in Papers of Air Vice-Marshal E-J Kingston-McCloughry, London, Imperial War Museum.
30. Middlebrook and Everitt, *The Bomber Command War Diaries*, 539.
31. Ellis, *Victory in the West*, 311–15; Copp, *Fields of Fire*, 104–6; Terry Copp, ed., *Montgomery's Scientists: Operational Research in Northwest Europe* (Waterloo, Ontario: Wilfrid Laurier University, 2000), 75.
32. Ellis, *Victory in the West*, 327–52. Copp, *Fields of Fire*, 135–46.
33. Quellien and Garnier, *Les Victimes Civiles Du Calvados*, 84.
34. Ibid.
35. Author's visits.
36. "Operation 'Overlord'—Preparatory Air Operations," WO 205, UKNA.
37. Boivin and Garnier, *Les Victimes Civiles De La Manche*, 100.
38. "Eighth Air Force, Normandy," FO 127 and map, "Eighth Air Force Tactical Operations in Support of Allied Landings in Normandy, 2 June–17 June 1944," AFHRC.
39. Jérémie Halais, *Saint-Lô Et Son Canton Dans La Tourmente De La Second Guerre Mondiale (1939–1945)* (St Lô: Société d'Archéologie et d'Histoire de la Manche, 2007), 95; "Eighth Air Force, Normandy," FO 727; Michelle Chapron, "Mémoires De L'été 1944," Témoignages écrits, MC, 1944.
40. Boivin and Garnier, *Les Victimes Civiles De La Manche*, 29.
41. Jean Roger, "Témoignages," Témoignages écrits, MC.
42. James A. Huston, *Across the Face of France: Liberation and Recovery, 1944–63* (West Lafayette, IN: Purdue University Press, 1963), 61.
43. Halais, *Saint-Lô Et Son Canton*, 96; Madame Legrand, "Souvenirs De Madame Legrand, Née Arthur," in Série 2J, Arch50; Boivin and Garnier, *Les Victimes Civiles De La Manche*, 29–30.
44. "Eighth Air Force, Normandy," Field Order 730; Harrison, *Cross-Channel Attack*, 321–35; Air Ministry, Air Historical Branch, "The Landings in Normandy," 217. 2nd Bombardment Division (2Div) Headquarters, Eighth Air Force, "Mission Logs 6–8 June," AFHRC.
45. Roger, "Témoignages," MC.

46. Boivin and Garnier, *Les Victimes Civiles De La Manche*, 230.
47. Quellien and Garnier, *Les Victimes Civiles Du Calvados*, 54.
48. Boivin and Garnier, *Les Victimes Civiles De La Manche*, 29.
49. Huston, *Across the Face of France*, 56.
50. US Strategic Bombing Survey, "Target Folder: Saint Lô," in RG 243 United States Strategic Bombing Survey, NARA.
51. Guillaume Mourier, *Les Sinistrés Saint-Lois Au 6 Juin 1944* (St. Lo: Société d'Archéologie et d'Histoire de la Manche, 2004), memoire, 23–24. Boivin and Garnier, *Les Victimes Civiles De La Manche*, 33.
52. Boivin and Garnier, *Les Victimes Civiles De La Manche*, 4, 30; Robert H. George, "Ninth Air Force, April to November 1944," Army Air Forces Historical Studies: No. 36 (Maxwell Air Force Base, AL: Air University, 1945), 84; Blumenson, *Breakout and Pursuit*, 146–74.
53. Blumenson, *Breakout and Pursuit*, 146.
54. Ibid., 234–72.
55. Boivin and Garnier, *Les Victimes Civiles De La Manche*, 29.
56. Boivin and Garnier, *Les Victimes Civiles De La Manche*, lists.
57. Catholic Online, "Saint Therese of Lisieux," www.catholic.org (accessed July 25, 2009); U.S. Centennial of Flight Commission, "Paul Cornu," www.centennialofflight.gov/essay/Dictionary/Cornu/D18.htm (accessed July 20, 2009); Institut National de la Statistique et des Études Économiques, *Résultats Statistiques Du Recensement Général De La Population, Effectueé Le 10 Mars 1946; Départment Du Calvados* (Paris: Presses Universitaires de France, 1951); Gwen Cannon, ed., *The Green Guide: Normandy* (Clermont-Ferrand, France: Michelin, 2006). Note: The population in 1936 was 15,150 in the city itself.
58. Meyer and Henschler, *The History of the 12. SS-Panzerdivision*, 17–19; "Weekly Intelligence Summary #1: For Week Ending 26 March 1944"; "Operation 'Overlord'—Preparatory Air Operations," WO 205, UKNA.
59. Joint Planning AEAF Committee, "Joint Planning Committee Meeting, Minutes, May 29, 1944," AIR 37/505, UKNA.
60. Mme. Dandais, "Souvenirs D'une Lexovienne (Lisieux)," Témoignages écrits, MC.
61. Meyer and Henschler, *The History of the 12. Ss-Panzerdivision*, 29, 36.
62. Gérard Hancoque, "Les Bombardements-Lisieux, Témoignages Écrits," Témoignages écrits, MC.
63. D'Este, *Decision in Normandy*, 140–41.
64. Quellien and Garnier, *Les Victimes Civiles Du Calvados*, 47.
65. Hancoque, "Les Bombardements-Lisieux, Témoignages Écrits," MC. Also reproduced in Boivin, Bourdin, and Quellien, *Villes Normandes Sous Les Bombes*.
66. Quellien and Garnier, *Les Victimes Civiles Du Calvados*, 47.
67. Ibid., 67; Andrée Petit, "Le Bombardment of Lisieux," Témoignages écrits, MC.

68. Petit, "Le Bombardment of Lisieux," MC; Quellien and Garnier, *Les Victimes Civiles Du Calvados*, 54.
69. "Eighth Air Force, Normandy," FO 727.
70. Ibid.
71. Ibid., FO 733.
72. United States Strategic Bombing Survey, "Interpretation Report No. Sa 1968 Towns Nw France," in RG 243 United States Strategic Bombing Survey, NARA.
73. Quellien and Garnier, *Les Victimes Civiles Du Calvados*, 54; Florentin, *Quand Les Alliés Bombardaient La France*, 415.
74. Copp, *Montgomery's Scientists*, 46.
75. Copp, *Cinderella Army*; Quellien and Garnier, *Les Victimes Civiles Du Calvados*, 54.
76. Boivin, Bourdin, and Quellien, *Villes Normandes Sous Les Bombes.*
77. http://www.ddaymuseum.co.uk/d-day/d-day-and-the-battle-of-normandy-your-questions-answered#casualities (accessed October 2016).
78. Office of Assistant Chief of Air Staff, Intelligence. *Sunday Punch in Normandy: The Tactical Use of Heavy Bombardment in the Normandy Invasion. An Interim Report* (Washington, DC: Center for Air Force History, 1945), 24.
79. Craven and Cate, *Argument to V-E Day*, 193.
80. Harris, *Despatch on War Operations.*
81. Ambrose, *D-Day*, 248.
82. D'Este, *Decision in Normandy*, 107–73; Hastings, *Bomber Command*, 69–151
83. Beevor, *D-Day*, 144–47; Atkinson, *The Guns at Last Light*, 85.
84. "Survey of Effectiveness of Bombing of Invasion Coast Defenses," "Eighth Air Force Tactical Operations in Support of Allied Landings in Normandy, 2 June–17 June 1944," AFHRC, 2.
85. Operational Research Section, "Bomb Damage Survey of Road Interdiction in French Towns," RG 18, NARA.
86. Testimony by Generalmajor Fritz Krämer, Fighting the Invasion: The German Army at D-Day, LC 4606.
87. P. A. Spayd and Gary Wilkins, eds. *Bayerlein: After Action Reports of the Panzer Lehr Division Commander, From D-Day to the Ruhr* (Atglen, PA: Schiffer Military History, 2005), 22; Carell, *Invasion!*, 112–15.
88. Complete United States Infantry Guide for Officers and Noncommissioned Officers: Reprinted from Government Publications (Philadelphia: J. B. Lippincott, 1917), 1753. This guide cites as an authority the *Annex to Hague Convention No. IV, 18 October 1907, embodying the Regulations Respecting the Laws and Customs of War on Land.*
89. Cited in Tami Davis Biddle, "Air Power," in *The Laws of War: Constraints on Warfare in the Western World*, ed. Michael Howard, George J. Andreopoulos, and Mark R. Shulman (New Haven, CT: Yale University Press, 1994), 148.

Conclusion and Observations

1. VII-Corps, Headquarters, "History of the VII Corps for the Period 1–31 July, 1944," World War II Operational Documents, CARL, Appendix A-5.
2. Ibid., Appendix A-1.
3. General narrative gleaned from Vincent J. Esposito, ed., *The West Point Atlas of American Wars*, vol. 2: *1900–1953* (New York: Praeger, 1959), 52–67.
4. Middlebrook and Everitt, *The Bomber Command War Diaries*, 524–29.
5. Freeman, Crouchman, and Maslen, *Mighty Eighth War Diary*, 261–71.
6. Andrew Knapp, note to author, November 2016.
7. Middlebrook and Everitt, *The Bomber Command War Diaries*, 591, 646.
8. Freeman, Crouchman, and Maslen, *Mighty Eighth War Diary*, 379.
9. Milner, *Stopping the Panzers*, 308.
10. Jochim Ludewig, *Rückzug: The German Retreat from France, 1944*, trans. David T. Zabecki (Lexington: University of Kentucky Press, 2012), 23, 33.
11. Milner, *Stopping the Panzers*, title. Milner's recent book is a necessary correction to the standard historical narrative and emphasizes Eisenhower and Montgomery's concern with the German counterattack threat.
12. "AWPD/1 Munitions Requirements," AFHRC, 1941.
13. United States War Department, *Field Manual 1-5, Air Corps Field Manual: Employment of Aviation of the Army* (Washington, DC: Government Printing Office, 1940).
14. Robert S. Ehlers Jr. *Targeting the Third Reich: Air Intelligence and the Allied Bombing Campaigns* (Lawrence: University Press of Kansas, 2009), 182–203.
15. Cited in Crane, *American Airpower Strategy in World War II*, 107–8.
16. Bourdin and Garnier, *Les Victimes Civiles De L'orne Dans La Bataille*, 5–7; Quellien and Garnier, *Les Victimes Civiles Du Calvados*, 5–20; Boivin and Garnier, *Les Victimes Civiles De La Manche*, 5–9.
17. Danièle Voldman, *La Reconstruction Des Villes Françaises de 1940 à 1954: Histoire d'une politique* (Paris: L'Harmattan, 1997), 17–40; Overy, *The Bombers and the Bombed*, 400; Leleu et al., *La France Pendant La Seconde Guerre Mondiale*, 245.

BIBLIOGRAPHY

Archives and Libraries

FRENCH ARCHIVES

Archives départementales du Pas-de-Calais (Arras) (Arch62)
Archives départementales de la Seine-Maritime (Rouen) (Arch76)
Archives départementales de la Manche (Saint-Lô) (Arch50)
Archives départmentals du Nord (Lille) (Arch59)
Archives départmentals et du Patrimoine (Rennes) (Arch35)
Archives municipales, Boulogne-sur-Mer (Boulogne-sur-Mer)
Mémorial de Caen (Caen) (MC)
  Collections témoignages écrits
Service Historique de la Défense (Vincennes) (SHD)
  Archives de Gendarmerie
Archives nationales (Paris) (AN)

UNITED STATES ARCHIVES

Air Force Historical Research Center (Maxwell Air Force Base, AL) (AFHRC)
Army History Education Center (Carlisle, PA) (AHEC)
  William J. Donovan Papers
Dwight David Eisenhower Presidential Library (DDEPL)
  Walter Bedell Smith Papers
  C. D. Jackson Papers
  Edward P. Lilly Papers
  Dwight D. Eisenhower: Papers Pre-Presidential
  Papers: Supreme Headquarters, Allied Expeditionary Force
Hoover Institution Archives and Library (Stanford, CA) (HIAL)
  Frederick L. Anderson Papers
Ike Skelton Combined Arms Research Library (Fort Leavenworth, KS) (CARL)
  CARL Digital Library
  World War II Operational Documents
  Obsolete Field Manuals
Library of Congress (Washington, DC) (LC)
  Papers of Carl Spaatz
  Papers of Hoyt S. Vandenberg

National Archives (US) (College Park, MD) (NARA)
Record Group 243 The United States Strategic Bombing Survey (USSBS)
US Army Center of Military History (Fort McNair, DC) (CMH)
Historical Reference Collection

UNITED KINGDOM
History Division, UK Ministry of Defense (London, UK) (MOD)
Imperial War Museum (London, UK) (IWM)
Papers of Air Vice-Marshal E-J Kingston-McCloughry
Papers of Field Marshal Viscount Bernard Law Montgomery of Alamein
Kings College (London, UK) (KC)
Papers of Ronald Edmona Balfour
National Archives (UK) (Kew Gardens, UK) (UKNA)
Royal Air Force Air Historical Branch (Northolt, UK) (AHB)
Air Battle Narratives

Unpublished Government Reports

AAF Evaluation Board in the European Theater of Operations. "Effectiveness of Air Attack against Rail Transportation in the Battle of France." AFHRC, 1945.

Air Ministry, Air Historical Branch. "RAF Narrative (First Draft): Air Defense of Great Britain, the Flying Bomb and Rocket Campaigns, 1944–1945." AHB, 1945.

———. "RAF Narrative (First Draft): The Campaign in France and the Low Countries." AHB, 1944.

———."RAF Narrative (First Draft): The Liberation of North West Europe; Volume I: The Planning and Preparation of the Allied Expeditionary Air Force for the Landings in Normandy." AHB, 1946

———. "RAF Narrative (First Draft): The Liberation of North West Europe; Volume II: Administrative Preparations." AHB, 1946.

———. "RAF Narrative (First Draft): The Liberation of North West Europe; Volume III: The Landings in Normandy." AHB, 1945.

Chief of the Army Air Forces. "AWPD/1: Munitions Requirements of the Army Air Forces." AFHRC, 1941.

Deputy Chief of Staff, Operations. "Eighth Air Force Tactical Operations in Support of Allied Landings in Normandy, 2 June–17, June 1944." AFHRC.

Harris, Arthur T. "The Employment of the Night Bomber Force in Connection with the Invasion of the Continent from the United Kingdom." In Appendices to Part VI of Notes of the Planning & Preparation of the Allied Expeditionary Air Force for the Invasion of Northwest France. AHB, 1944.

Headquarters, Eighth Air Force. "The Role of H2X on D-Day." Frederick L. Anderson Papers. HIAL, 1944.

Headquarters, Ninth Air Force. "Ninth Air Force Invasion Activities: April–June 1944." In Smith Papers 1941–1945. DDEPL, 1944.

Historical Sub-Section. "History of COSSAC (Chief of Staff to Supreme Allied Commander), 1943–1944." General Staff, Office of the Secretary. London: Supreme Headquarters, Allied Expeditionary Force, 1944.

Kingston-McCloughry, Air Vice-Marshal E-J. "The Transportation Plan." In Papers of Air Vice-Marshal E-J Kingston-McCloughry, edited by Allied Expeditionary Air Force (AEAF). IWM, 1946.

Office of Strategic Services. "Civil Affairs Handbook on France: Section Eleven Transportation Systems (Preliminary Draft)." William J. Donovan Papers. AHEC, 1944.

Office of Assistant Chief of Air Staff, Intelligence. Sunday Punch in Normandy: The Tactical Use of Heavy Bombardment in the Normandy Invasion. An Interim Report. Washington, DC: Center for Air Force History, 1945.

Robertson, Jenns. THOR (Theater History of Operations Reports). Maxwell Air Force Base, AL: Air Force Historical Research Institute. 2013.

Sandys, Duncan. "Investigation of the 'Heavy' Crossbow Installations in Northern France, Volume 1." CAB 80/92, UKNA, 1945.

Zuckerman, S., and E. S. D. Drury. "B. A. U. Report No 27. The Effects of Air Bombardment of German Defenses at Le Havre." AIR 37/1263, UKNA, 1945.

Thesis, Monographs, and Dissertations

Bender, Mark C. "Watershed at Leavenworth: Dwight D. Eisenhower and the Command and General Staff School." MMAS monograph, US Army Command and General Staff College, 1988.

Corrado, Giovanni. "Tactical Enthusiasm, Operational Blindness, and Civilian Casualties: Questioning the Allied Air Campaign against Italy during the Second World War." MMAS monograph, U.S. Army Command and General Staff College, 2015.

Folliot, Sandrine. "Sotteville-Les-Rouen Pendant La Seconde Guerre Mondiale Et La Periode De Reconstruction (1939–1965)." MA thesis, University de Rouen, 1990.

Foucrier, Jean-Charles. "Le Transportaton Plan, Aspects Et Représentations Une Histoire Des Bombardements Aériens Alliés Sur La France En 1944." PhD dissertation, Paris: Université Paris-Sorbonne, 2015.

Fromentin, Natacha. "La Gare D'amiens Et Le Réseau Amiénois (1939–1957)." MA thesis, Université de Picardie Jules Verne, 1999.

Gaetke, Kathryn. "Joint by Design: The Western Desert Campaign." MMAS monograph, US Army Command and General Staff College, 2015.

Hardy, Antoine. "La Défense Passive À Rouen Et Dans Son Agglomération." MA thesis, Université de Rouen, 2005.

Heathman, Jeremiah S. "The Bombing of Brittany: Failing to Solve the Problem." MMAS monograph, United States Army Command and General Staff College, 2010.

LeBlanc, Scott Simon Gerald. "Breaching the Ramparts: The 3rd Canadian Infantry Division's Capture of Boulogne in World War Two." MMAS monograph, US Army Command and General Staff College, 2016.

Van Esch, Joris Adrianus Cornelis. "Restrained Policy and Careless Execution: Allied Strategic Bombing on the Netherlands in the Second World War." MMAS thesis, United States Army Command and General Staff College, 2011.

Published Official Histories and Manuals

Blumenson, Martin. *The European Theater of Operations: Breakout and Pursuit.* United States Army in World War II. Washington, DC: Office of the Chief of Military History, 1960.

———. *The Mediterranean Theater of Operations: Salerno to Cassino.* United States Army in World War II. Washington, DC: Office of the Chief of Military History, 1969.

Carter, Kit, and Robert Mueller, eds. *The Army Air Forces in World War II: Combat Chronology.* Washington, DC: Air Force Historical Studies, 1973.

Chief of the Army Air Forces. "AWPD/1 Munitions Requirements of the Army Air Forces." Washington, DC: War Department, 1941.

Craven, Wesley Frank, and James Lea Cate. The Army Air Forces in World War II. Vol. 1, *Plans and Early Operations, January 1942 to August 1942.* Chicago: University of Chicago Press, 1948.

———. The Army Air Forces in World War II. Vol. 2, *Europe, Torch to Pointblank, August 1942 to December 1943.* Chicago: University of Chicago Press, 1948.

———. The Army Air Forces in World War II. Vol. 3, *Europe, Argument to V-E Day, January 1944 to May 1945.* Chicago: University of Chicago Press, 1948.

Ellis, L. F. *Victory in the West,* Vol. 1: *The Battle of Normandy.* London: Her Majesty's Stationery Office, 1962.

Gabel, Christopher R. *The U.S. Army GHQ Maneuvers of 1941.* Washington, DC: US Army Center of Military History, 1991.

Gendarmerie Nationale, Legion de Normandie, Compaignie de la Seine-Inferieure, Section de Rouen. "Registres De Correspondance Courante Au Départ (R/2), 24 Janvier Au 28 Août 1944." Gendarmerie Nationale, Section de Rouen Gendarme. SHD, 1944.

———. "Registres De Correspondance Confidentielle Au Départ (R/4), 20 Septembre 1940 Au 21 Décembre 1946." Gendarmerie Nationale, Compaigne de la Seine-Inférieure Gendarme. SHD, 1940–1944.

George, Robert H. "Ninth Air Force, April to November 1944." Army Air Forces Historical Studies: No. 36. Maxwell Air Force Base, AL: Air University, 1945.

Greenhous, Brereton, Stephen J. Harris, William C. Johnston, and William G. P. Rawling. *The Crucible of War, 1939–1945: The Official History of the Royal Canadian Air Force,* vol. 3. Toronto: University of Toronto Press, 1994.

Harris, Arthur T. *Despatch on War Operations, 23 February 1942 to 8th May 1945.* London: Frank Cass, 1995.

Harrison, Gordon A. *The European Theater of Operations: Cross-Channel Attack.* United States Army in World War II. Washington, DC: Office of the Chief of Military History, 1951.

Joint Chiefs of Staff. *Joint Publication 1-02, Department of Defense Dictionary of Military and Associated Terms.* Dec. 2014. Washington, DC: Department of Defense, 2010.

———. *Joint Publication (JP) 5-0, Joint Operation Planning.* Washington, DC: US Department of Defense, 2011.

Leighton, Richard M., and Robert W. Coakley. *The War Department: Global Logistics and Strategy, 1940–1943.* The United States Army in World War II. Washington, DC: Office of the Chief of Military History, 1955.

Matloff, Maurice. *The War Department: Strategic Planning for Coalition Warfare, 1943–1944.* The United States Army in World War II. Washington, DC: Office of the Chief of Military History, 1959.

Matloff, Maurice, and Edwin M. Snell. *The War Department: Strategic Planning for Coalition Warfare, 1941–1942.* The United States Army in World War II. Washington, DC: Office of the Chief of Military History, 1953.

Mulligan, Timothy P. *Records of the German Navy: Operational Commands in World War II.* Guide to Microfilmed Records of the German Navy, 1850–1945, no. 4. NARA, 2005.

Office of Statistical Control. "Army Air Forces Statistical Digest." Washington, DC: US Army Air Forces, 1945.

Pogue, Forrest C. *The European Theater of Operations: The Supreme Command.* United States Army in World War II. Washington, DC: Office of the Chief of Military History, 1954.

Ruppenthal, Roland G. *The European Theater of Operations: Logistical Support of the Armies,* Vol. 1: *May 1941–September1944.* United States Army in World War II. Washington, DC: Office of the Chief of Military History, 1953.

———. *The European Theater of Operations: Logistical Support of the Armies,* Vol. 2: *September 1944–May 1945.* United States Army in World War II. Washington, DC: Office of the Chief of Military History, 1959.

Saunders, Hilary St. George. *Royal Air Force:* Vol. 3, *The Fight Is Won.* London: Her Majesty's Stationery Office, 1954.

SHAEF Historical Division. "German Report Series: Atlantic Wall to the Siegfried Line, a Study in Command." CARL Digital Library. CARL, 1946.

Shortal, John F. *Organizational Development of the Joint Chiefs of Staff.* Washington, DC: Joint History Office, Office of the Chairman of the Joint Chiefs of Staff, 2013.

Stacey, C. P. *The Victory Campaign: Operations in North-West Europe 1944–1945.* Vol. 3, *Official History of the Canadian Army in the Second World War.* Ottawa: Queen's Printer and Controller of Stationery, 1960.

United States Strategic Bombing Survey. "Statistical Appendix to Over-All Report (European War)." Washington, DC: Government Printing Office, 1947.

United States Strategic Bombing Survey, Military Analysis Division. "V-Weapons (Crossbow) Campaign." United States Strategic Bombing Survey, European Division. 2nd ed. Washington, DC: Government Printing Office, 1945.

United States Strategic Bombing Survey, Physical Damage Division. "Gnome Et Rhone Aero Engine Factory, Limoges, France." Washington, DC: United States Strategic Bombing Survey, 1947.

United States War Department. *Field Manual 100-15*, Field Service Regulations: Larger Units. Washington, DC: Government Printing Office, 1942.

———. *Field Manual 1-5, Air Corps Field Manual: Employment of Aviation of the Army*. Washington, DC: Government Printing Office, 1940.

———. "Handbook on German Military Forces (Tm-E 30–451)." *In War Department Technical Manual*. Washington, DC: Government Printing Office, 1945.

Watson, Mark Skinner. *The War Department: Chief of Staff: Prewar Plans and Preparations*. The United States Army in World War II. Washington, DC: Office of the Chief of Military History, 1950.

Webster, Charles, and Noble Frankland. *The Strategic Air Offensive against Germany, 1939–1945*. Vol. 2, *Endeavor*. London: Her Majesty's Stationery Office, 1961.

———. *The Strategic Air Offensive against Germany, 1939–1945*. Vol. 3, *Victory*. London: Her Majesty's Stationery Office, 1961.

Local and Regional Studies

Bailleul, Laurent. *Les Sites V1 En Flandres Et En Artois*. Hazebrouck: S. A. Presse Flamande, 2000.

Bataille, Guy. *Boulogne Sur Mer: 1939–1945*. Dunkerque: Westhoek-éditions, 1984.

Battesti, Michèle, and Patrick Facon, eds. *Les Bombardements Alliés Sur La France Durant La Seconde Guerre Mondialle: Stratégies, Bilans Matereriels Et Humains*. Cahiers Du Centre D' Études D'histoire De La Défense, No 37. SHD, 2009.

Beaudufe, Christopher. *Le Sacrifice Des Normands: L'été 1944*. Paris: Perrin, 2004.

Boivin, Michael, Gérard Bourdin, and Jean Quellien. *Villes Normandes Sous Les Bombes (Juin 1944): Les Normands Témoignet*. Caen: Presses Universitaires de Caen, 1994.

Boivin, Michael, and Bernard Garnier. *Les Victimes Civiles De La Manche Dans La Bataille De Normandie: 1er Avril-30 Septembre 1944*. Caen: Centre de recherche d'historie quantitative, 1994.

Bourdin, Gérard, and Bernard Garnier. *Les Victimes Civiles De L'orne Dans La Bataille De Normandie: 1 Avril–30 September 1944*. Caen: Éditions-Diffusion du Lys, 1994.

Capillier, Thierry. *Boulogne, 40–44: Une Exposition Basée Sur Les Témoignages De Six Boulonnais*. Boulogne-sur-mer: Archives Municipales, 2005.

Chapron, Michelle. "Mémoires De L'été 1944." Témoignages écrits MC, 1944.

Chazette, Alain, Jacky Laurent, Alain Destouches, and Jacques Tomine. *Forteresse Boulogne-Sur-Mer 1939–1944: Occupation-Fortifications-Libération*. Paris: Éditions Histoire et Fortifications, 2007.

Chevalier, Hugues. *Bombes Et V1 Sur Le Pas-De-Calais 1944: Raids Alliés, Crashes, Destructions...* Vottem, BE: Snel Grafics à Vottem, 2009.

Chion, Thierry. *Pompiers sous les bombes: Rouen 1940–1944.* Louviers: Ysec Médias, 2013.

Dandel, M., G. Duboc, A. Kitts, and E. Lapersonne. *Les Victimes Civiles Des Bombardements En Haute-Normandie: 1er Janvier 1944–12 Septembre 1944.* Cormelles-le-Royal: Mandragore, 1997.

Dejonghe, Étienne, and Yves le Maner. *Le Nord-Pas-De-Calais Dans La Main Allemande.* Lille: La Voix du Nord, 1999.

Desquesnes, Rémy. *Le Mur De L'atlantique, De Dunkerque Au Tréport.* Lille: Editions Ouest-France, 2014.

———. *Les Poches De Résistance Allemandes Sur Le Littoral Français, Août 1944-Mai 1945.* Rennes: Editions Ouest-France, 2011.

Detrez, Chanoine L. *Quand Lille Avait Faim.* Lille: S. I. L. I. C., 1945.

Dubuisson, Émile. "Un Porte Mutilé—18 Juin 1940–9 Mai 1945." In *Chronoiques D' Un Port En Guerre: Dunkerque, 1939–1945,* edited by Patrick Oddone and Catherine Lesage. Dunkerque: Musée portuaire, 2010.

Gosset, André, and Paule Lecomte. *Caen Pendant La Bataille.* Paris: Carrefour des Lettres, 1974.

Goupil, M. Bernard. "Caen et Ses Ruines." Témoignages écrits MC, 1944.

Halais, Jérémie. *Saint-Lô Et Son Canton Dans La Tourmente De La Second Guerre Mondiale (1939–1945).* Série 8j: Travaux Universitaires. St Lô: Société d'Archéologie et d'Histoire de la Manche, 2007.

Hardy, Antoine. "La Défense Passive À Rouen." Études normandes, no. 1 (2008).

Itsweire, André. "Douanier À Dunkerque, Et Observateur Privilége." In *Chronoiques D' Un Port En Guerre: Dunkerque, 1939–1945,* edited by Patrick Oddone and Catherine Lesage, 108–47. Dunkerque: Musée portuaire, 2010.

Jarry, Maud. "Le Bombardement Des Sites V En France (Été 1943–Été 1944)." In *Les Bombardements Alliés Sur La France Durant La Seconde Guerre Mondiale: Stratégies, Bilans Matérials Et Humains,* edited by Michèle Battesti and Patrick Facon, 39–48. Vincennes: Cahiers du Center D'études D'historie de la Défense, 2009.

Hautefeuille, Roland. *Constructions Speciales: Histoire De La Construction Par "L'organizaton Todt," Dan Le Pas De Calais Et Le Cotentin, Des Neufs Gránds Sites Protégés Pur Le Tir Des V1, V2, V3 Et La Production D'oxygène Liquide. (1943–1944).* Tourcoing: Jean-Bernard, 1985.

Lantenois, Jean-Claude, and Michel Chaubiron. *Dunkerque, 1940–1945: Guide Historique & Touristique.* Paris: Ysec, 2007.

Le Trevier, Paul. *Objectif Rouen: 1er Raid Américain Sur L'europe.* Le Mesnil-Esnard: Comever-De Rameau, 2005.

Le Trevier, Paul, and Daniel Rose. *Ce Qui S'est Vraiment Passé Le 19 Avril 1944.* Le Mesnil-Esnard: Comever-De Rameau, 2004.

Lippe, Théo. *La Bosse De Beton* [in French]. Brussels: Private, 1973.

Marin, Gaston. "Les Bombardements De L'agglomération Mantaise Pendant La Duxième Guerre Mondiale." *Le Mantois 13: Bulletin de las Société "Les Amis du Mantois"* no. 13 (1962): 22–36.

Maurois, André. *Rouen Dévasté.* Paris: Les Editions Nagel, 1948.

Mourier, Guillaume. *Les Sinistrés Saint-Lois Au 6 Juin 1944.* St. Lo: Société d'Archéologie et d'Histoire de la Manche, 2004.

Nobécourt, R.-G. *Rouen Désollé.* Paris: Éditions Médicis, 1948.

Oddone, Patrick. "L'arrondissement De Dunkerque À L'épreuve Des Bombes Alliées (16 June 1941–29 Novembre 1943)." *Revue Historique de Dunkerque et du Littoral,* no. 5 (2005): 167–86.

Pailhès, Gontran. *Rouen Et Sa Région Pendant La Guerre, 1939–1945.* Rouen: H. Defontaine, 1949. Luneray: Editions Bertout "La Mémoire Normande," 1993.

Pessiot, Guy. *Histoire De Rouen 1939–1958: La Guerre 39/45 Et La Reconstruction En 900 Photographies.* Rouen: Editions PTC, 2004.

Quellien, Jean, and Bernard Garnier. *Les Victimes Civiles Du Calvados Dans La Bataille De Normandie: 1er Mars 1944–31 Décembre 1945.* Caen: Editions-diffusion du Lys, 1995.

Villatoux, Marie-Catherine. "Les Bombardements De Royan (Janvier Et Avril, 1945)." In *Les Bombardements Alliés Sur La France Durant La Seconde Guerre Mondialle: Stratégies, Bilans Materériels Et Humains, Cahiers Du Centre D' Études D'histoire De La Défense, No 37,* edited by Michèle Battesti and Patrick Facon, 125–34. Vincennes: Ministère de la Defense, 2009.

General Secondary Sources

Abbott, H. Porter. *The Cambridge Introduction to Narrative.* New York: Cambridge University Press, 2008.

Alary, Eric, Bénédicte Vergez-Chaignon, and Gilles Gauvin. *Les Français Au Quotidien, 1939–1949.* Paris: Perrin, 2006.

American Battle Monuments Commission. *American Armies and Battlefields in Europe.* Washington, DC: US Army Center of Military History, 1938. Reprint 1992.

Amouroux, Henri. *La Grande Histoire Des Français Sous L'occupation, Un Printemps De Mort Et D'espoir Joies Et Douleurs Du Peuple Libéré, September 1943–6 Août 1944.* Paris: Éditions Robert Laffont, 1999.

d'Ambrières, René. "Les Pelabon : entre industrie et patriotisme, ou des ANF aux Mureaux en passant par Londres." *Bulletin de la Sabix* 48 (2011): 79–85.

Ambrose, Stephen E. *Band of Brothers.* New York: Simon & Schuster, 1992.

———. *D-Day: June 6, 1944.* New York: Simon & Schuster, 1994.

Anderson, Benedict. *Imagined Communities.* New York: Verso, 1983.

Atkinson, Rick. *The Guns at Last Light: The War in Western Europe, 1944–1945.* The Liberation Trilogy. New York: Henry Holt, 2013.

Aulich, James. "Memory, What Is It Good For? Forced Labour, Blockhouses, and Museums in Nord-Pas De Calais, Northern France." In *Contested Spaces: Sites,*

Representations, and Histories of Conflict, edited by Louise Purbrick, James Aulich, and Graham Dawson. New York: Palgrave Macmillan, 2007.

Auphan, Paul, and Jacques Mordal. *The French Navy in World War II*. Annapolis, MD: Naval Institute Press, 2016.

Baldoli, Claudia, and Andrew Knapp. *Forgotten Blitzes: France and Italy under Allied Air Attack, 1940–1945*. New York: Continuum International Publishing Group, 2012.

Banks, Arthur. *A Military Atlas of the First World War*. Barnsley, UK: Pen and Sword, 1989.

Barbier, Mary Kathryn. *D-Day Deception: Operation Fortitude and the Normandy Invasion*. Stackpole Military History Series. Mechanicsburg, PA: Stackpole Books, 2009.

Barnett, Correlli. *Engage the Enemy More Closely: The Royal Navy in the Second World War*. New York: W. W. Norton, 1991.

Barzman, John, Corinne Bouillot, and Andrew Knapp, eds. *Bombardements 1944: Le Havre, Normandie, France, Europe*. Mont-Saint-Aignan: Presses universitaires de Rouen et du Havre, 2016.

Beevor, Antony. *D-Day: The Battle for Normandy*. New York: Viking, 2009.

Besselièvre, Jean-Yves. "Les Bombardements De Brest (1940–1944)." In *Les Bombardements Alliés Sur La France Durant La Seconde Guerre Mondialle: Stratégies, Bilans Materériels Et Humains, Cahiers Du Centre D' Études D'histoire De La Défense, No 37*, edited by Michèle Battesti and Patrick Facon, 103–24. Vincennes: Ministère de la Defense, 2009.

Biddle, Tami Davis. "Air Power." In *The Laws of War: Constraints on Warfare in the Western World*, edited by Michael Howard, George J. Andreopoulos, and Mark R. Shulman, 140–59. New Haven, CT: Yale University Press.

———. *Rhetoric and Reality in Air Warfare: The Evolution of British and American Ideas About Strategic Bombing, 1914–1945*. Princeton Studies in International History and Politics. Princeton, NJ: Princeton University Press, 2002.

Bishop, Stan D., and John A. Hey. *Losses of the US 8th & 9th Air Forces: Aircraft and Men, 1st April 1944–30th June 1944*. London: Bishop Book Productions, 2009.

Bradley, Omar N. *A Soldier's Story*. New York: Holt, Rinehart and Winston, 1951.

Brereton, Lewis H. *The Brereton Diaries: The War in the Air in the Pacific, Middle East, and Europe, 3 October 1941–8 May 1945*. New York: William Morrow, 1946.

Brinkley, Douglas. *The Boys of Pointe Du Hoc: Ronald Reagan, D-Day, and the U. S. Army 2nd Ranger Battalion*. New York: Harper Perennial, 2006.

Brokaw, Tom. *The Greatest Generation*. New York: Random House, 1998.

Brooks, Stephen, ed. *Montgomery and the Battle of Normandy: A Selection from the Diaries, Correspondence and Other Papers of Field Marshal the Viscount Montgomery of Alamein, January to August 1944*. London: History Press for the Army Records Society, 2008.

Brown, Anthony Cave. *Bodyguard of Lies: The Extraordinary True Story behind D-Day*. Guilford, CT: Lyons Press, 1975.

Buckley, John. *Air Power in the Age of Total War.* Bloomington: Indiana University Press, 1999.

———. *Monty's Men: The British Army and the Liberation of Europe, 1944–1945.* New Haven, CT: Yale University Press, 2013.

Cabell, Charles P., Jr. *A Man of Intelligence: Memoirs of War, Peace, and the CIA.* Colorado Springs, CO: Impavide Publications, 1997.

Caesar, Julius. *The Conquest of Gaul.* Translated by S. A. Handford. Penguin Classics. New York: Penguin Books, 1982.

Cannon, Gwen, ed. *The Green Guide: Normandy.* Clermont-Ferrand, France: Michelin, 2006.

Carell, Paul. *Invasion! They're Coming! The German Account of the D-Day Landings and the 80 Days Battle for France.* Translated by David Johnston. Atglen, PA: Schiffer Military History, 1995.

Chandler, Alfred D. Jr., and Stephen E. Ambrose, eds. *The Papers of Dwight David Eisenhower*, vol. 3, *The War Years.* Baltimore: Johns Hopkins Press, 1970.

Churchill, Winston S. *Closing the Ring. The Second World War*, vol. 5. Boston: Houghton Mifflin Company, 1951.

———. *The Grand Alliance. The Second World War*, vol. 3. Boston: Houghton Mifflin Company, 1950.

———. *The Hinge of Fate. The Second World War*, vol. 4. Boston: Houghton Mifflin Company, 1950.

———. *Their Finest Hour. The Second World War*, vol. 2. Boston: Houghton Mifflin Company, 1949.

———. *Triumph and Tragedy. The Second World War*, vol. 6. Boston: Houghton Mifflin Company, 1953.

Clarke, James. *A Topographical and Historical Description of Boulogne and Its Vicinity.* London: J. S. Hodson, 1835.

Clausewitz, Carl Von. *On War.* Translated by Michael Howard and Peter Paret. Indexed edition. Princeton, NJ: Princeton University Press, 1984.

———. *Vom Kriege.* Frankfurt / M, GE: Ullstein GmbH, 1991 [1832].

Clodfelter, Mark. *Beneficial Bombing: The Progressive Foundations of American Air Power, 1917–1945.* Lincoln: University of Nebraska Press, 2010.

Clout, Hugh. "Place Annihilation and Urban Reconstruction: The Experience of Four Towns in Brittany, 1940–1960." *Geografiska Annaler. Series B, Human Geography* 82, no. 3 (2000): 165–80.

Cohen, Eliot A. *Supreme Command: Soldiers, Statesmen and Leadership in Wartime.* New York: Free Press, 2002.

Copp, Terry. *Cinderella Army: The Canadians in Northwest Europe, 1944–1945.* Toronto: University of Toronto Press, 2006.

———. *Fields of Fire: The Canadians in Normandy.* Toronto: University of Toronto Press, 2003.

———. ed. *Montgomery's Scientists: Operational Research in Northwest Europe.* Waterloo, ON: Wilfrid Laurier University, 2000.

Corvisier, André. *Histoire Militaire De La France, 3: De 1871 Á 1940.* Paris: Presses Univ. France, 1992.

Cox, Sebastian, ed. *The Strategic Air War against Germany, 1939–1945: Report of the British Bombing Survey Unit.* London: Frank Cass, 1993.

Craig, Gordon A. *Europe since 1914.* New York: Holt, Rinehart, and Winston, 1966.

———. "The Political Leader as Strategist." In *Makers of Modern Strategy from Machiavelli to the Nuclear Age*, edited by Peter Paret, 481–509. Princeton, NJ: Princeton University Press, 1986.

Crane, Conrad C. *American Airpower Strategy in World War II: Bombs, Cities, Civilians, and Oil.* Lawrence: University Press of Kansas, 2016.

Creveld, Martin Van. *Supplying War: Logistics from Wallenstein to Patton.* Cambridge, MA: Harvard University Press, 1977.

D'Este, Carlo. *Decision in Normandy.* New York: HarperPerennial, 1994.

———. *Eisenhower: A Soldier's Life.* New York: Henry Holt, 2002.

Dallek, Robert. "Roosevelt as War Leader." In *The Oxford Companion to World War II*, edited by I. C. B. Dear and M. R. D. Foot, 960–66. New York: Oxford University Press, 1995.

Dancy, Peter G., and Franz-Antal Vajida. *German Aircraft Production, 1933–1945.* Warrendale, PA: Society of Automative Engineers, Inc., 1998.

Danchev, Alex, and Daniel Todman eds. *War Diaries, 1939–1945: Field Marshal Lord Alanbrooke.* Berkeley: University of California Press, 2001.

Dancy, Robert G. *Flying Bomb Launching Sites: A Description of What Was Still to Be Seen of Some of the 1944 V1 Launching Sites in Northern France About 60 Years Later.* Self-published, 2009. http://www.christianch.ch/history/V1_sites_rgd.pdf.

Darlow, Stephen. *D-Day Bombers: The Veterans' Story: RAF Bomber Command and the US Eighth Air Force Support to the Normandy Invasion, 1944.* London: Grub Street, 2004.

———. *Sledgehammers for Tintacks: Bomber Command Confronts the V-1 Menace, 1943–1944.* London: Grub Street, 2002.

Davies, Norman. *No Simple Victory.* New York: Penguin Books, 2006.

Davis, Richard G. *Bombing the European Powers: A Historical Digest of the Combined Bomber Offensive, 1939–1945.* Maxwell Air Force Base, AL: Air University Press, 2006.

———. *Carl A. Spaatz and the Air War in Europe.* Washington, DC: Center for Air Force History, 1993.

Dear, I. C. B., and M. R. D. Foot. *The Oxford Companion to World War II.* New York: Oxford University Press, 1995.

de Gaulle, Charles. *The Complete War Memoirs of Charles de Gaulle.* Translated by Jonathan Griffin and Richard Howard. New York: Carroll & Graff, 1998. Originally published 1955–59, Simon & Schuster.

Delaney, Douglas E. *Corps Commanders: Five British and Canadian Generals at War, 1939–45.* Studies in Canadian Military History. Vancouver: University of British Columbia Press, 2011.

Diamond, Hanna. *Fleeing Hitler: France 1940.* Oxford: Oxford University Press, 2007.

Dinardo, Richard. *Germany and the Axis Powers: From Coalition to Collapse.* Lawrence: University of Kansas Press, 2005.

Dodd, Lindsey, and Andrew Knapp. "'How Many Frenchmen Did You Kill?' British Bombing Policy Towards France (1940–1945)." *French Historical Studies* 22, no. 4 (Spring 2008): 469–92.

Dodd, Lindsey. *French Children under the Allied Bombs, 1940–1945, An Oral History.* Manchester: Manchester University Press, 2016.

———. "'It Did Not Traumatize Me at All': Childhood 'Trauma' in French Oral Narratives of Wartime Bombing." *Oral History* 41, no. 2 (Autumn 2013): 37–48.

Dolski, Michael R. "'Portal of Liberation': D-Day Myth as American Self-Affirmation." In *D-Day in History and Memory: The Normandy Landings in International Remembrance and Commemoration*, edited by Michael Dolski, Sam Edwards, and John Buckley. Denton: University of North Texas Press, 2014.

Dornberger, Walter. *V-2.* New York: Viking, 1954.

Doughty, Robert A. *The Breaking Point: Sedan and the Fall of France, 1940.* Hamden, CT: Archon, 1990.

———. *Pyrrhic Victory: French Strategy and Operations in the Great War.* Boston: Belknap Press, 2005.

Douhet, Giulio. *Command of the Air.* Translated by Dino Ferrari. New York: Coward-McCann, 1942. Washington, DC: Air Force History and Museums Program, 1942. Reprint 1998.

Downes, Alexander B. *Targeting Civilians in War.* Ithaca, NY: Cornell University Press, 2008.

Dungan, Tracy D. *V-2 Combat History of the First Ballistic Missile.* Yardley, PA: Westholme, 2005.

Eden, Paul. *The Encyclopedia of Aircraft of World War II.* London: Amber Books, 2004.

Ehlers, Robert S., Jr. *Targeting the Third Reich: Air Intelligence and the Allied Bombing Campaigns.* Lawrence: University Press of Kansas, 2009.

Eisenhower, David. *Eisenhower: At War 1943–1945.* New York: Random House, 1986.

Eisenhower, Dwight D. *Crusade in Europe.* Garden City, NY: Garden City Books, 1948.

Esposito, Vincent J., ed. *The West Point Atlas of American Wars,* Vol. 2*: 1900–1953.* New York: Praeger Publishers, 1959.

Fischer, David Hackett. *Champlain's Dream: The European Founding of North America.* New York: Simon & Schuster, 2008.

Flaubert, Gustave. *Madame Bovary.* Paris: Michel Lévy frès, 1856. Reprint 1994, Hertfordshire, Wordsworth Editions Limited.

Florentin, Eddy. *Quand Les Alliés Bombardaient La France.* Paris: Perrin, 1997.

Freedman, Lawrence. *Strategy: A History.* New York: Oxford University Press, 2013.

Freeman, Roger A., Alan Crouchman, and Vic Maslen. *Mighty Eighth War Diary*. London: Arms and Armour Press, 1990.

Frieser, Karl-Heinz, and John T. Greenwood. *The Blitzkrieg Legend: The 1940 Campaign in the West*. Annapolis, MD: Naval Institute Press, 2005.

Fussell, Paul. *Wartime: Understanding and Behavior in the Second World War*. New York: Oxford University Press, 1989.

Futrell, Robert Frank. *Ideas, Concepts, Doctrine: Basic Thinking in the United States Air Force, 1907–1960*. 2 vols. Vol. 1, Maxwell Air Force Base, AL: Air University Press, 1989.

———. "The U.S. Army Air Corps and the United States Air Force, 1909–1973." In *A Guide to the Sources of United States Military History*, edited by Robin Higham, 404–29. Hamden, CT: Archon Books, 1975.

Garnier, Jacques, ed. *Dictionnaire Perrin: Des Guerres Et Des Batailles De L'historie De France*. Paris: Perrin, 2004.

Gilbert, Martin. *The First World War: A Complete History*. New York: Henry Holt and Company, 1994.

Gildea, Robert. *Fighters in the Shadows: A New History of the French Resistance*. Cambridge, MA: Belknap Press, 2015.

———. *Marianne in Chains: Daily Life in the Heart of France during German Occupation*. New York: Metropolitan Books, 2003.

Gooch, John. "Churchill as War Leader." In *The Oxford Companion to World War II*, edited by I. C. B. Dear and M. R. D. Foot, 235–42. New York: Oxford University Press, 1995.

Greenfield, Kent Roberts. *The Historian and the Army*. The Brown & Haley Lectures. New Brunswick, NJ: Rutgers University Press, 1954. Presentation.

Greenhalgh, Elizabeth. *The French Army and the First World War*. Armies of the Great War. Cambridge: Cambridge University Press, 2014.

Hall, R. Cargill, ed. *Case Studies in Strategic Bombardment*. Washington, DC: Air Force History and Museums Program, 1998.

Hargreaves, Richard. *The Germans in Normandy*. Barnsley, South Yorkshire, UK: Pen & Sword, 2006.

Hart, Stephen Ashley. *Montgomery and "Colossal Cracks": The 21st Army Group in Northwest Europe, 1944–45*. Westport, CT: Praeger, 2000.

Hastings, Max. *Bomber Command: The Myths and Reality of the Strategic Bombing Offensive 1939–45*. New York: Penguin, 1979.

———. *Overlord: D-Day and the Battle for Normandy*. New York: Simon & Schuster, 1984.

Henshall, Philip. *Hitler's Rocket Sites*. New York: St. Martin's, 1985.

Herrmann, David G. *The Arming of Europe and the Making of the First World War*. Princeton, NJ: Princeton University Press, 1996.

Hesketh, Roger. *Fortitude: The D-Day Deception Campaign*. New York: Overlook Press, 2002.

Heuser, Beatrice. *The Evolution of Strategy: Thinking War from Antiquity to the Present*. New York: Cambridge University Press, 2010.

Hinsley, F. H., E. E. Thomas, G. F. G. Ransom, and R. C. Knight. *British Intelligence in the Second World War, Its Influence on Strategy and Operations*, vol. 3, part 2. New York: Cambridge University Press, 1988.

Hitchcock, William I. "The Price of Liberation." *MHQ: The Quarterly Journal of Military History* 21, no. 3 (Spring 2009): 20–29.

Holborn, Hajo. *A History of Modern Germany: 1840–1945*. New York: Alfred A. Knopf, 1975.

———. "The Prusso-German School: Moltke and the Rise of the General Staff." In *Makers of Modern Strategy from Machiavelli to the Nuclear Age*, edited by Peter Paret, 281–95. Princeton, NJ: Princeton University Press, 1986.

Holland, Matthew F. *Eisenhower between the Wars: The Making of a General and Statesman*. Westport, CT: Praeger, 2001.

Holt, Tonie, and Valmai Holt. *Major & Mrs Holt's Battlefield Guide to the Normandy Landing Beaches*. Barnsley, South Yorkshire, UK: Leo Cooper, 2000.

Horne, Alistair. *To Lose a Battle: France 1940*. New York: Little, Brown, 1969. Revised and updated 1990, New York: Penguin Books.

———, and David Montgomery. *The Lonely Leader: Monty, 1944–1945*. London: Pan Books, 1995.

Horne, John, and Alan Kramer. "German 'Atrocities' and Franco-German Opinion, 1914: The Evidence of German Soldiers' Diaries." *Journal of Modern History* 66, no. 1 (1994): 1–3.

Hughes, Thomas Alexandar. *Over Lord: General Pete Quesada and the Triumph of Tactical Air Power in World War II*. New York: Free Press, 1995.

Huston, James A. *Across the Face of France: Liberation and Recovery, 1944–63*. West Lafayette, IN: Purdue University Press, 1963.

Imlay, Talbot, and Martin Horn. *The Politics of Collaboration during World War II: Ford France, Vichy and Nazi Germany*. New York: Cambridge University Press, 2014.

Institut National de la Statistique et des Études Économiques. *Résultats Statistiques Du Recensement Général De La Population, Effectueé Le 10 Mars 1946; Départment Du Calvados*. Paris: Presses Universitaires de France, 1951.

Isby, David C., ed. *Fighting the Invasion: The German Army at D-Day*. Kindle edition. NewYork: Skyhorse Publishing, 2000.

Jackson, Julian. *The Fall of France: The Nazi Invasion of 1940*. New York: Oxford University Press, 2003.

Jackson, Peter. *France: The Dark Years 1940–1944*. New York: Oxford University Press, 2001.

———. "Recent Journeys along the Road Back to France, 1940." *The Historical Journal* 39, no. 2 (June 1996): 497–510.

Jones, Benjamin F. *Eisenhower's Guerrillas: The Jedburghs, the Maquis, & the Liberation of France*. New York: Oxford University Press, 2016.

Jones, R(eginald) V. *Most Secret War: British Scientific Intelligence 1939–1945*. London: Hamish Hamilton Limited, 1978.

Jones, Tobin. *617 Squadron, the Operational Record Book, 1943–1945*. Bicester, UK: Binx Publishing, 2002.

Kennedy, Paul. *Engineers of Victory: The Problem Solvers Who Turned the Tide in the Second World War*. New York: Random House, 2013.

Kiesling, Eugenia C. *Arming against Hitler: France & the Limits of Military Planning*. Lawrence: University of Kansas Press, 1996.

Kimball, Warren F., ed. *Churchill & Roosevelt: The Complete Correspondence*. Vol. 3, *Alliance Declining, February 1944–April 1945*. Princeton, NJ: Princeton University Press, 1984.

King, Benjamin, and Timothy J. Kutta. *Impact: The History of Germany's V-Weapons in World War II*. Rockville Centre, NY: Sarpedon, 1998.

Kingston-McCloughry, E. J. *The Direction of War*. New York: Frederick A. Praeger, 1958.

Kitson, Simon. "Criminals or Liberators? French Public Opinion and the Allied Bombing of France, 1940–1945." In *Bombing, States and Peoples in Western Europe 1940–1945*, edited by Claudia Baldoli, Andrew Knapp, and Richard Overy, 279–97. London: Continuum International Publishing Group, 2011.

Klemann, Hein, and Sergei Kudryashov. *Occupied Economies: An Economic History of Nazi-Occupied Europe, 1939–1945*. New York: Berg Publishers, 2012.

Knapp, Andrew. "The Destruction and Liberation of Le Havre in Modern Memory." *War in History* 14, no. 4 (2007): 476–98.

———. *Les Français Sous Les Bombes Alliées, 1940–1945*. Paris: Tallandier, 2012.

Kubiak, Jeffrey J. *War Narratives and the American National Will in War*. New York: Palgrave Macmillan, 2014.

Lacroix-Riz, Annie. *Industriels Et Banquiers: Français Sous L'Occupation*. Nouvelle édition. Paris: Armand Colin, 2013.

Lagrou, Pieter. *The Legacy of Nazi Occupation: Patriotic Memory and National Recovery in Western Europe, 1945–1965*. New York: Cambridge University Press, 2000.

Larrabee, Eric. *Commander in Chief: Franklin Delano Roosevelt, His Lieutenants & Their War*. New York: Harper & Row, 1987.

Leleu, Jean-Luc, Françoise Passera, Jean Quellien, and Michel Daeffler, eds. *La France Pendant La Seconde Guerre Mondiale, Atlas Historique*. Paris: Editions Fayard, 2010.

Lemay, Kate C. "Gratitude, Trauma, and Repression: D-Day in French Memory." In *D-Day in History and Memory: The Normandy Landings in International Remembrance and Commemoration*, edited by Michael Dolski, Sam Edwards, and John Buckley. Denton: University of North Texas Press, 2014.

Lewis, Adrian R. *Omaha Beach: A Flawed Victory*. Chapel Hill: University of North Carolina Press, 2001.

Linn, Brian M. "*The American Way of War* Revisited." *Journal of Military History* 66, no. April (2002): 501–33.

Longmate, Norman. *The Doodlebugs: The Story of the Flying-Bombs*. London: Hutchinson, 1981.

———. *Hitler's Rockets: The Story of the V-2s.* Yorkshire, UK: Frontline Books, 2009.

Lormier, Dominique. *Les Poches De L'atlantic: Médoc-Royan-Ile D'oléron-La Rochelle-Ile De Ré, 1944–1945.* Saint Paul: Lucien Souny, 2008.

Low, Andrew S., and Lloyd W. Prang, eds. *The Liberator Men of Old Buc: The Story of the 453rd Bombardment Group in World War II, 29 June 1943–15 September 1945.* Rev. ed. Tuleta, TX: The 453rd Bomb Group Association, 1999.

Ludewig, Jochim. *Rückzug: The German Retreat from France, 1944.* Translated by David T. Zabecki. Lexington: University of Kentucky Press, 2012.

Lytton, Henry D. "Bombing Policy in the Rome and Pre-Normandy Invasion Aerial Campaigns of World War II." *Military Affairs* (April 1983): 53–58.

MacIsaac, David. "Voices from the Central Blue: The Air Power Theorists." In *Makers of Modern Strategy: From Machiavelli to the Nuclear Age*, edited by Peter Paret, 624–48. Princeton, NJ: Princeton University Press, 1986.

Mahoney, Kevin. *Fifteenth Air Force against the Axis: Combat Missions over Europe during World War II.* Lanham, MD: Scarecrow Press, 2013.

Mazower, Mark. *Hitler's Empire: How the Nazis Ruled Europe.* New York: Penguin Press, 2008.

McArthur, Charles W. *Operations Analysis in the United States Army Eighth Air Force in World War II.* History of Mathematics. New York: American Mathematical Society, 1991.

McGrath, John T. *The French in Early Florida.* Gainesville: University Press of Florida, 2000.

McManus, John C. *The Dead and Those About to Die. D-Day: The Big Red One at Omaha Beach.* New York: NAL Caliber, 2014.

McNeill, William H. "The Care and Repair of Public Myth." *Foreign Affairs* 61, no. 1 (1982): 1–13.

McPhail, Helen. *The Long Silence: Civilian Life under the German Occupation of Northern France, 1914–1918.* New York: I. B. Tauris, 1999.

Meilinger, Phillip S., ed. *The Paths of Heaven: The Evolution of Airpower Theory.* Maxwell Air Force Base, AL: Air University Press, 1997.

Merriman, John. *A History of Modern Europe: From the Renaissance to the Present.* 2nd ed. New York: W. W. Norton, 2004.

Meyer, Hubert, and Harri H. Henschler. *The History of the 12. SS-Panzerdivision "Hitlerjugend."* Winnipeg: J. J. Fedorowicz, 1994.

Meyer, Leo J. "The Decision to Invade North Africa (Torch)." In *Command Decisions*, edited by Kent Roberts Greenfield, 173–98. Washington, DC: Office of the Chief of Military History, 1960.

Middlebrook, Martin, and Chris Everitt. *The Bomber Command War Diaries: An Operational Reference Book.* New York: Viking, 1985.

Millett, Allan R., Peter Maslowski, and William B. Feis. *For the Common Defense: A Military History of the United States from 1607–2012.* Rev. and exp. ed. New York: Free Press, 2012.

Miller, Donald L. *Masters of the Air: America's Bomber Boys Who Fought the Air War against Nazi Germany.* New York: Simon & Schuster, 2006.

Miller, Roger G. "A 'Pretty Damn Able Commander'—Lewis Hyde Brereton: Part II." *Air Power History* 48, no. 1 (2000): 22–44.

Milner, Marc. *Stopping the Panzers: The Untold Story of D-Day.* Lawerence: University Press of Kansas, 2014.

Milward, Alan S. *The New Order and the French Economy.* Oxford: Clarendon Press, 1970.

Montgomery, Bernard. *The Memoirs of Field-Marshal the Viscount Montgomery of Alamein, K.G.* London: Collins, 1958.

Murray, Williamson. *Strategy for Defeat: The Luftwaffe 1933–1945.* Maxwell Air Force Base, AL: Air University Press, 1983.

Nossiter, Adam. *France and the Nazis: Memories, Lies and the Second World War.* London: Methuen, 2001.

O'Brien, Maeve. "'Something in Me Said, Now, You Must See This': Reconciliation of Death and 'the Empty Beaches of Memory' in Sylvia Plath's 'Berck-Plage.'" *Plath Profiles: An Interdisciplinary Journal for Sylvia Plath Studies* 6 (Summer 2013): 95–108.

Orange, Vincent. "Coningham, Air Marshal Sir Arthur." In *The Oxford Companion to World War II*, edited by I. C. B. Dear and M. R. D. Foot, 262–63. New York: Oxford University Press, 1995.

Ousby, Ian. *Occupation: The Ordeal of France, 1940–1944.* New York: Cooper Square Press, 2000.

Overy, Richard. *The Air War, 1939–1945.* New York: Stein and Day, 1980.

———. *The Bombing War: The Allied Air War over Europe, 1940–1945.* New York: Viking, 2014.

———. *The Bombing War: Europe 1939–1945.* London: Allen Lane, 2013.

———. "Strategic Bombardment before 1939: Doctrine, Planning, and Operations." In *Case Studies in Strategic Bombardment*, edited by R. Cargill Hall, 11–91. Washington, DC: Air Force History and Museums Program, 1998.

———. *Why the Allies Won.* New York: W. W. Norton, 1995.

Pape, Robert S. *Bombing to Win: Air Power and Coercion in War.* New York: Cornell University Press, 1996.

Paret, Peter, ed. *Makers of Modern Strategy: From Machiavelli to the Nuclear Age.* Princeton, NJ: Princeton University Press, 1986.

Paxton, Robert O. *Vichy France: Old Guard and New Order, 1940–1944.* New York: Columbia University Press, 1972. Reprint 2001.

Plath Sylvia. *Ariel.* London: Faber and Faber, 1965.

Pogue, Forrest C. *George C. Marshall: Organizer of Victory, 1944–1945.* New York: Viking Press, 1973.

Porch, Douglas. *The Path to Victory: The Mediterranean Theater in World War II.* Old Saybrook, CT: Konecky & Konecky, 2004.

Porter, David. *The Kreigsmarine, 1939–1945: The Essential Facts and Figures for the German Navy. World War II Data Book.* London: Amber Books, 2010.

Probert, Henry. *Bomber Harris: His Life and Times.* London: Greenhill Books, 2001.

Rein, Christopher M. *The North African Air Campaign.* Lawrence: University Press of Kansas, 2012.

Richards, Denis. *The Hardest Victory: RAF Bomber Command in the Second World War.* New York: W. W. Norton, 1994.

———. *Royal Air Force: Volume I, the Fight at Odds.* London: Her Majesty's Stationery Office, 1953.

Rigby, David. *Allied Master Strategists: The Combined Chiefs of Staff in World War II.* Annapolis, MD: Naval Institute Press, 2012.

Roberts, Mary Louise. *D-Day through French Eyes, Normandy 1944.* Chicago: University of Chicago Press, 2014.

Rostow, W. W. *Pre-Invasion Bombing Strategy: General Eisenhower's Decision of March 25, 1944.* Ideas and Action. Austin: University of Texas Press, 1981.

Ryan, Cornelius. *The Longest Day.* New York: Simon & Schuster, 1959.

Saward, Dudley. *Bomber Harris.* Garden City, NY: Doubleday & Company, 1985.

Schaffer, Ronald. *Wings of Judgment: American Bombing in World War II.* New York: Oxford University Press, 1985.

Sherry, Michael S. *The Rise of American Airpower: The Creation of Armageddon.* New Haven, CT: Yale University Press, 1987.

Shirer, William L. *The Collapse of the Third Republic: An Inquiry into the Fall of France 1940.* New York: Simon & Schuster, 1969.

———. *The Rise and Fall of the Third Reich: A History of Nazi Germany.* New York: Simon & Schuster, 1960.

Sinnigen, William G., and Arthur E. R. Boak. A History of Rome to A.D. 565, 6th ed. New York: Macmillan, 1977.

Smith, Leonard V. *France and the Great War, 1914–1918.* New Approaches to European History. Edited by William Beik and T. C. W. Blanning. New York: Cambridge University Press, 2003.

Spayd, P. A., and Gary Wilkins, eds. *Bayerlein: After Action Reports of the Panzer Lehr Division Commander, From D-Day to the Ruhr.* Atglen, PA: Schiffer Military History, 2005.

Süss, Dietmar. *Death from the Skies: How the British and Germans Endured Aerial Destruction in World War II.* Oxford: Oxford University Press, 2014.

Symonds, Craig L. *Neptune: The Allied Invasion of Europe and the D-Day Landings.* New York: Oxford University Press, 2014.

Tedder, Arthur William. *With Prejudice: The War Memoirs of Marshal of the Royal Air Force Lord Tedder, G. C. B.* Boston: Little, Brown, 1966.

Temkin, Moshik. "'Avec un certain malaise': The Paxtonian Trauma in France, 1973–1974." *Journal of Contemporary History* 38, no. 2 (April 2003): 391–406.

Tirman, John. *The Deaths of Others: The Fate of Civilians in America's Wars.* New York: Oxford University Press, 2011.

Tooze, Adam. *The Wages of Destruction: The Making and Breaking of the Nazi Economy.* New York: Penguin Books, 2006.

Trevor-Roper, H. R. *Blitzkrieg to Defeat: Hitler's War Directives 1939–1945*. New York: Holt, Rinehart, and Winston, 1971.

Uziel, Daniel. *Arming the Luftwaffe: The German Aviation Industry in World War II*. London: McFarland, 2012.

Van Der Vat, Dan. *The Atlantic Campaign*. Edinburgh: Birlinn, 1988.

Vinen, Richard. *The Politics of French Business, 1936–1945*. New York: Cambridge University Press, 1991.

———. *The Unfree French: Life under the Occupation*. New Haven, CT: Yale University Press, 2006.

Voldman, Danièle. *La Reconstruction Des Villes Françaises de 1940 à 1954: Histoire d'une politique*. Paris: L'Harmattan, 1997.

Wakelam, Randal T. *The Science of Bombing*. Toronto: University of Toronto Press, 2009.

Weigley, Russell F. *The American Way of War: A History of United States Military Strategy and Policy*. Bloomington: Indiana University Press, 1973.

———. *Eisenhower's Lieutenants, the Campaign of France and Germany, 1944–1945*. Bloomington: Indiana University Press, 1981.

White, Hayden. *The Content of the Form: Narrative Discourse and Historical Representation*. Baltimore: Johns Hopkins University Press, 1987.

Wieviorka, Olivier. *Divided Memory: French Recollections of World War II from the Liberation to the Present*. Translated by George Holoch. Stanford, CA: Stanford University Press, 2012.

———. *The French Resistance*. Translated by Jane Marie Todd. Cambridge, MA: Belknap Press, 2016.

———. *Normandy: The Landings to the Liberation of Paris*. Translated by M. B. DeBevoise. Cambridge, MA: Harvard University Press, 2008.

Wilt, Alan F. *The Atlantic Wall: Hitler's Defense in the West, 1941–1944*. New York: Enigma Books, 1975.

Winter, Jay. *Sites of Memory, Sites of Mourning: The Great War in European Cultural History*. Cambridge: Cambridge Press Syndicate of the University of Cambridge, 1998.

Wood, Edward W., Jr. *Worshipping the Myths of World War II: Reflections on America's Dedication to War*. Washington, DC: Potomac Books, 2006.

Wright, Gordon. *France in Modern Times*. New York: W. W. Norton, 1995.

Wynn, Humphrey, and Susan Young. *Prelude to Overlord*. Novato, CA: Presidio, 1983.

Yung, Christopher D. *Gators of Neptune: Naval Amphibious Planning for the Normandy Invasion*. Annapolis, MD: Naval Institute Press, 2006.

Zaloga, Steven J. *The Atlantic Wall (1): France (Fortress)*. Oxford, UK: Osprey, 2007.

———. *German V-Weapon Sites 1943–1945*. Oxford: Osprey, 2007.

Zaloga, Steven J., and Jim Laurier. *V-1 Flying Bomb 1942–1952: Hitler's Infamous "Doodlebug."* Oxford: Osprey, 2005.

Ziemke, Earl F. "Rundstedt." In *Hitler's Generals,* edited by Correlli Barnett, 175–208. New York: Grove Weidenfeld, 1989.

Zinn, Howard. *The Bomb.* San Francisco: City Light Books, 2010.

Internet Pages

"Annuaire Des Mairies Et Villes De France." http://www.annuaire-mairie.fr.

Carville, Daniel. "France-Crashes 39–45." http://francecrashes39-45.net.

Joubert, Henri. "Mai 1944: Premier Bombardement." Témoignages écrits, *La gazette de l'île Barbe* (2004). http://www.jaillard.net/58-angers.php.

Movies

Ducellier, Jean-Pierre, and Raymonde Gilmann. "Les 60 Ans Des Bombardements D'amiens." Les 60 ans des bombardements d'Amiens.

Le Trevier, Paul, and Nicolas Jallot. "From Rouen to Hiroshima," France 5/France Télévision, 2015.

INDEX

ABOUT THE AUTHOR

After twenty years of enlisted and commissioned service in the US Army, **Stephen A. Bourque** obtained his PhD at Georgia State University and taught history at several military and civilian schools and universities, including the School of Advanced Military Studies, US Army Command and General Staff College, where he is professor emeritus.

The Naval Institute Press is the book-publishing arm of the U.S. Naval Institute, a private, nonprofit, membership society for sea service professionals and others who share an interest in naval and maritime affairs. Established in 1873 at the U.S. Naval Academy in Annapolis, Maryland, where its offices remain today, the Naval Institute has members worldwide.

Members of the Naval Institute support the education programs of the society and receive the influential monthly magazine *Proceedings* or the colorful bimonthly magazine *Naval History* and discounts on fine nautical prints and on ship and aircraft photos. They also have access to the transcripts of the Institute's Oral History Program and get discounted admission to any of the Institute-sponsored seminars offered around the country.

The Naval Institute's book-publishing program, begun in 1898 with basic guides to naval practices, has broadened its scope to include books of more general interest. Now the Naval Institute Press publishes about seventy titles each year, ranging from how-to books on boating and navigation to battle histories, biographies, ship and aircraft guides, and novels. Institute members receive significant discounts on the Press's more than eight hundred books in print.

Full-time students are eligible for special half-price membership rates. Life memberships are also available.

For a free catalog describing Naval Institute Press books currently available, and for further information about joining the U.S. Naval Institute, please write to:

Member Services
U.S. Naval Institute
291 Wood Road
Annapolis, MD 21402-5034
Telephone: (800) 233-8764
Fax: (410) 571-1703
Web address: www.usni.org